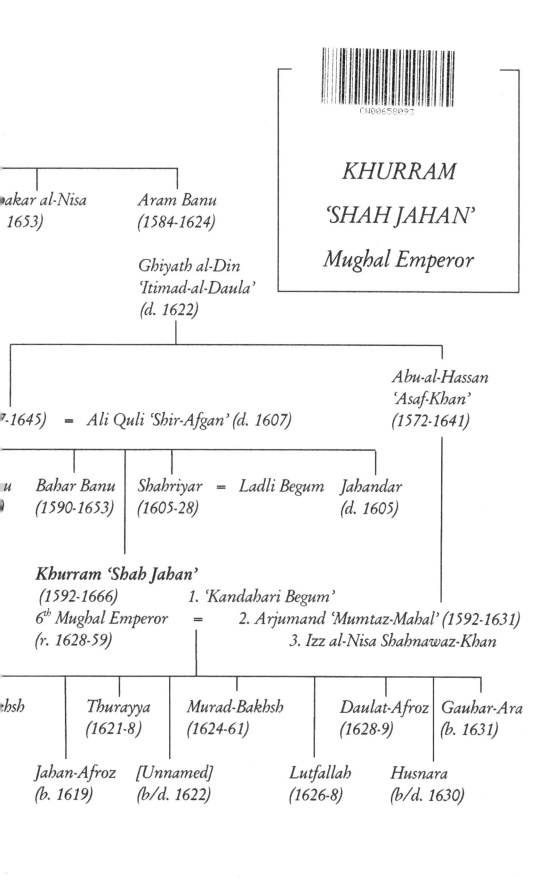

KHURRAM
'SHAH JAHAN'
Mughal Emperor

akar al-Nisa   Aram Banu
1653)   (1584-1624)

                      Ghiyath al-Din
                      'Itimad-al-Daula'
                      (d. 1622)

                                              Abu-al-Hassan
                                              'Asaf-Khan'
-1645)   = Ali Quli 'Shir-Afgan' (d. 1607)   (1572-1641)

u   Bahar Banu   Shahriyar = Ladli Begum Jahandar
     (1590-1653)   (1605-28)   (d. 1605)

     Khurram 'Shah Jahan'
     (1592-1666)   1. 'Kandahari Begum'
     6th Mughal Emperor   =   2. Arjumand 'Mumtaz-Mahal' (1592-1631)
     (r. 1628-59)   3. Izz al-Nisa Shahnawaz-Khan

hsh   Thurayya   Murad-Bakhsh   Daulat-Afroz Gauhar-Ara
         (1621-8)   (1624-61)   (1628-9)   (b. 1631)

     Jahan-Afroz   [Unnamed]   Lutfallah   Husnara
     (b. 1619)   (b/d. 1622)   (1626-8)   (b/d. 1630)

SHAH JAHAN

SHAH JAHAN

HAUS PUBLISHING
LONDON

First published in Great Britain in 2009 by
Haus Publishing Ltd
70 Cadogan Place
London SW1 9AH
www.hauspublishing.com

Copyright © Fergus Nicoll, 2009

The moral right of the author has been asserted

A CIP catalogue record for this book
is available from the British Library

ISBN 978-1-906598-18-1

Typeset in Optima by MacGuru Ltd
info@macguru.org.uk
Printed in China by SC (Sang Choy) International Ltd.

CONDITIONS OF SALE
All rights reserved. No part of this publication may be reproduced, stored in
a retrieval system, or transmitted in any form or by any means, electronic,
mechanical, photocopying, recording or otherwise, without the prior permission
of the publisher.

This book is sold subject to the condition that it shall not, by way of trade
or otherwise, be lent, re-sold, hired out or otherwise circulated without the
publisher's prior consent in any form of binding or cover other than that in which
it is published and without a similar condition including this condition being
imposed on the subsequent purchaser.

Contents

Maps and Illustrations

Preface

Every day of the year, even on the stupefying days of summer heat, the tourists come to the Taj Mahal, bearing their Baedekers, their Guides du Routard, their Chikyu no Arukikatas. They gaze up and ponder over the flawlessly inlaid Koranic quotations on the tomb's towering portals, stroll the leafy paths of the well-watered garden and pose for photographs with a backdrop of breathtakingly beautiful white marble that was iconic centuries before Diana, Princess of Wales, commandeered the world's greatest icon of enduring royal love to signal her own marital discontent.

The Taj Mahal: eighth wonder of the world, one of those places that many visitors fear will be a cliché, a disappointment – until they arrive. Commissioned in 1631 by the Emperor Shah Jahan after the death in childbirth of his beloved second wife Arjumand Mumtaz-Mahal, the glittering monument took twelve years to complete, at a cost of five million silver rupees. Contemporary writers acclaimed the masterpiece with rapturous descriptions of the funerary complex, from the tiniest chip of carnelian inlay on the royal sepulchre to the towering minarets and the vast market square abutting the principal gate. Today's visitors are fired by the emotion of the story of love and death – and by the fluent fabrications of the tour guides, who tell of Shah Jahan blinding his architects and cutting off his craftsmen's hands, lest they try to reproduce such a marvel. The tourists venture across the Yamuna River, seeking a different camera angle or perhaps examining the dust and ruined masonry in the Moonlight Garden on the other bank for proof of the fabled Black Taj. Nor is it only the half-million or so foreigners that are captivated by this most solid of myths each year. The Taj Mahal may be the primary image with which India markets itself to the world but the magic works at home too. For the vast majority of the crowds are Indians: more than two million in 2006; Hindus and non-believers as keen to explore the atmosphere at this Muslim tomb as those of the Muhammadan faith.

Yet in the long and frequently bloody tale of the rise and fall of Emperor Khurram 'Shah Jahan' – general, rebel prince and patron of the arts – the tomb to Mumtaz-Mahal plays but a small part. His is a complex and conflicted tale of romance and violence, of marital fidelity and fratricidal betrayal, of exquisite artistry and ugly intolerance. For the Mughal court was a world where brutally violent politics, internecine conflict, pedantic quadruplicate bureaucracy and high art all coexisted under the same royal roof. Before his usurpation by his own son, Shah Jahan reigned for 32 years as an enlightened despot: a man seen variously as a virtuous supporter of Sharia law and a monster of moral depravity. Between these extremes lies the truth of the man.

Shah Jahan was a soldier who loyally served his father, Emperor Salim Jahangir, in a series of campaigns against enemies both internal and external – before turning renegade and launching a disastrous attempt on the throne that left him in the wilderness, his every step dogged by imperial troopers, for six arduous years. As emperor, he moved away from the free-for-all hybridised religion of his grandfather Akbar to a more entrenched and conservative Islam, yet managed Sunni-Shiite sectarian tensions and the rival ambitions of subordinate Hindu princes to preserve the integrity of a multi-faith court, bureaucracy and army. Above all, he was a creative man and an aesthete: accomplished in and appreciative of the disciplines of the poet's metre and the architect's drawing-board – a man whose legacy will for ever be measured in the stones that he had laid: the fortresses, mosques, schools, caravanserais and gardens now crumbling in all corners of his vast empire.

In reconstructing this intriguing tale from contemporary documents, including the vivid pen-portraits and panegyrics of court biographers, Shah Jahan's own stern edicts and a surprising volume of correspondence with the neighbouring Persian Empire, many aspects of the conventional wisdom have had to be revisited. For the first time it is revealed why, despite Mumtaz-Mahal's aristocratic upbringing and influential position within the polygamous harem – attributes that enabled her to become Shah Jahan's closest political confidante – she was cast aside for five years between their engagement in Kabul on 4 April 1607 and their eventual marriage at Agra on 10 May 1612. For the first time, too, the emperor's staggering personal wealth is made clear, with the ruling family and no more than seven hundred named individuals dividing between them a treasury that dwarfed that of any contemporary European monarch and enabled Shah Jahan to spend eye-watering sums on vanity projects such as the eleven-million-rupee Ornamented Throne.

Most significantly, however, Shah Jahan's place in history as the fifth emperor of the Mughal dynasty has had to be reappraised. Compelling contemporary evidence, including corroborative testimony from neighbouring Persia, makes it clear that, by the time a bloody chain of events culminated in his coronation on 14 February 1628, Shah Jahan had murdered two brothers and at least six more male relatives, one of them the legitimately crowned Emperor Dawar-Bakhsh Shir-Shah. This redefines the man routinely eulogised in simplistic terms as lover, warrior and master architect as Shah Jahan the Regicide, confirming him in fact as the *sixth* of the Mughal royal dynasty to take the throne of Hindustan.

Acknowledgements

It may seem impertinent for a European to take on the life of one of the most celebrated emperors of the subcontinent; foolhardy, too, for a writer with a modest grasp of Arabic and Sanskrit but with no Hindi or Urdu, let alone medieval Persian. For as I was told during my travels, true understanding can only be reached by reading every line of every contemporary manuscript, in the original – and then reading *between* the lines. After all, each writer had an agenda, be it political, religious, or merely sycophantic; objectivity was rarely in the job description. Not for nothing did Muhamamad Hadi, amanuensis to an emperor, write wearily of the travails of the 'thirsty wanderer in the desert of history'. But how refreshing, once achieved, is that first glimpse over the high red sandstone wall into the lush tranquillity of the Mughal pleasure-garden; and how much more easily done when standing upon the broad shoulders of the giants of Mughal scholarship in India, Pakistan, Iran and beyond.

So I owe an enormous debt of gratitude to many for their magisterial written work, the generously shared personal insights, tolerance of persistent and probably exasperating questions, their kindly corrections and long heart-to-heart conversations. My bibliography illustrates the full scale of my debt but certain individuals belong on a personal roll of honour. Above all, Dr Yunus Jaffery worked through a blizzard of manuscripts and photographed inscriptions, translating the essential accounts that form the backbone of Shah Jahan's story with painstaking attention to detail, good humour and risqué asides. A chance encounter with his sister Nuzhat Khatoon at the Library of Congress in Washington had led me to Ustaz Dr Jaffery's modest home in Old Delhi. Professor Ram Nath, doyen of Mughal architecture, endured days of questions with patience and charm, filling out his analysis with pencil sketches and effortless quotations in Persian and Sanskrit. Professor Ebba Koch discussed details of her exemplary volume on the Taj Mahal and recommended important supplementary reading. Professor S. Qalb-i-Abid and his colleagues at the University of Punjab in Lahore were generous with their time and advice on the city's Mughal past. Professor Wheeler Thackston, Professor Sanjay Subramanyam and Dr Jim Benson responded to my emails with helpful suggestions and useful translations. Dr Muhammad Irfan and his fellow archivists at the National Archives of India in New Delhi opened the vaults to reveal priceless documents and volumes that could be found nowhere else.

To tread the ground where history was made is always a powerful motivator. The structures of the past, still massive and obdurate after the passage of four hundred years, cast a spell over the traveller, transporting him back to the 17th century and allowing him to clarify important questions that go far beyond the physical concerns of architecture and archaeology. Thanks, therefore, are due to those who oiled the wheels of progress: in Ajmer, Syed Azam Hussein and Dr Syed Badiul Hasan Chisty; in Burhanpur and Mandu, Sunil Gupta and Sanjiv Srivastav; on Jagmandir Island in Udaipur Lake, Chandra Bhan Singh. In Delhi, Anu Anand and Tarquin Hall provided hospitality, advice and good whisky, while colleagues at the BBC Delhi Bureau kindly lent me room to work and generous advice on miscellaneous linguistic questions. I am greatly indebted to the Society of Authors for a generous grant that enabled me to take the necessary time to follow in Shah Jahan's footsteps and look for evidence of his passing.

Most of my archive work on sources in English, Persian and Sanskrit was done at the Indian Institute, part of Oxford University's wonderful Bodleian Library, where Dr Simon Lawson took great delight in tracking down obscure items from the stack. Staff at London University's School of Oriental and African Studies, too, were most helpful in identifying elusive manuscripts and key texts in their impressive collection of primary and secondary sources.

This book would not have happened at all but for the dedication of Jaqueline Mitchell, who not only commissioned it but supervised its final stages with her customary care and precision. At Haus Publishing, Barbara Schwepke gave the project her personal commitment and considerable enthusiasm. And Mandy Little has monitored progress throughout, celebrating the highs and sympathising with the lows as only a really good agent knows how.

Tracing the life of Khurram Shah Jahan has taken me many thousands of miles from home; yet even in the most remote village and in the most frustrating circumstances of tricky travel and elusive evidence, this 'thirsty wanderer' always had the luxury of an unbreakable connection to home. So the biggest thanks are due to my wonderful family: Kate, Flora and James.

Note on Transliteration and Calendars

To make life easier for the non-specialist reader, it has been decided to avoid the use of diacriticals in the text. Given the range of languages and alphabets used across the Mughal Empire – including Persian, Turkish, Sanskrit and Bengali – and the lack of consistency in the various transliteration conventions, it seemed better to avoid potential distractions. Thus in the text I do not differentiate between the various Arabic forms of d, h, th, etc., or the various Sanskrit forms of n, r, s, etc. I have dispensed with the Arabic or Persian letters *ain* (ﻉ) and *hamza* (ﺀ) altogether. Thus, for example, whereas in an academic work one would expect to see the name of one influential courtier rendered as Ghiyāth al-Dīn I'timād al-Daula, I give simply Ghiyath al-Din Itimad-al-Daula. The second part of his name is fully hyphenated because it is a title and, like many central figures in this story, Ghiyath al-Din was more widely known by the honorific ('Pillar-of-the-State') than by his given name. Like other such titles, it was a compound name, a unique phenomenon that I have chosen to clarify by hyphenating the elements and by italicising them at first reference only. Other important examples include Shah Jahan's second wife, Arjumand Abu-al-Hassan *Mumtaz-Mahal* ('Most-Exquisite-of-the-Palace') and Mir Abd-al-Karim *Mamur-Khan* ('Master-Architect'). As for the eponymous emperor himself, it has been decided to let colloquial usage have the final say and render his given name and title as Khurram *Shah Jahan* ('Lord-of-the-World'); the same concession to convention has been made in the cases of the royal titles *Jahangir* ('World-Seizer') and Aurangzeb *Alamgir*.

The Mughal court operated on three very different calendars, which were used indiscriminately in official court documents (including imperial memoirs and biographies) and translated inconsistently in contemporary European sources. The Ilahi calendar (twelve solar months, 365 days) followed the signs of the Zodiac and was introduced to the Mughal dominions by the Emperor Akbar. New Year's Day was known as Nauruz and fell on 20 March, the Spring Equinox. The years of an emperor's reign were calculated from the first Nauruz after his actual coronation. Nauruz fell on the first day of Fawardin (Aries) and the remaining eleven in sequence were: Urdibihisht (Taurus), Khurdad (Gemini), Tir (Cancer), Amurdad (Leo), Shahriwar (Virgo), Mihr (Libra), Aban (Scorpio), Azar (Sagittarius), Dai (Capricorn), Bahman (Aquarius) and Isfandarmudh (Pisces). Because the Mughals were Muslim rulers, they also used the Islamic calendar (twelve lunar months, 354 days), which began with the migration of the Prophet Muhammad from Mecca to Medina in 622 AD. The months of the shorter Islamic year are: Muharram, Safar, Rabi I, Rabi II, Jumada I, Jumada II, Rajab, Shaban, Ramadan, Shawwal, Dhu al-Qada and Dhu al-Hijja. It is worth noting that, because the months in the lunar calendar 'slip' in relation to the longer solar calendar, when Shah Jahan died in prison, it was a week after his 74th birthday by the solar calendar, while by lunar reckoning he had lived 76 years and three months. The third calendar in use in Mughal documents was the Turkish duodenary (twelve-year) solar cycle, which also began on 20 March. This was mainly used in financial affairs because tax revenues depended on the farming seasons and the slipping of the lunar calendar meant a lack of consistency with the harvests. The twelve years in the cycle were named after animals: Mouse, Cow, Leopard, Hare, Crocodile, Snake, Horse, Sheep, Monkey, Fowl, Dog and Hog.

To complicate matters further, Western accounts used European calendars – but while the Gregorian reckoning (known as New Series) replaced the Julian calendar (Old Series) in most of Catholic Western Europe in October 1582, it was not adopted in Anglican Britain until 1752. Thus important English sources such as Peter Mundy and William Finch use the Old Series calendar, while the French Jesuit, Pierre du Jarric, and the Italian Pietro Della Valle use the modern Gregorian dating, befitting their Catholic patrons. After much deliberation and in the interest of consistency and ease for the reader, I have converted all dates to the New Style, leaving references to the other calendars largely to the source notes.

Principal Characters

Emperors

Jalal al-Din Akbar 3rd Mughal Emperor (r. 1556–1605); father of Salim, Murad and Daniyal

Salim Jahangir 4th Mughal Emperor (r. 1605–27); Akbar's eldest son; Shah Jahan's father

Dawar-Bakhsh aka Bulaqi and Shir-Shah; 5th Mughal Emperor (r. 1627); Jahangir's grandson; Khusraw's son

Khurram Shah Jahan 6th Mughal Emperor (r. 1628–58); Jahangir's third son

Aurangzeb Alamgir 7th Mughal Emperor (r. 1658–1707); Shah Jahan's third son

Royal Family

Arjumand Abu-al-Hassan aka Mumtaz-Zamani and Mumtaz-Mahal; Shah Jahan's second wife; mother of 14 children

Daniyal Jahangir's younger brother

Dara-Shikuh Shah Jahan's first son and heir apparent; executed by Aurangzeb Alamgir

Izz al-Nisa Begum Shah Jahan's third wife; Abd-al-Rahim Khan-Khanan's granddaughter

Jahan-Ara Shah Jahan's eldest daughter

Kandahari Begum Shah Jahan's first wife

Khusraw Jahangir's eldest son

Ladli Begum Nur-Jahan's daughter by Ali Quli Beg; married to Shahriyar
Manmati aka Jagat Ghosaini and Bilqis-Makani; Shah Jahan's mother
Mihr al-Nisa aka Nur-Mahal and Nur-Jahan; Jahangir's last and most important wife; Mumtaz-Mahal's aunt
Murad Jahangir's younger brother
Murad-Bakhsh Shah Jahan's fourth son
Pervez Jahangir's second son
Rajakumari Man Bai Jahangir's mother
Shahriyar Shah Jahan's youngest half-brother
Shah-Shuja Shah Jahan's second son
Suleiman-Shikuh Dara-Shikuh's eldest son

Politicians, officers and courtiers

Abdallah Khan aka Firoz-Jang; general under Jahangir and Shah Jahan
Abd-al-Rahim Khan aka Khan-Khanan; Prime Minister and general
Abu-al-Fadl al-Allami Court annalist and general
Abu-al-Hassan Ghiyath al-Din aka Itiqad-Khan, Yamin-al-Daula, Asaf-Khan and Umdat-al-Sultana; Mumtaz-Mahal's father; Ghiyath al-Din Beg Itimad-al-Daula's son
Ali Quli Beg aka Shir-Afgan; Mihr al-Nisa Nur-Jahan's first husband
Anup Singh aka Rai and Singh-Dalan; hunt-master; officer under Jahangir
Ghiyath al-Din Beg aka Itimad-al-Daula; Jahangir's chancellor; Mumtaz-Mahal's grandfather
Iraj Abd-al-Rahim aka Shahnawaz-Khan; Abd-al-Rahim Khan Khan-Khanan's son; father of Shah Jahan's third wife
Maharana Karna Singh Ruler of Mewar; Shah Jahan's friend and ally
Mir Muhammad Amin aka Mir-Jumla; diamond merchant; official in Golconda; Shah Jahan's Prime Minister
Mir Muhammad Baqr aka Iradat-Khan and Azam-Khan; general under Shah Jahan
Mirza Abu-Talib aka Shayista-Khan; general under Shah Jahan; Abu-al-Hassan Asaf-Khan's son
Mirza Aziz Kokaltash aka Azam-Khan; childhood friend of Akbar; Khusraw's father-in-law
Muhammad Sharif Mumtaz-Mahal's uncle; coup-plotter against Jahangir
Muhammad Sharif aka Mutamid-Khan; military administrative officer; historian
Pir Khan Lodi aka Khan-Jahan; Jahangir's foster-son; rebel against Shah Jahan
Raja Bhagwan Das Rajput prince; Jahangir's father-in-law

Raja Jai Singh aka Mirza-Raja; officer under Shah Jahan

Raja Man Singh Rajput prince; Khusraw's brother-in-law

Reza Ghulam Bahadur aka Khidmatparast-Khan; Shah Jahan's preferred assassin

Saida Gilani aka Bibadal-Khan; Superintendent of Goldsmiths; poet

Sundar Das aka Raja-Vikramaditya; Shah Jahan's chef de cabinet; general

Zamana Beg aka Mahabat-Khan; supporter of Jahangir; Commander-in-Chief

Artists and architects

Mir Abd-al-Karim aka Mamur-Khan; architect under Jahangir and Shah Jahan

Mullah Murshid aka Makramat-Khan; chief architect of the Taj Mahal

Non-Mughal personalities

Imam Quli Khan Ruler of Badakhshan

Malik Ambar General of Ahmadnagar; originally Ethiopian slave

Muzaffar Hussein Mirza Persian governor of Kandahar; father of Shah Jahan's first wife

Roe, Sir Thomas English Ambassador and chief trade delegate

Shah Abbas Ruler of Persia

Shah Abbas II Ruler of Persia

Shah Safi Ruler of Persia; nephew of Shah Abbas

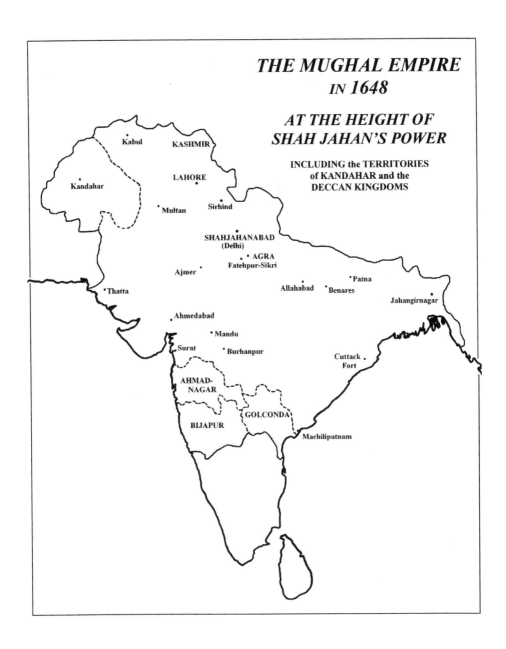

THE MUGHAL EMPIRE
IN *1648*

**AT THE HEIGHT OF
SHAH JAHAN'S POWER**

INCLUDING the TERRITORIES
of KANDAHAR and the
DECCAN KINGDOMS

1

'Prince of Good Fortune'

I do not think that in all the seven regions
There is any city of the grandeur and beauty of Lahore.

Talib al-Amuli[1]

When Jahangir sat on the throne of empire,
The world attained the splendour of the divine shadow.
Illuminator of crown and throne he was;
Generous, merciful and lucky.

Muhammad Hadi[2]

The baked-brick imperial fortress towered over the sweltering landscape as the royal convoy drew slowly nearer to the Ravi River. It was a fearsomely hot and humid day in the middle of August and the travellers had been taking their marathon journey through the plains of Lahore Province in carefully measured stages of no more than five or six miles a day, slogging through the mud of the recent monsoon rains. But at last they had reached the city itself: Lahore, the northern capital of the empire, 'mother of the cities of Hind', 'the grand resort of people of all nations'. At the heart of the cavalcade rode *Sultan* Khurram, prince of the Mughal realm, third son to the new king but now unquestionably his favourite. The boy who would himself one day wield absolute power as the Emperor *Shah Jahan*, 'King of the World', was returning to the city of his birth on the orders of his father the emperor.

It was Khurram's first major expedition out of the imperial capital at Agra and it was to prove one of the most important of his life. At fifteen and at a time of grave national crisis, he proudly bore new state responsibilities. For the past several weeks, since his oldest half-brother had ridden from Agra to raise mutiny against the empire and their father had ridden in urgent pursuit, Khurram had been designated *Wali-Ahad*, titular head of the Regency Council and charged with guarding the royal palace at Agra, under the watchful guardianship of the great Rajput prince Raja Rai Singh.[3] In the words of the contemporary historian Muhammad Sharif *Mutamid-Khan*, the emperor had 'made Khurram the king of the banner of unity and made him sit on the throne of empire … and gave into his charge the treasury and the female apartments'.[4] Having proven that his was a wise head on a young body, Khurram was now entrusted with the transport and care of the entire imperial household. The most distinguished member of the harem was his grandmother, Her Majesty Guljar Begum the Queen Mother, a lady born into the Kachwaha Rajput royal family of Amber – from the north-eastern plains of Rajasthan – and married into the Mughal dynasty.

Before he left Lahore the following year, Khurram would be formally designated as Crown Prince and heir apparent to the imperial crown, proud holder of his first military rank and enhanced status in the court's administrative structure. He would also be engaged to be married.

The logistics involved in transporting the royal harem over the 440-mile journey from Agra to Lahore had been complex – especially during the tail end of the rainy season -- but, in the capable hands of the court's huge camp-management team, Khurram and the royal ladies were able to enjoy a tranquil and luxurious passage along the mulberry-lined 'Long Walk'. This was but the western part of an astonishing avenue that stretched from the old fort at Attock on the Indus, via Delhi, Agra, Allahabad and Benares all the way east to the Bengal coast – a twelve-hundred-mile phenomenon described by one European traveller as 'the most incomparable show of that kind that ever my eyes surveyed'. A Cornish trader, Peter Mundy, counted not just mulberries but a wide variety of luxuriant broad-leaved evergreens 'distant one from the other about eight or nine ordinary steps … for the ease of travellers and for shade in hot weather'.[5] In later years, additional marker stones would be set up at every *kos* – a distance of around two-and-a-half miles – and wells dug at every third marker 'so that wayfarers could travel easily and comfortably and not suffer from thirst or the heat of the sun'.

Sites for overnight stops had been carefully selected every five or six miles, the campgrounds fitted out with every conceivable comfort brought along with the imperial retinue from Agra. Even in the stifling humidity, the ladies enjoyed excursions and diversions en route, especially hunting and visiting holy shrines. When not carried in curtained palanquins, the younger maidens rode on horseback, their modesty protected behind draped white veils, their tunics and colourful turbans decorated with Persian brocade and floral embroidery in stiff gold. But the end of even this agreeable and luxurious expedition must have come as a relief when, on Wednesday 16 August 1606, they reached Dhar village on the northern bank of the Ravi.[6] There to welcome them was Khurram's father, the Emperor himself: Salim Jahangir, the 'Seizer of the World'.

At thirty-seven, Jahangir had been impatient to come into his inheritance. A veteran *bon viveur*, party host, alcoholic and drug addict, he was erratic and unpredictable in his behaviour. One day he might be kindness and justice personified, his spare hours filled with philosophical and religious discussion and remarkable scientific experiments prompted by a boundless curiosity for the natural world. The next – usually after a heavy drinking session – he might swerve into arbitrary judgments and sadistic violence.[7] But he was consistent in remaining a stickler for royal protocol, especially for 'observing the formalities the young owe their elders', as he put it in his journal.

Now, on the bank of the Ravi, the reception committee had to be lavish, for the focus of the Emperor's loyal attention was his mother, the Hindu queen honoured with the title *Maryam-Zamani*, the 'Mary of the Age' a figure of immense influence in the administration of empire who was renowned 'from Bengal to Kandahar' for her charitable donations.[8] Jahangir's relationship with his mother was typical of the early Mughal princes: intense and devoted. While royal fathers became rivals, even blood enemies, royal mothers were venerated. Small wonder that Jahangir, like his father before him, confounded Jesuit missionaries by wearing and hanging on his palace walls images of the Christian Virgin Mary – though he disappointed the proselytising fathers by showing little interest in their wider teachings.[9] Now, Jahangir's reception to welcome Maryam-Zamani was organised in the imperial pavilion, a great tent in which, even in this northern outpost of empire, no luxury was stinted. Foreigners were routinely astonished at the opulence of the imperial appointments – especially by the so-called Mass of Clouds canopy, which required a team of three thousand 'skilful tentmen' to erect, assisted by 'the traction of a thousand kinds of mechanical science and pitched with a hundred contrivances'.[10] William Hawkins, a contemporary English merchant, saw this formidable construction and wondered at something 'so rich I think the like cannot be found in the world'.

This tent is curiously wrought and hath many awnings joining round about it of most curious wrought velvet, embroidered with gold, and many of them are of cloth of gold and silver. … I may say it is at the least two acres of ground, but so richly spread with silk and gold carpets and hangings [as] in the principal palaces, rich as rich velvet embroidered with gold, pearl, and precious stones can make it.[11]

It was too early in the day for the king to have been drinking heavily and he was on his best behaviour, perhaps keen to impress his mother – widowed just ten months earlier – with the dignity of his royal bearing. To receive Prince Khurram and the ladies of his household, the emperor wore tapered white silk trousers, embroidered with floral motifs; over them flowed a calf-length skirt of India's finest muslin, floating and diaphanous. Instead of a crown, he wore a simple silk turban, bound up in which was a single ruby worth one hundred thousand silver rupees – a gift from his grandmother at the time of his birth.[12] His necklaces more than made up for the relative lack of show in his headgear. In swags of pearl, emerald and diamond – these last the fruit of the empire's most productive mines at Barakar – they hung in ropes over his salmon-pink chemise, elegantly matched by the jewels sewn into his cuffs and collar. A curved sword, hilt and scabbard encrusted with jewels, hung at his left hip. The king's bare feet sank into the soft deep flowers of the Persian carpets scattered across the floor of the pavilion.

As for Prince Khurram, the pallor of his face was exacerbated by the heat and by a nagging illness that had dogged him during the journey north. He had his father's straight, sharp nose, though his moustache was as yet no more than a shadowy fuzz on his top lip. His ancestral roots were buried in Central Asia but generations of intermarriage with royal women of Rajasthan had blended his forefathers' Asiatic genes with Indian features. Like Jahangir, the prince wore beautifully tailored ceremonial attire: a gold embroidered tunic over white muslin shirt and aquamarine trousers. Like his father, he wore ropes of pearls and emeralds round his neck, while diamonds sparkled in his scarlet turban.

The ceremonies of welcome and tribute were elaborate, formulaic and fundamentally un-Indian. They were cultural imports, brought with Jahangir's invading ancestors from the mountains of Central Asia and little changed in the centuries since. Jahangir himself wrote that these Mughal rites of obedience stemmed from the customs of Genghis Khan and the rules of Timur 'the Lame' of Samarkand. At the seventeenth-century Mughal court, such deference was usually paid only to the emperor but on this occasion it was the king paying tribute to his mother. First came the formal *korunush* obeisance: the palm of the hand held to the forehead. Then Jahangir prostrated himself on the carpet at full length, before finally picking himself up and bowing in the *taslim* salute: touching the ground with the back of his right hand, then rising and bringing his right palm up to the crown of his head. It was a perfectly executed display of humility from the most powerful man in the land and when the rituals were complete it was time to decamp for the city.[13]

Khurram's grandfather, the lately deceased Emperor Jalal al-Din Muhammad Akbar, had lavished a great deal of care and attention on the reconstruction of Lahore, which had served for many years as his capital, the 'Seat of the Sultanate'. The huge baked-brick walls had been thrown up half a century before Khurram's arrival, their two vast gateways on the east and west sides providing the only entry or escape. Back in the 1550s, Akbar had observed that the ancient hilltop citadel was set too far back from the Ravi on its northern side, wasting the defensive potential of the natural barrier. So Akbar had filled in the sloping gradient between hillock and riverbank by piling chamber on top of subterranean chamber, raising the ground level to create a commanding plateau – as well as providing cool summer quarters in the rooms beneath, their windows looking out over the stream of the Ravi. The new north wall of the fortress, with the river lapping at its buttresses, presented an imposing, impregnable obstacle to any would-be assailant.

Sprawling below the towering walls of this renovated Imperial Fortress – the *Shahi Qila* – lay the narrow, twisting lanes of the town itself. This was where the bulk of the city's mercantile business was done and contemporary accounts make it clear that Lahore was a place 'of very great trade, wealth, and delight, lying more temperately out of the parching sun than any other of the emperor's great cities'.[14] The town lay at a crucial point on the trade route from the plains of Hindustan to Kabul and Kandahar. It was a settlement worth protecting and by Khurram's arrival in late 1606 the construction of further fortifications, walls and ditches around the perimeter, was already well underway, built around nine imposing gates on the landward side and three more giving directly onto the river.

Returning from Dhar village on the other side of the Ravi that August afternoon, the reunited royal family now crossed the river on a succession of broad-beamed and canopied ferryboats, disembarking at the western gate in the town's northern riverside wall. The townspeople thronged the waterside, penned back by imperial guards and Rajput cavalry. They cheered the emperor and the handsome young prince – their first glimpse of Khurram – as they rode past. They then fell silent in respect as the harem palanquins were carried, eight men apiece, up the slope to the castle gate. The royal ladies lay inside, reclining on silken cushions, scrupulously screened from public view, their purdah unbroken.

The real red-carpet treatment began as the emperor and his family entered the fortress itself, passing through Akbar's vast eastern gate. This massive structure was proof of the fort's practical military character. Its foot-thick hardwood gate, plated and studded with iron, opened between chunky octagonal bastions with crenellated battlements towering overhead. But the functional was, as so often in Mughal design, veiled by the aesthetic. The imposing brickwork of the gateway was layered over with thick plaster and painted with exquisite floral decorations in a swirl of bright colours. The hard, hot stone of the fortress steps was veiled too, in a continuity of tradition that stretched back to the days of Jahangir's forefathers. The entire passageway from the gate up to the royal residence in the northeast corner of the castle – a distance of several hundred yards – was draped and decorated with luxurious and immensely valuable cloth, to protect the feet of the imperial family as they dismounted. Imperial servants had laid a continuous carpet of brightly coloured Chinese silk, velvet from Europe, pashmina from the Himalayas, *kamkhab* brocade from the Persian city of Yazdi and *zarbaft* silk, woven with a weft of gold, to cushion the way as Khurram and his reunited clan passed on into the heart of the fort's household complex.

With the emperor again in residence, Lahore Fort resumed its role as nerve centre of the entire Mughal Empire. It had been eight long years since Akbar had last resided in the citadel; now the pomp and pageantry of the imperial entourage returned and the empty buildings of state once again resounded to the hubbub of daily court life, with its daily sessions of government business, administration of justice, military parades, elephant fights and other entertainments. These were months of peace and relaxation for the royal family. But where the emperor slept, there too was the emperor's work – and the labour of running an empire was a sleepless obligation. Jahangir performed his daily chores and logged them in his journal: housekeeping on an imperial scale, with its promotions and dismissals, gifts given and received, scientific experiments and religious holidays. In these tasks he had the constant support of two armies: both his soldiery and a parallel administrative army, an intricate and highly formal structure of bureaucrats, practitioners of Islamic law and law enforcement officers, all spread across the nation's provinces.[15]

The arrival of Prince Khurram presented Jahangir with an excellent opportunity to forge still closer ties with one of his most important advisers: Ghiyath al-Din Beg, a distinguished courtier who had served under Akbar and been retained by his heir Jahangir. A grey-bearded man of upright bearing and pale complexion, Ghiyath al-Din had decades earlier abandoned his home in Persia and travelled east. Bandits plundered his property on the way through the plains and his family fortune was reduced to two mules and their saddlebags. But compensation for this misfortune was at hand. At a remote caravanserai, the penniless Ghiyath al-Din fell in with a wealthy trader, who was able to make valuable introductions at court. Such an opening, to the patronage of Akbar the Great, was not one to be wasted. The Persian scholar's talents had been rewarded and he had risen steadily through the court hierarchy, wholly and effortlessly assimilated into Agra society. In time, he would reach the rank of *Wazir*, Chief Minister to the emperor, ennobled with the title *Itimad-al-Daula*, Pillar of the State.[16]

The fact that this distinguished adviser was a Persian and a Shiite to boot in no way diminished his prospects. Nor did it pose an obstacle to

a marriage between his family and that of the emperor himself. It was
the custom for Mughal princes to marry the daughters of the aristocracy,
a class that embraced without prejudice the traditional old families who
had travelled with Khurram's own ancestors from Central Asia, nobles of
impeccable Persian pedigree and India's own Hindu royalty, children of
the respected but subordinate kingdoms subsumed into the empire. So, as
the royal matchmakers cast about for an eligible wife for Khurram, it would
have been no leap of faith to scrutinise the family of Ghiyath al-Din, at
that time serving as Master of the Royal Household. Anyone familiar with
the affairs of the court aristocracy would have known that Ghiyath al-Din's
daughter, Mihr al-Nisa – a Sun Among Women – had already been married
off at the age of seventeen to a tough army officer named Ali Quli Beg
and was now sharing his quarters in Bengal.[17] It would be several years
before Mihr al-Nisa came to the royal court, in the wake of her husband's
disgrace and murder, and when she did it would be Jahangir's eye that she
would catch.

Akbar's
Eastern Gate
at Lahore Fort,
Shah Jahan's
birthplace

No daughter, then, but there was a grandchild. The eldest son of the
Master of the Royal Household, a promising young man named Abu-al-
Hassan, had a young daughter who *was* available: Lady (*Banu*) Arjumand.
At thirteen, she was just ten months younger than Khurram and, if stories at
court were to be believed, her looks, education and deportment matched
her political eligibility.[18]

Many tales have sprung up around the couple: Khurram and Arjumand, childhood sweethearts; Shah Jahan and *Mumtaz-Mahal*, the 'Most Exquisite of the Palace', the King and Queen whose love was immortal. Most of these tales are, unfortunately, of doubtful provenance and negligible value, the product of later fevered romanticism. But they speak to an abiding popular need to gloss the often ruthlessly pragmatic political manoeuvrings of emperors and their ministers with more human emotions. The most frequently repeated account of Khurram's fateful first meeting with Arjumand centres on the annual *Mina* Bazaar.

This special Jewel Market was an important part of the prolonged New Year festivities in mid-March, during which the women of the royal family and selected ladies of the nobility would gather in the palace precincts to 'play shop'.[19] The designated courtyard was screened off with sheets of colourful silk and brocade to ensure that the women would be seen by none other than their immediate family, their female servants, their posses of armed eunuchs and selected guests. It was therefore an irresistible opportunity for nobles with hopes of advancement to show off an eligible daughter to a young prince. Unsurprisingly, such a private and exclusive event – revolving around the mysterious invisible women of court – provoked salacious commentary. The Oxford-educated adventurer Thomas Coryat never even entered the palace grounds, let alone witnessed the Mina Bazaar, but, assuming that the fair was an opportunity for the lascivious emperor to indulge a roving eye, he wrote that the king became 'broker for his women' and 'by this means he attains to the sight of all the pretty wenches of the town'.[20]

In fact, the Mina Bazaar was a modest and never less than wholly stylish occasion, its twin-aisle format based on a typical pilgrim bazaar at Mecca in which precious souvenirs were sold to the faithful. Ladies associated with the court were given the opportunity to supplement their allowances by selling jewels, precious cloth, perfume and flowers to the male elite of the court: 'sultans, princes and nobles'.[21] For such a high-ranking clientele, it was demeaning even to ask the price of a choice item; when the vendor murmured the traditional market hustler's opening gambit, 'Pay me what you think it's worth', disproportionate sums changed hands in short order.

Not that the goods in the Mina Bazaar were shoddy or substandard. In an eloquent and flowery nineteenth-century treatise on the Jewel Market, Iradat-Khan described the shining array on sale, among them 'gems and rubies of Badakhshan, coral and multi-coloured stones like the rainbow … the best of the mines and the best of the oceans'. Solid gold roses with 'dew-drops' of pearl nestled on cushions of red satin. Necklaces and strings of pearls were modelled by statuesque slave-girls from Abyssinia and

Persia. Moving down past the material stalls, among great rolls of Chinese cloth and scarlet velvet, a browsing prince might find a young lady selling 'embroidery like a spring-time garden and printed satin that is so smooth that a rose-petal would feel like emery-board in comparison'.[22]

And, according to plausible tradition, it was on just such an occasion that Khurram and the young Arjumand first set eyes on one another. Before any engagement could go ahead, however, many consultations and formalities were required. Even though the betrothal was a political fix between Jahangir and his head of household, Ghiyath al-Din, no important family matters could be decided upon without the advice of the Queen Mother. Maryam-Zamani continued to wield considerable authority in any question involving the royal harem and her residence within the palace compound was the focus of many important functions and celebrations, including marriage ceremonies: if Khurram were to be married to the Lady Arjumand, the Queen Mother's blessing was a prerequisite.

There was also the vexed question of Khurram's own status as the emperor's third son. From his first four wives and one harem concubine, Jahangir had produced four boys and two girls, the most recent a sickly infant son named Shahriyar. The eldest son, nineteen-year-old Khusraw, had been born to a Hindu princess, Rajakumari Man Bai; but he had destroyed his own chances of inheriting the throne by launching an armed uprising against Jahangir within a month of his father's accession. Indeed, as will be seen, it was Khusraw's rebellion that had brought the emperor to Lahore, as the renegade had hoped to use the city as a fortified base for his rebellion. Brutal reprisals had followed the suppression of the revolt and Khusraw languished, blinded, in a subterranean dungeon in the northern sector of the Imperial Fortress. His mother, distraught, had taken her own life.

Khurram's next eldest half-brother, Pervez, was seventeen, the son of a Muslim lady known as Sahib-Jamal. He had been brought to Lahore in the wake of Khusraw's rebellion much more urgently than Khurram himself. Pervez had been out campaigning against the ruler of the Kingdom of Mewar, one of the independent Rajput principalities governed by a proud dynasty of the Hindu *kshatriya* warrior-caste and a constant thorn in the side of the Mughals. As the teenaged prince was so inexperienced, Jahangir had placed one of his most experienced officers, the elderly Mirza Jafar Beg *Asaf-Khan* in a superintendent position. The twenty thousand cavalry under Pervez's command – a huge expeditionary force designed to stamp out the last stubborn resistance against Mughal dominion – scored some early successes in the hills around the new Mewari capital at Udaipur. But Khusraw's rebellion prompted Jahangir to order his son to relocate to Lahore with all speed, giving the Maharana of Mewar time to regroup for the next encounter.

In the incipient power-struggle between the rival princes, then, the rebellion of Khusraw frustrated the ambitions of Pervez and benefited Khurram. A clear-cut victory in Mewar would have boosted immeasurably Pervez's claim to the succession; certainly it would have been outscored Khurram's nominal responsibility for the imperial capital and treasury. Jahangir had already fantasised in his journal that, with victory over Mewar in the bag, Hindustan could be left in the care of Pervez while he, the king, set out to achieve his father's and grandfather's dream and reconquer his ancestral lands in Central Asia.[23] Khurram would simply have been sidelined.

Jahangir appears to have dedicated the winter of 1606–7, spent at Lahore, to intense deliberation over the question of the succession. His journal at first indicates a clear preference toward Pervez. There were a number of high profile ceremonies and generous gifts that appeared to indicate favouritism, culminating in a uniquely Mughal promotion, to the rank (*mansab*) of Ten Thousand, bringing him to the level of the now disgraced Khusraw. This figure served three purposes: it denoted the number of foot soldiers that a member of the nobility was required to contribute to the national army though his own personal militia; it also established his position in the court pecking order, in direct relation to the numerical status ascribed to other individuals; and, as a loyal military corps at the heart of his retinue, this large group of retainers represented an important personal power base.[24] Shortly after his promotion came an opulent marriage ceremony on 28 October, in which Pervez was wed to his first cousin Lady Jihan, the daughter of Emperor Jahangir's younger half-brother, Prince Murad, another resolute drunkard. But by the New Year in spring, the emperor – without revealing his reasons – appears to have decided that the empire's best hopes lay with Khurram. He promptly began to pile on the honours.

On 30 March 1607, shortly after the conclusion of the prolonged festivities that marked both the spring equinox and Jahangir's formal accession to the throne, Prince Khurram was granted the authority to authenticate all imperial decrees, a gesture of trust that carried with it the formal title of Master of All Correspondence.[25] The prince was also given his first military rank, a banner of his own, drums to be beaten on parade and a traditional Central Asian *tuman tugh*, the yak-tail standard of a divisional commander. Finally – and perhaps cherished above all other honours – he was awarded the *lal purdah*, a scarlet silk curtain to draw across the entrance to his tent, in replacement of the silver drape customarily used by princes. The curtain was a vestige of ancient days, when the entrance to a clan leader's tent was screened to prevent anyone outside getting a clear bow-shot at the chieftain. Red was usually the prerogative of the king alone. From now on, the royal chroniclers would refer to him as *Shah buland iqbal*: the Prince of Good Fortune.

Khurram's new formal ranking of Eight Thousand still fell short of Pervez's – and it was an obligation that demanded considerable wealth. A body of fighting men might have been a useful power-base but a Mughal officer needed a substantial and regular income to raise, arm, train, accommodate and pay so many soldiers, as well as the mounts and equipment required by their Five Thousand cavalry counterparts. Given that both infantrymen and cavalry were paid at least 25 rupees per month, maintenance of Khurram's private militia contribution at the 8,000/5,000 level necessitated an income of nearly four million rupees per year, not including grooms and other ancillary personnel. Until that spring, Khurram had received a daily allowance commensurate with his status as a minor from the central treasury at Agra. With his appointment as Prince of Good Fortune, however, came the assignment of a *jagir*, an estate whose revenue went directly into Khurram's purse.[26] Nor was it just any estate that he now received. The provincial district of Hissar Firoza, a fertile territory one hundred miles west of Delhi, had traditionally been the gift of the emperor to his heir apparent. The courtier Muhammad Amin al-Qazvini described the event marking the awarding of the estate in highly emotional terms. It was a day 'more shining than the sun … one of the best days of the year', he wrote, before recalling that the stewardship of Hissar Firoza had been handed down, generation to generation, from Emperor to heir apparent.

'According to the ancestral custom,' Jahangir said, 'I have given my able son the said territory as a token of his rising to future greatness'. And, to discharge the duties of the government, he gave his kinglike enlightened son a great golden seal, to approve and confirm each and every warrant of government, and ordered that all orders be passed to the high-honoured prince and be signed with his own hand … in the hope of increasing the empire's endless wealth.[27]

Five days after this ceremony, Jahangir was on the verge of departure from Lahore. He had been in the city for nearly a year and felt the urge to mount a hunting expedition in the mountains around Kabul, a land cherished as the 'country of perpetual spring'. Like his predecessors, the emperor felt strongly his ancestral roots in the mountains of Central Asia and the attraction of the north was a powerful draw, especially when the weather grew intolerably hot in the plains of Hindustan.

But there was one more important item of business to be accomplished: the formal betrothal of Prince Khurram and Lady Arjumand. The arrangements had all been made, although the engagement gifts would take several months to select and present to the girl's father, Abu-al-Hassan

Ghiyath al-Din. Peace within the royal household was guaranteed as the Queen Mother's permission had been secured for the match – described by one courtier as the 'grafting of that rose of the garden of chastity and perfection with that fresh bush of the orchard of dignity and pomp'. That lush horticultural metaphor was appropriate indeed, for it was in Maryam-Zamani's private garden that the ceremony would take place, late at night on 4 April 1607.[28]

The Mughal garden was essential to the atmosphere of verdant luxury, coolness and ease that was so prized by the imperial family and the nobility. Khurram's ancestors had always planted gardens to serve the noble families of their imperial cities: in Kabul and Lahore, in the Kashmir valley and – perhaps most importantly – in Agra and Delhi, where they helped mitigate the fearsome heat of summer. More than simply places for physical restitution, Mughal gardens were objects of the most profound aesthetic thought – a complex Persian carpet, to be gazed upon from above; a representation of the centrality of water to life in both mountains and plain; and a glimpse on earth of Paradise to come. Like all Lahore's gardens, the Queen Mother's was more lush foliage than open lawn, densely planted with trees and bushes selected for their pleasing fragrance and merciful shade. One German traveller named Johann Albrecht de Mandelslo, describing a royal garden between Ahmedabad and Agra, noted that 'there was such abundance of trees, and they were planted so close, that we could walk about the garden in the shade, which was a great refreshing to us'.[29] William Finch, a trader selling indigo in the city market on behalf of the East India Company, eloquently described a typical Lahore garden experience; for a seventeenth-century European, it must have presented a mesmerising variety of exotic flavours.

In the midst of the garden is a very stately recreational terrace with fair buildings overhead, and a tank [large square pool] in the centre, with large and goodly galleries along the four sides thereof, supported with high stone pillars. Adjoining to this is a garden of the King's, in which are very good apples (but small), mulberry white and red, almonds, peaches, figs, grapes, quinces, oranges, lemons, pomegranates, roses, stock-flowers, marigolds, wall-flowers, irises, pinks white and red, with divers sorts of Indian flowers.[30]

The betrothal ceremony was a splendid example of the court at play in its richest and brightest attire. Gold, diamonds and pearls shone under the lamps; silk rustled as celebratory toasts were proposed; jewel-encrusted goblets of Persian wine and double-distilled liquor held high in acclaim. Fireworks crashed and boomed in glittering showers over the citadel: free entertainment for the masses in the crowded lanes of Lahore city below. Typically for this early period of Khurram's life, the most detailed and highly coloured account of the engagement comes from Muhammad Amin Qazvini. Deploying the traditional overwrought epithets of the court panegyrists – in which 'that bright Venus of the sphere of chastity' was hailed as 'worthy of conjunction with that auspicious star of the sky of fortune' – the poet embellished the event with swirling Persian flourishes of his own.

In short, His Majesty, who with his illuminating intelligence possessed clear knowledge of the inked letters inscribed on the foreheads of people and ... since he observed the lustre of happy fortune and worthiness on the shining forehead of that second Maryam, *Mumtaz-Zamani* ['Most Exquisite of the Age'] ... he asked her mother to produce that pearl of the casket of chastity in the inner apartments of the royal palace for the ceremony of betrothal to that star of the constellation of sovereignty. ... And that wise Lady ... made the Lady Mumtaz-Zamani kiss the carpet before that Solomon-like king. And His Majesty, having received her auspicious arrival with honour and respect, turned that heavenly assembly into the highest paradise through the blossoming of the garden of courtesy and blooming of the flowers of kindness. And, in a manner which befits the monarchs of pomp and glory, having performed the ceremony of betrothal, he embellished with the ring of luck the happy and fortunate finger of that worthy lady.[31]

At the centre of attention sat Khurram himself, a young man with many reasons to look forward to a long, contented, wealthy and very powerful life. He was the apple of his father's eye: freshly promoted, general to many thousand men, entrusted with a serious administrative appointment at the apex of the state bureaucracy and now engaged to be married to a gorgeous young lady of impeccable pedigree and no less impressive connections. In time, however, he would learn that the winds of political change can be fickle and harsh, the machinations of the all-powerful hostile as well as favourable. Khurram would discover that his temperamental father was not to be counted on and that other political priorities might assert themselves to delay the consummation of his own happiness.

Jahangir's 420-mile journey from Lahore to the hunting grounds around Kabul was achieved in a marathon seventy-two-day trek. That languorous average of fewer than six miles a day can largely be accounted for by the emperor's incorrigible enthusiasm for hunting and drinking, both of which prompted frequent and prolonged halts en route. It was all too easy to allow distractions to get in the way of business. And when camp was reached, the fixtures and furnishings enjoyed by the emperor made Khurram's earlier expedition from Agra to Lahore look positively tawdry. A king, as the Hindu courtier Chandrabhan the Brahmin would later observe, was meant to travel in style.

Wherever the sublime standards are displayed ... at every stage is pitched a complete set of tents, consisting of the sacred sleeping apartments, the baths, the Ordinary Audience Hall, apartments for the women, fitted up with windows, and other accommodations ... such as [various tents] made of satin, velvet, broad cloth embroidered with gold. The pavilions of the ... auspicious Monarch, together with those of the renowned Princes, ... the principal nobility and of all the other attendants, are placed in due order, at fixed distances.[32]

The latter stage of the journey to Kabul had been on a route described by Joannes de Laet, a Flemish geographer, as usually 'infested by Pathan brigands; and although the king has established twenty-three guard-stations of troops at regular intervals, none the less travellers are frequently robbed by these brigands'.[33] But the emperor travelled not just in style but also in formidable numbers. The focal point of the expedition was always the king, riding a favourite elephant or horse from the royal stables, or carried in a 'litter of gold and silver, inlaid and enamelled'. Around him rode the royal household, with the princes of the line, Khurram and Pervez, occupying places of honour. Their sisters, Sultan al-Nisa and Bahar, travelled with their two-year-old half-brother Shahriyar in the section of convoy where the royal ladies enjoyed security and privacy in their silken litters. This substantial mobile harem – amounting to as many as one thousand women, including their own army of servants – were carried in palanquins, six bearers apiece, or upon elephants, 'or else in cradles hanging on the sides of dromedaries, covered close and attended by eunuchs'.[34] Around them marched in close order the harem's own corps of elite guards, hardened fighters from the royal Hindu households of Rajasthan, loyal servants of their Muslim overlord – protecting his womenfolk, as one courtier put it, 'like a mountain of iron'. At the rear of the vast column, under even closer guard, travelled Prince Khusraw the traitor, his legs in chains.

After the royal family came the nobility. Each khan brought his own military detachment, raised from his own provincial estates, its size corresponding to his formal rank at court. Each too brought his family and household. Thousands of porters trudged in the rear, carrying the innumerable impedimenta of an army and an imperial court on the march. Vast numbers of camp followers swelled the host, to such an extent that at every night's camp a substantial market sprang up around the administrative core, catering to every requirement from grain and weaponry to clothing and books. 'When he rides on progress or hunting,' noted William Hawkins, the English merchant, 'the compass of his tents may be as much as the compass of London and more; and I may say that of all sorts of people that follow the camp there are two hundred thousand, for he is provided as for a city.' [35]

The logistics of such a vast operation were handled by the imperial Ministry of Furnishings, whose duties extended to pitching camp every night. The department in fact ran two complete operations, setting up one camp while the second – the 'forward camp' – leap-frogged ahead of the emperor's retinue to locate the next suitable halt. There the ground would be levelled and the huge array of lavish facilities taken for granted by Jahangir and his family would be erected. The foreman of this team would also be responsible for constructing bridges over any rivers that lay in the path of the expedition. One such bridge, sturdy enough to hold Jahangir's largest elephant without wobbling, took three days to build. Ministry officials also carried and maintained a good supply of boats that might be necessary when a river was too broad to be bridged or when the emperor simply fancied a recreational fishing expedition.

Jahangir's destination, the ancient mountain city of Kabul, was a large and attractive place, endowed with two fortified citadels and many comfortable and secure caravanserais for travelling merchants. It was a key point on the imperial trade routes: west into Persia and east towards China. Contemporary accounts describe the city as a 'great resort of merchants'. There was 'very much merchandise of silk and cloth, and of precious stones, both rubies, diamonds, and pearls', while 'great quantities of silk, musk, rhubarb and other merchandise are … brought to this province from China'.[36]

It was the court astrologers, both Hindu and Muslim, who had advised the emperor that the year AH 1016 would be one of particular auspiciousness for Prince Khurram. So, to celebrate his sixteenth birthday, they now cast a special horoscope and found it 'portentous'. So remarkable were their predictions that they urged the emperor to break with tradition and grant Khurram the unprecedented honour of an additional *Tuladan* weighing ceremony. This practise had been adopted by Khurram's liberal grandfather, the late Emperor Akbar, for whom the ceremony was carried out twice a year, on important solar and lunar calendar events. It was one of a number of ancient Hindu rituals – in which the ruler's weight in gold and precious stones was originally distributed to Brahmin priests for the maintenance of temple precincts – appropriated by Akbar to enhance his own legitimacy in locally recognizable terms. The emperor was weighed several times in succession against a variety of valuable items, which were then distributed as alms to the poor. At solar celebrations, Akbar had been weighed twelve times, starting with gold coins; at the lunar ceremony, he was weighed eight times, beginning with silver. Jahangir, now just twenty months on the throne, had maintained the biannual tradition. The opulence of one such occasion moved an elderly visitor from Samarkand to compose a short, elegant verse that played on the Persian word *mizan* – used both for the scales of the weighing apparatus and the zodiacal month of the emperor's enthronement.

When the Emperor sat in the scales, I said,
'The Sun of the World is in the house of Libra!' [37]

Just four months earlier, Prince Khurram had himself been weighed, as convention dictated for a prince of the royal line, on the occasion of *Nauruz*, the Spring Festival, when Aries began and the court devoted itself to an eighteen-day jamboree that also marked the second official anniversary of his father's accession to the throne.[38] Now, the astrologers had urged a second ceremony, placing the prince – now assumed to be the heir apparent – on a par with the only other man to be accorded such an honour, the emperor himself. And so, on 30 July 1607, the cream of the royal Mughal court turned out in all their finery at Khurram's Orta-Bagh mansion for an occasion whose opulence and profligacy effortlessly demonstrated the enormous wealth of the Mughals. The property had been assigned to the young prince upon arrival at Kabul. Dissatisfied with its layout, he had ordered a rapid and comprehensive interior redesign. The successful results – according to Jahangir, 'delightful and well-proportioned' – were an early hint of the design masterpieces to come.[39]

Now, Khurram sat patiently in the Orta-Bagh garden, in front of a truly princely pavilion, built between tall cypresses and shady mulberries. Stretched over his head was a crimson silk canopy, fringed with gold brocade. Underfoot was a thick layer of carpets, the finest made in Persia and Kashmir. The largest was densely knotted in azure-dyed wool, picked out with silver and white flowers. Its central motif, set in a blaze of scarlet, was a trio of dancing girls. As the prince watched his father approach for the ceremony, his gaze was levelled upwards – because he sat not on the traditional ceremonial divan of stiff gold cloth but at floor-level. His seat was a square cushion, its sides plated with gold and studded with blood-red carnelians, that formed one side of a huge set of scales. The enormous balance was shaped from long slender beams of intricately carved timber, gilded and bejewelled.

Prince Khurram is weighed at Kabul, July 1607

On a white silk sheet beside the scales were set out the counterweights for the Tuladan ceremony. First gold, then phials of quicksilver, bolts of silk, flasks of ambergris, musk, sandalwood and aloes. Brass trays with precisely laid out displays of jewellery, ornate weapons, swatches of the finest Bengali muslin – all lay waiting to be added in turn to the balance, more and more until the exact weight of the prince should be met. And

all the while an official from the state treasury noted down proceedings in his book.

By the prince's side, holding the ropes of the A-frame balance with a firm hand, was Abd-al-Rahim Khan. He had been Prime Minister under Akbar and retained in that office by Jahangir, not just in tribute to his long and faithful service but in recognition of the indispensable value of an adviser who was fluent in Persian, Arabic, Turkish and Hindi. A grey-bearded and dark-skinned figure, Abd-al-Rahim Khan was, at fifty, a veteran of the court administration and a polymath.[40] Poet, diplomat and soldier, he had distinguished himself in Akbar's campaigns in the southern Deccan and served as Jahangir's personal mentor since the emperor was thirteen. A sly and sometimes amoral pragmatist – the Niccolò Machiavelli of his time and place – his favourite axiom was 'Enmity to an enemy should come out under the guise of friendship'. With such various talents, it was no surprise that he was honoured at court with the simple title *Khan-Khanan*: the Khan of Khans. Dressed simply in plain white turban and trousers, with a white cotton stole draped round his shoulders and over his grey silk shirt, he now prepared to murmur blessings, prayers and Koranic quotations into Khurram's ear during the ceremony.[41]

Behind the Khan of Khans, in a dutiful row, stood the key figures of court: generals, ministers and trusted counsellors to the emperor. As Jahangir approached, each bowed to perform the taslim salute, touching the ground with the back of his right hand, then rising and bringing his right palm up to the crown of his head before finally saluting the monarch with the greeting *Hazarat-i alam-panah*, 'Lord Protector of the World'. Most prominent among these courtiers, at the right end of the row, stood Ghiyath al-Din Beg, grandfather of Khurram's bride-to-be. To his left stood Zamana Beg, the son of another influential Persian family who had migrated from Shiraz to set up home in Kabul. Zamana, charged with the care of the emperor's private apartments, was one of the emperor's most ruthless and feared acolytes: his title *Mahabat-Khan* – Master of Terror – summed up his willingness to do anything to forward his ruler's ambitions.

This pairing was a perfect example of the blend at court. Many of Akbar's loyal staffers were retained for their experience and to maintain a sense of continuity. But in this, the second year of Jahangir's reign, newcomers were also enjoying a rapid rise up the ladder of imperial favour. They were, in many cases, sneered at by veteran courtiers as arrivistes, boorish and headstrong, with a whiff of the provinces about them; but to the king they were loyalists, tried and tested during the long years when Jahangir was himself crown prince and a petulant heir apparent – when he and his coterie had grown increasingly impatient with the long wait to come into his inheritance.

Now, at a signal from the emperor, a group of functionaries began to pile leather sacks stuffed full of little gold coins onto the square pan on the opposite side of the balance holding the young prince. As the quantity of gold heaped up, Khurram began to ascend until his square seat came to a halt, swaying almost imperceptibly in a slight pendulum motion as another grey-bearded court flunkey added a few last mohurs to get the balance just right. The sixteen-year-old prince sat cross-legged in demure silence, his upright posture and calm stillness the result of physical fitness and an acute awareness of the dignity of the occasion. The ceremony was a formulaic ritual but still a powerful way of demonstrating the generosity of a leader to the poor who would receive the alms from the weighing scales – proof that, though youthful, he was already mindful of his responsibility to the less fortunate of the empire. It was also a clear statement on Jahangir's intent: here, under the eyes of the nations' most senior dignitaries, was their future leader. Prince Khurram was, literally, in the ascendant.

2
The Millennial Child

According to the will of the Almighty,
the King appeared in the world at the end of a thousand years.
He banished the abusive manners of oppression and tyranny from the
    world
and lighted up the solitary places of the infidels and the blind.

Muhammad Amin Qazvini[1]

A wide-awake shepherd makes for a flock that sleeps soundly.

Muhammad Sharif Mutamid-Khan[2]

The long tale of Prince Khurram Shah Jahan had begun fifteen years earlier on those same northern fringes of the empire. Khurram was born in the imperial mansion at Lahore Fort on 15 January 1592. In the context of his religion and his times, he was a millennial child. His birth-date – 30 Rabi I 1000 by the Muslim calendar – fell not just in the month of the Prophet Muhammad's own birth but in the thousandth year since he had made the *hijra*, his celebrated strategic relocation from Mecca to Medina. The kingdom's most respected and influential astrologers, both Hindus and Muslims, immediately fell to work on drawing up the new prince's horoscope. The stargazers noted that Khurram's birthday fell on the twenty-fifth day in the zodiacal month of Capricorn and observed from their charts additional planetary auspices that boded well for the infant's future. The celebrated Shiite cleric, Mullah Mahmud of Indjan, rejoiced in the birth of 'the star of the constellation of the caliphate', while another courtier, Muhammad Hadi, reached back into literary history for premonitions of this remarkable day.

It is also a sign of auspiciousness and divine guidance that at the beginning of every millennium a world ruler should come into existence to eradicate rebellion and ignorance from the world, just as the rising of this star was predicted 565 years ago by Afzal al-Din Hakim Khaqani:

'They say that every thousand years there comes into this world one who is privy to the people of perfection. One came before this, but we had not yet been born; one will come after this, but we will have sunk into grief.'

On the third day after his birth, His Majesty the Emperor Akbar went to the palace to feast his eyes on the baby's world-adorning beauty and such a celebration was held that the eyes of the world were dazzled.[3]

The birth of a prince was indeed an occasion for lavish celebrations. All the most influential nobles of the kingdom were expected to send gifts of tribute and congratulation to the royal family. Men of letters, musicians and singers contributed their own offerings of prose and poetry. The subsidised court poets waxed lyrical. One opined sycophantically that the creator of the world's wonderful works had opened his treasury and given the King a pearl; another boasted that a new star shone out, the equal of which had not before been seen. Others, in a blend of artistry and pedantry that was typical of the Mughal literati, were put to work to come up with appropriately sonorous chronograms whose constituent Persian letters, each assigned its own numerical value, added up neatly to 1,000: the Islamic year.[4] One Persian courtier wrote later that, at Khurram's emergence into the world, 'the world was so joyful that the old became as frolicsome in their happiness as green youths'.[5] This remark may have been a specific reference to Khurram's grandfather, the fifty-year-old emperor Akbar himself.

Khurram was born in the thirty-sixth year of Akbar's enlightened reign. It had been an extraordinary period in which Akbar – beginning at the age of just fourteen – had conquered a vast swathe of territory, hundreds of thousands of square miles of mountain, plain, field and river, embracing large portions of what we know today as northern and central India, Afghanistan, Pakistan, and Bangladesh. It was a period of constant campaigning and steady territorial expansion, as Akbar subjugated or negotiated treaties with smaller kingdoms and city-states, integrating them into the sprawling dominions of his greatly enlarged Mughal Empire. For the past half-century, Jalal al-Din Muhammad Akbar had ruled this vast territory with wisdom and liberality, taking a personal interest in the oversight of his empire's political, administrative, social and cultural development.

It was Akbar himself who named the newborn boy, giving him a typically straightforward, emotionally honest name that borrowed the Persian word for 'joyous': *khurram*. In so doing, he endeared himself to Hindu courtiers, who knew that truly auspicious birth-names were never chosen blindly. According to a verse by the poet laureate and Sanskrit scholar Faydi Mubarak, the name of a child born in Capricorn must begin with the letters *K* or *Kh*: Khurram fit the bill splendidly.[6] The little boy quickly grew to become his grandfather's favourite and many of the old emperor's personal characteristics were clearly appealing to the youngster.

Akbar was respected for his simple, direct and mostly courteous approach to everyone he encountered; an emperor as much loved as

feared. He had spent much of his childhood either in exile in Persia –
following his father Humayun's military defeats during the 1540s – or on
the long, weary road back to royalty, as Humayun fought his way over the
northern mountains via Kabul to reclaim his throne at Delhi. Deprived by
these wanderings of a settled education, Akbar made up for it by a tireless
curiosity: for spiritual meaning, for the best ways to achieve administrative excellence, even for the grimy skills of the carpenter, blacksmith or
armourer. A letter from Fr Anthony Monserrate, a Portuguese Jesuit priest
visiting Akbar in Lahore shortly before Khurram's birth, leaves us an elegant
and concise pen portrait of the emperor.

**The King is of good stature, sturdy of body, arms and legs, broad-shouldered. The configu-
ration of his face is ordinary, and does not reflect the grandeur and dignity of the person
because, besides being Chinese-like as the Mughals usually are, it is lean, sparse of beard,
wrinkled and not very fair. The eyes are small but extremely vivid ... and they also reveal
sharpness of mind and keenness of intellect.**[7]

That description of the emperor matches exactly Akbar's depiction in
contemporary portraits – most noticeably in his small round head, cropped
sandy hair and almond-shaped eyes – and speaks volumes for the dynasty's
roots in the mountains and plains of Central Asia. The name 'Mughal' itself,
a bastardisation of 'Mongol', emerged from those Asiatic origins – although
a more accurate correct dynastic label would have been 'Chagatay Turk',
indicating descent from the second son of Genghis Khan, or even 'Timurid',
for Khurram's family also claimed direct descended from the great four-
teenth-century warlord, Timur the Lame of Samarkand, remembered with
pride in Mughal family history as the Prince Temur Kuragan.

During the great years of the Mughal court, there were more than
nostalgic remnants of that lineage from the Central Asian steppe. Perhaps
the most significant baggage was the abiding idea that all the sons of the
chieftain had an equal claim to rule. Instead of following the principle of
primogeniture, a successor had to prove himself, preferably by building
his own political power base, backed by military muscle, and defeating
his brothers, uncles, nephews, cousins and occasionally sons to obtain
the leadership. This leftover from the centuries of rootlessness brought
upheaval to generation after generation of Mughals in the sub-continent
– with Khurram's later uprising against his father Jahangir forming just
one link in a seemingly inevitable chain of rebellion – although it did at
least guarantee a brisk turnover of military and bureaucratic talent, as the
survivors of each struggle for succession brought in their own adherents to
recreate the central core of power in their own likeness.[8]

There is a traditional saying in Arabic, cited at the Mughal court, that 'love of one's homeland is an article of faith'; during Khurram's childhood, this lineage would have been drummed into him as a core statement of his identity.[9] His destiny might be to rule all the vast lands of Hindustan – from the Kashmir Valley to the central Indian Deccan plains, from Baluchistan on the frontier with Persia to the Bengali port of Chittagong – but his origins lay emphatically in the mountains of the north. So his fingers would have traced down the family tree: through the generations immediately succeeding Timur and down through the centuries to the first Mughal rulers of the subcontinent. Each acquired, upon his coronation, honorific titles celebrating their pride in Islam; each acquired, upon his death, a further title by which he was referred in all future dynastic chronicles.[10]

The arrival of the Mughals in the first half of the sixteenth century was the last of the great cultural invasions of the South Asian sub-continent and with it Khurram's great-great-grandfather Babur created an empire that became an extraordinary cultural melting pot, a model of assimilation. Its human ingredients were Muslim and Hindu, Persian, Bengali, Gujarati and a myriad more besides, as well as those traditional tribal elements imported from Central Asia. And the military invasion of Khurram's forebears from outside the north-west frontier of the South Asian landmass was followed, at least as relentlessly, by a secondary invasion of immigrants. Individuals and families, holy men, fighters, literary personalities and plain adventurers, all trickled into an hospitable and wealthy environment of cultural and religious tolerance where they flourished, influencing society, religion and literature with their own mainly Persian or Arab values. So the administration of the empire, genuinely multi-cultural, evolved constantly, synthesising tribal practices from the Mughals' Central Asian past with a vast range of indigenous practices: local Hindu systems, structures of the pre-Mughal Delhi sultanate, as well as theoretical remnants of the great Arab dynasties at Baghdad, Damascus and Cairo.

Akbar's own tireless search for metaphysical answers embodied that process of assimilation and synthesis. His combined liberalism and intellectual curiosity made him a fascinating mentor and role model for his grandson Khurram, although it caused great friction at court and consternation among the established elite of the Sunni orthodoxy. The emperor encouraged the free celebration of all religious holidays: not just the Zoroastrian Spring Festival of Nauruz but the major Muslim festivals of Ramadan, the Eid al-Fitr and the Eid al-Adha, as well as the great Hindu celebrations of Dussehra and Diwali. Akbar's readiness to engage in a free-for-all discussion of religious ideas left outsiders amazed. 'If I had spoken thus against Muhammad in Turkey or Persia,' wrote Thomas Coryat after a typically feisty exchange of views, 'they would have roasted me upon

a spit; but in the Mughal's dominions a Christian may speak much more freely than he can in any other Muhammadan country in the world.'[11]

The zenith of Akbar's search for religious truth – or, for his detractors, the nadir – was the establishment, in 1582, of a new 'divine religion', the *Din Illahi*. To shape it, he cherry-picked aspects of theory and dogma from Islam, Hinduism, Jainism and Zoroastrianism, though conspicuously (and despite the best efforts of the relentlessly assiduous Jesuit missionaries) not Christianity. In addition, he assumed the role of *mujtahid* – the supreme guide to the interpretation of religion – and disciples of the new religion wore special badges to indicate their fidelity to this radical departure from the mainstream.[12] Orthodox Muslims of both Sunni and Shiite schools could only watch with outrage as the king convened a special council to endorse his new state religion and his own infallibility. Revenge came later. The Mughal historian Abd-al-Qadir Badauni, a conservative Sunni, wrote in highly pejorative terms of Akbar's delusion, ranting that the emperor had been led astray by 'bastards' and 'low irreligious persons' and ultimately 'plunged into scepticism'. 'To his entire satisfaction,' Badauni concluded, 'Akbar was able to carry out his project of overturning the dogmas and principles of Islam, to set up his novel, absurd and dangerous regulations and to give currency to his own vicious belief.'[13]

Whatever the spiritual complexities and internal rivalries at court, however, the fact remained that the Mughals were, in most respects, as different from the bulk of the Indian population as were the travellers and traders from Western Europe who noted their extravagances with such fascination. The point was not lost on more astute observers, even if it was coloured by a prevailing sense of cultural superiority: in a letter of July 1580 to a colleague in Goa, Fr Anthony Monserrate noted acidly that Akbar and his men were 'white men like us, very clever, and still have not a little of the barbarian.'[14]

The Mughal royal family itself became in time a microcosm of the larger cultural melting-pot. Khurram's own mother was a Hindu princess named Manmati Jagat Ghosain, the daughter of Udai Singh 'the Fat Raja' of Marwar. His fiefdom was an important principality in Rajasthan with an army of 80,000 soldiers; its admirers liked to boast of its distinguished lineage, status among other Hindu clans and military prowess. But Marwar was still subordinate to the empire and to have a daughter marry into the imperial family was a time-honoured way of improving prospects at court. There, like the majority of imperial womenfolk who were given honorifics and nicknames or known simply by reference to their places

Emperor Akbar and Crown Prince Salim (later Jahangir)

of birth, Manmati was called simply *Jodh-Bhai*, 'Sister from Jodhpur'.[15] Khurram's father, Crown Prince Salim – the alcoholic who would adopt the name Jahangir on his coronation day – was just twenty-two when Khurram was born. His wedding to Manmati Jodh-Bhai had been a characteristically lavish ceremony, featuring both Hindu fire-ceremonies, with priests chanting Sanskrit verses, and the full Muslim proprieties, in the presence of the *Qadi*, the senior Islamic jurist, and an array of military and civilian dignitaries. The occasion had prompted the Emperor Akbar to restore to the bride's father several districts of Rajasthan that had earlier been confiscated, to the extent that Udai Singh's revenues doubled.[16]

Manmati Jodh-Bhai was just one of a number of royal wives in a harem whose considerable size was commensurate with her husband's status as heir apparent. Salim's first wife was Rajakumari Man Bai, the daughter of Raja Bhagwan Das Kachwaha of Amber, a prominent Rajput prince who had done sterling service for Akbar.[17] They had been married in February 1585 and the dowry alone, including strings of Persian horses, elephants, slaves, utensils of solid gold, rare jewellery and 'seven hundred sets of costly dresses for the bride' was valued at two hundred thousand rupees.[18] This princess had already borne Salim two children: Princess Sultan al-Nisa and Prince Khusraw; after the successful production of a male heir, she was known in subsequent court records as *Shah-Begum*, the 'Royal Lady'.

Around each small sub-section of the royal family swirled a host of women and children. The imperial harem was a babel of tongues: Persian, Sanskrit, Hindi, Gujarati, the old Turkish of Central Asia and many other tongues beside. Each of Salim's wives and concubines brought her own staff to take care of all essential personal services. Each of these great ladies of court strove to assert the right to prevail in this hot-house of rival ambitions and fought to preserve their own traditional practises and religious affiliations. Khurram's other half-brother Pervez – his elder by three years – was the son of Sahib-Jamal, daughter of a respected Muslim religious personality. A second half-sister, Lady Bahar, was born to a third wife, *Malik-Jahan*, 'Queen of the World', the daughter of Raja Kalyan Das of Jaisalmer, another of Akbar's Rajput generals. In fact, official records indicate that Khurram's father had at least twelve more wives, including the (unnamed) daughters of Mirza Muhammad Hakim, a Muslim aristocrat well connected at court, Maharaja Rai Singh of Bikaner and various local chieftains from as far apart as Kabul, Kashmir and Khandesh.[19]

These inter-faith marriages made for good politics from the emperor's perspective: Muslim overlords assimilating their Hindu subordinates both martially and maritally. More remarkably, however, it meant that Khurram – ostensibly the latest generation in a proudly Muslim dynasty – had just one grandparent who was a Muslim: Akbar himself. Yet, while assimilation was both practical and relatively easy to accomplish, this did not mean that Hindu pride escaped undented. Indeed, Rajput sources occasionally betray the depth of resentment, with one commentator observing tartly that the name of Bhagwan Das was 'execrated as the first who sullied Rajput purity by matrimonial alliance with the Islamite'.[20]

Thus it was as a member of this crowded and multi-faith harem that the Princess Manmati gave birth to her first and only son. Despite the fact that she survived the birth – which, for all the wealth and comfort of the royal household, was certainly not guaranteed – the baby was taken away from her by Akbar and entrusted to the emperor's unmarried cousin, Ruqayya Sultan Begum. The trauma of this sudden deprivation is not recorded and Manmati is allowed to fade from the official history, her child-bearing function fulfilled.[21] There was likely a political dimension to Khurram's transfer to Ruqayya's household. Relations between Akbar and Salim were souring and the emperor may have wanted to move a healthy potential heir into his own household. Manmati's loss was the Lady Ruqayya's gain. But, as Muhammad Amin Qazvini noted with affectionate hyperbole, 'Mother Time, like the wet-nurse, began to rear Khurram up by the milk of understanding and by the tread of his faltering first steps he reached the head of honour on the high firmament'.[22] And despite the fact that the baby had been whisked away from his own household, Salim Jahangir recalled many years later, perhaps with rose-tinted hindsight, that Ruqayya had loved little Khurram 'a thousand times better than if he had been her own'.

Little by little as his years progressed, real potential was noticed in him. He served my exalted father [Akbar] more and better than any of my sons and my father was very pleased with him and his service. He always commended him to me. Many times he said, 'There is no comparison between him and your other sons. I consider him my [own] true son.' [23]

So Khurram's training for leadership began from his earliest years and at the feet of one of the greatest military leaders and most profound philosophical seekers of the age. That the emperor should be paying such close attention to the young prince, however, should have worried Salim, because it clearly indicated that Akbar was already looking to his grandson's generation for a successor. All three of Akbar's sons – Salim, Murad and Daniyal – were alcoholics and drug addicts, something that must have caused him considerable anxiety for the future of the kingdom he had worked so hard to build. Murad and Daniyal were the children of anonymous harem concubines of lesser distinction than Salim's Hindu mother but, as boys, they automatically took precedence over daughters born even to ranking queens of aristocratic birth. At the time of Khurram's birth, Murad was a tall, dark-skinned twenty-one-year-old, settling in to his new appointment as Governor of Malwa province, winning 'the standard, kettle-drums … banner and all the insignia pertaining to a prince royal'.[24] But for Murad, as for his party-loving brothers, performance and duty often came second to poetry, wine and late-night salons. Unlike Akbar, his sons had been born and raised in pampered luxury, untempered by deprivation or suffering, and he took a dim view of their carousing. Akbar certainly enjoyed a glass or two of wine on appropriate occasions and was not remotely troubled by any religious prescriptions to the contrary – but he was absolutely intolerant of anything that might detract from administrative competence. 'Indulging in intoxicants and being reckless,' he noted, 'is not the habit of emperors.'

It is best for them to be always wide-awake and watchful; the king is the guardian and watchman of the realm. Wantonness or intoxication is a dream; it does not behove one who is guardian or custodian; it behoves him to remain alert and cautious.[25]

The desire to inculcate exactly those qualities underpinned Akbar's close personal supervision of Khurram's education, both academic and physical. The prince naturally received the best that was available in the Mughal kingdom. Convention had long dictated that education began immediately after circumcision, at the precise, astrologically charted age of four years, four months and four days. Back in November 1572, Khurram's father Salim had himself been circumcised at that exact age, amid great celebrations. But Akbar had more recently issued an edict – just one in a series of liberal regulations that challenged convention – to the effect that no boy could be circumcised before the age of twelve and that circumcision could only be carried out with the boy's stated agreement. Still, the four years/four months/four days stipulation continued to apply to education. This meant that, since Akbar liked to use the solar calendar of the zodiac, Khurram began his formal tuition on 18 May 1596 with the *maktab* ceremony.

The celebration was led by the court's most distinguished scholars, Sunni, Shiite and Hindu, orthodox and Sufi, who put aside their differences for the day. Maulana Qasim Beg of Tabriz presented a selection of edifying texts in exquisite calligraphy. Then, on a sandalwood slate, he inked in the slender shape of the first letter of the Persian alphabet, *alif*, before demanding that Khurram copy his sample. With Akbar beaming from the wings, the young prince then touched the Koran to his brow, pledged to be guided always by its commandments and by the Hadith, the sayings and traditions of the Prophet Muhammad – before reciting the *fatiha*, the holy book's opening verse: *bismillah al-rahman al-rahim*, 'In the name of Allah, the compassionate, the merciful'. The ceremonial complete, the mullah was rewarded with a rich silk brocade robe – while the court poets jostled to come up with an ode that would win royal approval.

Perfect knowledge was his crown;
Nine circles of the sky were the lines of his education.
His divine heart knew God's secrets
And the *khutba* of kingship was written upon his forehead.
The secrets of the divine world were hidden in his heart;
The divine knowledge was in his mind.
He got the lesson from the unseen world
And the teachers from the School of Truth.
His essence was from the Ocean of Eternity
And knowledge was revealed in his speech.[26]

Qasim Beg supervised Khurram's early education with an exacting eye. The tutor was a Persian scholar, lyric poet and Sufi of high rank who had, like so many senior courtiers, travelled to the Mughal capital from his original home at Tabriz. The standard of literacy required was high; Qasim's successor, a distinguished medical doctor named Hakim Ali, was just as demanding. Dr Ali's is a story that illustrates the opportunities available to outsiders in the Mughal dominions. He had travelled from his hometown of Gilan in western Persia as a young and impoverished would-be medical man. He worked hard and eventually word of his skill reached the emperor's ear, prompting Akbar to subject the young foreigner to a test. He challenged Ali to identify correctly urine samples from sick and healthy individuals – as well as from donkeys and cows. Ali's successful labelling of the mixed-up samples gave him an opening at court, where he rose to become the emperor's personal physician and friend. Dr Ali was also a mathematician, a literary commentator and an architect of some standing. More useful politically was his developing relationship with Khurram's father, Crown Prince Salim, who profited from his confidant's 'great skill in the management of affairs and business of the world'.[27]

Over the next ten years, Khurram was subjected to a demanding timetable of lessons, all revolving around the Persian language, which Akbar had declared the *lingua franca* of state administration. Curricular emphasis was laid almost equally on acquiring literary merit and skills in polity. There were several key texts, mandatory in the education of a prince who enjoyed the patronage of the emperor. Among the poetic classics were the *Gulistan* ('Garden of Roses') and *Bustan* ('Fruit Garden') of the thirteenth century master Sheikh Muslih al-Din Sadi. Important works on morals and ethics included the memoir *Contemplation and Action* by Nasr al-Din Tusi and Jalal al-Din Davani's *Flashes of Illumination on Praiseworthy Ethics*. Other key items on the prince's curriculum included astronomy, arithmetic and geometry, medicine, logic and religion. The campaigns and policies of the prince's own ancestors, too, were a priority in the classroom. These were described in a range of memoirs, from the early Timurid period – written in the ancient family language, the Chagatay Turkic dialect of the northern mountains – right through to the elegant Persian compositions of Akbar's own chamberlain, Sheikh Abu-al-Fadl the Learned (*al-Allami*), which were worked up over time to become the most authoritative account of the Great Mughal's reign, the *Akbarnama*.[28] In the words of one of Khurram's most cherished teachers, all these texts would be of use when, as an adult, he joined 'the assemblies of the learned'.[29]

The little boy proved himself an able pupil – though to Akbar's disappointment Khurram's rapid acquisition of Persian was not matched by a similar interest in the old family Turkish. But with a man like Akbar as his ultimate mentor, Khurram knew that provable practical skills were cherished at least as dearly as abstract academic abilities. So, at the age of five, he began archery lessons with Mir Murad Juwaini, a senior officer who was subsequently promoted to military administrator of Lahore Fort and who claimed direct descent from the Prophet Muhammad. At the age of eight, Khurram started additional musketry lessons, as well as swordsmanship, cavalry techniques, spear work and wrestling – all under the watchful eye of Raja Salivahan, a trusted Hindu officer in Salim's personal militia.[30]

In addition to these core physical skills of a proudly martial society, the young prince became familiar with the great beast that defined the royal family's self-image: the elephant. Elephants were highly cherished and sought after in great numbers. In his youth, Akbar was known to mount his prized elephants by hopping first onto a lowered tusk, then clambering up the ridged trunk before finally vaulting into the canopied howdah – an acrobatic skill that earned him the label *Fil-Afgan*, the 'Overthrower of Elephants'. Imperial memoirs were peppered with affectionate accounts of favourite elephants, which were given names like 'Light of Nauruz', 'Mountain of Gold' and '*Sundara*', the Sanskrit for 'beautiful'. Carefully regulated elephant fights were an important event at court and thousands of these great beasts, symbols of power and royalty, were housed and pampered in their own quarters at the imperial Elephant House and lavishly fitted with golden ornaments.[31]

The Mughal capital during Khurram's childhood lay at Agra. Lahore had served its purpose as a base for empire building but Akbar's sprawling dominions had to be directed from a more central location. In October 1558, he found the perfect spot on the bank of the Yamuna River, whose broad and reliable flow allowed river traffic north to the derelict old city of Delhi and east to Allahabad, where it met the mighty Ganges. Akbar's grandfather, Babur, had visited the spot in the late 1520s and had a beautiful garden constructed on the eastern side of the Yamuna. Set in fertile arable land, this ancient settlement stood at a natural crossroads at the heart of the empire. The king's road west led, via Jaipur and Ahmedabad, to the Arabian Sea and the imperial port at Surat. North, beyond Delhi, lay Lahore and the mountain regions of Kabul and Kashmir. East, by road or river, stretched the provinces of Oudh, Bihar and Bengal. And south lay the long road to Ajmer and Burhanpur, essential bridgeheads for the almost incessant campaigning against the remaining independent principalities in the hills of Rajasthan to the south-west and the rulers of the three Shiite 'Deccan' states beyond the southern fringes of Hindustan – Ahmadnagar, Bijapur and Golconda – which together represented the last bulwark against total Mughal domination of the sub-continent.[32]

Like Lahore, Agra had had its own ancient fort before the arrival of the Mughals from the north, one that had been a conspicuous landmark, acclaimed by an eleventh century poet in the verse 'The citadel of Agra appeared in the midst of the dust like a mountain / Its ramparts and battlements like mountain peaks'. But time had wrought its customary damage and harsh reality belied the poetic hyperbole: as early as 1558, at just sixteen, the young Emperor Akbar gazed at a dismally crumbling brick structure on a dusty hummock of land and pledged to sweep away the rubble before laying the foundation stones of his own mighty red sandstone fort on the modest elevation beside the river. The first blocks of dressed stone were not laid until 1565 but thereafter the construction proceeded apace, funded by special taxes on the surrounding district. Akbar threw money – as much as three-and-a-half million rupees – as well as manpower into the construction of his new fortress, a project carried out under the watchful eye of Muhammad Qasim Khan, Head of the Imperial River Fleet.[33] A strange selection, perhaps, for site supervisor – but the Yamuna was vital for the transport of hundreds of tons of granite and sandstone. Eight thousand labourers manhandled the raw material on its river passage before passing it into the hands of the 'two thousand stone-cutters and the same number of sculptors and stone masons … engaged for the work'.[34] Construction took eight years but by 1573 Akbar's new Seat of the Caliphate had been born, a city lauded by the king's loyal retainer Sheikh Abu-al-Fadl as 'the centre of the circle of the throne and the ascension point of the light of fortune'. 'Abodes were distributed to the grandees,' he went on; 'fortune took up her dwelling there and auspiciousness laid her foundation in that rose-garden.'[35] It remained true that the seat of government went wherever the emperor went – and Akbar, Jahangir and Shah Jahan all travelled a great deal – but Agra would remain the principal capital until Shah Jahan began work on his own new capital at Delhi in 1639.

Like Lahore, the *Shahi Burj*, or 'Royal Bastion', of Agra Fort was built as a genuine military citadel, surrounding a comfortable homestead for the core of the royal household. Its seventy-foot walls bristled with the latest modern armaments, including finely worked brass cannons. The largest of these fearsome weapons, mounted next to the western gate that led to the crowded and dirty lanes of the city's main market, was fully fifteen foot long and had an astonishing three-foot calibre. The south-eastern gate was named *Hathi Pol*, Elephant Gate, after the gigantic statues overlooking the passage: 'two well-modelled elephants of polished black marble', their howdahs occupied by defeated Rajput princes.[36]

Inside the perimeter of the fortress, the grim demeanour was cast aside and an atmosphere of royal luxury revealed, for the castle was also a palace and it was in these cool and spacious suites that the young Khurram spent his days. The great doorways through the Hathi Pol – leading through and up and into the cool chambered mansions within the citadel – were solid hardwood, sheathed in beaten gold whose burnished surface was stamped with starbursts, foliage and splintered geometric patterns. The stonework surrounding the larger gateways was plastered over and painted in bright swirling patterns in silver and vivid blue; green and bright yellow; red and imperial purple. Flawlessly executed floral motifs were picked out on the red sandstone columns on each side. The stone lattice windows overlooking the Yamuna, where Akbar sat to watch his beloved elephants fight on the riverbank, were also plated with gold. The *pièce de résistance*, in the eyes of contemporary visitors, was the mansion that housed the emperor's own private chambers, the only structure that survived the modifications of Akbar's successors. Inside, wrote the Dutch merchant Francisco Pelsaert, all was 'very richly decked with alabaster', while the domes topping the structure were 'plated on the outside with gold, so that the look of it is not only royal on a close view, but imperial from a distance'.[37]

Around the base of the fort's indomitable walls sprawled the city itself, seven miles along the river and three into the surrounding countryside. The wealthiest and most influential citizens – members of the royal family and their closest courtiers – had their mansions, 'the costly palaces of all the famous lords', built along the southern bank of the river. This sector of the city was the preserve of the elite, who commandeered both physical space and limitless manpower to make their homes and gardens as opulent as possible. John Jourdain, another well-travelled employee of the East India Company who spent six months in Agra in 1610, when Khurram was 18, wrote that the city was by repute 'far greater than Grand Cairo'.

There is great resort of people to that city from all parts of the world, that you cannot desire anything but you shall find it in this city. It is very populous, insomuch that when you ride along in the streets you must have a man or two to go before to thrust aside the people, for they are so thick as in a fair in our country. ... This city is of great trade from all places. Here you may find merchants that will pass money to all places of the Indias, Persia and Aleppo.[38]

Just twenty miles from Agra lay one of the rare examples of failure by Khurram's beloved grandfather Akbar: the ghost city at Fatehpur-Sikri.[39] It had always been a guiding principle of the Mughals' master architects that no settlement would be founded without due regard to the pre-eminent considerations of security and water. They had found that riverside locations offered both; hence the construction of Agra and Delhi on the Yamuna, Lahore on the Ravi and Allahabad on the Ganges. Even Kabul in its mountain fastnesses had capacious supply tanks, replenished by rain and snowmelt. Sikri was a parched little village on an outcrop of the Aravalli hills, a community of stone-cutters and farmers – but its significance to Akbar had nothing to do with strategy or location.

Sikri was the home of a Sufi ascetic, Sheikh Salim Chishti, a member of an order established centuries earlier by his ancestor, Khawaja Muin al-Din Chishti. This Muslim holy man had become something of a patron saint to the Mughal ruling family and the Khawaja's burial place at Ajmer – a crowded complex of tombs, shrines and mosques – was the destination for frequent pilgrimages.[40] There were many who believed that to make seven pilgrimages to the Ajmer shrine – known locally as the *Dargah* – was the equivalent of performing the Hajj itself. Akbar himself had walked the full distance from Agra, 230 miles, at least twice, to pray for a son and heir. During one visit, the court poet Faydi noted piously that there was nothing undignified about the king being seen actually walking: 'On the chessboard also the king moves on foot'.[41] In response to these regular demonstrations of piety and humility towards his ancestor, Sheikh Salim made a dramatic prediction: the emperor's prayers would be rewarded with not one but three fine sons.

To maximise prospects for success, Akbar sent his pregnant Hindu queen, Guljar Maryam-Zamani, to Sikri to stay in Sheikh Salim's modest compound. On 30 August 1569, the first part of the prophecy was fulfilled. Overjoyed, Akbar ordered 'heaps and heaps of gold' to be scattered in the streets of Agra and every prisoner released amid lavish festivities. As

Gold coins showing the signs of the Zodiac

courtiers hastened to compose elegant chronograms marking the event, dubbing the baby 'the pearl of Akbar Shah's gem basket', the king himself opted for a typically straightforward name for the infant. He would be Salim, in honour of the holy man Sheikh Salim Chishti, though the little boy was as often known by the affectionate nickname 'Sheikhu Baba'. Another pregnant harem inmate was promptly despatched to Sikri, resulting in the birth of Murad on 7 June 1570.

The third part of the sheikh's prophecy had yet to come true – Prince Daniyal was not born until 10 September 1572 in the holy compound at Ajmer – when Akbar returned from campaigning in the south and turned his attention to the development of Sikri. The plaster was barely dry on the frescoed walls of Agra Fort but to celebrate the security of his clan's male line, he now declared that a 'City of Victory', *Fatehpur*, would be built at Sikri, close enough to permit easy and frequent visits from the new capital at Agra – and regardless of the problem posed by water shortages. His closest advisers, looking on the bright side in the time-honoured manner of royal sycophants, were soon rhapsodising that 'the portions of land which were lying barren like the dry hearts of lovers – yearning for a touch of an artist's hands – began to glow like the rosy cheeks of the beloved'.[42] Land was given free to those who had the money to build on it and the stonecutters and sculptors got busy, mining the local hills for their distinctive red sandstone.

The palace at Fatehpur-Sikri, completed in 1585, was never intended as a replacement for Agra but it was undeniably an aesthetic triumph: a new palace playground for the elite with all the required facilities and fancies to enable the emperor to do business and take his pleasure within an attractive and compact complex. Yet, while Akbar may have himself been a force of nature, he could not defeat nature. Such lavish facilities, especially the gardens, demanded huge quantities of water, which outside monsoon season had to be piped in. It was completely unrealistic. The palace, always receiving the priority supply, may have enjoyed 'a goodly tank of excellent water' but the town that grew around it was gasping. Illness and even death were the inevitable result of townspeople being forced to drink from tanks that were 'brackish and fretting [corrosive]'. So drought spelled speedy defeat for Akbar's 'City of Victory'.[43] The palace complex was inhabited as the centre of a working capital for just fourteen years. The eerie extent of the ghost city – spanning fully three miles across from the opposing gates in its surrounding wall, far larger than the royal complex on the hilltop that survives today – struck contemporary visitors like William Finch powerfully. 'In the midst it is all ruinate,' he wrote in 1610, 'lying like a waste desert, and very dangerous to pass through in the night, the buildings lying waste without inhabitants; much of the ground being now converted to gardens and much sowed with indigo and other grain, that a man standing there would little think he were in the midst of a city.'[44]

So faded Fatehpur-Sikri, though it did not altogether die. The core buildings within the central complex were viable, given a reduced but consistent water supply, and the settlement took on a new identity as an outpost of the capital, a holding-area from which to launch military expeditions into the western provinces of the empire – and a convenient place to camp out when the astrologers imposed delays on entering Agra. The significance of the 'City of Victory' would not be lost on Khurram himself when he camped here on the eve of his own triumphant coronation.

3
Salim's Rebellion

One who can keep fresh and green the four orchards of the world,
who plucks out by the root the thorns of tyranny and strife,
he is indeed capable of rulership.

Muhammad Sharif Mutamid-Khan[1]

The people also reported to the Emperor that Salim took
excessive droughts of opium and wine and that his acts of barbarity
were due to intoxication and temperamental disturbance.

Khwaja Kamgar Husaini[2]

As an adult prince and as Emperor, Khurram Shah Jahan would spend
many long years on campaign. As a child, however, Akbar chose to keep
him close under his wing. When Khurram was just six years old, in 1598,
his father Salim submitted a formal request that the boy be allowed a
leave of absence from his studies at court to accompany him on the latest
campaign against Mewar in Rajasthan, on what would have been the
young lad's first army campaign. Akbar was himself about to set off south,
determined to bring the Shiite states on his southern Deccan frontier into
his dominions. The Emperor refused, asserting, according to one account:
'I do not want Khurram to be a warrior; I want him to be a companion in
mysticism'.[3] For the young prince, this small but significant confrontation
over his own destiny would provide a valuable lesson: for even as Akbar,
now aged 56 and coming towards the end of his life, fought against the
Deccanis in the south, Salim moved to exploit the vacuum left at the heart
of the empire, unleashing a brutal dynastic struggle that was destined to be
repeated not just by Khurram against his own father but, fifty years later,
by his own son.

Akbar's war in the south had begun in earnest five years earlier: on
16 October 1593, Khurram's twenty-one-year-old uncle, Prince Daniyal,
was despatched by Akbar to the Deccan frontier, despite a debilitating
drink problem that nullified his official ranking as a commander of Seven
Thousand and rendered him useless as an expedition commander. The
Deccan was a rugged, mountainous territory to the south of Akbar's
sprawling dominions.[4] As the Himalayas and the Hindu Kush formed a

natural northern border to the great plains of Hindustan, so the Deccan represented its southern limits. The vast territory between was well watered by the Indus, the Ganges and the Narmada – and may have been enough to satisfy a less ambitious man. To take the Deccan presented a formidable challenge – one that would preoccupy successive generations of the Mughal dynasty and would, twenty years hence, present Khurram Shah Jahan with his greatest military triumph. It was divided into three autonomous territories – Ahmadnagar, Bijapur and Golconda – ruled by families with substantial wealth, armies and long-established Shiite connections to the great Safavid ruling family of Persia, far to the west over the Arabian Sea.[5] An uneasy truce had prevailed in the years since Akbar had pushed the boundaries of his realm against the northern frontiers of the Deccan states.

Now, irritated by the insulting meanness of a tribute sent by the ruler of Ahmadnagar, Burhan Nizamshah – an offering comprising just a dozen elephants, some local fabrics and a few jewels – Emperor Akbar sent Daniyal to teach the southerners a lesson. The prince was accompanied by his father-in-law, Abd-al-Rahim the Khan of Khans, as well as several other senior Rajput commanders and estate-landlords from the provinces of Delhi, Ajmer and Malwa. Their army, fully mustered, stood at an impressive 70,000 cavalry. But the prince had barely travelled 200 miles before drink-related ailments forced his return to his sickbed, leaving the campaign command to the Khan-Khanan.[6] This failure was the first of a series of toppling dominoes: Daniyal's replacement would be his elder brother Murad, whose premature death from alcohol poisoning would lead to Akbar's personal assumption of command and the vacuum left at the heart of the empire would be exploited by Khurram's father Salim. All that was still to come; in the meantime, the Deccan campaign ground to a halt before it had really begun.

It was not until February 1596 that Akbar authorised a fresh assault on the south. Hoping to capitalise on the opportunities presented by King Burhan's premature death and a savage conflict between Ahmadnagar and its eastern neighbours in Bijapur that had claimed the life of the new king, Ibrahim Nizamshah, Akbar despatched Prince Murad, again with the trusty Khan of Khans at his side.[7] Despite potentially disastrous rivalries and mutual antagonism between the senior Mughal commanders, a prolonged siege of Ahmadnagar Fort produced a negotiated surrender by the Deccanis and subsequent attempts at insurrection were beaten down. In short, modest victory was achieved – but if the power of Ahmadnagar's army were to be smashed and a firm Mughal foothold established in the south, real leadership was required. Akbar knew that, given his three disappointing sons, only he could do the job.

On 16 November 1598, at an auspicious hour identified by the court astrologers, the emperor marched from his temporary capital at Lahore for the south. Daniyal was fobbed off with a meaningless promotion and despatched to drink himself insensible at Allahabad, his career on hold. Murad was left to sulk at Burhanpur, the southern campaign headquarters on the Tapti River, refusing to reorganise his army and refusing to return to face his father's disapproval. Khurram's father, Salim, was no more welcome on Akbar's campaign than his brothers: he was appointed Governor of Ajmer and, with a high-ranking veteran, his brother-in-law Raja Man Singh, maintaining a watchful eye on the wayward prince, ordered to launch an offensive against the recalcitrant Maharana Amar Singh of Mewar, whose stubborn independence was a constant reminder that Mughal strength had not yet dominated all of northern India.[8]

Akbar's march to the Deccan was then delayed en route when Khurram was stricken with smallpox. The emperor called in his finest doctors to treat the prince, including his tutor Dr Ali Gilani and an even more skilled colleague known only as *Hakim-Misri*, 'the Egyptian doctor', whose knowledge of medicine was believed to be so comprehensive that if all the known tomes on medical research had disappeared he could have written them out from memory. In his relief at the boy's recovery, Akbar distributed lavish gifts and donations to the poor and released dozens of prisoners. The convalescent was scattered with tiny flowers wrought in gold and silver, which were then gathered and given to the poor. The Egyptian doctor was given the honour of a court title: *Jalinas-Zamani*, the Galen of the Age, a flattering allusion to the ancient Greek master-physician.

Even with Khurram on the mend, the campaign stuttered forward without urgency. Campaign planning only began in earnest at Agra, where the emperor delayed for a full year. And with his customary vast retinue, progress on the road was slow. Leaving Agra Fort on 27 September 1599 with his two favourite grandsons, Khurram and Khusraw, among his personal entourage, Akbar had an army of a hundred thousand men, infantry and cavalry, complemented by more than a thousand war-elephants. Reaching the hill country on the northern fringes of the Deccan, momentum slowed still further. The trackless terrain, with its sharply rising and thickly forested hills, made manoeuvres on the scale of a royal march almost impossible. According to the Jesuit observer, Fr Pierre du Jarric, 'the mountains were crossed by passes so rough and difficult that it sometimes took a whole day to cover a distance equal to the range of an arquebus', the low-velocity matchlock rifle of the period.[9]

Much had changed in the south by the time Akbar finally reached Burhanpur on 11 March 1600. Murad was dead, his excessive drinking having induced violent epileptic fits. Following an ancient Central Asian

Prince Khurram firing a matchlock rifle

tribal tradition, the news was brought to the emperor by a senior courtier bearing a blue handkerchief to indicate bad news; the king, however, was reported to be 'not in the least overcome with grief'.[10] There was, however, a glimmer of good news: Prince Daniyal had sworn off alcohol. Mightily relieved, the king summoned his youngest son from Allahabad and summoned him to assume the southern leadership, equipped not just with the rank of commanding general an earful of 'weighty counsels', but with the crimson silk curtain that was usually the sole preserve of the emperor himself. Daniyal had grounds for optimism: an unlikely interim commander, Abu-al-Fadl al-Allami, Akbar's court historian, had seized the initiative and thrown himself into the Deccan campaign with astonishing success, masterminding a succession of victories, including the capture of Asirgarh, a vast and impressive fortress that towered over the surrounding hill-country. So successful and instinctive was his soldiering, in fact, that Daniyal – aware that he was about to be eclipsed – wrote in warning: 'Your energy is impressed upon everyone. Your desire is to take Ahmadnagar before we arrive but you must restrain yourself from such action.'[11]

This progress in the Deccan, however, clouded Akbar's judgment and distracted him from a threat far to the north: for now the danger in the emperor's removal to the Deccan became apparent. Salim and his corps of experienced officers had launched a messy and inconclusive war of attrition in the Mewar hills. The Mughal forces were able to gain footholds in some areas but lost positions elsewhere; Rajput accounts boast that as many as eight minor forts were retaken from the invaders but at a heavy cost: 'the Mughals wreaked vengeance by putting vast areas to fire and sword and inflicting untold suffering on the inhabitants'.[12] Beyond the actual fighting, Salim, bitter at what he saw as an insultingly minor mission, fumed and fretted and contemplated the injustice of being thirty-one years old and not yet king. His paranoia and resentment was fed by a steady drip of insinuation and fearful logic from his acolytes and hangers-on, who pointed to Akbar's manifest lack of trust in his eldest son. And, to the injury of refusing him charge of the Deccan campaign in place of his hopeless brothers, had the king not added the insult of taking Khurram and Khusraw, Salim's own favourite sons, with him? Surrounded by sycophants and spies, Salim was justifiably convinced that Akbar's clear intention was to pass him over and install Daniyal, newly sober and kitted out with imperial tent and southern command, as heir apparent. And if Daniyal blew his opportunity, there was still Khusraw.

Salim's own retrospective account of this period is perhaps the most unblushingly dishonest and revisionist paragraph in his entire memoir. 'Short-sighted men,' he wrote several years later, 'tried to persuade me to rebel against my father. In the end their words and advice did not seem reasonable to me at all, for I knew how long a reign based on contention with my father would last. I was not led astray by the advice of these weak-minded people but rather, putting into practice what was required by intelligence and knowledge, went to pay homage to my father, my guide … and lord.'[13] In fact, Salim greedily seized the opportunity presented by his father's absence to establish his own kingdom. The location picked for his new capital was Allahabad, provincial capital of Bihar, where Salim took over Akbar's mighty fortress overlooking the confluence of the Yamuna and the Ganges.[14] Like Agra Fort, it was a structure of tall red sandstone walls, inside which was a three-storey palace containing 48 royal apartments, 'all wrought overhead with rich ornamental plastering and curious painting in all kinds of colours'.[15]

It was to this luxuriously appointed palace that Salim came in August 1600, abandoning his Mewar obligations and, en route from Rajasthan, crossing the Yamuna cheekily close to Agra. Hearing of her disaffected grandson's passage and 'astonished at his disobedience and at his not coming to pay his respects', Queen Maryam-Makani tried to stop him for a meeting and 'by her counsels guide him to the path of auspiciousness'. Salim, however, evaded her envoy and hurried on. At Allahabad, he seized the treasury, a fortune of more than three million rupees, and began distributing titles, favours and considerable land grants in Bihar and Agra provinces to his existing coterie and to any new arrivals.

Among the most prominent of his followers was Zamana Beg of Kabul, who had entered Salim's service as a freelance sword for hire. Salim found him so useful that he was awarded a land grant and given administrative responsibility for the Crown Prince's own staff of civil servants. Another close follower was Salim's foster-brother, Khubu *Qutb-al-Din-Khan*, 'Axis of the Faith'. Also, from the territories of Orchha, came Bir Singh Deo of the Bundela clan, a man with a profound family grievance against Akbar. Perhaps Salim's most aristocratic hanger-on was Khawaja Muhammad *Sharif-Khan*, the 'Noble Lord', one of Salim's childhood friends who had been selected by Akbar to serve as a messenger, carrying an order to end the mutiny. Sharif-Khan decided instead to throw in his lot with the rebels and acquired a host of spurious titles – Prime Minister of the Sultanate, Headman of the Kingdom – befitting his seniority in Salim's new pseudo-realm.

Down in the Deccan, Akbar appears not to have been too troubled at first by his eldest son's rebellion, treating it more as petulance than a real threat. Besides, he had serious business to attend to: to 'clear the territory of Ahmadnagar of the weeds and rubbish of rebellion', before pushing on south into Bijapur and even Golconda to the east. Ahmadnagar Fort was finally taken on 27 August, a much more decisive outcome than the earlier negotiated surrender. Bahadur, the new Nizamshah, was captured and more than fifteen hundred of his troops were put to the sword. Sheikh Abu-al-Fadl, meanwhile, busily oversaw the capture of another troublesome fort at Mali, while Daniyal neglected his administrative chores and tried to claim the credit for Abu-al-Fadl's work.

For the next few months, Akbar's officers were preoccupied with the administration of the forts and territories that had been newly occupied. But in April 1601, Akbar received news that Salim's rebellion had become more serious. Not content with awarding titles to his followers, the prince had come up with a few for himself. Indeed, he had had himself crowned with the formal name of *Abu-al-Muzaffar* (Father of Victory) Sultan Salim Shah *Ghazi*; this last epithet, 'Warrior of the Faith', a title that was designed to underline his credentials as an upholder of Islam. The new 'royal' seal bore the additional title 'Victor of the World and the Faith' Sultan Salim.[16] His throne, a great slab of black basalt, ten foot square and six inches deep, had been carved with elegant verses and the date of his bogus coronation. He even had his own currency minted, clear proof of his aspiration to form a parallel government.[17]

This harder edged threat – a rival kingdom at the heart of his own dominions – forced Akbar to abandon abruptly his personal leadership of the Deccan campaign on 30 April 1601. Abd-al-Rahim the Khan of Khans was initially left in supreme command, with the endlessly energetic Sheikh Abu-al-Fadl at his side, because Daniyal, now heir presumptive, had to stay with the king. But the emperor's precipitate abandonment of the campaign triggered immediate insurrection in his wake and, at the Narmada crossing, Daniyal was sent south again. Taking Khurram, Khusraw and his household with him, Akbar pressed on for the north, completing the immense journey through the blistering summer heat in a little over a hundred days. Along the way, he fired off messages to Salim, urging him to clear his mind of 'cobwebs of suspicion and refraction' and come in to the imperial palace with due humility.

But the rebellion stuttered on for another three years. In the summer of 1602, Salim mounted a half-hearted advance on Agra with an army of thirty thousand men. If he thought his father would simply buckle, he was mistaken. Akbar fired off a stern letter, warning that 'when paternal love begins to slacken and decay, contempt arises'.

Your unabated belligerence leaves me no option but to crush by force the threat of rebellion. This is my last warning against insurrection. … Unconditional submission may save you from going under the surge of my wrath. Unity of the empire will be preserved whatever the cost.[18]

It only took Akbar's appearance on the battlefield at Etawah to persuade the prince to retreat in ignominy to Allahabad. Salim's behaviour now became more and more erratic. Mixing wine with opium and drinking more than his constitution could handle, he became so unhinged that he spent evenings either in delirium, in a psychotic rage or simply in a stupor, 'as active as a design on a carpet or a picture on a wall'. Gruesome accounts came to court – the real court – of Salim's grotesque and extravagant punishments for those who failed to please him. In one typical incident, three courtiers were discovered to be planning to abandon Allahabad and transfer their loyalty to Prince Daniyal. One, a court reporter, was flayed alive in Salim's presence, another was castrated and the third flogged to death. 'With such punishment,' Salim's own amanuensis, Muhammad Hadi, later noted, 'great trepidation took root in everyone's heart and all avenues of escape were blocked.'[19]

But it was the assassination of Sheikh Abu-al-Fadl Allami that provoked the most profound rift between Akbar and Salim. An extraordinary polymath – diplomat, poet, annalist and now military commander – the sheikh was summoned by Akbar shortly after Salim's abortive march on Agra to put together an expeditionary force to move on Allahabad. After long months of hesitation, the emperor had finally decided to crush Salim's rebellion, which now threatened to become a prolonged standoff. As one European resident noted, 'many had adopted Salim's cause, preferring, as men are wont to do, to worship the rising rather than the setting sun'. To the rebel prince, an effective general like Abu-al-Fadl was a threatening adversary. Salim, blithely disregarding his own treasonous guilt, accused Abu-al-Fadl of fomenting discord at court. One Salim apologist, Khawaja Kamgar Khan, chipped in with the claim that Sheikh Abu-al-Fadl, 'intoxicated by the wine of fortune and vain of the influence he had obtained over the Emperor's mind, had lost his senses and … acted with rancour and animosity against his master's son'.[20] Perhaps the prince was already pondering a safe way of worming himself back into his father's affections. He wrote later, utterly without embarrassment, that he had ordered the sheikh's murder because in the end it had enabled him 'to proceed without disturbance of mind to kiss the threshold of my father's palace'.[21]

The assassination was arranged and carried out by Salim's crony, Raja Bir Singh Deo Bundela who was only too happy to carry out the mission because his ancestral lands had been repeatedly subjected to Mughal attack. He held Abu-al-Fadl personally responsible for the confiscation of prime family estates. The sheikh and his small entourage of three hundred newly recruited troops were waylaid and slaughtered not far from Gwalior on 22 August 1602. Salim gloated over the severed head, extemporising a poetic line, apparently without irony, to the effect that 'the miraculous sword of the Prophet of God severed the head of the rebel'. But when Akbar received the news a fortnight later he was 'extremely grieved, disconsolate, distressed and full of lamentation'. 'That day,' wrote Sheikh Abu-al-Fadl's deputy, the emperor 'neither shaved, as usual, nor took opium but spent his time in weeping and lamenting'.[22] The administration of state was put on hold for several days.

Alas for the celestial knowledge; it has turned to dust.
The pillars of science have moved and the nest of eloquence is empty![23]

Despite this callous murder, Akbar never overcame his reluctance to give up on Salim completely. Besides, the affair of Daniyal and his drink problem was not as happily resolved as had once appeared. Far off in the Deccan, bickering with Abd-al-Rahim Khan-Khanan, Daniyal had reneged on his pledge of abstinence and 'in consequence of such fire-water his disposition had become immoderate'. Once again despairing about the succession, Akbar sent an edict ordering that Daniyal be transferred from the Burhanpur citadel across the shallow flow of the Tapti by royal barge,

Forty-pillared hall at Allahabad Fort (18th century aquatint)

there to be confined in the quieter ambience of an old hunting-lodge in an area known as Zeinabad on a forced abstinence cure.

An opportunity for a rapprochement with Salim was soon presented by the death at the age of eighty-one of the emperor's venerable aunt, Gulbadan Begum, in February 1603. Forgiving him his past crimes, Akbar now permitted the disgraced Crown Prince to return to Agra and even presented him with his own turban, a clear symbol that he would inherit the throne. Salim exuded sentiments of regret, repentance and gratitude. 'If every hair in my body were to become a tongue,' he told his father, 'it would not be possible to thank you for even one of your thousand acts of kindness.' [24] In October, Akbar gave him another chance to prove his merit, another mission to the Mewar hills to finish off the Maharana.

It was all to no avail. Salim abandoned the Mewar expedition after just five miles and fled instead back to Allahabad and the intoxications of wine, opium and the illusion of power. There, in the words of Muhibb Ali, assistant to the late Sheikh Abu-al-Fadl and therefore a man who had good reason to hate the prince, Salim, 'from bad companionship, love of flattery, self-indulgence, presumption and harshness, took to disobedience and made many improper acts his glory'.[25] But another death in the royal family prompted another return to court in late 1604. Salim knew how badly the king would be affected by the death of his seventy-seven-year-old mother, Maryam-Makani, who had been widowed for the same half-century that Akbar had been on the Mughal throne. The emperor himself was distraught, shaving his head, beard and moustache, discarding all trappings of royalty and personally shouldering one corner of the *tabut*, the funeral bier, in the long cortege to Delhi. Again, Salim the renegade came in; again he paid his respects and asked for forgiveness. But this time, Akbar had tougher measures up his sleeve.

He first brought Salim into the female apartments and they dined together. After dinner, the king took him into his private room, pretending to consult him, and then slipped out himself and chained and locked the door with his own hand. The prince, as soon as he realised his situation, knocked his head on the stone like a madman and sank into the darkness of confinement. He tasted neither food nor drink for three or four days. The emperor, fearing the death of his … son, then brought him out and placed him in the Chahar-Bagh garden, opposite the fort on the other side of the river. He placed a guard of his trusted servants round the garden to watch the prince.[26]

Salim's return and detention was greeted at court with a wide range of emotions, most of them carefully concealed. Many were simply horrified at his rebellion against the venerable emperor; such treachery in their eyes negated any right to inheritance. Others recalled his drunken, eccentric and often barbarically violent behaviour and wondered how secure they might be in the court of Emperor Salim, which could reasonably be predicted to be a dangerous place of arbitrary and often very brutal punishment. Still others, increasingly open about their choice, had a specific alternative in mind: Khurram's eldest brother, Prince Khusraw.

Even as Salim's rebellion had been brought to an end, the fifteen-year-old Khusraw had taken in marriage the daughter of a very influential courtier. Mirza Aziz Kokaltash, Akbar's foster-brother and childhood friend, had fallen out with the emperor over the extent of his religious liberalism and had fled to self-imposed exile at Mecca. With the passing of the years, however, he had returned to a warm welcome and complete political rehabilitation. By April 1595, he had become imperial Chief Minister and been given the honorific *Azam-Khan*, the 'Resolute Lord'. Azam-Khan had recently been heard to say he would die happy were Khusraw's place on the throne to be secured, commenting he was 'willing that the fates should convey the good news of his sovereignty to my right ear and should seize my soul at the left ear'.[27] A growing number of influential courtiers and military officers shared his view, among them Khusraw's uncle, Raja Man Singh.

But Akbar had still not made up his mind over the succession. He would certainly have been dismayed to learn that on 15 May 1605, Salim's first wife, Rajakumari Man Bai, had been so distraught at the relentless family in-fighting that she had taken a suicidal overdose of opium at Allahabad. Salim, whose guilt was apparent to all, blamed her death on Khusraw's treacherous ambitions. But for Akbar, the number of viable successors was dwindling. In March 1605, his youngest son Daniyal finally succumbed to alcohol poisoning after a forty-day illness. Still languishing at the hunting lodge, denied access to the citadel at Burhanpur, let alone the decision-making centre so far away, and increasingly resentful at Salim's rehabilitation, he had resorted to paying accomplices to smuggle him liquor in various ingenious vessels. His last drink was a fiery cane-spirit, straight from a corked gun-barrel. So died Khurram's second uncle at the age of just thirty-two, leaving three sons whose fate would be tied up in the political machinations of their elders.

With both Daniyal and Murad dead, the path to the crown seemed open for the newly rehabilitated Salim. But Akbar, prone to worryingly serious illnesses, remained preoccupied with the future of his dominions. It was to quell this uncertainty and disquiet that he announced a special elephant fight on the bank of the Yamuna. Facing each other on the flat, sandy arena between the castle wall and the water would be Salim's favourite, Giranbar, and the pride of Khusraw's stable, *Apurva* the 'Incomparable', a tribute gift from the Raja of Udaipur.[28] Let these mighty beasts, the epitome of royalty, provide an omen for the future of the Mughal realm.

Two iron mountains moved from their places;
You'd have said that the earth moved from end to end.[29]

Prince Khurram sat at his grandfather's side, high in the king's balcony. Below, a huge crowd turned out, all the noblemen of Agra pushing their way forward to secure the best positions. On each side of the battleground, knots of close followers clustered around the protagonists, Salim and his son Khusraw, as they sat astride their finest war-horses. There were strict rules of engagement and protocol to be observed. A third elephant, the mighty Ranhatan, had been positioned to intervene on the loser's side if the winner should go berserk, beyond the control of his mahout.

Smashing through a token partition mud wall between them, Giranbar and Apurva began their fateful battle. It rapidly became clear to the spectators that Salim's beast was unstoppable. As Apurva retreated, bellowing in pain, into the current, Ranhatan emerged from his ambush position to drive off the rampaging Giranbar. Salim's supporters howled in protest. They had come to see blood and absolute defeat for the upstart Khusraw. They started to fling stones at Ranhatan and his mahout, who was hit in the head. Akbar promptly ordered Khurram to descend from the balcony, sprinting through the cool palace corridors and out onto the sand below, to mediate between the rival crowds of spectators and persuade his father to call off his thuggish supporters. Khurram also had the idea of using fireworks to scare the fighting tuskers apart. But before he could bring his tender diplomatic skills to bear, the rout was complete. Ginanbar had taken on Ranhatan too and forced him into the Yamuna, where only the arrival of a flotilla of boats was able to separate the enraged animals. With the Crown Prince and his son Khusraw screaming insults at each other and the cream of the imperial officer class reduced to rival baying mobs by the waterside, Akbar was prostrated by the high emotions of the day and a high fever developed.

The emperor had his omen.

4
Jahangir's New Order

Kingship regards neither son nor son-in-law;
In fact; a king can have no relations.

Emperor Jahangir[1]

Therefore don't get too close to kings;
And if you must get close to them, keep your distance.

Sheikh Farid al-Din Attar[2]

Akbar's last days were a prolonged misery of illness and suspicion. Plagued with severe abdominal cramps and diarrhoea, he took to his bed in the palace at Agra Fort. The emperor's favourite Egyptian physician, Hakim-Misri, had passed away, leaving his colleague Dr Ali Gilani unable to find a cure. After more than a week without treatment, the ailing emperor was driven to an uncharacteristic outburst of bitterness and rage. 'You were nothing but a foreign spice-seller!' Akbar ranted at the Persian immigrant, flinging a mug at his head. 'It was here that you took off the sandals of exile. We raised you to this rank in order that some day you might be of use!'[3] The constant nagging and slurs on his professional competence eventually persuaded Dr Ali to give Akbar a strong combination of kaolin and morphine. Unfortunately, the medicine merely provoked acute constipation instead and failed to end the agonising cramps. Akbar rejected this final attempt at treatment and the debilitating diarrhoea returned with a vengeance. His days were numbered and he lay fretting that his symptoms may have been those of poison.[4]

Throughout the king's terminal illness, the thirteen-year-old Khurram stayed at his side 'with firm heart and unshakeable resolve'. There was an element of personal risk because intense political manoeuvring was going on behind the scenes. His half-brother Khusraw's star was emphatically in the ascendant. The elder prince's main champions – his uncle Raja Man Singh and his father-in-law Mirza Aziz Azam-Khan – had control of the central state administration and were well placed to usher the dying king's grandson onto the throne in place of Khusraw's drunken father, Salim.

In July 1605, Khusraw was promoted to the extraordinary rank of Ten Thousand, receiving the war-drums and yak-tail emblem of high office. With such flanking manoeuvres underway, Salim judged it safer to stay away from the palace, despite his better claim to the succession. Later he would write bitterly in his memoir about 'short-sighted men, despairing utterly of pardon and forgiveness for the multitude of crimes and short-comings they had committed, [who] thought they could make Khusraw a puppet and take the reins of government into their own hands'.[5] He was probably justified in his suspicions. The historian Asad Beg Qazvini, a Salim loyalist, was quite explicit about the political positioning in the aftermath of the ominous and traumatic elephant fight.

During the emperor's illness, the weight of affairs fell upon Azam-Khan and when it became evident that the life of that illustrious sovereign was drawing to a close, he consulted with Raja Man Singh, one of the principal nobles, and they agreed to make Sultan Khusraw emperor. They were both versed in business and possessed of great power and determined to seize Prince Salim when he came, according to his daily custom, to pay his respects at court – thus displaying the nature of their mind, little considering that the sun cannot be smeared with mud nor the marks of the pen of destiny be erased by the pen-knife of treachery. He whom the hand of the power of Allah upholds, though he be helpless in himself, is safe from all evil![6]

Salim, rescued from this trap by the timely intervention of a loyal courtier, tried hard to keep Khurram away from the palace intrigues. The boy was too conspicuously and explicitly loyal to his father, as well as his ailing grandfather, for his own safety. Khurram's own future, of course, depended on a successful transfer of power from Akbar to Salim. For those who believed that the throne was indeed Khurram's destiny – manifested not least by the auspicious timing of his birth – it was a destiny that could only be reached if his father preceded him. Should Khusraw, his elder by just five years, prevail in the struggle for succession, Khurram would at best be sidelined and at worst be left dangerously vulnerable. But the young prince showed his mettle, staying loyally by Akbar's side, helping Dr Ali with his ministrations and vowing that 'as long as there is a breath of life left in my grandfather, there is no possibility of being separated from him'.[7]

With the hierarchy fragmented and rumours swirling, it seemed that the odds were heavily in Khusraw's favour. But his two main advocates lacked the necessary ruthlessness and sheer power of personality. When an anxious convention of the court nobility gathered in the imperial audience-chamber to debate the future of the throne, Raja Man Singh and Azam-Khan failed to convince them that their man was the best possible

Prince Khurram as a young man

candidate and that Akbar's gesture of handing the turban of succession to Salim should be overridden. Nor did the two conspirators have the manpower at their disposal to force the issue. As a result, in the words of an elderly official named Muhammad Faiz-Bakhsh, later recalling his youth at court, 'the schemes of their weaving broke up like a spider's web and not one of their aims was effected'.[8]

It was now that Salim made his move. He timed his final intervention perfectly. Aided by a senior courtier in charge of military logistics named Sheikh Farid Bukhari, he sneaked into the palace and to the emperor's bedside. Akbar, in his 'last agonies', opened his eyes to see what he had always longed to see: the face of his eldest son, smiling with affection and loyalty. It took no effort of will – though the physical strain of any movement was great – to signal to his closest servants that the turban and robes of kingship should be handed to his chosen successor. His opponents, derided in a later account as a 'band of ingrates … repented of their idle desires and, ashamed and humiliated, made obeisance before His Highness'.[9] Khusraw was bundled away and confined to quarters in the most secure tower of Agra Fort. At the last possible moment, Salim had played and won. He had secured his inheritance but – as one important history of the period noted – 'the snake of conspiracy and discord was only scorched and not killed'.[10]

The final decisive move was made none too soon and, for the time being at least, a brutal contest for power over the Mughal territories was narrowly averted. Jalal al-Din Muhammad Akbar died on Wednesday 26 October 1605, after half a century on the throne. 'Groans rose from Earth to Heaven', lamented one contemporary historian, while the courtier Muhammad Hadi wrote that 'the royal falcon that had soared to the apogee of world rule flew from this mortal world to the garden of eternity'.[11]

Such is the revolution of life
In this circle of evil and mortality.
It lasts for a few days and is over;
One rubs ones forehead on the earth and departs.
Pauper or king, it makes no difference.
Many a vessel is wrecked in this whirlpool;
No one is ever saved from this storm.[12]

On the street, there was very real public grief: a typical emotional reaction at 'the dreadful news, which came as a sharp and sudden blow', was recorded by a young Jain merchant named Banarasi Biholia in Jaunpur, at the eastern end of the empire. His account also reveals the extent to which news of the power struggle at court had trickled out to the provinces. Until news came from Agra that all was well in the capital, at which point 'the commotion subsided', there were profound fears of lasting insecurity – even, perhaps, that the fabric of empire was fundamentally damaged.

People suddenly felt orphaned and insecure without their sire. Terror raged everywhere, the hearts of men trembled in dire apprehension; their faces became drained of colour. ... The whole town was in a tremor. Everyone closed the doors of his house in panic; shop-keepers shut down their shops. Feverishly, the rich hid their jewels and costly attire under-ground; many of them quickly dumped their wealth and their ready capital on carriages and rushed to safe, secluded places. Every householder began stocking his home with weapons and arms. Rich men took to wearing thick, rough clothes such as are worn by the poor, in order to conceal their status, and walked the streets covered in harsh woollen blankets.[13]

Salim's first duty as the new emperor was to help carry his father's body from the great fortress at Agra to its last resting place. Khurram's loyal service by his grandfather's deathbed was rewarded with the other place at the head of the royal bier. Akbar died at the age of sixty-four, without resolving the mystery of his true religious belief – if indeed he had any to declare. The Din Illahi had been a hybrid imposition, never truly accepted by either Muslim or Hindu subjects. But Akbar was ultimately claimed as a Muslim and accorded the appropriate rituals of death.[14] Ancient custom dictated that a new gateway had to be punched in the fortress wall through which the departed would pass and a broad section of the red sandstone wall was temporarily dismantled. Akbar was taken in solemn procession to a 'sacred garden' five miles up the Delhi road known as Bihishtabad, a tranquil paradise where he had already initiated the construction of a red sandstone mausoleum. There the king was laid to rest amid a storm of lamentation and heartfelt panegyrics; over the next seven years, labourers worked to build a tomb truly worthy of such a great monarch.[15] Above the astonishing southern entrance to the vast walled garden, planted with fragrant flowering trees, the *Buland-Darwaza* or Gateway of High Fortune featured a simple quotation from the Koran: 'These are the gardens of Eden; enter them and live forever'.[16]

Crown Prince Salim was thirty-six when he ascended the Mughal throne at last on 2 November, a week after his father's demise. He inherited a treasury of staggering proportions. According to the precise accounts in the imperial ledgers, the state coffers were filled with 'gold coins ... silver coins ... precious stones, wrought gold and silver work and fine porcelain ... diamonds, rubies, emeralds, sapphires and pearls ... various figures cast in gold as elephants, camels, horses, etc. ... gold and silver cloths of Persia, Turkey, Gujarat and those imported from Christian countries ... cannons, guns, muskets ... arrow-proof coats worn when going to war'. The grand total at the bottom of this vast list was an astonishing 348 million rupees.[17]

Hindu astrologers grumbled superstitiously about picking a Saturday for the coronation but were overruled by their Shiite Persian colleagues, who insisted that it was a truly auspicious day. The splendour of the celebration – beginning several days of lavish banquets, military parades, pyrotechnic fireworks and musical concerts – was matched by the piled-high epithets of the new king's formal regal name: Nur al-Din Muhammad Jahangir Padshah al-Ghazi: Light of the Faith, Seizer of the World, King of Kings and Warrior of the Faith. Salim was also the first in the dynasty to abandon his own given name in favour of the self-selected honorific 'Jahangir', writing later that he had decided to do so to avoid being confused by historians with the sixteenth-century Ottoman sultans Selim I and II in Constantinople. To confirm his coronation, the *khutba* sermon was delivered from every mosque in the land, stating the name and titles of the new monarch. Hundreds of prisoners were released and the imperial secretariat began issuing its edicts and bureaucratic instructions in the name of Jahangir. Ambassadors from Persia, the Ottoman capital at Constantinople – as well as from the three Deccan states on the Mughal Empire's southern borders – all arrived with fulsome messages and generous gifts of tribute from their royal masters.

The court poets composed special verses to mark the coronation. The great Urfi of Shiraz and Naziri of Nishapur composed lengthy panegyrics, each such *qasida* pointing to the emperor's noble lineage, faultless character and limitless devotion to his poorest subjects. The elderly *Maktub-Khan*, 'Doyen of Writers', contributed a strikingly eloquent verse that the new emperor immediately resolved to quote in his own memoirs.

King of kings Jahangir, a second Timur,
Sat in justice on the victorious throne.
Success, fortune, victory, pomp and triumph
Are wrapped around him to serve with joy.[18]

Those of Jahangir's cronies that weren't already in Agra now rushed to the citadel to pay their respects. His substantial retinue, built up with great care since adulthood, now had the chance to transfer what they'd learned in the administration of the pseudo-capital at Allahabad and earlier to the running of the whole empire. As well as soldiers and administrators, there were poets and artists, refugees from the old Afghan kingdoms and individuals disaffected with Akbar who'd attached their own hopes to the rising star.[19] Hotfoot from Allahabad came Zamana Beg Mahabat-Khan, honoured by Salim during the prince's rebellion with the title 'Master of Terror' as a reward for the treacherous murder of the Raja of Bhojpur. This distinguished Rajput had been a guest in Salim's city but the mercurial prince had been jealous of the raja's retinue, ostentatiously clogging Allahabad's busy streets. Zamana was ordered to behead him in his sleep. Now at Agra, Mahabat-Khan was swiftly promoted to Commander-in-Chief. Another new arrival at court was Khawaja Muhammad Sharif-Khan – regarded by Jahangir as 'a son, brother, friend and comrade' – who secured the governorate of Bihar. This appointment allowed him to return to Allahabad in high honour. Salim's coterie from the years of rebellion became Jahangir's imperial elite, reaping at last the benefits of their fidelity to the prince.

Veteran courtiers, however, viewed these upstart young officers as toadies and arrivistes; fault-lines appeared rapidly at court. Mirza Aziz Azam-Khan, for so long the champion of Khusraw, found it difficult to stifle his resentment at Salim's elevation to the throne and was incorrigibly indiscreet. On one occasion, he was so bold as to criticise the new emperor's selection of courtiers – and begged to be released from imperial service to sweep Akbar's tomb complex at Bihishtabad. 'For fifty years under Akbar,' he wrote, 'the Chagatays and the Rajputs flourished and multiplied and ever remained faithful. Your Majesty arrived upon the scene and distanced both these communities and placed all power in the hands of the Khorasanis [Persians] and Shahzadas [Indian Muslims], who know nothing but mischief-mongering and treachery.'[20] Ever loyal to his master, though, Mahabat-Khan stood up to Azam-Khan robustly. 'I don't understand discussions,' he told the emperor; 'I'm a soldier. I have a strong sword and I'll strike his waist. If it does not divide him into two pieces, you can cut off my hand.'[21]

The new king was, however, no doubt aware of the widespread perception that his talents fell considerably short of those of his illustrious father. In his journal, he mused on power and justice, reflecting that 'whenever a just and equitable monarch's mind and intention are focused upon the people's welfare and the peasants' prosperity, the blessings of good crops and produce are innumerable'. 'It is hoped, he wrote,' that God will keep this supplicant firm in his resolve to do good.'[22] To that end, he introduced a set of twelve edicts on a wide range of themes, varying from efforts to boost internal trade and maximise imperial revenues to more socially oriented commandments.

1. **Ban on ad hoc taxes by provincial administrators**
2. **Construction order for caravanserais and mosques on rural routes**
3. **Ban on 'stop-and-search' of travelling merchants**
4. **Rules on inheritance; money from those without heirs to go to public works**
5. **Ban on manufacture or sale of wine or spirits**
6. **Ban on billeting troops in private homes**
7. **Ban on disfiguring punishments, e.g. cutting off the nose or ears**
8. **Ban on land confiscation by rural estate holders**
9. **Ban on estate holders marrying local people**
10. **Construction of hospitals and appointment of doctors, with royal funding**
11. **Ban on slaughtering animals on Thursdays and Sundays, as well as the emperor's birthday (18 Rabi I)**
12. **Promotion and pay-rises for Akbar's imperial officers**

This last measure was a pragmatic way of ensuring support within the palace power structure. It also gave a sense of continuity and avoided abrupt change. Some appointments surprised their recipients as well as the gossips at court. Raja Man Singh, so long an advocate of Khusraw's succession, was made interim Governor of Bengal, a prestigious and lucrative appointment. It was also one far from the machinations of Agra: his removal neatly halved the number of influential Khusravites in the capital. But he was sent on his way with a rich robe of honour, a jewel-encrusted sword and a fine horse.[23]

Another innovation was Jahangir's celebrated Chain of Justice, which stretched from the imperial audience-chamber, where it was fastened to two pillars, out through a window and down to a courtyard below. In theory, any citizen with a grievance could pull the chain and set the hundreds of small golden bells tied along its length ringing and 'straightway get justice against the oppressor'. In reality, the chain only highlighted the emperor's isolation from his people. No humble citizen could possibly be admitted into the imperial presence and any grievance had to be discussed through an obliging and possibly venal courtier. Only the highest ranking qualified for proximity. Payments and gratuities to lesser mortals were tossed by the emperor from a window into a silk sheet tied by its four corners to posts near the supplicant below. While the petitioner waited, he might peruse for his edification the verses extolling the king's virtues, painted on the wall below the royal balcony.

May praise of the king of the world be the remembrance of those who keep vigil by night;
May prayers for his fortune be the litany of those who rise with the dawn.
In whatever direction the lone rider wields his sword like the sun,
May the army of his enemy be dispersed as the stars.[24]

So, rhetoric and golden symbols aside, justice remained a very distant prospect. It was also always subject to Jahangir's fickle temper. On occasions, the new king could be lenient and exercise sound judgement, especially when cases of official corruption came to his attention. When one of the imperial staff stationed on the River Ravi at Lahore was found to have extorted a commission from merchants travelling south from Kashmir or Kabul to sell their goods to the royal household, Jahangir gave orders that the officer was to have his head shaved and be dragged in disgrace through the streets of the city.[25] But the emperor was equally capable of brutally draconian punishments. In an empire where the vast distances between trading centres could only be bridged by an efficient road and river network, highwaymen could not be tolerated. Robber-gangs were despatched en masse, their executions grisly and very visible. One account of a journey up the Agra-Lahore road in 1611 described tall way-markers made entirely of skulls cemented together: 'the heads of some hundred thieves newly taken'. The bodies of the miscreants were left to rot, impaled on stakes set at regular spaces for a mile along the highway. Another account, from the diary of the English ambassador, Sir Thomas Roe, in 1616, noted with outrage that the death penalty could be handed down without trial or even counter-argument: 'One hundred thieves were brought chained before him and accused. Without further ceremony, as in all such cases is the custom, the king bade carry them away and let the chief be torn with dogs, kill the rest.'[26]

At the root of his most violent punishments was the new emperor's continuing drink problem. Despite efforts to regulate his intake, he was often an aggressive and sadistic drunk. Much later in his reign, Jahangir instated a mandatory waiting-period between sentence and punishment, to pre-empt the alcohol-induced impetuosity that he himself recognised. Political prisoners – those, as Jahangir put it, 'whose release would occasion sedition in the realm' – were detained indefinitely in the main fortresses scattered across the empire, especially at Gwalior and Ranthambor. In the face of imperial displeasure, there was no right to appeal.

Jahangir's unpredictability also extended to the question of religious tolerance. The emperor maintained the family enthusiasm for the Sufi saints of the Chishti family – often in the face of frowns from the Sunni orthodox at court. He was capable of generous charity work and great kindness to his subjects. At the shrine of Khawaja Muin al-Din Chishti at Ajmer, the most powerful man in the land could be found on feast days, his queen at his side, cooking a special dish of sweetened rice for five thousand villagers in a vast cauldron and serving those in line with his own hands.[27] Nor was it just the Sufis that received the king's patronage. An imperial decree of 1610 ordered that animals must not be slaughtered during the holy days of the Jain minority's Paryushana festival.[28]

Yet at the same time, by the emperor's own account, Jahangir imprisoned three young Muslim men who had struck up an acquaintance with a Hindu *sannyasi*, or holy man, and subjected their companion to one hundred lashes with a whip. The holy man's teachings, wrote Jahangir, 'reeked of infidelity and heresy'. 'This special punishment was in order to maintain the religious law lest any other ignoramus be enticed into similar actions', the emperor noted piously and hypocritically, for he himself enjoyed a respectful and lasting relationship with a Hindu sannyasi named Jadrup and the pair would debate religion and philosophy for hours on end at an ashram outside Ujjain.[29] Barring such jarring contradictions, the multiculturalism of Akbar's day was alive and well.

Such was the climate of the new court in which Jahangir's maturing sons were now learning to find their place. At thirteen and as the third son, Khurram posed no threat to either father or brother. Enjoying the protection of his father's power and the comforts of the imperial apartments at Agra, he continued his studies, branching out into more complex lessons in language, philosophy, art, religion and warfare: all the essential aspects of Mughal statecraft. His eldest half-brother Khusraw, by contrast, seethed. The twenty-year-old prince was effectively a captive in a gilded cage: allowed to reside in a splendid mansion outside the fort and endowed with a generous donation of one hundred thousand rupees and the emperor's forgiveness. His backers had capitulated and little now remained of a power base from which to launch a coup within the confines of the court. For five months, Khusraw nursed his resentment at what might have been. Some Mughal historians have denounced Khusraw as 'an haughty spirit' or worse but these accounts overlook the qualities of the young man – and the fact that he had been taught by his grandfather to aspire to greatness and by his former supporters to aspire to his own father's throne. Escape must have been continually on Khusraw's mind but it was not until late March 1606 that he was seized by an unquenchable urge to make a bid for freedom. The decision was triggered by the din of the prolonged, eighteen-day Nauruz festivities, which formalised his father's recent accession as

well as marking the New Year festival. As the triumphant music reached his ears through his prison windows, Khusraw resolved to trust no more in uncle and father-in-law and make his own bid for power.

The first that Khurram knew of his brother's rebellion was the appearance in the late hours of the night of 15 April of Sharif-Khan, breathless and dishevelled, knocking frantically at the emperor's private apartments to seek an urgent audience. The general had just been informed of Prince Khusraw's escape from Agra Fort. The detainee had been given leave to make a late-night pilgrimage to Akbar's tomb at Bihishtabad, a daily routine in which he prayed by the simple stone cenotaph and distributed food to the poor. The officer corps had been complacent, the guards less than watchful, and Khusraw had made good his escape, turning immediately for the north.[30]

The prince initially hoped to use Lahore as the launch pad for his uprising. He had spent at least a dozen years in the city and, with additional contacts provided by his father-in-law Azam-Khan, the Punjab might have served as a profitable place in which to build a more solid body of partisan support. In this, he was confident of the support of Abd-al-Rahim Khan, the city's Chief Minister. But even as he rode north from Agra, the prince had a serendipitous meeting with one of Akbar's most loyal northern commanders, Hussein Beg Badakshi, who still served as Governor of Kabul and who argued forcefully that – just as it had been under the teenaged Akbar fifty years earlier – Kabul could be the first city of a new empire.

More importantly and closer to hand, Hussein Beg also controlled the formidably strong Rohtas fort in the Punjab, where he held a treasury of more than 400,000 rupees. The money, the fort and his men were all now placed at Khusraw's service, in memory of Akbar and in defiance of the disgraceful renegade now sitting on the throne. Khusraw then 'made a liberal distribution of his plunder amongst his soldiers,' noted a contemporary account, 'the report of which, being noised abroad, soon brought twelve thousand more men to his side, so that by the time he reached Lahore … he was at the head of a considerable force', made up of Chagatay clansmen who rejected the rule of Salim Jahangir, disaffected Rajputs, as well as various Afghan and Hazara tribes.[31] But on reaching Lahore, he found the mighty gates barred against him by the newly appointed governor, Dilawar-Khan, who had raced from Agra in just eleven days to strengthen the bastions and ramparts. Pitching his tents on the north bank of the Ravi, Khusraw resolved to besiege the city.

Back in Agra, Jahangir faced his first serious challenge with surprising calm, authority and energy. At first he planned to send Khurram in pursuit of his recalcitrant brother. But Sharif-Khan, whose negligence had allowed the prince's escape and left a blot on his own reputation, persuaded the king to let him make amends by leading the hunt for the rebel, in collaboration with Sheikh Farid Bukhari. Their brief was terse and explicit. Asked how to proceed in the event of Khusraw refusing to surrender, Jahangir replied simply: 'If he won't come to his senses without a battle … do whatever you have to do'.[32] The full Mughal army, whose commanders were all conveniently assembled in Agra for the Nauruz festivities, was well organised and ready for immediate departure. Jahangir's generals mounted an impressively rapid march, covering the 440 miles in just seventeen days. When Jahangir and the imperial retinue set off in the wake of the main force, Khurram was left to hold the fort at Agra.

Khusraw's rebellion was crushed swiftly and mercilessly. The decisive military engagement took place on 27 April 1606 on the riverbank not far from the walls of Lahore. The prince himself had turned from the siege too late to prevent the vanguard of Jahangir's army from crossing the stream and, in a confusion of disinformation and dreadful weather, the rebel troops were outmanoeuvred and outfought. 'A great storm of wind, rain and lightning was raging that day,' wrote a Dutch traveller; the rain fell so violently that it rendered the bows of Khusraw's men useless and their horses unmanageable.[33] At the critical moment, the imperial forces launched a devastating charge, screaming *'Padshah salamat!'* – 'Long live the king!' – and Khusraw's army panicked and fled. The prince made a run for it, heading for Kabul with a small group of close companions but was taken at a river crossing after just seventy-five miles. Khusraw was escorted in manacles to Lahore by a triumphant Mahabat-Khan.

The aftermath of Jahangir's victory was ruthless: mass execution, torture and imprisonment. One contemporary account describes Khusraw's 'captains being taken by the King and hanged upon flesh-hooks and stakes'.[34] The emperor made sure that his son was not spared the excruciating detail of his supporters' punishment, forcing him to ride along an avenue of death, lined with the bodies of his former comrades. 'Having taken his son,' another observer shuddered, 'he placed him to see the execution of those two thousand he had taken: the manner of the execution being terrible; for they were put into the ground upon sharp stakes, and so left to die.'[35] Others were hanged; as their bodies dangled, swinging in the wind, Mahabat-Khan gloated in Khusraw's ear from his position behind him in the elephant howdah, 'Sultan, see how your soldiers fight against the trees'.[36]

Among those executed was Arjun Dev, the fifth Guru of the Sikhs, whose possessions were also confiscated. It is far from clear that the guru had even supported Khusraw's rebellion; more likely he had simply accorded conventional hospitality – prayers, spiritual advice and the saffron *tilaka* on a guest's forehead – to a royal visitor passing the newly constructed Golden Temple at Amritsar on the great Agra-Lahore road. But Jahangir was not willing to take any risk with such an influential Punjabi community leader; he also found it irritating that Arjun Dev and his predecessors had represented an alternative source of authority to his own dynasty ever since the early years of the Mughal invasion. It has been argued that Jahangir would ideally have liked to end Amritsar's autonomy and force all Sikhs into the embrace of Islam, a recourse that would have been wholly objectionable to his father Akbar. For now, though, he had at least removed their leader.

Khusraw's chief commanders, Abd-al-Rahim Khan and Hussein Beg Badakshi, were subjected to a novel torture. Stripped naked, Hussein Beg was sewn into the hide of a freshly slaughtered ox, while his companion Abd-al-Rahim was stitched into the skin of an ass, also newly killed. As the men were paraded through the streets of Lahore in this humiliating condition, the hides dried in the sun and shrank, slowly crushing and suffocating the men inside. Hussein passed out and was summarily beheaded, his quartered body displayed by the roadside. Abd-al-Rahim survived both degradation and discomfort and was eventually ransomed for a small fortune by a loyal courtier.

With such brutal punishment the order of the day, with so many of his followers so 'barbarously mangled', many courtiers wondered what fate the young Prince Khusraw would meet. The relationship between Salim and Khusraw had for years been more that of rival brothers than father and son. The fact that Khusraw, with excessive familiarity, openly referred to Salim as *Shah-Bhai* or 'imperial brother' may have made it easier for Jahangir to harden his heart.[37] A Jesuit priest, Fr Fernão Guerreiro, provides a vivid and emotional account of the day of reckoning when 'His Majesty

... turning on him [Khusraw] a countenance full of wrath, upbraided him in the most bitter terms ... [and] to make his degradation complete, deprived him of his right to succeed to the throne, transferring these to his second son [Pervez].[38] Khusraw, still bound 'with a chain fastened from his left hand to his left foot, according to the laws of Genghis Khan', was then taken to his cell and blinded by having his eyes sewn shut, a method designed to be agonising but potentially reversible.[39] Cast out for good from the counsels of state and deprived of the trappings of royalty, Khusraw was then imprisoned in a windowless cell.

Jahangir's subsequent prolonged stay in the north, at Lahore and Kabul, through the spring, summer and autumn of 1607, was prompted by more serious considerations than relaxation and hunting. No sooner had the rebellion been dealt with than a new crisis emerged in the northeast – and it came as a direct result of Khusraw's mutiny. Persia, to the west, had been fomenting trouble around the city of Kandahar and Shah Abbas, now settled at his splendid new place in Isfahan, had seized the opportunity presented by the upheaval within the Mughal ruling dynasty to make his move on a long desired prize.

The presence of the sprawling Persian Empire was constantly in the minds of the Mughals, especially when it came to the long-cherished dream of regaining the ancestral homelands of Central Asia, not least because the Persians had rival ambitions on those territories they did not already hold. Successive Mughal emperors did their best to maintain cordial relations with the Safavid dynasty at Isfahan; indeed, it was only with Persia and the Ottoman Empire that the Mughals deigned to maintain diplomatic relations on a basis of equality. So there was a regular exchange of ambassadorial delegations, lavish gifts and long letters that offered mutual assurances of peaceful intent and eternal brotherhood in Islam.[40] But behind the diplomatic smiles and elaborate honorifics lay an acute understanding of realpolitik. For the previous fifteen years, Shah Abbas had maintained a regular correspondence with Akbar. More recently, during the struggle to succeed the Great Mughal, Abbas had hedged his bets, writing both to Daniyal and Salim, earnestly and disingenuously urging each to pursue a 'spiritual, not material friendship'.[41] For his part, Daniyal had kept the neighbouring ruler up to date on the struggling Deccan campaign in a series of clandestine letters, presumably in an attempt to enlist Persian support for his own candidacy in a prospective war of succession.[42] But there remained Mughal and Persian ambitions that were mutually conflicting – most overtly concerning the ownership of Kandahar.

Kandahar, a city of immense strategic and mercantile value, had changed hands since long before Khurram's birth but was finally annexed to the imperial dominions in 1595, when the prince was three. Akbar's victory was less a result of military heroism – though Abd-al-Rahim the old Khan-Khanan had led an effective campaign – than a windfall of treachery. The Persian governor, Muzaffar Hussein Mirza, had quarrelled with his imperial master and, disillusioned by 'the avarice of the Turkish mercantile elements in Kandahar, who could think of nothing but profits from Indian cloth and the accumulation of gold', had handed over this important fort to the Mughals.[43] During the long summer of 1605, even as Akbar lay dying and the Khusraw/Salim dispute simmered, there were two Persian ambassadors in Agra, leading the latest impressive delegation from Isfahan. They brought generous gifts, including hundreds of thoroughbred horses. But under the cloak of this benign goodwill mission, Ali Beg Yuzbashi and Darwish Beg were busily gathering information. They were able to transmit to Shah Abbas an accurate picture of the divisions at court, including Khusraw's 'great popularity among the masses': their conclusion was that 'a prolonged civil war seemed unavoidable'.[44] The Shah set his plans in motion, ordering the provincial governors of Farah and Sistan in the Khorasan region, backed by a detachment from Herat, to consolidate their forces and attack Kandahar.

But he was to be disappointed. Once securely on the throne, Jahangir dealt with this further crisis with creditable speed and efficiency. He had, after all, seen it coming. 'God forbid,' he had written in his journal, 'that the death of His Majesty and Khusraw's untimely rebellion might whet these people's appetites to make an attack on Kandahar.'[45] Fortunately, Jahangir could depend on a loyal and efficient governor, Shah Beg Khan, who fortified Kandahar against the expected attack. To buttress the beleaguered garrison, Jahangir sent another large contingent from Lahore under the command of a Mughal aristocrat of impeccable family credentials, Mirza Ghazi. This multi-talented poet and general, whose ancestors were from Central Asia's Khorasan region, now added Kandahar to the governorates of Thatta and Multan. The man who penned his eloquent qasidas under the nom-de-plume *Waqari* could now muster a personal following of 5,000 cavalry and infantry to match. Thwarted by this rapid counter-deployment, the Persian plans unravelled and Shah Abbas was forced to disavow any knowledge of the attempt on the fort. He dictated a swift and gushing letter to Jahangir, seeking to repair the damage caused by what he described as a 'slight misunderstanding'.[46]

Jahangir may have enjoyed his rival's discomfiture but he chose not to rub the Persian Shah's nose in it. After all, Kandahar had been secured easily enough – and there were many more compelling issues to occupy him at court once back in Agra. There was a substantial building programme underway, starting with the tomb of the late Emperor Akbar. Then there was his own second marriage, celebrated in 17 June 1608, to Raja Man Singh's great-granddaughter, a union secured with a gift of eighty-thousand rupees to the girl's family (though the imperial elephant-house benefited from the arrangement, receiving a reciprocal donation of sixty fine beasts). This was a highly political match: not just an affirmation of strong political ties between the Mughals and the Hindu ruling family of Amber in Rajasthan but also a clear sign that the divisions created by the feud with Khusraw, Man Singh's nephew, were set firmly in the past.

Not long afterwards, Jahangir turned his attention to other military matters. In August, Mahabat-Khan was despatched to tackle the recalcitrant Maharana Amar Singh of Mewar, whose subjugation had for so long been so fruitlessly delegated to Salim himself. Through the hills of Rajasthan, the Mughals 'swept the land like swarms of locusts, destroying and laying waste everything in their path ... like locusts, the invading force lost equally heavily, even though, again like locusts, more swarms kept coming'.[47] Sporadic campaigning had continued, too, in the Deccan, where the original expeditionary force had been assigned reinforcements of twelve thousand men and a generous treasury of a million rupees. But conclusive success against the Nizamshah of Ahmadnagar was elusive, so Jahangir decided to shake up the high command by appointing his hitherto undistinguished middle son, Pervez, to be nominal commander-in-chief. On 12 October 1609, Pervez was sent south, kitted out with many gilded treats. Hopes were not high, however. Even Jahangir was sceptical about prospects, while hard-bitten foreign traders like the Englishman Thomas Kerridge plainly despised the vacillating Pervez, 'whose capacity being weak and he given to womanish pleasures, there is no hope either of honour or content from him'.[48]

During this long period, Prince Khurram maintained an intense focus on building his own support base, constantly assessing his own status relative to that of his brother Pervez. Since the heady days of his betrothal to Arjumand Banu in late 1606 and his placement as effective heir apparent, some of the shine had gone off his position in the royal household. Jahangir's memoirs certainly recorded a gradual trend of favouritism – subtly larger gifts of golden daggers and choice jewels – towards Pervez. Khurram mocked and despised his middle brother as an inconsequential good-for-nothing but he had grounds for anxiety. Pervez had remained with his father through the long years of rebellion at Allahabad, while Khurram himself had been kept at Akbar's side wherever the old emperor travelled. Still, there was little concrete evidence to indicate that Jahangir had now changed his mind about the succession. Even the appointment of Pervez as commander-in-chief of a renewed Deccan campaign could be interpreted in two ways. Promoted to the rank of Ten Thousand, endowed with a massive war chest of 2.5 million rupees, substantial manpower and seasoned fighters among his top brass, the southern campaign looked like giving Pervez an excellent opportunity to prove himself where his uncles Murad and Daniyal had failed and so secure the status of favoured son. The seventeen-year-old Khurram, by contrast, languished in the tedium of the classroom and the military training academy, wholly bereft of any chance of glory. But Burhanpur was a very long way from Agra, while Khurram was given the valuable privilege of remaining at the heart of empire, playing an increasingly important administrative role – in short, learning the ropes and all the time building up his personal treasury and factional following.

There was one serious crimp in Khurram's otherwise smooth progression. His marital prospects had been damaged, if not effectively destroyed, by an incident in which he himself had played a telling role. In September 1607, during the long slow journey back from Kabul to Agra, the prince's own private secretary received a report from a spy planted in the household of the blind prince Khusraw to the effect that a plot to assassinate the emperor was in motion. Khusraw had recently been released from irons but was already planning another attempt on the kingdom. Anxious to win back his father's absolute favour, and with no hesitation about informing on his former rival, Khurram rushed to tell Jahangir about his brother's scheme. With minimum fuss, keen not to destroy the easy momentum of the march south by recreating the old schisms at the heart of court, the emperor coolly ordered the four ringleaders of the five hundred or so alleged conspirators to be 'executed by various tortures'.[49]

But there was a disastrous repercussion for Khurram. Among the conspirators thus executed – a quartet identified by a 'peculiar badge' given them in private audience by Prince Khusraw – was Muhammad Sharif, younger son of Ghiyath al-Din Itimad al-Daula, and uncle to Khurram's financée, Lady Arjumand. Even the venerable Pillar of the State could not escape guilt by association: Ghiyath al-Din was placed under arrest in the household of a noble named Qasim Beg *Dinayat-Khan*, subjected to an enormous fine of two hundred thousand rupees and disgraced.[50] Far more seriously for Khurram, his betrothed was now tainted by this criminal misdemeanour within her own family. Marriage with a prince of the royal line was now clearly impossible. Khurram's prompt and loyal action had won him praise from his father – but lost him a greater prize.

Within a short time, however, a replacement bride materialised from an unexpected quarter. When Jahangir came to reconsider the Persian question at the end of 1609, pragmatism as always came to the fore. It would be madness to antagonise such a powerful personality, not least because a declaration of open hostilities between Agra and Isfahan would likely prompt Shah Abbas to send arms, men and money to his Shiite allies in the three Deccan kingdoms. That would doom the campaign led by Pervez. Persia's duplicity over Kandahar, then, had to be set aside and relations smoothed. As always, a politically expedient marriage would provide the answer – and with Khusraw in prison and Pervez already bound for Burhanpur and the southern front, Khurram was the logical choice. The decision to shape this purely strategic alliance came as mixed news to the young man. On the one hand, he had been denied the consummation of his long-standing betrothal to the Lady Arjumand; set against that was the renewal of his central position in his father's attentions and in the politics of the moment. If he could not command, he could at least prove his loyalty as a reliable instrument of practical government.

And so it was that the eighteen-year-old Khurram was compelled to make his first marriage to a young Persian maiden. The young lady in question (like Arjumand, a complete stranger to the prince) was the virgin daughter of a recently deceased Persian dignitary from the northern mountains at Kandahar, Mirza Muzaffar Hussein. He was not only great-grandson of Shah Ismail I, sixteenth-century founder of the Safavid dynasty and ancestor of Shah Abbas, but also cousin to the Persian ruler. Subsequent Mughal court recorders and biographers, however, merely accord the princess the blandly descriptive label *Kandahari-Begum*, a clear indication of her lesser status in a court where most epithets and titles were fulsome and flowery, and none bother with personal details of appearance or education.[51]

The process of arranging the marriage appears to have taken some time. The emperor Jahangir recorded two related entries in his memoirs, nearly a year apart. The first appeared as just one item of business in a typically humdrum account of the day's court transactions, regional promotions, salary checks and other miscellaneous imperial housekeeping chores. 'On Sunday the fifteenth of Ramadan 1018 [12 December 1609],' he noted, 'I sent fifty thousand rupees as a wedding pledge – *sachiq* – to Kandahari Begum's house.' Eleven months later – and a full month after the wedding celebration itself – the diary note was somewhat more enthusiastic but still comparatively brief.

On this day, the seventeenth of Aban [7 November 1610], when the banquet was held, I went to Baba Khurram's house and stayed the night there. I gave more of the amirs robes

of honour and several prisoners in the Gwalior fortress were released. … I gave a bit of gold and silver and some of every sort of grain to trusted men to distribute among the poor of Agra.[52]

Khurram's official biographer, Muhammad Amin Qazvini, was far more eloquent in his description of the marriage. Indeed, effusive compliments were the order of the day and his delirious account left no superlative unexplored. The festive assembly was arranged in a beautifully appointed mansion that was traditionally assigned to the widowed mother of the ruling emperor – currently the Dowager Queen Guljar Maryam-Zamani – and located inside the thick walls of Agra Fort adjacent to the palatial State House. The astrologers duly consulted, the marriage – 'a banquet of joy and pleasure' – was held at an auspicious hour.

After the conjunction of those two luminaries of the zenith of happiness and felicity, His Majesty … took the trouble to grace Khurram's residence, which … had lately taken on the appearance of the celestial garden of the houris, on account of the construction and furnishing of attractive edifices and faultless villas. And for one night and day, the emperor adorned the assembly of joy and pleasure and decorated the banquet of delight and cheerfulness. Khurram, having spread carpets from the lofty royal audience hall to the special seat in his own palace that had been allotted for the emperor … presented by way of *peshkash* offering costly gifts comprising jewels, studded utensils and rich stuffs. And through the emperor's kindness and consideration, everything had the honour of royal acceptance.[53]

5
In The Shadow of Nur-Mahal

Nur-Jahan, albeit in appearance a woman,
In the ranks of heroes is a tiger-hunting woman.
Ghulam Hussein Salim Zaydpuri[1]

Emperor Jahangir takes pride in her
As she possesses the ability to defeat even the heavens
Through her wise and clever devices.
Kami Shirazi *Khallaq-al-Mani*[2]

Khurram's comprehensive rehabilitation – and the temporary eclipse of Pervez – came on 16 January 1611, the day that Khurram helped save his father's life. It happened during a hunting expedition in the administrative district of Bari, shortly before the prince's twentieth birthday. This dramatic encounter, in which Khurram gave 'a raging lion a taste of his bloodthirsty sword', was the first of many incidents recorded in the Mughal annals and immortalised in lavish paintings, celebrating the prince's personal bravery, physical fitness and martial prowess.[3] The royal party had turned west off the Agra-Gwalior road and travelled, with customary lack of haste, into the scrubby hill-country of eastern Rajasthan. Forgoing his usual massed entourage, Jahangir was travelling light: hunting with just Khurram, a small number of aristocratic friends and his closest servants, while the hunt professionals used cheetahs to drive deer through the arid undergrowth.

This kind of chase was certainly nowhere near as dangerous as hunting lions and tigers, which was frequently a hair-raisingly close-range experience, even for the usually well-cushioned emperors. In 1597, when Khurram was just six, his father Salim had nearly been killed on a lion hunt. The elephant on which he was mounted had killed a litter of cubs but the enraged mother had sprung upon the prince. Salim had finally stunned the lioness with a blow from the butt of his musket, leaving one of his troop of guards to finish her off with his sword.[4]

Now, in the hills of Bari district, the sun was setting on the end of a successful day's hunting. The Muslims among the imperial staff had just completed their evening prayers when word suddenly came from the beaters in the surrounding bush that a huge, powerfully built lion had been seen in the vicinity, prowling around the cow-pens owned by local villagers. Jahangir jumped to his feet immediately. His usual evening drinking session was already underway and the news made him highly excitable. Ignoring the pleas of his hunt managers, who pointed out that dusk was falling and that nobody, not even the emperor, went hunting lion without a sturdy elephant to ride on, Jahangir leapt on his lavishly caparisoned horse and cantered off into the evening. Khurram scrambled to gather his weapons, musket and sword, and galloped off in his father's dusty tracks, followed by Raja Ram Das, a local dignitary enjoying the hunt, and the emperor's ever-present wine-bearer, known only partly in jest as *Hayat-Khan*, the 'Master of Life'.

The chief huntsman for the expedition was Anup Singh Badgujar, a Rajput of distinguished but penniless origins. He had been dragged to court in chains in Akbar's day, charged with shooting a royal cheetah. In fact, it had been a mistake. Anup Singh had been out hunting deer and had shot at an animal flashing through the woodland in a blur of movement. Only when he tracked the dying beast did he see the glorious markings of the cheetah – and the golden collar that revealed the identity of its royal owner. Horrified, Anup Singh had tried to bury the evidence but was soon discovered. Typically, Akbar found more merit in his marksmanship than blame for his error and employed him forthwith.[5] Now, Anup too grabbed up a large-calibre musket and its tripod mount and hastened to catch up with his master, desperate to forestall disaster.

By the time the small rescue party caught up with the emperor, he had already flung himself off his horse and fired two shots at the lion, which lay, wounded and snarling, in the undergrowth. But even as they galloped up, the lion charged. Jahangir ordered Anup Singh to hand over his powerful gun but without its tripod his aim was off. The bullet missed, there was no time to reload and the lion began to close in. Clustered round their king, prince and servants alike put their own bodies between Jahangir and the beast. Anup Singh lashed out at the lion's head with his tripod and had his hands savaged by sharp teeth. As the lion fell upon the hunt master, Khurram and Raja Ram Das slashed at its shoulders and flanks with their blades. Jahangir noted with relief that one blow to the shoulder 'really cut in' and the lion retreated, streaming blood from a dozen wounds.[6]

As camp followers and lesser servants rushed after the lion into the bush, firing repeatedly, the shocked hunting party assessed the damage. Jahangir was overcome with gratitude – despite having been stamped on by his rescuers, so keen were they to put themselves between him and the lion. Anup Singh was given the title *Singh-Dalan*, 'Lion Crusher', and promoted. Raja Ram Das, wounded numerous times with tooth and claw, received special imperial attention. 'That captain,' a contemporary traveller recorded, 'having first received thirty two wounds; whom therefore the King took up into his own palanquin, with his own hands also wiped and bound up his wounds, and made him a captain of five thousand horse, in recompense of that his valorous loyalty'.[7] Turning at last to his son, the emperor 'drew the prince's still blood-stained sword from its scabbard with his own blessed hand and inspected it, praising and extolling the hand and arm of the regal lion-hunter who had been nurtured by divine power'.[8]

Khurram's reward came two months later, at the Feast of Culmination, which brought the eighteen-day Nauruz Spring Festival to a noisy conclusion. As always, the entire court was festooned with drapes of the finest and most vividly coloured materials. Each day's entertainment was prepared and funded by one of the great nobles of court, who also hosted the king and presented him with lavish tributes. Amid all the promotions, rewards and mutually exchanged gifts recorded in Jahangir's journal – the jewelled daggers, bolts of exquisite cloth, elephants with gilded tusks and glossy Arab stallions – came the elevation of Prince Khurram to the rank of Ten Thousand foot and Five Thousand horse. At last his status formally matched that of his elder brother, Pervez. The hunting incident had removed any doubt about Khurram's personal courage – and his latest promotion entrenched his position as heir apparent.

The court to which the imperial hunting party returned that spring was an establishment on the verge of profound change, much of it centred on the personality of the emperor's third wife, Mihr al-Nisa, whom he had met at the New Year festival in March 1611 and was to marry that summer. She would come to wield unprecedented influence not only over her husband, the emperor, but also over his sons. Her appearance at court stemmed from a complex chain of political events and, at the time of her arrival in the royal harem at Agra, her prospects were dismal. Yet in very short order, this steely lady was able to build up a personal power-base at the heart of empire, gathering around herself and her loyalists within the royal household the elite of the mainly Persian aristocracy. And all this was achieved despite the rigorous maintenance of strict purdah. She was, literally, the power *behind* the throne – monitoring the affairs of state from the privacy of a small carved stone window near the king's own seat.

Mihr al-Nisa, that 'Sun Among Women', had seen some turbulent times since her marriage at seventeen to Ali Quli Beg Istalju. Her father, Ghiyath al-Din Itimad al-Daula, had lost his position as the king's most favoured minister and she, like Khurram's original fiancée, Arjumand Abu-al-Hassan, shared the family disgrace. Her husband, meanwhile, had fallen foul of the brutal politics of the Mughal succession. Originally a key part of Prince Salim's coterie – and such a loyal protégé that, after a particularly impressive shooting performance, Salim had dubbed him *Shir-Afgan*, the 'Tiger Killer' – Ali Quli had changed sides after the prince's rebellion and backed the Khusravite movement, endorsing what at that time appeared to be the Emperor Akbar's own choice of successor. When Salim ultimately secured the throne, Ali Quli had unexpectedly received a generous land allocation from the new Emperor Jahangir at Burdwan in Bengal, where he settled with his wife and infant daughter, Ladli.[9] But in the summer of 1606, Jahangir abruptly reversed his conciliatory approach, summoning Ali Quli to court to quiz him in person about rumours that he'd supported Khusraw's recent abortive uprising at Lahore. When the emperor's childhood companion and foster-brother, Sheikh Khubu Qutb-al-Din-Khan, 'Axis of the Faith', arrived to deliver the summons the following May, Ali Quli attacked and killed the envoy before himself being overcome and hacked to pieces by the armed entourage surrounding the emperor's friend.[10]

When news of this grim and bloody encounter reached Jahangir in Kabul, he was disconsolate. The death of Qutb-al-Din-Khan was the worst thing that had happened since Akbar's demise. And as for Ali Quli, a man once counted as a close friend, the emperor wrote: 'It is hoped that the disgraceful wretch's place will be forever in hell'.[11] Qutb al-Din's cousin was despatched to escort Ali Quli's family to court, for, as was traditional, his entire property was forfeit to the emperor upon his death. It was an ill-omened start to the life of Mihr al-Nisa at court: humiliated and disgraced by association with her husband's murder of the king's closest friend. Worse still, by the time she arrived at court in Agra, her own father, Ghiyath al-Din Itimad al-Daula – tarnished not only by the action of his son-in-law in Bengal but also by his own son Muhammad Sharif's association with the Khusravite assassination plot against the emperor on the road between Kashmir and Kabul – was languishing under arrest in the house of Qasim Beg Dinayat-Khan and in no position to argue for her.

For four long years, she was forced to live in obscurity, secluded in the women's quarters of Khurram's own childless foster-mother, Ruqayya Begum, who became her sponsor and protector at court. But then came an extraordinary reversal of fortunes: from despised chattel to imperial wife. On the first night of the Nauruz New Year festival, 20 March 1611, she 'caught the King's far-seeing eye' when he attended the Mina Bazaar – the same annual event at which Khurram had met Lady Arjumand five years earlier. Mihr al-Nisa was shopping with her patroness, Ruqayya Begum. Accounts by contemporary European travellers asserted that formal marriage was not uppermost in the emperor's mind, yet the marriage of an infatuated Jahangir and Mihr al-Nisa was indeed formally celebrated on 3 June 1611 – although, quite inexplicably, the king neglected to include it in his own memoir.[12] It was for the young widow, as the veteran courtier Muhammad Hadi observed, a case of 'all's well that ends well'.

The days of misfortune drew to a close and the stars of her good fortune commenced to shine and to wake as if from a deep sleep. The bride's chamber was prepared, the bride was decorated and desire began to arise. Hope was happy. A key was found for closed doors, a restorative was found for broken hearts; and on a certain New Year's festival she attracted the love and affection of the King. She was soon made the favourite wife of His Majesty. In the first instance she received the title of *Nur-Mahal*, 'Light of the Palace'.[13]

The figure of Nur-Mahal stands out in Mughal history as prominently as almost any king – and certainly far more than any other queen. She polarised opinion at court, prompting slavish loyalty from her own supporters and equally venomous disapproval from her critics. The latter included conservative Muslims like the historian Muhammad Salih Kamboh, who asserted that 'a woman in power can only lead to the ruin of a country'.[14] As much as any other political figure closely involved in the harsh struggle to win and hold on to power, her record and reputation have been subjected to the distortions of propagandists. So, while one account describes the 'golden opinions' won from the people by the new queen, who was 'just to all who begged her support ... an asylum for all sufferers', others denounce her as 'the leaven of confusion and trouble for India' and a 'villainous strumpet'.

Partisan commentary aside, Nur-Mahal undoubtedly wielded tremendous influence over the king, beginning almost immediately. The first demonstration of this was the rapid promotion of her family and friends to ever more central positions at court, to the extent that the Mughal kingdom was soon administered by an elite within the elite, intensely loyal to her. The rehabilitation of Nur-Mahal's father Ghiyath al-Din Itimad al-Daula was accelerated to the point where, on 4 August 1611 – just two months after the royal wedding – he was appointed to the post of Wazir, the imperial Chancellor responsible for the nation's finances. His disgrace by association with his son's treason was forgotten and over the next eight years, Itimad al-Daula's personal ranking at court rose to Seven Thousand, a status matched by a generous allocation of revenue-generating estates.

Queen Nur-Jahan hosts Jahangir and Khurram (lower right) in the harem

Nur-Mahal's elder brother Abu-al-Hassan experienced a dizzy rise too. He was immediately granted the imperial honorific *Itiqad-Khan*, the 'Master of Conviction', and made Chief Steward of the Royal Household, while his own sons were given unprecedented opportunities. This was clinically efficient faction building, based on neither religion, ethnicity nor ideology

but on simple self-interest. Around them, this quartet – the emperor, his queen, her father and her brother – gathered a powerful clique of affiliates, each of whom brought his or her own substantial contingent of soldiers, administrators, religious personalities, artistic figures and other hangers-on to buttress the power and income of the collective.[15]

Nur-Mahal's power stretched into every corner of the empire – and it was achieved despite the fact that she never appeared in public. Yet, while royal women may have been invisible, they were almost always present: discreetly located behind the elegant latticework *jali* screens in the audience-chambers of court, they monitored all the functions of state, heard the emperor's petitioners and had opinions on even provincial business transactions. Effortlessly superseding Jahangir's earlier wives, Nur-Mahal now became the driving force within the harem, the Senior Queen of a court-within-the-court, sophisticated, cultured and politically astute. Far from being restricted to merely passive roles, the imperial women played an important role in the administrative machinery of the state. They were well financed, too. Jahangir had marked his coronation with a dramatic increase in the allowances granted to harem residents and Nur-Mahal rapidly acquired substantial estates whose revenues brought hundreds of thousands of rupees annually into her private coffers.

Official documents in the name of Nur-Mahal – and, in her later incarnation, in the name of *Nur-Jahan*, 'light of the world' – reveal the extent to which she wielded influence, both in her own right and through her brother the Chief Steward. Her tone was always one of unquestionable authority.[16] Typically peremptory notes urged immediate compliance with Jahangir's imperial edicts on land distribution or advised on the imminent arrival of the tax collector. 'Muhammad Hashim has been deputed by Her Majesty to collect the revenue from Amber District,' said one; 'when the said official reaches there, he should take necessary steps immediately and remit the cash to the Treasury at Agra. He should not act contrary to or deviate from the said orders.' [17]

Nur-Mahal was but following the precedent of earlier generations of royal women. Akbar's widow, Guljar Maryam-Zamani, was well known and widely respected for her many varied and vigorous trading interests, including a small fleet of ships to take 1,500 passengers at a time on the Hajj pilgrimage to Mecca. Maryam-Zamani also had the authority, in her capacity as Queen Mother, to address issues of provincial embezzlement.[18] There were plenty of stories to illustrate the influence of royal women. On one occasion, Jahangir had convened a meeting of senior nobles to discuss the fate of a recalcitrant member of the nobility; a majority advocated execution but then the emperor's aunt, Salima Sultan, called out from behind the purdah screen to insist that the entire harem had assembled to demand mercy.[19] Most crucially, influential women at court were seen as well-placed conduits to pass on messages and petitions to the emperor or his powerful sons.

The influence of such royal women was all-pervasive. Their greatest and most visible legacy is the sheer number of tombs, mosques, gardens and caravanserais endowed by their capacious purses. They patronised charities for the poor, supervised almshouses and soup-kitchens – and made sure that the nation's leading religious figures had their establishments maintained to a suitable standard. Every Eid – the festival that ended the fasting month of Ramadan – the poor were fed at their expense. The Queen Mother was further celebrated for donating ten per cent of her privy purse in charity on every Muslim and non-Muslim holiday.[20]

The sheer size of the women's apartments in the main Mughal strongholds at Agra and Lahore indicates just how substantial the harem was. So, when a foreign traveller wrote in sniggering terms of a place where the emperor 'keeps a thousand women to serve his lustful desires', he might have misunderstood the purpose of the harem but he was not far wrong on numbers. The harem grew exponentially in times of war as the relatives of defeated vassal princes were taken into confinement. In just one campaign by Akbar's generals, for example, sent 'to chastise the Afghans of Swat and Bajaur', Mughal forces 'killed a great many of them and sent the wives and family ... with all their friends, nearly four hundred in number, to court'.[21] Yet, despite these many temptations, not one of the Mughal emperors treated the harem as a glorified bordello – even if many outsiders believed that all high-ranking Mughals were devoted to their 'fleshly pleasures'.

The harem may have been comfortable, even luxurious, but it was a gilded cage. The primary value of female descendants lay in their marriageability; young women were cynically used as chattels of the state, best deployed when used in marriage to seal a political bond. Unfortunately, there were usually more women than opportunities for advantageous marriages, especially once the empire was secured and fewer strategic contracts required. This meant that most harem inmates were forced to forgo not just marriage but sex of any kind and many princesses died as virgin spinsters, never having travelled beyond the harem. Furthermore, when women were discovered taking part in acts of sexual impropriety, punishment could be severe. A noblewoman in Nur-Mahal's personal entourage who was 'taken in the king's house in some action with an eunuch' was executed by being buried 'up to the armpits in the earth hard rammed ... to abide three days and two nights without any sustenance, her head and arms bare, exposed to the sun's violence'. She lasted a day and a half; the offending eunuch was trampled by elephants.[22]

The elevation of Nur-Mahal to the rank of Primary Queen transformed the lives of both the emperor and his favourite son. Jahangir recognised in her a soulmate as well as a woman whom he could trust to share the burden of running the vast imperial machine. She hunted as enthusiastically as he did, blasting tigers and other game with impressive accuracy from within her modestly curtained howdah. She shared his adoration of the northern mountains, especially the Kashmir Valley, and, like him, her favourite palace was Akbar's fastness at Lahore, which she and Jahangir fortified, modernised and adorned with extensive and expensive redevelopment programmes over the following decade. She was involved in the planning of all key events of state, consulting the Hindu and Muslim astrologers to make arrangements for the solar and lunar weighing ceremonies. Above all, it was a complementary relationship in which power was shared – her greater strength of character and lack of personal weaknesses balanced by his imperial status. And it was rooted in personal adoration, a mutual obsession romanticised in a celebrated poem.

'Thy collar, my love, has not been dyed with saffron,' said Jahangir;
'Engrained therein is the pallor of my face.'
And it is the ruby-drops of my heart which have lent their hue
To those ruby buttons on thy silken coat,' answered Nur-Mahal.[23]

While his father rediscovered love, Khurram obtained a crucial ally in his personal search for status and power. He was already an important personality at court, accorded a rank that commanded respect and a considerable following. He had also, at nineteen, recently become a father for the first time. A daughter, Purhunar, was born to Queen Kandahari Begum on 21 August 1611 and effortlessly swallowed up in the harem. The infant was entrusted to the care of a governess known only as *Akbarabadi-Mahal*, the wife or sister of one of the emperor's closest companions and a lady whose position as wet-nurse to the royal line afforded her wealth and status within the household.[24] Meanwhile, Khurram's relationship with his new step-mother was becoming one of the defining political developments in the entire family history: an alliance between a clever, ruthless and arrogant young prince and an equally astute and ambitious queen with the ear of the emperor. Over time, the make-up of the ruling clique and the weight of influence within it would critically shift – but it would take another marriage to cement Khurram's place within the Nur-Mahal junta.

Ghiyath-al-Din
Itimad-al- The court that Nur-Mahal had now joined in such an influential capacity
Daula was, however, an establishment of entrenched routine and convention,

where change was conceded grudgingly. It was a place of immense wealth and opulence, its appointments and sheer style estimated by astonished foreigners to exceed anything then available in Europe's royal capitals. Records show that the emperor's annual income from of his crown lands held steady at around 250 million rupees, a figure estimated by contemporary English traders as equating to nearly thirty million pounds sterling – at a time when the Chancellor of the Exchequer in London was receiving just £425,000 a year from public taxation.[25] Small wonder that East India Company agent Nicholas Withington was moved to write: 'As concerning the greatness of this king, the Great Mughal, his state is so great in comparison to most Christian kings that the report would be almost incredible.'[26] Apart from the revenues of the efficient imperial tax system, the king's wealth stemmed from the ancient tribal prescription that he inherited the entire estate of every citizen who died. He might choose to allot the income to another individual, perhaps to the widow or eldest son of the deceased, but it was his absolute right to seize it all: 'It returns,' as one foreign diplomat put it, 'like rivers to the sea, both of those he gave to and of those that have gained by their own industry.'[27]

Everything at court hinged on status, on the concentric circle of authority stretching away from the personality of the emperor like diminishing ripples on one of Jahangir's beloved Kashmiri lakes. At the symbolic centre stood the great black stone throne that Jahangir had had brought by the eunuch *Daulat-Khan* from Allahabad on 25 September 1610 to be the focus of all formal court occasions. At its furthest extremes were the tens of thousands of functionaries belonging to court and camp: the soldiers, the cavalrymen, the porters, gunners, water-carriers, elephant-keepers, grooms, carpet-layers, cooks, the tent squads, the gardeners and lantern-bearers. All were paid monthly out of the royal treasury at Agra – wages as negligible as three rupees handled with the same attention to detail in paperwork and procedure as the most lavishly endowed courtier.

The strict hierarchical disposition of the aristocracy was carefully calibrated. In November 1611, just a handful outside the royal family held a rank of between Nine and Twelve Thousand; eighteen individuals were named at Five Thousand and twenty-two at Three Thousand. As for the lower echelons in the pecking order, precisely 2,950 men were identified as holding ranks from Two Thousand sliding down the scale to Twenty.[28] With each ranking went a commensurate income, either derived in regular allowances from the treasury or in grants of lucrative estate lands, ranging from small-holdings to entire provinces. The sons of the most eminent nobles at court, such as the Chief Minister, Chancellor and Commander-in-Chief, began receiving their own rankings at the age of fourteen or fifteen. So too did the offspring of the oldest Mughal families; as their patron since ancestral times, the emperor was responsible for their welfare, reducation and training. They were allotted the honour of carrying the royal sunshade, sword, shield, bow or even spectacles.

But the subservient relationship of every man and boy in this hierarchy to the emperor himself was always clear. It was perhaps mostly starkly illustrated in this extract from the account of Captain William Hawkins, who in 1612 observed the ritual surrounding the return of a court official from a provincial posting.

First, the nobleman stays at the gate of the palace till the Vizier, the Lieutenant-General and the Knight-Martial come to accompany him unto the King. Then he is brought to the gate of the outermost railings … where he stands in the view of the King, in the midst between those nobles. Then he touches the ground with his hand and also with his head, very gravely, and does thus three times. This done, he kneels down, touching the ground with his forehead; which being once done, he is carried forward towards the King, and midway he is made to do this reverence again. Then he comes to the door of the red rails, doing the like reverence the third time; and having thus done, he comes within the red rails and does it once more upon the carpets. Then the King commands him to come up the stairs or ladder of seven steps, that he may embrace him.[29]

A typical day began with the dawn prayer, the first of the five that Muslims are obliged to perform. Jahangir sat afterwards on his sheepskin prayer-mat in contemplation, running his prayer-beads through his fingers, facing Mecca in the west. At sunrise he made the first of three daily appearances before his people; this time he crossed the palace to face the eastern dawn and the crowd already gathered below. This important ceremony was a modern hangover from the ancient Persian and Indian rules of kingship, which stipulated that the monarch be accessible, at least visually, to every one of his subjects every day. It was crucial to be seen to be in good health and in control.[30] On his appearance at a special balcony window in the outside wall of the palace – a place known as the *jharoka darshana* for its dual purpose as a 'see-and-be-seen' venue – the masses below erupted with cries of *Padshah salamat*: 'Long live the King!' Jahangir then returned to his private quarters to spend the morning with his household.

The next part of the day, when the real work was done, began at noon with the emperor's second appearance at the jharoka darshana. Again, the people were compelled to assemble to acclaim their monarch. Twice a week, elephant fights, 'the bravest spectacle in the world', were staged for his pleasure on the riverbank below. The serious business of court took place during the mid-afternoon, when Jahangir appeared before his elite class, the nobility who ran the empire on his behalf. The English merchant William Finch, selling indigo for the East India Company at Agra and

Lahore, left a vivid description of the strict formalities observed when attending an imperial audience.

You enter into a spacious court with guardrooms round about, like shops or open stalls, wherein his captains according to their degrees keep their seventh day watches. A little further you enter within a railing into a more inward court, within which none but ... men of sort are admitted, under pain of swacking by the porters' cudgels, which lay on load without respect of persons. Being entered, you approach the King's durbar or seat, before which is also a small court enclosed with rails, covered over head with rich drapes to keep away the sun. Aloft in a gallery the King sits in his chair of state, accompanied with his children and Chief Vizier (who goes up by a short ladder forth of the court). No other without calling dares to go up to him, save only two fan operators to gather wind; and right below him on a scaffold is a third, who with a horsetail makes havoc of poor flies. ... Within these rails below, none under the degree of Four Hundred horse are permitted to enter. ... Here every day, between three and four o'clock, the King comes forth and many thousand resort to do their duties, each taking place according to his degree. Here he remains, hearing of matters, receiving news by letters read by his Vizier, granting suites, etc., till shutting in of the evening, the drum meanwhile beating, and instruments playing from a high gallery on the next building opposite.[31]

The final part of the day, once business was over, was unmistakably Jahangir's favourite. Justice had been seen to be done; sentences had been served; executions carried out. After observing the final prayer of the day, he abandoned himself to relaxation: pleasant company, good food, plenty of alcohol and a few pellets of the finest opium. And, before close of day, there came one final appearance by one of his ubiquitous secretariat, ready to take down his master's musings on the day's developments. Drunk or sober, Jahangir rarely missed an opportunity to set down in writing the great political headlines of the day, the promotions, the gifts given and received – and his own scientific observations on the flora and fauna of his kingdom that piqued his interest.

It took a perceptive eye to appreciate that the emperor was as much in thrall to this exacting timetable as his courtiers. For officers of the state, it must have been immensely disrupting to have to break off all and any engagements three times a day in order simply to take part in a compulsory ceremonial. The emperor himself, though, was hardly exempt. In the febrile atmosphere of court, where rivalry constantly simmered and would-be successors looked for signs of weakness, these routine appearances were essential. Sir Thomas Roe, the tetchy ambassador from the Court of King James in London, visited Jahangir frequently in the Exclusive Audience Hall and made meticulous observations about Mughal politics and society. Decisions might be the sole preserve of the king, he saw, but

Arjumand
'Mumtaz-
Mahal'

'the course is unchangeable … so he is in a kind of reciprocal bondage, for he is tied to observe these hours and customs so precisely that if he were unseen one day and no sufficient reason rendered the people would mutiny; two days no reason can excuse, but that he must consent to open his doors and be seen by some to satisfy others.'[32]

Nur-Mahal's understanding of how to manipulate the machinery of court grew rapidly, assisted by her father and brother. Aware, perhaps more than anyone then in Agra, of the binding power of a good political marriage, the queen began to engineer the return to prominence of her young niece, the Lady Arjumand. Sidelined for more than four years, her prospects atrophied by the disgrace brought on the family by the treasonous plotting of her uncle Muhammad Sharif, Arjumand had languished in her father's harem. Her aunt plucked her from obscurity, patching up the marriage contract with Prince Khurram and reminding the emperor of the promises that had been made in Lahore back in the heady days of spring 1607, when the Khusravite rebellion had been crushed and the ascent of Khurram had begun. The wheels turned swiftly after that. During the Nauruz marking the start of Jahangir's seventh year on the throne, Khurram was promoted again, to the rank of Twelve Thousand.

The festival season was barely over before the emperor gave the nation's elite an excuse to begin the party all over again. After a hiatus in their engagement of nearly five years, Prince Khurram took Arjumand Abu-al-Hassan for his second wife on Friday 10 May 1612.[33] She was a little over nineteen, with many child-bearing years ahead of her. He was twenty years old, still not yet in his prime, on the cusp of greatness. It was a splendid occasion, with nobles, priests and slaves moving in grand procession into the Ordinary Audience Hall, to the accompaniment of musicians, dancers and acrobats. There had been many customary procedures to be fulfilled before the great day dawned. The bride's family had signalled their assent to the match by presenting betel leaves. Then, following the handover of the *sachiq* wedding gift, the hands and feet of both bride and groom had been traced with beautiful patterns in henna.

Jahangir himself took charge of the banquet arrangements, 'having obtained various articles of gold, jewels, stuffs and so forth … on such a scale as befits the emperors of very great grandeur'.[34] Now Khurram, heir to the throne, his forehead wreathed by the emperor himself in a *sehra* headband of pearls and jewels, vied with his new father-in-law, Abu-al-Hassan Itiqad-Khan, to mount the most ostentatious display of wealth and happiness, handing out robes of honour in gold-embroidered cloth and thick brocade. The procession then advanced, with drums thrashing and horns blaring, to the home of the bride, Arjumand, where the Muslim wedding ceremony – its precise timing dictated by the court astrologers – was conducted by the Qadi in front of the emperor. Muhammad Amin Qazvini's verse summed up the splendour of the occasion.

At a time when the ascendant star was favourable
The eyes deserved meeting each other …
A night brighter than the day of youth,
Adding to pleasurable delight and fulfilment of desire.[35]

The proud emperor was determined to put his personal stamp of approval on his favourite son's wedding day. First, he paid a personal visit to the mansion of the bride's father to award him yet another, higher title to mark the occasion: *Yamin-al-Daula*, 'Right-hand Man of the State'. The streets of Agra were brought to a standstill as the imperial convoy traversed the short distance from the fortress walls to Yamin-al-Daula's riverside estate, where 'for one night and day the emperor illumined the assembly of that feast of joy and pleasure'. Then Jahangir moved in stately progression back to the fort, where he paid his respects – another essential ceremony – to the ladies of the royal harem, who were about to be joined by the woman whom everyone knew was likely in time to be the nation's Primary Queen. There he feasted 'in the company of all the veiled ladies from behind the curtains of chastity and the concealed ones from the mansion of sovereignty'.

Khurram, too, had formalities to observe. A prince had to be seen to be both entertaining in style and according the emperor all the obligatory tributes: in this context, Khurram was more his father's subject than son. So he spread his most intricately woven and brightest carpets and scattered gold coins to the well-wishers thronging outside the citadel walls. The formal offering to the king – known as *peshkash* – was a glut of 'peerless jewels and heart-pleasing stuffs and precious objects'. The emperor, casting an experienced eye over the gifts, graciously condescended to accept the tribute in its entirety. Three weeks later, Jahangir paid another personal visit, this time to Khurram's own home for a further overnight stay. 'He presented offerings for my inspection,' the king noted with approval in his journal, 'arranged favours for his mother and stepmothers, as well as the harem servants, and gave robes to the senior officials.' [36]

And so Lady Arjumand Abu-al-Hassan, daughter of a Shiite Persian clan, entered into South Asia's greatest ruling family, travelling to her new harem in a six-man litter caparisoned in gold. All that remained was to identify an appropriately regal honorific, 'to distinguish with greater honour one from among those who grace the royal bedchamber of fortune'. After canvassing opinion among the elders of court, Khurram focused on Arjumand's 'weighty dignity', her intellectual capabilities and her beauty. She was, he concluded, simply the finest woman in the whole royal household, the 'Most Exquisite of the Palace'. The name has echoed down through history: *Mumtaz-Mahal.*

6

Shah Jahan:
Soldier of the Empire

Victorious emperors satisfy their driving passion
For the virgin lady of sovereign rule
Only when the glare of their flaming sword
Has erased the name of their malicious enemy from life's tablet.

Muhammad Baqir Najm al-Thani [1]

… Still there remained
For Amar the sad task of bending down before
The Moslem Prince, owning his own defeat,
A degradation that hurt his feelings more
Than any torture, death or exile from
His country, for in his heart he cursed
The bitter fate that gave to him no choice
But to give in and to be the first
Rana of Mewar ever to bow before a man.

S.O. Heinemann [2]

To cement his position, Khurram needed now only to add a reputation for military success. His opportunity came with the conquest of the Rajput principality of Mewar in 1613–15. In addition to his qualities of obedience, education and military training, the prince was also a confirmed abstainer – somewhat conspicuously in a court where so many red-letter days culminated in alcoholic parties. Khurram never clearly defined this abstinence as religiously motivated; it may equally have been prompted by the evidence daily before his eyes of his father's gradual physical disintegration and unpredictable temperament, both caused by the king's constant intake of strong liquor. Whatever the reason, his reluctance to join in the more frivolous social activities of court added to his reputation as a young man of iron discipline, stern and humourless.

For Jahangir, now well into his eighth year of rule, there was only the question of where this model son might be best deployed. Since the crushing of Khusraw's rebellion, imperial administration had all been easy sailing: a time of consolidation, a time to enjoy using treasury funds and architectural experts to expand and enhance the great edifices of state in Agra and Lahore. Now, it seems, a sudden steely determination set in. Should Khurram be pointed west, where Mewar remained stubbornly resistant to the best efforts of the Mughal military, or south, where Akbar's dream of expansion into the Deccan Hills remained just that, a dream? Jahangir, on the crest of a surge of optimism, decided to take them on one by one.

Of the two challenges, the obstinacy of the Sisodia Mewaris was the greater irritation. The emperor found the Hindu rulers 'overly proud of the impregnability of their mountains and dwelling'.[3] This pride was quite justified; contemporary accounts noted with awe Mewar's 'strong position and vast wilderness, high mountains and deep valleys which, by preventing an army from obtaining a foothold in that country rendered it invincible'.[4] The Maharana of Mewar – held by many Hindus, not just within his own kingdom, to be a direct descendant of the Sanskrit epic hero Rama – was the most influential and important in the hierarchy of the independent rulers of Rajasthan. His credentials were matched by his courage. He and his forefathers had over the previous century been forced to defend their homeland against serial onslaughts. Meanwhile, the kingdoms of Bikaner, Jaisalmer, Marwar, Jaipur, Kota and a handful of even tinier Rajput princi-palities had been picked off, one by one, by the advancing Mughal armies: forced to pay the tribute of the vassal and, worse, to bow their heads in unprecedented humiliation to the silken carpets of their Muslim overlord.

The current lord of Mewar, Amar Singh, had reason to be proud that his ancestors had held out so long, even at the cost of the fortress capital at Chittor, which had been sacked by Akbar in 1568. But the kingdom was exhausted by decades of conflict and vulnerable. Maharana Amar Singh presided over a new capital at Udaipur, built on the artificial Lake Pichola. The passes leading into this tranquil oasis through the surrounding mountains were sealed with massive stone gates and thick walls that climbed rock and crag to block any future Mughal advance. Thus had he resisted no fewer than four successive campaigns launched against him by Jahangir.

The first, under the nominal leadership of the seventeen-year-old Prince Pervez, had been aborted almost before it began when the expeditionary force was recalled to Lahore following the May 1606 Khusravite uprising. Mahabat-Khan's follow-up campaign in July 1608 had enjoyed more success; it 'crashed through Amar Singh's defences, destroyed everything in their path and took prisoner countless numbers of Rajput warriors'.[5] This drive was reversed, however, by a bold and devastating night-time attack in which the desperate Rajputs sent herds of buffaloes, laden with barrels of gunpowder, into the main Mughal camp. As Mahabat-Khan retreated, demoralised, the Rana's forces rebuilt their defences. Jahangir's third campaign was led by Abdallah Khan Bahadur *Firoz-Jang* – 'Victorious in War' – commanding a force of 12,000 men. To maximise chances of success, the scar-faced general adopted a ruthless carrot-and-stick approach with his own troops: they were paid four times as much as on any other expedition, but slackers who fell behind on a march were beheaded. Junior officers who failed to pass soldiers' grievances up the chain of command had their beards and moustaches shaved off. Such brisk leadership got results. 'At the mere sound of the trumpet,' his secretary wrote later, 'four thousand horsemen immediately reported for duty and none remained absent'.[6] On the ground, Firoz-Jang adopted a brutal policy of land clearance; he 'had the forest cut down and all narrow passes in the mountains opened and widened by great numbers of stone-cutters'.[7] Despite this uncompromising approach, the expedition was again inconclusive. A fourth venture, under a Pathan chieftain named Raja Basu, one of Jahangir's cronies from the old days in Allahabad, proved no more successful and the maharana himself continued to elude the Mughal grasp. Jahangir wrote querulously in his journal: 'The Rana's country has been trampled under the feet of my victorious forces but still the affair has not been settled satisfactorily'.[8] The stage was set for the prince to achieve what so many had failed to do before him.

Before Khurram's appointment as force commander, however, Jahangir decided to relocate the imperial court to Ajmer, which would serve as the field headquarters for the final push on Mewar. The journey was taken in hand with a lack of urgency that was wholly at odds with the gravity of the mission. Departing from Agra on 17 September 1613, Jahangir and his retinue moved south-east towards the Rajasthan hills at a dawdling rate. Apart from lengthy hunts, there were two reasons for the dilatory progress: the court astrologers had determined that the king must not enter Ajmer until 18 November, at a precisely defined hour, and Jahangir himself had decided that the final stretch of the journey towards the Sufi shrine of Khawaja Muin al-Din Chishti, still the patron saint of the family, should be done on foot. By the time he dismounted, however, the imperial entourage was just a little over two miles from the Dargah: a rather half-hearted effort, almost a parody of his father's celebrated pilgrimages.

After paying their respects, Jahangir and Khurram led the imperial household on through the streets of Ajmer to a substantial rectangular fort a short distance away. The town was the capital of a fully-fledged imperial province that, in time of war, could contribute as many as 86,500 horsemen and 147,000 infantry to the imperial army. Though the vast majority of Ajmer's residential districts were packed with houses of timber and straw – prone to raging fires that blazed through the narrow lanes most summer nights – the governor's residence, now commandeered by the emperor himself, was an edifice of imposing dimensions. Built by Akbar back in 1570 as a base for his own, partially successful, operations against the Rajput kingdoms, it featured typically immense and towering bastions at each corner and long, crenellated walls. By Jahangir's standards, needless to say, this sturdy fortress was rather too starkly functional and minimally adorned. Still, even as he mulled over cosmetic improvements and more comfortably appointed quarters, he found time to attend to both duty and pleasure. The following morning, the king appeared at the lattice jharoka darshana window above the fort's front gate to shower largess upon the pilgrims who had been at the shrine. Immediately departing for a tour of the province, he managed to fit in a few days' snipe-shooting on Pushkar Lake, a small body of water in the hills above Ajmer, surrounded by ancient Hindu temples and shrines. Pushkar swiftly became one of Jahangir's favourite venues for his weekly drinking parties and other recreations.

By 26 December 1613, Jahangir's generals had assembled their reinforcements, numbering 12,000 cavalry and infantry, completed their drills and assembled their equipment. Everything was in place for a final assault on Mewar. Standing before his father in the central Assembly Hall at Ajmer Fort, the 21-year-old Khurram received the honours appropriate to the commanding general of such an important mission. Surrounded by his most senior courtiers, the emperor bestowed upon his favourite son a gold-brocaded coat, decorated with jewel-studded flowers and heavily ornamented sleeves, as well as a cummerbund studded with gems. A turban fringed with pearls and a gold-spun scarf completed the outfit, which was set off by a jewelled sword and ornamental dagger. Finally, four fine beasts were led forward by the servants of the royal menagerie: two splendid Arab horses with gilded saddles and two of Jahangir's finest elephants, *Fateh-Gaj* ('Victorious Elephant') and *Kopara* ('Piece of Mountain').[9] More important than all the finery, however, was another promotion: his personal cavalry was boosted to Six Thousand, which, in addition to his infantry force of Twelve Thousand, put him third only to the emperor himself and the despised Pervez, whose last Deccan posting, though unsuccessful, had commanded a promotion to Fifteen Thousand. There was one last piece of personal business, too: the prince swore a vow that he would donate 1,000 gold coins to the Chishti shrine if victory were secured.

Not everyone, however, was happy about the prince's appointment. Even as the gilded ceremonies were taking place at Ajmer Fort, the elderly retainer Mirza Aziz Azam-Khan was slogging away in the Mewar hills with a substantial body of men.[10] The arrival of the prince on the scene promised to deny him any reward for his efforts: indeed, when Khurram reached the battlefront, Azam-Khan simply withdraw his own forces in a huff. The prince's reports to his father complained of the old warrior's disloyalty and outright interference – symptoms of exactly the kind of internal rivalry that had drained the effectiveness of so many Mughal campaigns in both Rajasthan and the Deccan in the past. Nor did the wily Khurram neglect to remind his father of Azam-Khan's support, all those years earlier, for Prince Khusraw in the struggle for the succession. Jahangir was left in no doubt as to whom to support: Mirza Aziz Azam-Khan was sacked and imprisoned at Gwalior Fort.[11]

Such ruthlessness in disposing with potential competition within his own ranks was more than matched by Khurram's leadership in the field. Learning from the successes and failures of the past, he pursued a policy of saturation warfare, exploiting to the full his superiority in numbers over the Rana of Mewar and, as succinctly put by the English merchant Nicholas Withington, 'continually for two year's space plying him with a world of soldiers'.[12] The campaign was relentless, pausing neither for monsoon rains nor the grinding heat of high summer. It was a strategy designed simply to wear the Rajputs down until the maharana was forced to surrender.

It was also the opportunity for Khurram to try out his closest allies and acolytes in action. Handpicked to replace Azam-Khan and his cronies, these included several men who would make up the core of the prince's support base, through good times and bad, in the years to come. It went without saying that the head of the prince's personal household, Sundar Das, travelled with him into Mewar, as did Abdallah Khan – a tough general who was now Governor of Gujarat – Seif-Khan and Dilawar-Khan, who had successfully defended Lahore Fort against Khusraw's siege.[13] Among the new arrivals was Muhammad Sharif *Mutamid-Khan*, a Persian émigré serving as a military administrative officer. There were some who were less than impressed by the calibre of the new men, with one court wag improvising a sarcastic verse to the effect that 'Khanship became cheap during Shah Jahangir's reign!'[14] The Mughal state's Rajput clients were also essential in prosecuting a successful campaign. Men like Raja Suraj Singh and Raja Udai Singh knew the mountainous country well and were able to recommend targets and pre-empt outflanking manoeuvres by the Mewaris.

As the campaign ground on into the summer of 1614, the embattled maharana was forced further and further into the hills. His armies were scattered and demoralised. Khurram's men rampaged through the territory, burning villages and selling captives into slavery. His roadblocks prevented the passage of reinforcements, weapons or food supplies into the theatre of operations. Mewar was slowly starving. The death-knell for the resistance was the loss of their capital. 'When Sultan Khurram arrived at Udaipur,' wrote the contemporary chronicler Kamgar Khan, 'he detached bodies of troops into all parts of the country, and so completely hemmed the Rana up in the mountains that all supplies were cut off. A malignant disorder raged amongst the [Mewari] troops from a stagnant air and desertions became very frequent.'[15] On the run and filled with depression, Amar Singh contemplated the end of his dynasty. He wrote gloomily to a friend, comparing his predicament with the luxurious life of the Rajput rulers who had earned only disgrace by capitulating to the Mughals: while they, he wrote, were 'making merry on the balconies of their palaces, I am roaming as a denizen of the forest'.[16]

Throughout the long campaign, Khurram's motivation was further boosted by a succession of letters from Ajmer containing good news. On 2 April 1614, Mumtaz-Mahal gave birth to a second daughter, to whom Jahangir gave the name *Jahan-Ara*, the 'World Adorner'. Khurram may have been disappointed not to have been presented with a son and heir – but he could not know how much he would depend on this girl, his most loyal and spiritually inclined child, in his later years. The little girl was given to Huri Khanam Begum, the wife of a distinguished courtier, to be nursed.[17] Jahan-Ara's education would be entrusted to the sister of Jahangir's poet laureate, Talib Amuli. This lady, named Sati al-Nisa Khanam, had travelled to the Mughal court from her home in the Caucasus and become 'chief maid and seal-bearer' to Mumtaz-Mahal. There she was acclaimed for her 'eloquent tongue, knowledge of etiquette … housekeeping and medicine … the art of reading the Koran and … Persian literature'.[18]

Also in the imperial post came evidence that Queen Nur-Mahal was bolstering her position. During the long Nauruz festivities formally marking Jahangir's ninth year on the throne, her brother, Abu-al-Hassan Yamin-al-Daula was accorded another, greater honorific, *Asaf-Khan* – the name by which he is known in all regional histories and one that compared the holder to Asaf ibn Barkhiya, chief minister to the Prophet Solomon.[19] Best of all, the same Spring Festival brought Prince Khurram, still hard at work in Mewar, a short but affectionate letter written in the emperor's own hand.

O my son, dear to the heart of this father, may God make this world-brightening Nauruz auspicious and grant you further victories![20]

One event that Khurram did *not* hear about was a sudden onset of illness that laid the emperor low for some time in early August 1614. Ever mindful of the risks of perceived vulnerability, Jahangir concealed his predicament from the court. The only person he trusted was his queen, Nur-Mahal Begum, the one who, as he put it, 'I thought had more affection for me than any other'.[21] When at length he recovered and was strong enough to venture outside Ajmer Fort, Jahangir made the short expedition on 2 September to the shrine of the family saint, Sheikh Muin al-Din Chishti. In gratitude and relief, the king now declared himself a committed follower of the saint and had his ears pierced and decorated with golden rings as proof of his subservience. Courtiers and other toadies promptly rushed to acquire the latest accessories *du jour*.

To monitor the relentless pursuit of the enemy, Khurram pitched camp on a hillside above Udaipur. His well-appointed tents were now inside the vast Rajput defensive wall, at the head of a valley overlooking the lake and the maharana's now abandoned long white palace. Already, the nobles among his corps of officers were eying up suitable locations on the lake to build the homes that would be needed by an army of permanent occupation. The army paymaster and annalist Mutamid-Khan dutifully recorded some of the less pleasant sectarian consequences of the war. Khurram's generals, he reported, smashed and stripped down Hindu temples in the vicinity to use the stone for their own mansions. 'Temples were destroyed,' he gloated, 'and foundation-stones of mosques were laid; instead of the conch blowing [in Hindu ceremonials], the cry "Allahu Akbar!" resounded'.[22] Having shown so forcefully that inter-faith harmony was a lower priority than making an example of the vanquished, whatever their creed, by the beginning of 1615 Khurram was on the verge of a famous victory.

The depredations of the Mughal army, coming on top of the grinding toll of years of war, left the maharana with no choice but to surrender. In consultation with his senior chieftains, many of whom had had their families captured and imprisoned by the invaders, Amar Singh agreed to send envoys to Prince Khurram seeking terms. The rana's main aim was to avoid the personal humiliation of having to bow before Jahangir at Ajmer. He was fortunate to find both Khurram and Jahangir in magnanimous mood, although there were four key preconditions to any peace treaty.

1. **Maharana Amar Singh was obliged to surrender in person to Khurram but did not have to face the emperor;**
2. **Crown Prince Karna Singh was obliged to travel as a hostage to the interim Mughal capital at Ajmer;**
3. **Mewar would become a vassal of the Mughal state, subject to tribute payments and the levy of one thousand cavalry on demand; and**
4. **The Mewaris were forbidden ever again to rebuild or reoccupy Chittor Fort.[23]**

In his memoir, Jahangir noted that this merciful response was dictated by Khurram's own recommendations and by his own desire, 'insofar as possible, not to ruin ancient families'. It may have helped that Khurram and the Mewari heir apparent, Karna Singh, rapidly became firm friends.[24]

On Sunday 14 February 1615, the victorious commander received the ruler of Mewar and his eldest son at Gokunda, north-west of Udaipur. The ritual of submission was brief but telling: the maharana was obliged to bend and grasp Khurram's ankle and beg for forgiveness. As Abd-al-Hamid Lahori put it in his official court biography of Khurram Shah Jahan, the defeated king 'rubbed the forelock of politeness on the ground as servants do and executed the rituals of humility. With his own blessed hand the Prince lifted his head … soothing him with hope-increasing and fear-erasing words.' [25]

Not surprisingly after such a long and costly conflict, the ritual exchange of gifts that sealed the peace was a little uneven. The rana was presented with a hundred robes of honour and fifty horses to distribute among his

Surrender of the Maharana of Mewar

entourage; for himself and for Karna Singh, there were elephants with silver howdahs, horses with ornamented saddles, as well as the customary jewelled swords and splendid robes. From his depleted treasury, the defeated lord of Mewar was able to muster a tribute of gold and jewels including a rare ruby, in addition to seven elephants and some particularly delicious Rajput sweets. As had become customary since the days of Akbar, Karna Singh was formally assimilated into the ranks of the court nobility with a rank of Five Thousand.

These ceremonies, however, paled into significance when compared to the welcome accorded to Khurram on his return to Ajmer. He had secured for his father a long-coveted prize, one that enabled Jahangir to boast for the first time that he had succeeded where Akbar the Great had failed. On the first day of March, the victorious army made its triumphant

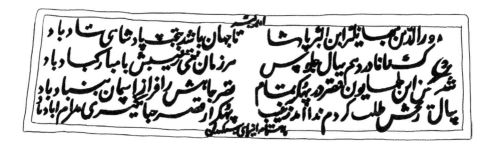

entrance into the temporary capital, having been greeted at the city gates the previous day by the massed ranks of the nobility and their full retinues. Their commanding officer, surrounded by his general staff, advanced into the Exclusive Audience Hall at the centre of Ajmer Fort. Jahangir stepped forward and embraced his son, deliberately breaching the conventional sanctity of the emperor's personal space and setting off a buzz of comment. Lavish gifts again changed hands, with Khurram handing over the rana's offerings, including the huge ruby and a flawless 'crystal chest made by the artisans of Venice filled with precious gems'.[26] Nor had Khurram forgotten his pious pre-campaign vow. He now donated 1,000 gold coins to the Chishti shrine and capped the gift by pledging to build a new and splendid mosque within the shrine complex, in gratitude to the powers of the saint buried within.

Pushkar inscription marking Khurram's victory over the Rana of Mewar

The celebrations lasted for weeks. Jahangir was so delighted that he gave orders that a large granite boulder not far from the fortress wall be carved into the shape of a reclining elephant. On the elephant's right flank, a Persian verse was carved: 'This piece of rock is the Elephant of Jahangir'.[27] Up the hill at the Pushkar Lake camp-ground, where in Khurram's absence the emperor had enjoyed the fresh air and excellent duck-shooting (as well as the brisk demolition of a couple of Hindu idols that irritated him), a small lake-side palace was constructed for the emperor's pleasure. A white marble inscription shows that this modest complex was commissioned by Anup Rai Singh-Dalan, the hero of the 1611 lion-hunting incident. The inscription can still be found amid the dilapidated ruins, known today as the Jahangiri Mahal.

Allahu Akbar!
Shah Nur al-Din Jahangir, son of Akbar Padshah:
May he rule in contentment from the imperial throne as long as this world lasts.
He captured the country of the Rana in the tenth year of accession.
May every moment bring him a fresh and auspicious victory, direct from the unseen world.

This auspicious palace was built on his command at Puhkar [*sic*]:
May the palace of his glory be based on heaven.
When I sought the chronogram, there came a voice from the unseen world:
'May the palace of Jahangir at Puhkar flourish for ever!' [28]

As the immediate sense of triumph began to fade during the spring of 1615, life at Ajmer settled back into the usual placid round of prescribed daily rituals, exchanges of wildly expensive gifts and tributes, as well as the obligatory hunting parties. Content with the climate in this temperate hilly region, Jahangir showed no interest in returning to Agra, a capital deprived of its *raison d'être*, its mighty fort and surrounding aristocratic mansions all running on skeleton staff in their owners' absences. Before long, however, urgent news came to Ajmer that made staying there imperative: plague was spreading through the empire and the capital itself had not been spared from the calamity. Banarasi Biholia was a young Jain merchant struggling to build up a business trading cloth between Jaunpur and Agra.

The city was suddenly in the grip of a raging plague, the one which was later to be known as the First Plague. Mortal disease, called the disease of the clot, spread rapidly over the city. Its distinctive symptom was the appearance of a clot on the body, an invariable sign of instant death. There was no cure for it. Doctors, too, were dying like rats. No one dared touch food for fear of contagion. People fled from Agra in a great exodus.[29]

The pestilence appeared to have emerged first in the rural areas of the Punjab and spread rapidly along the empire's trade routes. Lahore was the first imperial city to be hit, to devastating effect. The plague swept the population away in their thousands, rich and poor, Muslim and Hindu. 'In Lahore,' wrote Mutamid-Khan, 'its ravages were so great that in one house ten or even twenty persons would die and their surviving neighbours, annoyed by the stench, would be compelled to desert their habitations.' [30] Contemporary accounts tracked the spread of the disease as it rampaged south along the Sirhind-Delhi road, emptying villages and leaving behind an eerie silence. The superstitious watched the behaviour of rats and mice in their homesteads: if the rodents were seen rushing about in a frenzy before expiring, it was a cue to leave immediately for the most remote jungle that could be found. Human company was to be feared and shunned. No place in all Hindustan was free from the dreadful visitation, nor was the plague entirely eradicated for another eight or nine years.[31]

Small wonder, then, that the court elected to remain in the relatively isolated comfort of the old stone fort in Ajmer. The emperor made his provincial appointments, promoted those deemed most worthy and punished slackers. Senior nobles, ever ambitious for preferment and fearful of actual or potential rivals, queued to offer the emperor increasingly opulent gifts. Mahabat-Khan and Abd-al-Rahim the old Khan of Khans were both lobbying fiercely for the right to absolute sole leadership of the southern campaign in the Deccan, which after Mewar now offered the best prospects for military glory. They made such lavish presentations – jewels, silverware, elephants, ornamental weaponry and embroidered cloth from the lands beyond Mughal control at the tip of the sub-continent, all worth hundreds of thousands of rupees – that they risked draining their personal treasuries and bankrupting the fiefdoms whose taxes made them so fabulously wealthy.

For Khurram, resident on the outskirts of Ajmer beside Pichola Lake, it was a time of security and ease, during which good news came thick and fast. On 1 May 1615, his position at court was elevated still further with an increase to the rank of Fifteen Thousand foot and Seven Thousand horse – further reward for his Mewar success. He had again drawn level with Pervez and in the long, acrimonious race for the succession, the younger prince now looked to be overwhelmingly the favourite.[32] This welcome development, however, was comprehensively overshadowed by what had happened earlier that week. On Monday 29 March, Mumtaz-Mahal had safely delivered her third child and Khurram's first son.[33] Just as he had been formally named by his own grandfather, so now the prince turned to Jahangir for a name. After much deliberation – and, given the outcome, presumably a word or two from his Persian wife, Nur-Mahal – the emperor decided on *Dara-Shikuh*, 'Glory of Darius', a nod to the great Emperor of Persia in the 5th century BC. The court poets hastened to compose elegant verses to mark the occasion and, as so often, the prize went to the master, Abu-Talib Kalim. His verse included a typically polished phrase to describe the new prince, a chronogram as precisely chiselled as the finest lattice stone window: *Gul awwalin gulistan shahi*, 'The first flower of this royal garden'.[34]

And so the year drifted by, the royal family largely untroubled by the deadly sickness rampaging through the land. Jahangir rarely bothered to mention it in his journal, apart from mild speculation about possible causes, including 'the putridity of the air arising from the dryness and lack of rain': 'one can only bow to divine destiny,' he concluded.[35] The king was more concerned with his meticulous notes on the minutiae of court procedure and keeping score of the wild boar, deer and other wildlife that he slaughtered in droves during his regular trips up to Pushkar Lake. His other favourite location – visited more than twice as often as Pushkar, for pure relaxation – was a garden he called *Chashma al-Nur*, the 'Fountain of Light', an idyllic spa palace he had constructed around a waterfall and stream in a ravine out in the hill-country two miles from the fort. An eloquent Persian inscription by the senior court goldsmith Saida Gilani records the completion of the complex in 1615. When the 'king of the seven climes … visited this fountain,' it said, 'through his bounty water began to flow and dust turned to elixir'.[36] Visitors who were allowed to penetrate the secretive, winding entrance through the mighty boulders and scree slopes marvelled at 'a place of much melancholy delight and security, only being accompanied with wild peacocks, turtles, fowl and monkeys that inhabit the rocks hanging every way over it'.[37]

Periodically, Jahangir and his favoured son crossed the town to pay their respects at the Chishti shrine, scattering thousands of rupees and various valuables for their fellow pilgrims. This pious side of the emperor's nature, however, was more than offset by his enthusiasm for vivacious drinking parties. As always, however, Prince Khurram declined alcohol, a fact confirmed by Sir Thomas Roe, who lingered doggedly at court for more than a year in hopes of securing preferential trading status for East India Company merchants based at Surat on the west coast. Sir Thomas makes for an entertaining guide to Mughal mores – proud, peevish and constantly exasperated by his hosts' endless wiles and prevarications – but he was also alert to political and personal nuances at court. At Ajmer, he observed how, while the emperor and most of his nobles drank heavily and 'became the finest men I ever saw, of a thousand humours … his son Khurram, Asaf-Khan and some old men forbore'.[38] The prince's conspicuous refusal to imbibe led to a memorable argument between father and son on 14 January 1616 at the beautiful Daulat-Bagh garden, laid out along the watercourse that emptied Pichola Lake. Relaxing at the top end of the garden on the long terrace where cooling breezes blew off the water, Jahangir forced Khurram to break his own rule of abstinence.

It was the eve of the prince's twenty-fifth birthday. The customary weighing ceremony, approved by the court astrologers, had gone off smoothly and the ensuing party was well underway. Noticing that the man of the hour was ignoring the offered goblets of wine, Jahangir pressed him – though, as he noted in his memoir, 'it took great persistence to get him to drink'.[39] Implicitly questioning the prince's masculinity, he pointed out that Khurram was a man with a son of his own and that 'monarchs and princes have always drunk'. His son tried to resist but the order, for such it was, was not to be refused, even when the dipsomaniac emperor – with breathtaking hypocrisy – presumed to quote the celebrated 10th century Persian physician 'Avicenna'.

Wine is the enemy of the intoxicated and the friend of the sensible.
A little opium is good; too much is the venom of a snake.
All in all, excess is injurious;
But if taken in small doses, it can do the power of good.[40]

Aside from his ill-mannered insistence on forcing his son to break his pledge, Jahangir was at least telling the truth in respect of the Mughal dynasty's enthusiasm for wine. Just as they had no time for the conventional Islamic proscription of representational art – portraiture was always a popular and high-quality art form at court – so the ruling family had traditionally scorned the Koranic command to shun alcohol.[41] Their kind of Islam, no doubt to the rage of the orthodox Sunni and Shiite scholars at court, was a Central Asian hybrid in which age-old social traditions still played an important part, outweighing the strictures of Arabian-style conservatism. An elderly visitor from Samarkand, known as al-Asamm the Minstrel, detailed during successive visits to Jahangir the enthusiasm of the emperor's predecessors for wine. Humayun, Babur, Akbar – all had rejoiced in wine, he noted, quoting relevant verses by each of the carousing kings.[42]

The slow pace of life at Ajmer Fort enabled Prince Khurram to spend time with his family, though there were times of sadness as well as joy. His senior queen, Mumtaz-Mahal, demonstrated her commitment to her child-bearing obligations, handing him a second son, Shah-Shuja, on 3 July 1616. The newborn boy was acclaimed as 'the second star of the royal heaven' and the birth went some way to mitigating the loss of the queen's eldest child, Hur al-Nisa. The three-year-old girl had succumbed to smallpox a fortnight earlier, causing at least as much grief to her doting grandfather, Jahangir, as Khurram himself. The emperor was so distressed that he had to ask Ghiyath al-Din Itimad al-Daula, great-grandfather to the dead child, to complete the daily entry in his journal. The elderly courtier contributed a moving account of the death of this 'heavenly daughter, a newcomer to the garden of felicity', as well as the helpless and protracted grief of the king, who ordered 'the room where that bird from paradise had lived to be walled up, never to be seen again'.[43] To make up for his personal bereavement, Jahangir took the infant Shah-Shuja into his own household. There, he would be cared for personally by his newly renamed queen. Nur-Mahal – closest of all the king's wives, most respected of all his counsellors – was now dubbed *Nur-Jahan*, 'Light of the World'.

With the Mewar question conclusively resolved, Jahangir turned his attention south again, to the Deccan. Like Mewar before Khurram's decisive intervention, the campaign against Ahmadnagar had stuttered forward in the years since his uncles, Murad and Daniyal, had succumbed to drink. Pervez still held the nominal command, with Abd-al-Rahim the elderly Khan of Khans at his side and recently reinforced by the despatch of both Mahabat-Khan and *Khan-Jahan* Lodi with a total of 30,000 men, a full complement of artillery and war elephants, as well as a war-chest containing three-hundred thousand rupees.[44]

What worried Jahangir most was that the three kingdoms of the south were now effectively working together to the extent that they could field a large, unified army to repel any Mughal incursions. During the winter of 1609–10, the East India Company indigo trader William Finch described how successive imperial campaigns had faced dogged resistance from the 'three great kings' of Ahmadnagar, Bijapur and Golconda, who 'gathered great forces, making head [quarters] near Burhanpur, upon the Mughal's frontiers … both armies lying abroad in tents'.[45] These nations were ruled by dynasties that stretched back in unbroken line for centuries. They were proud, independent and – barring occasional violent spats – more or less comfortably co-existent neighbours. There was also the vexed question of whether these Shiite kingdoms were receiving more than just moral support from Persia. In 1613, Shah Abbas sent out three separate ambassadorial missions from Isfahan; a Persian account of the envoys' journeys described how 'to each prince he sent a friendly letter and appropriate presents, including horses and other wonderful gifts'.[46]

The ruler of Ahmadnagar – Jahangir's first objective in what he hoped would be an exercise in west-to-east domino toppling – was technically the five-year-old Burhan Nizamshah III. In fact, because Burhan was so young, the real power was held by one of the era's most dynamic characters: the Nizamshah's fearsome regent, *Malik* Ambar, a district chieftain or 'petty king' within the Ahmadnagar kingdom. What made Ambar such an extraordinary figure in the political and physical landscape of southern India was that he was a black African from a family of Abyssinian slaves. Mughal sources – with a contempt he scarcely deserved – labelled him simply Ambar the Ethiopian (*habashi*) or Ambar the Ill-Starred (*badakhtar*). How he rose from such mean beginnings is a tale that has been lost, though he appears to have travelled to India via Baghdad and spent some time in the service of the court of Bijapur before reaching Ahmadnagar. His career breakthrough must have happened by February 1596 – even as Akbar's forces were pressing against Ahmadnagar's northern frontiers – when the name of 'the Malik' began to crop up in the correspondence of Portuguese merchants seeking to expand trading opportunities from their western port base at Goa.[47] In the years since Jahangir's succession, Malik Ambar had been busy, patching over internal divisions and political rivalries, as well as forging a renewed alliance with the Adilshah of Bijapur. Using the time-honoured method of sending his son to marry into the Bijapuri royal family, the wily general secured his eastern flank against surprise attack, leaving him free to stand up to the Mughal advance.

Malik Ambar was an organised and effective campaigner, a much greater challenge for the Mughals than the Maharana of Mewar. He had beaten back the best efforts of both Abd-al-Rahim the Khan-Khanan and Raja Man Singh. The latter officer arrived with 10,000 rein-

forcements and one thousand war-elephants, so that, according to William Finch, 'all the plains for a great distance were covered with tents very brave to behold; with the army came divers great boats for the transportation of forces over waters.' [48] The Raja's early boasts about grinding the pride of the Deccanis into the dust, however, proved to be embarrassingly hollow. In a classic example of psychological warfare, Ambar had a forged letter produced, purporting to come from the court at Agra and reporting the sudden death of Jahangir. This plausible but bogus order summoned the entire southern command urgently to the capital for the selection of a new emperor. The generals 'set fire to all their baggage and tents and fled'; by the time the fraud was exposed, Ambar had gained considerable territory.[49]

Sir Thomas Roe, Ambassador of King James

The deployment of Prince Pervez had made little difference either. Malik Ambar had pushed forward relentlessly, recapturing Ahmadnagar Fort in May 1609 and slaughtering the surrendering garrison. He had at least ten-thousand men at his command – a small force compared to the imperial invaders but one that was highly motivated and made up of troops from all three Deccan states. The relentless bickering and back-biting among the Mughal high command only contributed to Ambar's success. He maintained this punishing momentum for the next several years, penning the Mughal forces back into the walled city at Burhanpur.

Not surprisingly, Jahangir now resolved to give Khurram a chance. The decision was taken on 22 June 1616, during the prolonged period

of grieving for Khurram's infant daughter Hur al-Nisa, a time when the
king, reluctant to stay in the ill-omened fortress, moved to his son's Ajmer
mansion outside the castle walls for two weeks. Giving Khurram the
southern command had profound implications for the succession. Pervez
was only too aware of the risk to his own future and wrote to his father
complaining that replacement by his younger brother would be an intoler-
able dishonour that would be met with force. He would, however, obey
an order to fall back to Allahabad with his closest advisers – but only if
his replacement were Prince Khusraw. Pervez knew that the appointment
of his eldest brother, currently detained up at Pushkar under the watchful
eye of Anup Rai the Lion-Killer, would be far too risky for the king. As
for Jahangir, he would have nothing to do with this haggling. Sir Thomas
Roe noted in his journal that Jahangir's response to the threat of conflict
between the two brothers was dispassionate at best. '"Let them fight," he
quoted the king as saying; "I am well content; and he that proves himself
the better captain shall pursue the war."' [50] This ruthless answer was a stark
illustration of the Mughal approach to inheritance. Primogeniture should
never be assumed: the succession was simply the prize for the survival
of the fittest and war was as good a way as any of measuring a prince's
capacity to rule. With his customary careful and accurate analysis, Sir
Thomas bemoaned the emperor's tactics as fundamentally dangerous for
the stability of the empire.

**Thus he nourishes division and emulation between the brothers and puts such power in
the hand of the younger, supposing he can undo it at his pleasure, that the wisest foresee
a rending and tearing of these kingdoms by division when the king shall pay the debt to
nature [i.e. die] and that all parts will be torn and destroyed by a civil war.[51]**

That 'rending and tearing' was still some way in the future. For
now, Khurram's prospects were enhanced not just by his father's blatant
favouritism but by evidence from the Khan of Khans and other front line
commanders of worsening splits within Malik Ambar's tripartite southern
alliance. During the autumn of 1615, an embassy had come to Ajmer
from the ruler of Bijapur, Ibrahim Adilshah, bringing a gift of lavishly-
accoutred elephants and apologising for the offences perpetrated by the
rulers of the Deccan and offering the restoration of Ahmadnagar Fort and
other Mughal territories that had been won by Ambar.[52] Worse still for the
southern general, his own forces were riven by racial stresses caused by
the pre-eminence of Abyssinians in the Nizamshah's army. It was a perfect
time to strike back.

The first victory was secured even before Khurram left for the south,
by Iraj Abd-al-Rahim *Shahnawaz-Khan*, the son of the veteran Khan of

Khans. Selecting a defendable position at Roshangaon village, within an ox-bow of the River Dudhana, the officer deployed his guns with care and awaited the advance of Malik Ambar's 40,000-strong army. At dawn on 13 February 1616, the imperial artillery began its bombardment; after a lull, the cavalry and infantry followed up with a screaming advance. As Jahangir noted with relish and pride in his journal, the 'lions of the thicket of bravery drew their swords and charged the enemy's vanguard, showing their mettle and scattering the foe. … There were mountains of slain men.'[53] Ambar's youthful Abyssinian cavalry, the cream of his army, was pinned down in a gully, 'huddled together as if they had been chained'. 'In this position,' a contemporary southern historian noted, 'they were mown down by the Mughal artillery like leaves of trees under a destroying wind'.[54] Shahnawaz-Khan's rampaging forces followed on, burning and looting freely, destroying Ambar's field headquarters before retiring in satisfaction to Burhanpur and the warmth of their commander's gratitude.

It is ironic, then, that Pervez was replaced just as he was finally achieving results. It could even be argued that, as in Mewar, Khurram's arrival came just as the exhausting campaigns of many others were reaching fruition, enabling him to claim credit for their labour. Events unfolded rapidly, at least by the languid standards of the Mughal court. On 7 April 1616, Prince Khurram received another promotion, to the heady rank of Twenty Thousand foot and Ten Thousand cavalry. On 10 July, Pervez finally bowed to the inevitable and left Burhanpur: instead of standing to fight his usurping brother, he proceeded meekly to Allahabad and an uncertain future. He was not even permitted to pay his respects to his father, although according to Sir Thomas Roe, the emperor was overruled by Queen Nur-Jahan, 'yea, although the king had fallen down and taken his mistress by the feet to obtain her leave to see his son'.[55]

Jahangir's plans then hit an unexpected obstacle. The petulant complaint from Pervez that he would accept dismissal only if he were replaced by Khusraw had reminded Khurram of the danger of leaving a rival so close to the throne when he was about to depart for war. No-one but Nur-Jahan, of course, knew about the king's most recent illness – but the queen had already decided that her own future advantage lay best with Khurram. So the prince now stated a precondition for his leadership of the Deccan campaign: that his eldest brother should be 'remanded to his personal custody … to prevent Khusraw from seizing an opportunity to instigate further mischief in his absence, which might require the army to return to eradicate the evil and hence leave the work of the Deccan unfinished'.[56] Jahangir was a drunkard but he was no fool: he surely knew the risks involved in ceding custody of the prisoner. Through the months of Ajmer's blistering summer, he held out against the combined will of Nur-Jahan and his talented but ruthless son. He was aided in his resistance by Khusraw's jailer, Anup Rai Singh-Dalan, one of the many who still admired the prince despite his rebellion nine years earlier and consequent disgrace – and who now pledged to die with all his Rajput officers in defence of Khusraw. Eventually, however, the pressure told. On 27 October, Jahangir ordered Anup Rai to remove Khusraw from his Pushkar lodging and escort him to the household of Khurram's father-in-law, Abu-al-Hassan Asaf-Khan. The entire court, including Khurram, seems to have been unaware that Asaf-Khan was fostering other plans for Khusraw and had at this stage no intention of transferring him to his half-brother's tender mercies. Sir Thomas Roe was not alone in interpreting the emperor's concession as a death sentence.

His sister and divers women in the seraglio mourn, refuse their meat, cry out of the king's dotage and cruelty and profess that if he [Khusraw] die there will be 100 of his kindred burn for him [i.e. as suttees] in memory of the king's bloodiness to his worthiest son. ... The common people all murmur; they say the king has not delivered his son's but his own life into the hands of an ambitious prince and a treacherous faction ... The truth is uncertain and it is dangerous to ask.[57]

The final pre-departure ceremony came on 10 November, by which time Khurram's forward camp was already ten days gone on its march south. As evening fell, the prince paraded before the emperor in silver tunic, encrusted with pearls, alongside his senior officers, white plumes of egret feathers in their turbans. Along with the traditional parting presents – jewelled robes, horses, an elephant and a carriage sent as a gift by King James in London – Jahangir now awarded his son a title unprecedented in the Mughal dynasty: henceforth he should be known only as Shah Sultan Khurram. For one observer in the Audience Hall, it could not have been a clearer message. A new Persian ambassador, Muhammad Reza Beg, had just arrived with fraternal greetings from Shah Abbas at Isfahan. Jahangir's reply was clear from Khurram's promotion: a calculated snub to the Shah of Persia, indicating that, far from being an equal, he ranked no higher than the Mughal Crown Prince.

And so Shah Khurram departed for the south, a special sword – the first to be seized during Akbar's war on Ahmadnagar – strapped at his hip. He went with acclaim and blessings dinning loud in his ear, from his father, from senior officials at court, even from visiting petitioners like Dastur Kaikobad Mahyar, a Parsee who included the prince in his laudatory poems.

You are the king of the world, cheerful and famous.
May your place be always on the throne.
God has made you a leader of leaders and has
Placed illustrious persons under your orders.
Go now with a large army to Deccan and extirpate its
Seed from the root with your sword![58]

Extirpation may have been the long-held Mughal aspiration in the south but Shah Khurram was enough of a pragmatist to value compromise as an essential aspect of statecraft. While his objective was a reassertion of military strength, it was too much to hope that a repeat of the Mewar campaign's saturation warfare would be easily achieved in a far larger territory. So, as he travelled with his closest friends and generals on the long march south, the prince debated the advantages of an alternative, diplomatic solution. It was far easier to offer a demoralised and divided opposition a seat at the negotiating table than to risk casualties or even defeat by compelling them to fight for their lives. For despite Malik Ambar's defeat in February, the Deccanis had not given up. An official chronicle of Ambar's Bijapuri allies, the *Futuhat Adilshahi*, describes how a force of 20,000 southern cavalry had rallied and 'ravaged [the territories of] Khandesh and Berar and expelled the Mughal officers from their posts'.[59]

As soon as he arrived at the imperial fortress at Burhanpur, therefore, Khurram gave orders for a dual track campaign. With Bijapur, he would pursue diplomacy, attempting to achieve an irrevocable split from Malik Ambar. Against the Abyssinian general and his nominal overlord, the Nizamshah of Ahmadnagar, he would wage a relentless campaign. Both tactics began in early 1617 and both began to show promising results within months. By March, the Adilshah of Bijapur had sent an urgent delegation to Burhanpur, swearing fealty and pledging military support in reclaiming any lost Mughal lands. On the military front, Shah Khurram was able to deploy his forces to such effect that Ahmadnagar Fort was recaptured at the beginning of July. This crushing blow gave the prince the momentum he needed and the confidence to make one final diplomatic play: he sent an impressive embassy to Malik Ambar and to Ibrahim Adilshah. The envoys were splendidly dressed and accoutred and surrounded by a dazzling display of Mughal cavalry in full parade dress. They bore a simple enough message, offering peace with just two conditions: surrender the land that was ours and pledge to pay the vassal's tribute to the rightful emperor in perpetuity. Malik Ambar – his right flank exposed by the unreliability of his erstwhile ally, Bijapur – had little option but to capitulate.

Shah Khurram's envoy hastened north with the good news: arriving at court on Thursday 19 July 1617, he was first received by Queen Nur-Jahan, who relayed the tidings to the hung-over king. It was far from the sweeping victory that Jahangir had planned but, in comparison to the embarrassing failures that had gone before, it was an eminently satisfying conclusion to the campaign. Confiding his relief to his journal, the emperor noted that 'the troublemakers who had dared to rebel had admitted their inability and powerlessness by submitting to pay tribute and taxes … more than they have ever given to any ruler in their times.' [60] Other observers were less impressed. Sir Thomas Roe, who heartily detested the triumphant prince, noted acidly in a letter to his diplomatic counterpart at Constantinople that the united Deccan kings had been 'persuaded to part with some rotten castles that may pretend a shadow of yielding somewhat, for which they are pleased here to think themselves worthy of the glorious praises due to an honourable conquest'. [61]

By the time Shah Khurram's envoy reached the emperor, Jahangir had moved his court from Ajmer – where he had resided for nearly three years – and was comfortably ensconced at Mandu, an ancient citadel that was 400 miles closer to the action in the Deccan. This was one of the great military bastions on the southern fringes of the empire, with a plausible claim to be the largest fortified city in the entire medieval world. Shaped like a vast irregular starfish, the settlement occupied a sprawling plateau atop a virtually unassailable mountain in the south-western ranges of the Malwa Hills. A precipice dropping 1,200 ft on the southern side separated it from the plains of Nimar, while a deep ravine encircled the remaining sides with cliffs and rocky water-courses. Where nature had not provided a natural defence, the city's rulers had built mighty walls along an extraordinary circuit of some thirty miles' perimeter. [62] Not surprisingly, it had taken Akbar's commanders a great deal of time and effort to subdue the place known to its rulers as *Shadiabad*, the 'City of Joy'.

Jahangir now devoted his time to planning a sensational welcome for his prized son. News brought from Burhanpur by the post-runners made him ever more excited about being reunited. First, towards the end of August, came an official report that Bijapuri envoys had arrived at Shah Khurram's fortress audience hall with a gratifying tribute of jewels, utensils encrusted with gems, prime stock elephants and a stable of Arab horses to match. A second notice at the beginning of September informed the emperor that his son had unilaterally taken on a further challenge: the capture of Kangra fortress.

Kangra was about as far from Burhanpur as was possible to travel and stay within the bounds of the vast empire. A hilltop citadel of vast stone bastions and seven closely guarded gates, it lay in the hill country north of Lahore and, despite being so close to Akbar's one-time capital, remained one of the few citadels never to be taken. One contemporary chronicler noted its cultural importance to the region's Hindus as a centre of scholarship and science, adding that its temple contained 'more than 1300 books written by Brahmins of old times'. The account went on to describe it as 'that inaccessible asylum, which no Delhi sovereign had hitherto thrown his lasso over ... famous for its strength.'[63]

Jahangir had already tried to subjugate the recalcitrant clan at Kangra, sending Sheikh Farid Bukhari Murtaza-Khan, who 'took with him many thousand stone- and wood-cutters on account of the vast jungle and the narrow pathway'.[64] The campaign, however, had been left rudderless by the sudden death of the enterprising general in the field in May 1616. Shah Khurram now informed his father that he was deploying Raja Jawhar Suraj Mal in an effort to force the capture or surrender of the fortress. Suraj Mal was an influential landlord in the Kangra region but he had a bad reputation as a corrupt trouble-maker who had fallen out with the late Murtaza-Khan. He had found forgiveness from the emperor, who had 'drawn the pen of pardon across the book of his crimes', and solid service in the Deccan had repaired his battered name.[65] It was a risky appointment and one that Shah Khurram would have cause to regret: victory over Kangra would not be achieved for another four years and it would not be under the leadership of Raja Suraj Mal.

With the Deccan victory secured, however, it was an advantageous time for Prince Shah Khurram to take steps to consolidate his own personal following. Writing to Jahangir at Mandu, he proposed that Abd-al-Rahim the Khan of Khans should be given the governorate of all the newly secured southern lands: Khandesh, Berar and Ahmadnagar. The old officer's son, Iraj Shahnawaz-Khan, who had inflicted the only significant defeat on Malik Ambar, was now despatched from Burhanpur with 12,000 troops to garrison the territory and ensure its continuing security. Both appointments – making the father governor and the son de facto commander-in-chief of the southern districts – served to guarantee their future loyalty to Shah Khurram but there was a more traditional way of tying the knot more firmly.

In time-honoured fashion, the prince now took Shahnawaz-Khan's young daughter, Izz al-Nisa Begum, to be his third wife, not bothering to consult his father first. Later accounts, like that of the contemporary court biographer, Muhammad Amin Qazvini, have insisted that the marriage was forced upon the prince – presumably because, being an exercise in clinical realpolitik, it detracted somewhat from Khurram's image as the loving husband of Mumtaz-Mahal. But even Qazvini conceded that the wedding on 2 September 1617 was a full 'bond of matrimony through a religion-sanctioned marriage ceremony.' [66] Needless to say, no Mughal historian thought it worth recording what Queen Mumtaz herself made of her husband's third marriage. She may, however, have been distracted: only the previous day, she had produced yet another child, a girl this time, named *Raushan-Ara*, the 'Bright Adorner'.

All seemed to be going well for Shah Khurram. What he did not know, however, was the extent of the scheming underway within the royal palace at Mandu against his interests. Much has been written about the Nur-Jahan junta: the invincible quartet of the Primary Queen, her father the 'Pillar of the State', her brother Asaf-Khan and her son-in-law Prince Khurram. In reality, however, this was a time of shifting alliances, of constant re-assessments, where back-stabbing was the norm and no allegiances could be taken for granted. The initial plotting centred on the figure of Khusraw. After so many years of incarceration and disgrace, his prospects looked dim indeed but it was conspicuous that Asaf-Khan had not handed the prisoner on to Shah Khurram on the eve of the Deccan campaign. It emerged that he and his sister had other plans, specifically to marry him to Nur-Jahan's daughter from her first marriage, Ladli Begum, and re-create him as the heir apparent, in place of the redoubtable Shah Khurram. Sir Thomas Roe reported to his colleagues in mid-August 1617 that, far from being executed as many had feared, Prince Khusraw had been freed to 'take air and pleasure at the banqueting house by me.' By the end of the month – and with an unmistakeable whiff of *Schadenfreude* towards the detested Khurram – the ambassador noted that 'this day Nur-Mahal feasted Asaf-Khan and the Prince Sultan Khusraw; as is reported, to make a firm alliance and that he will bring away a wife … This will beget his full liberty and our proud master's ruin.' [67]

What these conspirators did not expect, however, was that the dignified Khusraw would simply decline to be their puppet. His reason was equally inexplicable to them: love. His wife, the daughter of Mirza Aziz Azam-Kahn, had stuck by him through the long years of imprisonment and blindness; he now absolutely rejected the notion of acquiring a second bride for reasons of political expedience. According to the Italian adventurer, Pietro Della Valle, even she could not persuade him to accept a pragmatic path to freedom.

Insomuch that whilst he was in prison and was told by reiterated messages that if he would marry Nur-Mahal's daughter he should be immediately set free, nevertheless he would not do it. His wife, on the contrary, who loved him as well as he loved her, obtained to be the person allotted to serve him in the prison and accordingly went thither and lived with him so long as he was there, never ceasing to persuade him to marry Nur-Mahal's daughter, so that he might be delivered from those troubles; that for her part she was content to live with him as a slave, provided she saw him free and in a good condition; but he never could be prevailed with.[68]

Khusraw's refusal temporarily stymied the plotters, leaving the field open again for Shah Khurram. It now remained only for him to take his household north to Mandu to receive his father's gratitude in person. It was a vast entourage that now set out from Burhanpur: Shah Khurram took with him 25,000 cavalry, more than a third of the entire southern army. This made for slow progress. Logistical delays were compounded by torrential monsoon rains and it was not until October that he finally arrived at Mandu's mountain-top castle. His reception must have exceeded even his wildest dreams: unspoilt by any hint of the Nur-Jahan/Asaf-Khan conspiracy or by any lasting rancour on Jahangir's part over his son's recent unsanctioned marriage.

On 11 October 1617, at a precise time dictated by the court astrologers, the prince climbed the steps to the royal audience hall in the *Jahaz-Mahal*, the elongated 'Ship Palace' that was the epicentre of the ancient royal compound. The monsoon rains had filled the artificial lakes on either side of the palace to bursting and the terraces and pavilions were similarly filled with military officers, governors summoned from the provinces, court officials and ambassadors, all on hand to see Prince Shah Khurram honoured. After marching down the terrace, his progress interrupted by the formal obeisances appropriate to approaching the king, the prince ascended to the royal balcony via the special red ladder leaning against the low marble railing of the gallery.[69] As his third son approached, Jahangir was so overcome with emotion that he leapt to his feet and rushed forward to embrace him.

At the core of all such ceremonials were the gifts of tribute made by Mughal officers for their overlord: a clear restatement of the old clan values that had lasted since the days of Genghis Khan. First to step forward was Khan-Jahan Lodi, offering a thousand gold coins and a chest of jewels. Then came Abdallah Khan, followed by Mahabat-Khan and a succession of lower-ranking officers from the Deccan campaign command. The final tribute was presented by the envoys of the Adilshah of Bijapur, whose surrender had broken the spine of Malik Ambar's tripartite alliance. Shah Khurram's turn to give tribute, however, would have to wait, for the king was overwhelmingly eager to bestow his own gifts on the twenty-five-year-old hero.

In a booming voice, Jahangir declared that his favourite son would now bear the rank of Thirty Thousand foot and Twenty Thousand horse – unprecedented in the annals of the dynasty – and would henceforth be known only as *Shah Jahan*, 'King of the World'.[70] Furthermore, he would be allowed to sit in a carved sandalwood chair close to the imperial throne, another privilege never bestowed before.[71] Then the emperor descended the stone stairway from the balcony to a large display of trays containing offerings. 'From these trays,' reported Inayat-Khan, another of Shah Jahan's official chroniclers, 'the Emperor picked out various articles of gold and silver and sprinkled them with his own hands over the auspicious head.'[72] The prince was now in a seemingly unassailable position. He had the support of an effective and loyal coterie of officers, a network buttressed by marriage ties and debts of favours to be repaid. He had the secure dynastic future of a man with sons and, above all, a clear indication from the emperor himself that the succession was secured. 'Truly,' reflected Jahangir in his memoir, 'he is a son worthy of kindness and affection, and I am highly pleased with him. May God grant him long life and success.'[73]

7
The Wolf Cub

For one rose it is necessary to endure the trouble of a hundred thorns.
Nur al-Din Abd-al-Rahman Jami[1]

The time will come when all in these kingdoms will be in combustion and a few years' war will not decide the inveterate malice laid up on all parts against a day of vengeance.
Sir Thomas Roe[2]

Shah Jahan had every reason to believe that the Mughal throne would one day be his. But his impatience would be his undoing: precipitate action against his father would bring about his own downfall within five years, triggering a long period in the wilderness. For now, however, father and son enjoyed the post-campaign lull together: as a relief from the vicarious rigours of the Deccan fighting, Jahangir arranged an excursion to the coast, taking Shah Jahan on an extensive rambling tour of Gujarat province. Indeed, just as he had been awarded the province as his own fiefdom by Akbar, so now Jahangir handed it on to Shah Jahan. With this assignment – the control of one of the most lucrative sources of revenue in the empire – went additional privileges. In February 1618, the king accorded his favoured son the unprecedented honour of granting his own protégés the insignia of royal favour: robes of honour, banners, drums and ornate weapons. 'Until now,' noted Jahangir, 'it has not been customary in this dynasty for a prince's liegeman to be given the privilege of a banner and drums. ... My affection for this son of mine, however, is so great that I cannot disappoint him in anything. ... Now in the full bloom of youth and prowess, everywhere he goes he accomplished his missions to my satisfaction.'[3] The first recipient of this new largess was *Rustum-Khan*, Shah Jahan's nominee as provincial governor. The king also presented his son with the huge ruby that had adorned his own turban since birth, a precious gift from his late grandmother, exclaiming in impromptu verse:

May you live a thousand years long!
And may every month of every year be like the precious months of spring.[4]

The Gujarat expedition was enlivened by regular elephant hunts, not the usual killing-spree but a round-up of the finest beasts for the royal filkhana. Records note that 185 tuskers were captured, a third of them by Shah Jahan's own scouts and elephant keepers. Thus the imperial camp progressed in stately and languid fashion through the western districts until, in late August 1618, the royal household prepared to begin its long return journey to Agra amid the torrential rains of monsoon season. The most serious delay – indeed, the gravest threat to the ruling family itself – came at Ahmedabad. The excursion had been prolonged by renewed reports of plague outbreaks at Agra but it soon became clear that the sickness did not respect rank or royalty and both Jahangir and Shah Jahan were laid low and were lucky to survive the pestilence. After a prolonged recuperation, the royal family was at Dohad, still only half-way to Agra, when, on 3 November 1618, one of the most important events of the year occurred: the birth of Shah Jahan's third son.[5] It was deemed improper to conduct the full ceremonials of birth, along with the ritual naming, at such a spot, so it was not until the imperial retinue reached Ujjain that Jahangir came up with a suitable name: *Aurangzeb*, the 'Throne Adorner'. As always, the poets were quick to produce suitably grandiose epithets to grace the occasion and the infant boy. 'Gem of the crown of throne-adorning kings', one dubbed him, while Saida al-Gilani countered with 'the world-illuminating sun'.[6] Shah Jahan no doubt echoed his father's prayers when he heard that Jahangir had written in his memoir of Aurangzeb's birth: 'It is hoped that his advent will prove fortunate and auspicious to this eternal dynasty'.[7]

The mood began to change during the winter of 1619/20, on one of the emperor's periodic holidays in Kashmir.[8] Something that occurred during that spring of 1619 – or perhaps it was someone with an alternative agenda for the inheritance – appears to have planted a seed of alienation, even animosity, between Jahangir and Shah Jahan. The nimble Mughal biographer, Sheikh Farid Bakkhari, later wrote that 'spiteful persons had alienated the temperament of the king … and moving the chain of sedition did not allow sincere attachment between the father and the son'.[9] The journey to Kashmir was undoubtedly stressful: the 940-mile trek from Agra into the mountains was always a risky one, especially when the imperial retinue was forced by the inhospitable terrain to travel light.

The multitude marching under the imperial banners was like a horde of locusts, emptying the land of food for miles around. So on Kashmir trips, the minimum of personnel was taken along and local porters, used to the altitude, were hired to 'carry heavier burdens than could men of Hindustan'.[10] Kashmiri weather was also notoriously hostile to travellers. The emperor himself was fortunate to survive one night when he was caught by a blizzard while still out hunting with his immediate entourage. He and his harem were forced to shelter in the private tents of Muhammad Sharif Mutamid-Khan, the court official charged with preparing the way on this hostile route through the mountains. Fortunately, Mutamid-Khan had with him 'sufficient number of tents, carpets, sleeping garments, cooking utensils and other paraphernalia ... that there was enough for everyone. God be praised!'[11] There was no sign of Shah Jahan being on hand to help out.

The more superstitious traced the problem back to the appearance in January 1619 of a comet in the skies over northern India.[12] In fact, the comet was blamed for a variety of misfortunes. On 18 April 1619, Shah Jahan's beloved mother died. Honoured henceforth as the 'Bilqis of the Age', the Rajput queen Manmati Jagat Ghosain was buried with full royal honours in the riverside garden of Muzaffar Khan at Agra.[13] The prolonged recurrence of plague throughout the empire was also thought to have been precipitated by the comet. Indeed, it was Mutamid-Khan himself, in his later biography of Jahangir, who described the coming of the comet as the trigger for maladies, unnatural occurrences and internecine strife.

It was in consequence of its appearance that a pestilential disorder spread throughout this extensive country of Hindustan ... and continued to rage for eight years. It was also through the effects of this phenomenon that a misunderstanding arose between His Majesty and the fortunate Prince Shah Jahan. The disturbances which thus originated lasted seven or eight years. What blood was shed in the country! And what families were ruined![14]

It is certainly striking how, during the spring and summer of 1619, Jahangir began referring to his son increasingly rarely in his journal; when he did, he stopped using the formal title 'Shah Jahan' and reverted to the prince's given name, Khurram. On 16 December 1619, passing through Sirhind, the emperor recorded in his journal the birth of Arjumand Mumtaz-Mahal's seventh child and fourth son. As always, family custom prevailed: Shah Jahan presented the emperor with a thousand gold coins, requesting the honour of a name for the infant. Deciding at last on *Umid-Bakhsh*, 'Bestower of Hope', the king offered no more than minimally formulaic expressions of good will and hopes for the auspicious future of the dynasty. Unfortunately, the birth of the new prince heralded bleak times – and the baby did not live to see his third year.[15] Still, thirteen days later, the emperor did visit Shah Jahan in his personal quarters for Umid-Bakhsh's birth celebrations, which of course included another lavish gift from the prince to the king. The present, worth 140,000 rupees, included an elephant in prime condition and a Venetian sword, its hilt and scabbard encrusted with sapphires. So, as the year drew to a close, all was still well, at least on the surface.

Then, on 19 January 1620, Shah Jahan left the imperial travelling party and made his own way to Lahore to inspect on his father's behalf the major programme of modifications that Jahangir had ordered at the fort. This immense project had been initiated back in 1612, when the king had sent Khawaja Jahan Dost Muhammad to lay the foundations of a new residential complex stretching across the northern half of Akbar's castle complex. From the spring of 1617, the work had been taken on and completed by Abd-al-Karim *Mamur-Khan*, the 'Doyen of Architects'. Of all the new buildings, additions, extensions and re-decorations – many of which would be later demolished and overbuilt by Shah Jahan himself – the greatest artistic triumph at Lahore Fort was the celebrated Picture Wall, running along the northern and north-western faces of the citadel. It presented a vibrant array of colourful glazed tiles in the Old Persian style – but on a monumental scale. Fighting elephants, their trunks entwined; fairies with outstretched wings; procession scenes with Mughal officers in their parade finery: all were realised with consummate skill and sense of proportion, surrounded by geometric designs and swirling arabesques.[16]

The prince was gone for ten days, exactly the amount of leave granted by his father. On his return to the imperial party, however, something had caused a final souring of the atmosphere. Even when Shah Jahan embarked on an ambitious project to create a new garden for his father on the eastern shore of Dal Lake, the old appreciation was gone. The prince had observed that a beautiful stream, bubbling up from a natural spring at Shalimar, could be channelled and controlled to create pleasing waterfalls and pools. Around the central watercourse, he visualised beds of roses, narcissi and violets, giving colour to a garden made fragrant by the flowers of blue jasmine, peach and almond. There would be fruit trees aplenty, of course: the famous Kashmiri apple, delicious pears and the apricots that had been introduced by Akbar and had grafted well in the Himalayan climate. It would, in time, become one of the most gorgeous and celebrated gardens in the entire empire but the emperor could muster little enthusiasm for his son's role. Instead, his journal shows a conspicuous rise in the profile of Asaf-Khan, brother of Queen Nur-Jahan and father to Shah Jahan's second wife, Mumtaz-Mahal.[17]

Promoted to the rank of Five Thousand in July 1617, Asaf-Khan had
been a member of the king's entourage during the entire five-year trek
through Ajmer, Mandu and Gujarat. He acquired a reputation for spending
a fortune on splendid mansions and beautiful gardens and endeared
himself to his master by throwing huge parties and presenting gifts of
tribute worth hundreds of thousands of rupees. Trusted, too, to investi-
gate complex fraud cases with probity and impartiality, it is small wonder
Jahangir regarded Asaf-Khan as one of his indispensable servants. But his

blossoming left Shah Jahan in the shade. There was certainly a degree of personally animosity between them, too. Back in Mandu, in the wake of Shah Jahan's triumph in the Deccan, Asaf-Khan had confided to Sir Thomas Roe that the arrogant prince was 'ravenous and tyrannical and wearied all nations'.[18] What Asaf-Khan had *not* confided to the Englishman was that, after Khusraw's frustrating refusal to play a part in his plot to replace Khurram as heir apparent, a fall-back plan was already well underway. When it came to fruition, it would precipitate a national crisis of unprecedented proportions.

The impression of Shah Jahan's gradual eclipse was confirmed by a sense of diminishing returns when it came to rewards for military success in the Kangra campaign. In August 1618, Shah Jahan had received news that Raja Suraj Mal, the local landowner he had sent to subdue the fortress in the northern Punjab, had fallen back into his old ways and become 'treacherous and rebellious', a betrayal that prompted the emperor and his courtiers to label him variously as 'that shame-faced accursed one' and an 'ungrateful bastard'.[19] In his place, the prince despatched his trusted chef de cabinet, Sundar Das – a man now more widely known by the title *Raja-Vikramaditya* – 'King Sun of Valour'.[20] After urgent preparations, he hastened north with reinforcements of 2,000 cavalry, 500 infantrymen and additional artillery. Progress since then, however, had been slow and Jahangir's irritation at the lack of military success was exacerbated by continuing reports that the delinquency of the prince's previous choice as commander, Raja Suraj Mal, had worsened. The renegade was still causing violent trouble in the Kangra vicinity, impeding the ongoing campaign, and Jahangir knew whom to blame. 'Although it was terribly unwise and imprudent,' he wrote, 'to let this ingrate back into the hill country, since my son had taken charge of the campaign, there was nothing I could do but leave Suraj Mal subject to my son's will and order'.[21]

Eventually, Raja-Vikramaditya managed to put these distractions behind him and focus on the siege of Kangra itself, a strategy that involved simply starving the previously impregnable garrison into submission. Victory came at last on 26 November 1620, when the defenders, reduced to eating straw, sued for mercy. Receiving the news at Lahore Fort, en route from Kashmir back to Agra, Jahangir rejoiced but saw no reason to give Shah Jahan much credit for his protégé's energetic prosecution of the war. On 7 December, the emperor visited his son's new mansion – outside the imperial precincts – and deigned to accept the traditional tribute presents. No reciprocal gift was forthcoming. And when it came to selecting a new governor for the conquered fortress, Jahangir picked his own man, Abd-al-Aziz Khan Naqshbandi, who had served as Raja-Vikramaditya's aide-de-camp (and Jahangir's personal spy) for the past eighteen months.[22] The emperor displayed the heavy-handed side of his personality when he subsequently staged a triumphant state visit to Kangra. Adding insult to the injury of their defeat, he gleefully rubbed the noses of the Hindu residents firmly into the dirt. First he arranged for the Muslim call to prayer and the khutba prayer to echo over the fortress. Then he had a cow slaughtered and, the *pièce de résistance*, commissioned a brand new mosque inside the citadel. The event was acclaimed in verse by the peerless Saida Gilani.

Nur al-Din Jahangir, son of Akbar the King,
Is a monarch who has no equal in the world.
The cloud of his sword, whereof a drop can raise a flood,
Took the Kangra Fort with the aid of God.
This mosque, radiant with light,
Where the foreheads of worshippers
Beam with lustre, was built on his order.
And an invisible voice gave the date of construction:
'The mosque of King Jahangir is luminous!' [23]

Shah Jahan may have hoped to secure greater credit from the next crisis to hit the empire. The disintegration of the Deccan ceasefire he had achieved in July 1617 was a set-back but gave him the opportunity for another high-profile victory. From the distant south came a steady stream of reports that Malik Ambar had rearmed, re-established diplomatic and military ties with Bijapur and Golconda and was sweeping back into territories that the peace deal had placed firmly under perpetual Mughal control. Abyssinian raiders were reported to be plundering homesteads at will across the territories of Ahmadnagar and Berar. Finally came word that Ahmadnagar Fort itself was under siege. Worse, garrisons from several frontier posts had been forced to fall back on the walled city of Burhanpur, where Abd-al-Rahim the Khan of Khans still governed the southern watches of empire. Despite his recent and, so far, unexplained slip from royal favour, Shah Jahan was again the default choice to restore order in the Deccan. But there were costly delays. By the time his most senior officers – especially Raja-Vikramaditya – were freed for this new assignment by the successful conclusion of the Kangra campaign, the imperial army in the south had suffered a series of military setbacks. Malik Ambar's forces now numbered more than 60,000 cavalry, contributed by all three states of the repaired tripartite alliance, and they inflicted several punishing reverses on the Khan-Khanan's troops. Even when a picked force of seven thousand Mughal horsemen mounted a daring raid on

Ambar's base camp near the garrison town of Balapur, it was a pyrrhic victory that left Abd-al-Rahim's army dangerously depleted. Its lines of communication overstretched and food supplies running short, he again retreated to Burhanpur.

Jahangir responded to the crisis in two ways. His first response was to send a heavyweight diplomatic mission to Shah Abbas in Persia, whom he suspected of aiding and abetting the Shiite alliance threatening the Mughals' Deccan holdings. The embassy was led by Mirza Barkhodar *Khan-Alam*, a veteran diplomat with experience of negotiating with both Persians and Deccanis. With him went generous gifts garnered during the recent Gujarat tour and – more pointedly – from the booty of the first Deccan campaign. When the mission finally reached the city of Qazvin it caused open-mouthed amazement. Never since the founding of the Safavid dynasty, said veteran Persian courtiers, had the Mughals – or the Ottomans, for that matter – come with such a magnificent retinue. Jahangir was, quite simply, showing off and Khan-Alam's mission was a naked display of wealth, power and reach.

He had with him some seven or eight hundred retainers of the royal household, personal attendants, servants and zookeepers, together with ten huge elephants, quipped with gold howdahs and embellished with all kinds of trappings, and a variety of animals, including tigers, leopards, antelope, Indian lambs, cheetahs, rhinoceroses, talking birds and water-buffalo which pulled various types of litters.[24]

According to contemporary Dutch chroniclers, the embassy was accorded a lavish reception, including feasts and hunting trips. Shah Abbas himself greeted Khan-Alam and embraced him in a friendly manner. But the Persian ruler had his own agenda. His confidential message to the ambassador as he departed for Agra, accompanying an official open letter of friendship, was one that would be remembered in years to come, one that had nothing to do with the Deccan states but a territory far to the north: Kandahar. 'Verbally he asked [the envoy] to remind the king that Kandahar belonged to him, having inherited it from his father and grand-father, and that it had been delivered into Akbar's hands by an unworthy subject of his. "My brother will have done a very good thing," he said, "if he gives it back."' [25]

The emperor's second response to the Deccan flare-up was to deploy maximum force under the best available commander. So it was that, on 13 January 1621, Shah Jahan was once again charged with the restoration of Mughal honour in the south. His father sent a formal order out to his commanders, calling on them to 'crush the rebels with a stern hand'.[26] In his own journal, Jahangir noted grimly that 'six hundred and fifty officers, a thousand *ahadis* [irregulars not assigned to individual fief-holders], a thousand musketeers, fifty thousand mounted and infantry artillerymen, in addition to the thirty-one thousand cavalry who were already in the province ... a huge arsenal and many elephants' should be enough to do the trick.[27]

En route to the front, in a conscious echo of his great ancestor Babur, Shah Jahan made a very public declaration of his abstinence from alcohol. Reaching the River Chambal, he had his household staff bring out all the casks of wine and spirits from the stores and toss them into the water. He then smashed up the gold and silver ornamented drinking-cups and distributed the mangled remnants to poor villagers in the vicinity.[28] The next major river crossing, much closer to the action, saw the prince and his huge army on the Narmada at New Year. But with their commander in such a grim and determined mood, the Spring Festival of 20 March 1621 brought little cheer to the officer corps of the expeditionary force.

By Saturday 4 April, Shah Jahan had reached the imperial fortress at Burhanpur, where his exquisitely appointed mansions stood atop a formidable citadel that had loomed over the River Tapti for two centuries. Behind and below lay one of the wealthiest cities of the empire.[29] Despite the tensions prompted by renewed conflict, a massive enlargement project was underway, very similar to the work just completed at Lahore, including a substantial extension northward along the Tapti waterfront. The cliff-like façade was richly decorated with coloured tile work in the Old Persian style – revealed today by the few faded remnants of coloured panels on the towering wall – while its myriad windows admitted the cool river air into the darkened summer-apartments within.[30] The superstructure of Akbar's stolid old fort would be improved, too, in line with Jahangir's fastidious demands for comfort and aesthetics. Shah Jahan absorbed the changes with interest but architectural projects would have to wait until peace-time: there was a war to be fought and the prince was in no mood to delay.

The sheer bravado of Malik Ambar in launching such effective raids deep into Mughal territory had stung. Shah Jahan now divided his army into five divisions, under the leadership of Raja-Vikramaditya, Mirza Darab *Darab-Khan* (the Khan of Khan's second son), Abdallah Khan, Khawaja Abu-al-Hassan and Raja Bhima. This last officer was the brother of Shah Jahan's friend, the former Crown Prince of Mewar, Karna Singh, who had recently inherited the kingdom and been permitted to return to his capital at Udaipur.[31] Honouring the terms of the February 1615 peace treaty, Maharana Karna Singh sent a contingent of 3,000 Rajput cavalry. Shah Jahan's five divisions, of 30,000 men apiece, were now despatched to take on Malik Ambar in a mighty pincer move. Simultaneously, as he had

Burhanpur Fort towers over the Tapti River

done four years earlier, the prince sent delegations to the weaker willed elements of the enemy alliance, the Qutb al-Mulk at Golconda and the Adilshah of Bijapur. The message to both was equally uncompromising, 'earnestly pointing out that the tribute that they used to pay to his father had not been paid for three or four years. … He added that he would not agree to any delay but had the intention of sending his army to exact it by force and, in addition, to attack and drive them out.'[32]

Shah Jahan's six-week military offensive was no less ruthless. In a series of bloody encounters, his generals forced Ambar's troops relentlessly back, to the point where the Malik was compelled to rescue his nominal overlord, the Nizamshah of Ahmadnagar, and transfer him to a safer refuge in the fortress at Daulatabad. On the Mughals pressed until they reached the enemy headquarters at Khadaki and 'so destroyed the city, which had taken twenty years to build, that it is not known if it will regain its splendour in another twenty years'.[33] Malik Ambar rallied his tri-state army, buttressed by his special Abyssinian troops, but to no avail. Shah Jahan's generals drove him back with heavy losses until, as before, negotiation remained his only option. 'When Ambar saw destruction in the mirror of his situation,' noted one imperial biographer, 'he approached the Raja [Vikramaditya] with representations of repentance and humility.'[34]

Surrender cost the southerners dearly, for Shah Jahan was in no mood to be merciful. At the centre of the second peace treaty between the Deccan states and the mighty Mughal Empire was a massive punitive indemnity of five million rupees. These were war reparations on an unprecedented scale and the three states were forced to argue bitterly among themselves about who could afford to pay the larger share.[35] In addition to this draining financial payment, Shah Jahan stipulated a full return of Mughal territories to his jurisdiction, along with a buffer zone fifteen miles wide, to be maintained on the southern side of the border as a no-man's-land, beyond which no Deccani soldier would ever be permitted to step. When word of this sensational victory reached Jahangir at Agra on 25 May 1621, he was delighted. Referring to Khurram by the honorific Shah Jahan once again, he crowed over the discomfiture of 'the treacherous trickster, the damned Ambar'. 'Our fleet-steeded heroes,' he gloated, 'lit out in pursuit and ground many of the enemy into the dust of annihilation with their vengeful swords.'[36] But Shah Jahan's own reward was hardly commensurate with his triumph, especially when set against the glorious receptions and honours previously piled upon him. The prize was a single ruby – though a fabulously valuable one with an extraordinary history. It had come to Agra only that February as a gift from Shah Abbas of Persia and, to Jahangir's amazement, had been the personal property of the grandson of Timur Leng of Samarkand. Hardly a trinket, then, to be inscribed with the proud lineage of the Mughal dynasty's founding fathers.

With every military success, Prince Shah Jahan had become a greater force to be reckoned with. He was now thirty years old, in the prime of life, self-confident to the point of arrogance and dangerously independent. He had built up a considerable personal following, a substantial treasury and commanded the finest cavalry in all the Mughal army. Jahangir could surely not have underestimated his son's thirst for power and potential for rebellion. The emperor had staged his own surprisingly long-lasting but ultimately abortive rebellion to seize the throne from Akbar, an episode he could no more have forgotten that than his eldest son's mutiny almost exactly sixteen years earlier. The recent machinations by the Queen and her coterie to rehabilitate the thirty-five-year-old Khusraw had served as a reminder of princely ambitions, unsettled Shah Jahan's hopes of succession and brought instability to the heart of the court. Put simply, Jahangir knew the risks. He knew too the pithily relevant axiom of the great poet Sheikh Muslih al-Din Sadi, which the emperor himself had borrowed in writing contemptuously of a treacherous subordinate.

At the last a wolf cub will surely become a wolf,
Even though he may be raised by man.[37]

Now, as Jahangir had served his father, so he was served by his son. Shah Jahan's rebellion, however, was at least as much about self-preservation as it was about ambition. Always a ruthlessly clear thinker, the prince had grounds for profound anxiety about his own future. He may have been bruised superficially by the lacklustre response from his father after the successful prosecution of the second Deccan campaign. After the plaudits and extravagant gifts that had followed earlier military successes, a single ruby – and without a hero's welcome at court – may have appeared to be damning with faint praise. Shah Jahan could, though, have put such a slight down to his father's fading competence; after all, his abilities were much impaired by decades of steady consumption of drugs and alcohol. But in that very frailty – in the room it left for mischief making by Queen Nur-Jahan – lay Shah Jahan's greatest anxiety. Loyal accounts, like that of Nawab Shamsam al-Daula Shahnawaz-Khan, made it clear that Shah Jahan's mutiny in the seventeenth year of Jahangir's reign happened as a direct result of Nur-Jahan's scheming.[38]

The particulars are that when Nur-Jahan got complete sway and had control of political and financial matters, and nothing but the name of the king remained to Jahangir, she fell to thinking that if Jahangir's long illness ended in his death, the empire would become Shah Jahan's. Though he was perfectly friendly to her, how would he permit her to exercise all this power? Therefore she married the daughter that she had by [her first husband, Ali Quli] Shir-Afgan to Sultan Shahriyar ... and set about patronising him. She became hostile to Shah Jahan and turned Jahangir's feelings that way also.[39]

The conspirators had found an alternative at last to the principled Khusraw. Shah Jahan's youngest half-brother Shahriyar was just sixteen years old, similar in age to Nur-Jahan's daughter Ladli. More importantly he was much more malleable than the queen's former protégé, Shah Jahan, who thus found himself faced with yet another threat to what he saw as his hard-earned inheritance. For Nur-Jahan, this was a way of securing her own future influence at court, long after the anticipated death of Jahangir, whose increasingly frequent bouts of acute asthma forced an acceleration of the queen's planning. She turned to Shahriyar, 'confident that from his weak capacity he would be the mere pageant of a king, whom she could manage at her pleasure'.[40] During Shah Jahan's five-month absence in the south, Shahriyar had been boosted to become the centre of attention at court, securing military promotion to the rank of Eight Thousand foot and Four Thousand horse on New Year's Day and the hand of Ladli Begum on 23 April 1621. Muhammad Sharif Mutamid-Khan, by now attached to Shah Jahan's entourage at Burhanpur in an administrative capacity, observed events at first hand. He believed that Nur-Jahan's manoeuvrings were jeopardising the security of the state and that the replacement of his master by the youth he derided as 'Shahriyar the Bastard' would be unacceptable.[41]

So, just as the taste of wine was agreeable to her taste, so the intoxication of power took root in that short-sighted woman – which is typical of women, who only cause chaos. … She started to train him [Shahriyar] and her design was that, in the event of Jahangir's death, she will keep him as her puppet and all the powers of the treasury and the elephant-stable and all the affairs of the state will be in her hands. And with these absurd ideas, she started to create chaos and came into direct hostilities with the Prince of Good Fortune [Shah Jahan].[42]

Ruthlessly assessing the threat posed by each of his half-brothers in turn, Shah Jahan resolved first to deal with Khusraw, the problem closest at hand. On the eve of his second Deccan campaign, he had finally secured guardianship over the eldest prince. Jahangir must have known that the risks involved had not diminished but, in what one account suggests was a decision taken 'in an hour of drunkenness', Khusraw was removed from Asaf-Khan's household to the care of one of Shah Jahan's divisional commanders in the Deccan and transferred south to Burhanpur.[43] Some have suggested that the handover bore all the signs of personal inter-vention by Nur-Jahan, who had already transferred her ambitions to a Shahriyar succession and had resolved to dispatch both his rivals by deliv-ering one up to be murdered by the other, who would subsequently be condemned.[44]

On Monday 22 February 1622, Shah Jahan ordered his rival to be strangled by an executioner named Reza Ghulam Bahadur in the palace at Burhanpur Fort. The murder was arranged to look like suicide by hanging, timed to happen when Shah Jahan was out hunting twenty-five miles away. Khusraw's body was discovered at dawn by his faithful wife, who 'filled the whole palace with her shrieks'.[45] The corpse was paraded through the streets of the walled city in a bogus display of grief and respect, stage-managed by Shah Jahan's officers, before being consigned to the earth in a makeshift tomb. The body was subsequently moved to join that of his mother, the Rajakumari Man Bai, in the tomb complex at Allahabad, where the burial of 'an innocent martyr' attracted the devotions of a small minority ready to anoint the murdered Khusraw as a true saint.[46] Few were convinced by Khurram's crocodile tears; one English merchant commented sardonically on the prince's brazen attitude, noting that he was 'not being dismayed in the world's eye'.[47] But Shah Jahan loyalists like Muhammad Salih Kamboh argued that it was 'entirely lawful for the great sovereigns to rid this mortal world of the existence of their brothers and other relations, whose very annihilation is conducive to common good'.[48]

The murder, so half-heartedly concealed, provoked outrage across the empire. To the west at Surat, traders muttered darkly about business prospects being adversely affected by 'the doubtful events and revolts which may succeed in this country' as a result of the killing. Others looked forward to the day when Khurram would pay a moral price for his crime. 'The yet deferred vengeance for Sultan Khusraw's unnatural fratricide,' wrote three shocked English merchants in June that year, 'shall undoubtedly fall heavy upon the bloody abetters, who may conceal it … per the distance of place and connivance of friends; but there is an omniscient power, the King of Kings, that never leaves unpunished the unnatural and treacherous effusion of innocent blood.'[49]

Who now stood in Shah Jahan's way? Pervez had never been openly ambitious but had been increasingly visible at court, securing some valuable presents from key figures at court and doing his best to stay close to the king, who in turn began calling him 'my favourite son' and 'my felicitous son'. But because he had neither played for political stakes with any seriousness nor led any strikingly successful military campaign, Pervez was bereft of either powerful supporters at court or a heavyweight military force in the provinces. Shahriyar by contrast, though seven years Shah Jahan's junior, wholly untried in combat and derided by his elder half-brother as nashudani, 'worthless', had secured the patronage of the best possible champion: the queen, whose ambitions were plainly to be seen.[50]

Nur-Jahan had recently been deprived of her most loyal adviser by the death at an advanced age of Ghiyath al-Din Itimad-al-Daula on 5 February 1622. Her personal clout was, however, greatly increased when she was allotted his entire fortune, a rare exception to the rule that all property devolved to the emperor himself.[51] She immediately commissioned a magnificent tomb for him on the east bank of the Yamuna, an architectural gem of perforated marble screens in complex ornamental patterns, decorated with geometric panels of colourful inlaid stone and intricate pietra dura illustrations.[52] The queen had also been granted the extraordinary honour of having her drums beaten after those of the king, once a prerogative of Shah Jahan himself. Worse still for the prince, her additional wealth enabled her openly to attempt to secure the loyalty of influential courtiers, bribing them with lavish receptions and robes of honour presented on her behalf at key court events. They, equally sensible of Jahangir's ever-diminishing faculties, now began to cluster to Shahriyar – partly because of the evident support that came from the queen and partly because no one at court believed that Khusraw's demise had been anything but deliberate: a kingdom under Khurram Shah Jahan would be a place of fear. The queen, having achieved the first part of her plan by effecting Khusraw's murder, now wasted no opportunity to fan the embers of outrage against Shah Jahan, her aim being simply to destory the reputation of Shahriyar's remaining rival.

The trigger for Shah Jahan's rebellion was the struggle for ownership of Kandahar, a crisis that had been largely dormant since the brief excitement of 1607–8, when Jahangir's forces had thwarted the Persian effort to use provincial levies to capture the contested trading centre. In the interval, Shah Abbas had sent from Isfahan no fewer than four lavishly appointed embassies, each bringing fulsome messages of goodwill and friendship. But the Persian king was troubled by the successes of Shah Jahan in the south and each of his many letters to Jahangir conveyed the same emphasis on the 'traditional ties of attachment and devotion' binding the Persian royal family to the Shiite rulers of the Deccan. The kings of Bijapur and Golconda, he wrote, had been 'unremitting in expressing their traditional loyalty'. Harping on the same theme in successive letters, he pleaded that if the southern rulers had offended the Mughal sovereign in any way, their 'chastisement' should be left to him. 'It is not worthwhile,' he added, 'for great monarchs to deny repose to submissive vassals'. And, in an important letter during the winter of 1616–17 – as report after report reached him of Shah Jahan's relentless campaign successes – Abbas had begged Jahangir to rein in his armies.

Let the people of the world witness how the mutual affection of two sovereigns led one of them, on a mere message from the other, to forgive enormous offences and forgo the acquisition of extensive dominions.[53]

But the Shah's appeals had fallen on deaf ears, despite the diplomatic blandishments carried back to Persia by Jahangir's own splendidly equipped envoys. So, to draw the Mughal war machine away from the south, Abbas again struck at Kandahar. Provided by his ambassadors with sound intelligence on the deployment of the opposition, Persian troops made their move on the city at the end of May 1622 with considerably more efficiency and drive than they had fifteen years earlier, capturing the fortress after a siege that lasted 45 days. The Shah himself was close by, pretending to be enjoying a hunting expedition in his Khorasan territories. As a further decoy, he had written a civil note to the Mughal governor of Kandahar, Abd-al-Aziz Khan, inviting him to come out of the citadel to 'kiss his stirrup' in hospitality. Unleashing his troops, however, he watched with satisfaction as 'daring spirits, clinging to the walls by their fingernails, within seventeen days made breaches in the walls and by means of tunnelling riddled the defence like a honeycomb.' The Mughal defenders cracked and capitulated on 21 June.[54] As an explicit statement of the city's new ownership, Shah Abbas was formally identified as ruler in the khutba prayer and the names of the Twelve Imams of the Shiite faith were recited in the town's Jami Mosque for the first time in thirty years.

Shah Jahan was still at Burhanpur on 27 March 1622 when Jahangir, en route *to* Kashmir for his traditional summer holiday in the mountains, sent the first letter summoning his son to a new war. The attack horrified the emperor, who now resolved to commit the armies of the Deccan, Gujarat, Bengal and Bihar to a massive retaliatory campaign, initially headquartered at Lahore.[55] The order sent to Shah Jahan was terse: to come 'as quickly as possible with all the soldiers, elephants and artillery he had in his governorate so that … he could be sent with an innumerable army and uncountable treasury and make Shah Abbas realise what it meant to break his oath in ingratitude'.[56] Shah Jahan was sufficiently impressed and, quelling his resentment at the dim reception accorded to his recent triumph, decamped for the long march north.

My army is tired and my general, Raja Bhima, has yet to return from collecting Your Majesty's tribute from the people of Gondwana. Given the heavy rain, it will also be difficult to bring my artillery carriages through the mud of the Malwa Hills. I have decided, therefore, to wait at Mandu until the appearance of *Suheil*, the southern pole star, indicates clearer weather.[57] After the monsoon, I will then raise my banners to recapture Kandahar.

I do not seek to make unreasonable demands for money, men or elephants – but I feel that Your Majesty should grant me the fiefdom of the Punjab, which lies on my route and can provide my army with the necessary provisions. In addition, I desire ownership of Ranthambor Fort [in Rajasthan], so that the women of my household may be kept safe there pending my resolution of the Kandahar campaign.[58]

He had barely travelled one hundred miles, reaching the hilltop fortress at Mandu in April, when he stopped in his tracks. It was a sudden, almost instinctive volte-face, based on some hard-headed calculations. His father was barely functioning at the levels required of an emperor of such massive dominions, instead serving as the puppet and mouthpiece of the queen. His younger brother Shahriyar was by the emperor's side, surrounded by the queen's cronies, including the influential Asaf-Khan. He was thus at the heart of decision-making and well placed to denigrate his brother and to jump at an opportunity that might present itself with any sudden deterioration in Jahangir's health. Shah Jahan, meanwhile, was about to take himself and the cream of his loyal forces into the northern mountains to retake a town whose importance was as nothing when the throne itself was in the balance – and at a time when injury or even simple delay could forever jeopardise his chances of succession.

His new intentions were openly declared to his father in a letter of response ferried back to Kashmir by the same imperial envoy. Kandahar, Shah Jahan argued, was in a different league from the campaigns that he had waged so far on his father's behalf: the Persians were fearsome fighters and to rush the Mughal response to the affront was to invite disaster. The prince then added some conditions of his own.

This request for control over the fertile and lucrative province of Punjab was an impertinent demand indeed – especially given that Shah Jahan already held the governorships of the occupied Deccan, Gujarat, Mewar, Malwa, Ahmadnagar and Khandesh – not to mention his older estates and holdings further north. Appointment to the Punjab governorate would make the provincial capital, Lahore, Shah Jahan's city – and it was well known to all that Lahore was, of all the imperial cities, the favourite not just of Jahangir but Nur-Jahan too. Had not the Queen written the verse: 'We have bartered our souls for Lahore / And have given lives to acquire this second paradise'?[59]

Jahangir was infuriated by his son's greed and effrontery: the redeployment of Shah Jahan from the south, in partnership with Pervez, had been a decision made in good faith, based on proven military experience. Now, faced with naked insubordination and troubled by the presence of a substantial force of uncertain loyalty at Mandu, one of the empire's strongest fortresses, Jahangir and Nur-Jahan resolved to return at once from Kashmir to the secure bastion at Lahore. According to Inayat-Khan, a biographer who was above all a Shah Jahan loyalist, the febrile atmosphere surrounding Jahangir was fomented by toadies of the empress 'whose coin of sincerity was impure' and malcontents who misrepresented practical military suggestions as insupportable procrastination: the emperor's mind was estranged from the prince, Shah Jahan's partisans concluded, and as a result 'the fire of intrigue and disturbance kept burning in Hind for the next four or five years'.[60] And from that day until the day of his death, the emperor referred no more to his son in his memoir as Khurram, let alone Shah Jahan; instead, he was labelled *bi-daulati*: a 'stateless' outcast.

But Jahangir was not wholly degraded nor completely Nur-Jahan's creature. There were residues of both imperial dignity and love for his errant son and he had not given up hope of his rehabilitation. Yet he knew that this mutiny at Mandu was likely to be but a precursor to an outright attempt on the throne. So, in an effort to 'guide him to wakefulness from his slumber of heedlessness and conceit' and dissuade him from his 'vain desires and loathsome aims', he sent Shah Jahan a highly personal and emotional letter, in which he mixed rebuke and cajolery. The sheer force of language – in which the once-acclaimed Shah Jahan is branded a 'vile-mannered child' – shows that this came directly from the desk of an emperor in whom anger, frustration and regret jostled for supremacy.[61]

Woe to his judgment! That, having obliterated the filial obligations of obedience which are the bond of father and son, he has placed his steps beyond the path of submission and obedience and ... raised his hands to the sword of opposition to his father with the intention of securing the crown and the throne.

If he has a desire to strike with the sword and conquer lands, then what could be better than to go with the hosts of well-wishing generals and their devoted soldiers to Persia and fight a war with Shah Abbas, because the inhabitants of Kandahar have violated their obligations to me. ...

Therefore it is necessary that my son ... should rub the face of thankfulness on the world-decorating threshold so that the royal favours and benevolence may be included in the conditions of that son.[62]

Just as he had been forgiven by Akbar for his petulant attempts to create a rival kingdom, so Jahangir now hoped that Shah Jahan would accept his magnanimous forgiveness and reinstatement after a rebellion driven by youthful impetuosity. The appeal did not work. On the contrary, Shah Jahan was still examining the potential of the Kandahar threat to advance his own prospects. One immediate possibility was a military collaboration with the Persians: allowing the Shah to engage Jahangir's forces redeploying in great numbers to the north, he might use his own army to strike directly at the capital. In the short term, the crisis at least gave him the opportunity to strengthen his position relative to his two remaining brothers. He struck rapidly at his most immediate rival, sending troops to secure a fiefdom at Dholpur that had just recently been allocated to Shahriyar. It was petty and vindictive way to begin an uprising.

Jahangir responded angrily, ordering Shah Jahan to stay at Mandu and be content with the provinces already assigned to him. His army, however, should continue its march north because he had assigned it a new commanding officer: Prince Shahriyar. Rubbing salt into Shah Jahan's emotional wounds, the king promoted his younger rival again, to the rank of Twelve Thousand, still 18,000 short of Shah Jahan's own status. A high-ranking envoy sent to court by the 'Outcast' – whose aim was that 'with the aid of cajolery and civility the storm of the dust of discord might be made to subside and relations of amity and harmony between the Emperor and the Prince might not cease' – was denied audience.[63] Worse was to follow. The prince was sacked from his various provincial governorships and tersely informed that he could take his family wherever he fancied setting up a permanent home, just as long as it was in the southern fringes of the empire. And then, when Jahangir reached Lahore on 25 October 1622, a devastating blow: he ordered that the revenues of Shah Jahan's fertile estates at Hissar Firoza be confiscated and diverted to the Kandahar campaign treasury. The properties were transferred to Shahriyar. The trappings of the heir apparent had been removed.

8
Rebellion and Exile

Who strives to win Ambition's crown
Must crouch on bended knee
To quaff, until his thirst be slaked,
The bitter tasting sea.

Abu-Talib Kalim[1]

Since the Grand Mughal's decease, sundry competitors aimed at the
succession and with none of them accepted in general, it gave liberty to
each to gather head and ill humours of the land to break out.

Thomas Kerridge, East India Company[2]

Shah Jahan had gambled on forcing an improvement of his position in
relation to his brothers and the queen – and had lost badly. His great
military successes, his titles and robes of honour, his ranking at court and
swollen entourage, all had evaporated in this unexpected humiliation.
The young man who had always had everything his way suddenly found
his prestige in the dust, his prospects dismal. His only remaining option
was open rebellion. Had he known what the next five years would bring
– successive military defeats and a life on the run, harried by pursuing
armies, season after season, over thousands of weary miles – he may have
hesitated to launch his uprising. For if ever a man reaped what he sowed
it was Shah Jahan. He now set his sights on Agra – exactly as his father,
Crown Prince Salim, had done twenty years before – seeking to take
the seat of government and home to the bulk of the imperial treasury. In
launching his rebellion, he had with him the core of his princely retinue:
Sundar Das Raja-Vikramaditya, Raja Bhima of Mewar and *Afzal-Khan*, the
'Superior Master', all of whom had joined him from the Deccan general
staff, taking care to bring with them, by way of funds, the most recent
tributes from the Deccan principalities.

Shah Jahan may also have hoped to win an open declaration of support
from a few important court insiders, not least Nur-Jahan's brother and his
own father-in-law, Abu-al-Hassan Asaf-Khan. Rumours had certainly begun
to swirl around the empire that Asaf-Khan had defected to Shah Jahan. This
allegation – and the resulting suspicion of the queen – may have stemmed
from Asaf-Khan's all too honest declaration that, in his opinion, only Shah

Jahan could tackle the Persian incursion effectively. Defenders of Asaf-Khan's loyalty, however, insist that, 'at the time when there was the dust of trouble between Jahangir and Prince Shah Jahan, [only] intriguers and evil-thinking persons suspected Asaf-Khan of favouring the prince, and alienated the mind of the Begum from a brother who was the pillar of the empire'.[3] Nur-Jahan, perhaps as a way of forcing her brother to reveal his true loyalties, had him sent to Agra to transfer the entire content of the royal treasury to a safer location; en route, he was given the additional and, under the circumstances, somewhat pointed title: *Umdat-al-Sultana*, 'Support of the Sultanate'. Asaf-Khan, however, is mentioned no more in connection with the attack on Agra and his precise role in the protection of the fortress and its treasury remains obscure; but the fact that he did not support Shah Jahan indicates that he had committed himself, for the time being at least, to the queen's faction and to the Shahriyar option for the succession.

In fact, Agra Fort was already well defended as Shah Jahan closed in on the city. The hero of the hour was Jahangir's senior eunuch, the Commandant of Agra Fort, whose title, *Itibar-Khan*, 'Master of Favoured Position', reflected his status in the royal household. He now marshalled the city's defenders, fortified the red sandstone citadel and saved the imperial treasury from the insurgents. As Shah Jahan's forces swarmed in from the south-west, they found the massive gates of Agra Fort closed against them. They vented their frustration on the merchants and inhabitants of the sprawling city on the Yamuna. Word travelled fast along the imperial trade routes. By 20 March, the Italian traveller Pietro Della Valle, at Surat, was able to report the sensational news that 'Sultan Khurram had taken and sacked the city of Agra, except the castle, and that his army and himself had committed very great cruelties there in spoiling and discovering the goods and money of the citizens; particularly that he had tortured and indecently mangled many women of quality and done other like barbarities, whereby he rendered himself very odious to the people.'[4] Whether or not these atrocities had been embellished in the spreading of the tale, war had come to the heart of the Mughal Empire. Even the notoriously unrestrained Prince Salim had not gone so far. And Jahangir, now dictating his memoirs to his amanuensis Mutamid-Khan, bewailed the actions of his 'undutiful son'.

What weighs heavy on my heart and galls me is that at such a time when my son and loyal amirs [generals] should be endeavouring without partisanship to further the Kandahar campaign, in which lies the honour of this reign, this unhappy wretch is chopping away at the roots of his own fortune and making himself a stumbling block in the path of the campaign.[5]

As at the very beginning of his reign, when the Khusravite uprising threatened to deny him his throne, Jahangir now rose to the occasion with unexpected determination and drive. Even as the court made its stately way from Lahore towards Agra, the emperor made his deployments. Mir Abd-al-Salam *Islam-Khan*, a distinguished diplomat of Persian origin, was sent north as mentor to Prince Shahriyar, who now had Eight Thousand horse added to his rank of Twelve Thousand infantry, as well as the Kandahar command.[6] Then Jahangir summoned Prince Pervez from Allahabad. And to face the threat of Shah Jahan in the south, he ordered down from Kabul the one general in whom unquestioning obedience was matched by military capability: Mahabat-Khan, the man labelled 'Master of Terror' for his murderous loyalty. On 22 March 1623 – with Shah Jahan frustrated by his failure to break into Agra Fort and uncharacteristically hesitant – Jahangir gave the order to his massed forces to move forward. Twenty-five thousand cavalry were marshalled in four divisions, under the banners of Abdallah Khan, Asaf-Khan, Lashkar-Khan and Fidai-Khan. The ground selected for the first encounter, on 28 March, was a small settlement called Baluchpur, near Delhi. Examined objectively, the result appears to have been less than conclusive, with both sides suffering demoralising setbacks. But for Shah Jahan, a man playing for the highest stakes, failure to win amounted to defeat.

On Shah Jahan's side, the vanguard was led by his finest officers, Raja-Vikramaditya, Darab-Khan and Raja Bhima, who now arrayed their forces and advanced. Clouds of arrows sang through the air; muskets blasted between the advancing lines. Suddenly, Abdallah Khan – commander of the imperial vanguard – broke away from the main body of his army and led his troops directly into Shah Jahan's front line, which ceased firing, parted and let them through. This was the first serious betrayal of the uprising, in the full throes of battle. Raja-Vikramaditya, who had wooed Abdallah Khan and engineered the defection, directed his elephant-driver to seek out Darab-Khan, to inform him of this heartening news. Yet even as he advanced to congratulate his brother officer on the event that must decide the day, a bullet came whizzing out of the mêlée and took him in the head. Sheikh Farid Bakkhari describes how the Raja's sudden death evened up the sense of demoralisation.

By his fall, the thread of Shah Jahan's army snapped into disorder. … On the imperialists' side, the desertion of Abdallah Khan threw the royal army out of order; while on the prince's side the killing of Raja-Vikramaditya rendered the hand and heart of the army idle. Towards the closing hours of the day, the armies on both sides withdrew to their quarters and stayed there.[7]

The folly of Shah Jahan's gamble was now truly revealed. Even with Jahangir's vanguard gutted by the treachery of its commander, his own forces were clearly not courageous enough to hold their ground in the wake of their general's death. Few of his remaining officers were of similar calibre to Raja-Vikramaditya. After overseeing the honourable cremation of his stalwart Hindu general, Shah Jahan now ordered a strategic retreat towards Ajmer and then Mandu. The irony could not have been lost on him that he was now fleeing through a succession of territories whose subjugation or negotiated surrender had made his own reputation. And as a figure who had once been the incarnation of Mughal oppression, he may have been surprised by the warm welcome accorded him by some of those he had defeated in the past. In the Kingdom of Mewar, Maharana Karna Singh gave him private accommodation on Jagmandir Island, a short distance over the lake from his own rapidly growing palace. The *Gol-Mahal*, or 'Round Palace', on the island is a small and simple stone building but, as Kaviraj Shyamaldas later wrote, in giving a 'safe haven' to the exile, 'the dynastic ideal of doing the right thing at the right time and helping in distress without taking into account any other implications was upheld by the Rana'.[8] As a symbol of eternal friendship, Prince Khurram and Rana Karna exchanged turbans.

The prince's route south was a replay of his past glories, except in retreat instead of on the offensive, in much greater haste and in abject disgrace. Close behind followed a substantial expeditionary force, under the joint command of Prince Pervez and Mahabat-Khan. They were swiftly deployed after the inconclusive Battle of Baluchpur by Jahangir, who also moved with his entire administrative staff south to Ajmer. With this imperial army snapping at his heels, Shah Jahan reached the protected heights of Mandu in the early summer. There he paused to scribble urgent letters pleading for help. He reminded the Shah of Persia of how his great-grandfather Humayun had been able to count on Persian support during his years of exile: 'It is the hereditary practise of this family,' he wrote, 'to seek succour from the family of prophetic descent and this suppliant is merely following the example of his ancestors.'[9] Shah Jahan also wrote to Malik Ambar, to the south, requesting a military alliance against the empire.

Such humiliating correspondence dealt with, there was some good news. At Mandu, Shah Jahan collected a huge sum of money: one million rupees, the bulk of the Gujarat treasury, brought to him by a loyal provincial official. Despite the money, however, morale was dropping like a barometer before a storm. Rustum-Khan, one of his most trusted officers, defected to Mahabat-Khan's army during a skirmish north of the Narmada. There were also two further stinging defeats, inflicted on Shah Jahan's demoralised forces on 20 June 1623 and in mid-July, forcing him to flee

Jagmandir Island: Shah Jahan's refuge during his rebellion

further south. Leaving a substantial rearguard and hauling his boats up well away from the riverbank, the rebel prince crossed the Narmada, making for Burhanpur and the hilly terrain of the Deccan.

Here there was another unexpected reverse. Darab-Khan's father, Abd-al-Rahim the Khan of Khans, was a man of divided loyalties. He had been appointed by Shah Jahan as his proxy governor in all the southern provinces but prior to that there had been a lifetime of loyal service to Jahangir and to Akbar before him. In an effort to distance himself from Shah Jahan, the old general now wrote a secret letter to Mahabat-Khan, pleading that what he called his 'imprisonment' by the prince should not be taken as treason – and that only constant surveillance had stopped him from fleeing the 'discomfort' of the rebel camp.[10] The letter was discovered by Shah Jahan's agents and the elderly Khan of Khans held under close surveillance. His son, Darab-Khan, despite his military skills, was also suspect by association and was forcibly detained. But, in a desperate attempt at dialogue, Shah Jahan gambled on trusting the Khan-Khanan with one last diplomatic mission. He was to return to the Narmada, Shah Jahan's last line of defence against the emperor's army, and there approach Mahabat-Khan directly with a message of peace. Instead, the old seneschal promptly defected.

At this stage, Shah Jahan was still travelling with his entire household in tow. At Asirgarh, however, he resolved to leave all 'non-essential' members of the harem in the security of the mountain-top fortress, taking with him only his three wives, his children and the maidservants and eunuchs necessary to keep the mobile household running smoothly. For Mumtaz-Mahal, abandoning either her husband or her children was out of the question.

The intimacy, deep affection, attention and favour which His Majesty had for the Cradle of Excellence exceeded by a thousand times what he felt for any other [wife]. And always that Lady of the Age was the companion, close confidante, associate and intimate friend of that successful ruler, in hardship and comfort, joy and grief, when travelling or in residence. … The mutual affection and harmony between the two had reached a degree never seen between a husband and wife among the classes of the sultans or among the other people. And this was not merely out of sexual passion: the excellent qualities, pleasing habits, outward and inward virtues and physical and spiritual compatibility on both sides caused great love and affection and extreme affinity and familiarity.[11]

Shah Jahan's desperate letters from Burhanpur appealing for help all failed. The call to Shah Abbas of Persia fell on deaf ears. Far from being ready to conspire with Shah Jahan to split the Mughal army by attacking from his new base at Kandahar, the wily Persian ruler – well furnished, as always, with political as well as military intelligence – was already in correspondence with Queen Nur-Jahan and even Prince Shahriyar himself. Abbas had clearly decided which faction had the best prospects of success. His reply to Shah Jahan read like the advice of a tetchy uncle: submission and good behaviour, he advised, were the best way back into Jahangir's favour, especially for one who was 'still in the incipient phase of his princely career'.[12]

God, he said, had enjoined sons to obey their parents; the prince should seek to do his father's will, thus removing his father's ground for complaint against him and removing the need to take military action against him. If the prince would take this advice, he said, he would be applauded and esteemed.[13]

The rebuff stung. And if Shah Jahan, departing from Burhanpur and crossing the swollen Tapti River amid heavy rains, had hoped to receive hospitality on a Mewari scale from his old enemy, Malik Ambar of Ahmad-nagar, he was swiftly disabused of such optimistic notions. The kingdom of the Nizamshah had experienced the full force of Mughal imperial anger all too recently and Ambar was not foolish enough to risk Jahangir's displeasure by harbouring a wanted man. Still, the wanted man in question travelled with a vast army – eight hundred elephants, 1,400 horse and around ten thousand infantry – and it was only prudent of Malik Ambar to let Shah Jahan pass on through to Bijapur. Shah Jahan may have hoped to bully the Bijapuris into supporting him, as he had bullied them into submission when splitting the tripartite Deccani alliance. But Bijapur too declined to host the rebels. Even the Qutb al-Mulk of Golconda, further to the east, begged Shah Jahan to leave his territory as soon as possible, though the Sultan did provide cash and assistance and issued orders to his border guards that the prince was to be given safe passage from his territory into Orissa. This long loop through the southern quarter of India put Shah Jahan at the uttermost extreme of the Mughal Empire – but it also created an opportunity to transform defeat into victory. A lightning advance up through Orissa and into Bengal could be followed by a swing west into the imperial heartland, he must have reasoned, and a forced march via Bihar and Allahabad would take him upriver to Agra, where this time the defenders of the royal fortress might be defeated. Were such a strategy to work, Pervez and Mahabat-Khan would be outflanked and humiliated.

The first sighting of Shah Jahan's army as he emerged from Golconda came on 5 November 1623 at the port town of Machilipatnam, on the Bay of Bengal south-east of Hyderabad, where the kingdom met Mughal territory.[14] To reach the sea, the prince had taken his men through some formidable terrain. He had crossed the frontier between the mountains of the Deccan plateau and the swamps and rivers of Orissa at Chatar Diwar Pass, a rocky defile where the Qutb al-Mulk dynasty had built a solid stone fortress. There, legend had it, 'a force of three hundred to four hundred thousand soldiers may be held up by a regiment of five hundred matchlock-men'.[15] But the laissez-passer from Golconda served its purpose and Shah Jahan was free to launch his attack on the eastern outposts of his father's empire. At Machilipatnam, the arrival of such a vast army provoked amazement and fear. Two employees of the East India Company, Thomas Mills and John Dod, recorded the devastation caused by the arrival of the ravenous horde. Many inhabitants, they reported, simply packed their belongings and fled, despite Shah Jahan's repeated pledges 'that none of his people should use the least violence'.

He approached Masulipatam [sic] and pitched his tents about a mile and a half off in a fair green environ with much paddy and other grain in the ground fit for his present occasion ... where he and his people might be best accommodated with such provisions and necessaries as they wanted after so great a travail in these boisterous times of rains and foul weather. ... They have made a dearth and scarcity of all things and more especially the commodity for the bellies, as rice, sugar, butter, wheat, hens and all other such kind ... besides the elephants hath destroyed many hundreds of coconut and toddy palms,

a misery most lamentable to behold. … His army consists, as near as I can gather, about 4,500 horse, 500 elephants, 10 or 12,000 attendants and camels, most part for carriage; so that he is to the number of 16,000 persons, one and other, besides women of his own and others of his great men about him.[16]

Shah Jahan's conquest of Orissa was achieved with brisk efficiency, aided by the cowardly imperial governor, Mirza Ahmad Beg Khan. Local sources confirm that he failed even to attempt to delay the invaders, let alone engage them in open battle, instead falling back in disarray, first on Cuttack Fort, then on Burdwan, the old Bengal fiefdom where Nur-Jahan's first husband, Ali Quli, had come to grief. By December 1523, Shah Jahan was pleasantly accommodated at Cuttack, attended upon by local Hindu chieftains and land-owners who had fallen foul of the ambitious Ahmad Beg, as well as Portuguese merchants based at Hugli.[17]

The annexation of Bengal followed almost as smoothly. Leaving Muhammad Taqi behind as governor of 'liberated' Orissa and honoured with the title *Shah-Quli-Khan*, Shah Jahan pressed on into the empire's north-eastern corner. The decisive battle for Bengal on 20 April 1624 was the first major victory secured by Abdallah Khan Firoz-Jang – replacing Raja-Vikramaditya as Shah Jahan's commander-in-chief. Jahangir's governor, Ibrahim Khan *Fateh-Jang*, was taken by surprise by the speed of Shah Jahan's advance from the south. Yet even as he 'sank in the river of bewilderment', he was able to muster the courage to rebuff a rebel offer of safe passage to the imperial capital. 'I have no other aspiration,' he replied,' than that, in the discharge of my obligations for past royal favours … I may sacrifice my life and obtain the felicity of martyrdom.' [18] In the ensuing battle, seeing that his forces were being soundly defeated in a 'labyrinth of destruction', he made one last suicidal charge into the ranks of the enemy. Bengali historians were critical of his impetuousness. 'Ibrahim Khan's death vindicated his honour as a man,' wrote one, 'but it did not fulfil his obligations as a commander. … Thereafter Bengal easily passed into Shah Jahan's hand.' [19]

Nauruz saw the prince celebrating in style at Jahangirnagar, where he distributed the Bengal treasury among his top brass: a quarter of a million rupees, bales of silk, rare perfumes and dozens of captured war-elephants.[20] Ending months of close detention, he ordered Darab-Khan to be released and charged instead, under oath, with the governorship of this lucrative province. Raja Bhima and Firoz-Jang were sent west to reconnoitre the route into Bihar. Significantly, it began to look as if support for the emperor among the provincial nobility had started to ebb. The imperial garrison at Patna, the Bihari capital, yielded without a fight. Rohtas Fort, a formidable bastion that would have taken valuable time to besiege and subdue, was surrendered 'without movement of the sword or the spear' by Sayyid Mubarak, who hastened to pay his respects in person to Shah Jahan.[21] Even closer to the centre of power, Mirza Rustum surrendered Allahabad Fort, the ancient castle at the merger of the Yamuna and the Ganges, where Prince Salim had set up his pseudo-capital and where Pervez had nursed his wounded pride.[22] The advance appeared to be irresistible.

But a rude shock awaited the rebel army as in August 1624 they moved confidently westwards. Their manoeuvre had been anticipated as much as six months earlier – although Prince Pervez had not actually left Burhanpur until 24 March.[23] Far from waiting to be outflanked, he and Mahabat-Khan had driven their army up through India's west and central districts to cut off Shah Jahan's advance. Commandeering a substantial flotilla of river-boats from local land-owners, they had then moved rapidly downstream towards Allahabad. By mid-August, the two armies were in sight of each other and for two full weeks they maintained formation, each waiting the other's move, on the bank of the Tons River, a tributary of the Ganges.[24]

The imperial army greatly outnumbered the rebel force and the majority of Shah Jahan's commanders advised a strategic retreat. There were two conspicuous exceptions. Firoz-Jang counselled a northward circling manoeuvre, attacking Agra via Lucknow and Delhi and by-passing Mahabat-Khan's formidable army. Raja Bhima of Mewar, by contrast, expressed his displeasure at the delay and urged an immediate attack. According to the account by Mutamid-Khan, the Rajput general threatened to withdraw his troops if Firoz-Jang's tactics were adopted:

His voice prevailed and the ranks were formed for battle … and arrows and bullets fell like hail.
From both sides, the artillery of the gunners commenced scattering fire on the hosts.
From the smoke of the gun-wagons of the two forces, you might say a pitchy cloud had formed.
Cannon-balls showered like hail; yea, a storm of destruction blew. …
From blood, yea, on every side a stream flowed; on every side showered stone-rending arrows;
They passed right through every body that they lodged in.
From swords and spears, breasts were torn to shreds; the corpses of heroes fell on the ground.
But the Imperialists, like stars, hemmed in the army of the Prince.
They surrounded them in that battle, yea, as the ring encircles the finger.[25]

Realising the danger posed by Raja Bhima's sheer force of personality, the imperialists made him their principal target. Resisting a powerful charge by the Mewari battalions at the centre of their line, Mahabat-Khan's troops rallied and surged against the raja's personal bodyguard. Too strong and too numerous for the Rajput swordsmen, they forged a path through and cut Raja Bhima down. Dismayed, Shah Jahan's gunners abandoned their cannons and fled, leaving their prized artillery pieces in the hands of the royal forces. This bleak reversal of fortunes was compounded by betrayal. There were conspirators among the Bengali boatmen who had been conscripted with their vessels to move the rebel army upstream. Letters reveal that contact had already been made with Mahabat-Khan, pledging not only to slip away at a crucial moment in the battle but also to work against their commander's interests in Bengal itself. Exposed by treachery and cowardice, beset on three sides, deprived of his boats and guns, Shah Jahan himself held his ground until an arrow took his horse out from underneath him. The prince was lucky to escape alive, evading the onslaught of successive attackers until Abdallah Khan Firoz-Jang, riding to the rescue, plucked him from the field of battle.

This sudden defeat at the Battle of the Tons effectively sounded the death-knell for Shah Jahan's ambitions for the crown. In the words of one disapproving Deccan chronicler, 'the ungrateful are humiliated'.[26] In despair, the prince fell back on Rohtas Fort, rejoining his family and closest advisers. The only decision remaining to him now, he knew, was the choice between humiliating retreat and even more ignominious surrender. But even as he arrived at Rohtas, his favourite wife, Mumtaz-Mahal, was again in labour, a rate of productivity that led to her being acclaimed as a 'mine teeming with gems of royalty'.[27] Her tenth child and fifth son, Sultan Murad-Bakhsh, was born on 8 October 1624.[28] Even in these desperate days of flight, the niceties had to be observed. The astrologers opined that the birth had happened 'at an auspicious hour when Venus and Jupiter were in the ascendant', while such poets as remained with Shah Jahan cast about for suitable honorifics, finally coming up with 'The Desire of the King of the World, Emperor of Faith and Governments'.[29] As Shah Jahan turned south again, back towards Orissa, the baby had to be left behind with a wet-nurse. The ever-loyal Mumtaz-Mahal, however, accompanied her husband into what would be a prolonged exile, all the while buttressing his flagging resolve with assurances that the failure on the Tons had been the fault of his generals, not his strategy. 'They ought to die by taking poison,' she said with contempt, 'and should not show their face to Your Royal Highness'[30]

Territory gained in the east now proved impossible to hold; his victories were shown to be as ephemeral as smoke. Even as he retreated, Shah Jahan summoned Darab-Khan from Bengal, knowing that every available soldier would be needed. But Darab-Khan pretended that he was cut off at Jahangirnagar and unable to make the assigned rendezvous. Unfortunately

سیده جوک حاکم ایل بهه سالار عمل ها مسلم

for the turncoat governor, however, his treachery was seen as equally perfidious by the emperor, who called him an 'ill-starred wanderer in the valley of perdition' and had him executed the following year. His head was sent to his father, Abd-al-Rahim, the Khan of Khans, wrapped in a napkin like a melon.[31] Mahabat-Khan, living up to his name, dealt with other rebel stragglers in a similarly brisk fashion, having them executed and their heads sent to Jahangir. His prize was another promotion: he was awarded Abd-al-Rahim's title 'Khan of Khans' and his status as Commander-in-Chief (*sipahsalar*) was confirmed. But there were critics, too, who took issue with Mahabat-Khan's new title – *Mutamin-al-Daula*, 'Trustworthy One of the State' – arguing that the general had failed in his central duty: capturing Shah Jahan and bringing him to justice.[32]

Instead of performing the duties in accordance with the instruction and expectations of the king, he entertained other designs of deceit.
In the beginning he exerted himself more but later on acted with short-sightedness.
Three times the rebels [i.e. Shah Jahan and his retinue] fell a prey to his hands but defeat after defeat was inflicted on him.
Nor did he exert sufficiently to capture them and the rebels were able to escape far from the field of battle.
He did not even chase the rebels and thus brought tumult and unrest to the world.[33]

For Shah Jahan, the following eighteen months were the bleakest time of his life: on the run and harried by imperial troopers. Even when his reduced entourage achieved another marathon trek through southern India – reversing the confident swing through the Deccan of two years before – the only safe haven he could find was in the territory of his former enemy, Malik Ambar.[34] Prince Pervez, anticipating another attempt on the empire by the western route, had dashed back from Allahabad and sealed off any possible advance.

By the spring of 1626, Shah Jahan was in desperate straits, his abject defeat compounded by severe illness. Profoundly depressed and surrounded by a diminishing band of demoralised courtiers, he was faced with little choice but complete capitulation. His last attempt to establish a secure base within Mughal territory failed when a prolonged siege of Burhanpur Fort, carried out in alliance with Malik Ambar's Deccani auxiliaries, failed to break the will of the stubborn defenders. Finally, on the verge of physical and mental exhaustion, Shah Jahan wrote to his father on 2 March 1626, begging for forgiveness for his own errors and clemency for his followers' misplaced loyalties.[35] Touched by his son's humility and moved by the abject state to which he was reduced, Jahangir rose to the occasion with commendable decency. The emperor was, however, experi-

Abd-al-Rahim the Khan of Khans

enced enough to lay down two non-negotiable conditions for Shah Jahan's pardon. If the prince were to be forgiven, Jahangir wrote in his own hand, he would have to send his two eldest sons, Dara-Shikuh and Aurangzeb, to court as hostages. Second, the fortresses of Rohtas, on the Bihar-Bengal border, and Asir, not far from Burhanpur, must be surrendered by the Shah Jahan loyalists who still held them.[36]

Shah Jahan was now reduced to a status no higher than that of a vassal prince. Humbled, he complied with his father's terms, sending the eleven-year-old Dara Shikoh and his eight-year-old brother to Agra, along with a small contingent of personal servants and a lavish tribute to the emperor. But Shah Jahan's wilderness years were far from over. Rejecting the emperor's offer of control over the small territory of Balaghat on the southern fringes of empire, the prince took to the road again, adopting the life of his nomadic ancestors. The business of empire had been hijacked by Shah Jahan's rebellion for more than four years. Its total collapse left him a discredited wanderer in the hinterlands of internal exile, his fortunes at their lowest ebb.

The taming of Shah Jahan should have brought lasting peace to the Mughal kingdom and satisfaction to its reigning emperor and queen. But there was no respite from the intense plotting and counter-plotting over the succession and peace proved elusive for the now chronically ailing Jahangir (who despite the protracted crisis had kept to his regular timetable of long Himalayan holidays). With Shah Jahan roving the western fringes of empire, disgraced and effectively removed as a plausible candidate, it might have appeared that the last serious obstacle to Nur-Jahan's plans for Shahriyar's succession had been removed. Indeed, contemporary accounts like that of Kami Shirazi, a sycophantic Nur-Jahan loyalist, formally identified Shahriyar – by now returned from the abortive attempt to retake Kandahar – as 'the heir to the throne'.[37] Mughal politics, however, were rarely so simple: there were other causes to be championed. The man with the highest profile was an unlikely figure, the previously negligible Pervez. Thanks to the military genius of Mahabat-Khan, Jahangir's new Commander-in-Chief, the twenty-five-year-old prince had achieved rank far beyond expectations and celebrity to go with it. More significantly, he owed nothing to Nur-Jahan.

There were also those at court who still mourned the murdered Prince Khusraw and looked to his young child, Dawar-Bakhsh *Bulaqi* – a nickname that suggests a prominent nose-stud or ring – as a candidate of unimpeachable birthright, the eldest son of the eldest son. The young man had been given the governorship of Gujarat, promoted to the rank of Eight Thousand and was subsequently referred to by Jahangir as 'my son'.[38] Indeed, some sources indicate that the emperor personally favoured the Bulaqi option – not least in grief and regret for handing Khusraw into the hands of his executioner – and may even have made out some sort of 'testamentary disposition' to that effect.[39] And the English traveller, Sir Thomas Herbert, was later informed that when Jahangir was on his death-bed, 'he made all his Amirs or noblemen swear by their Koran to make his grandchild Sultan Bulaqi "Mughal", or Emperor, after him and to exclude Khurram for ever'.[40]

Faced with this threat to her own plans, Nur-Jahan began a typically systematic drive to consolidate Shahriyar's position. Pervez, she calculated, would be emasculated without the support of Mahabat-Khan. In making her move, the queen had the full collaboration of her brother Abu-al-Hassan Asaf-Khan, who had been brought back to the emperor's side from an appointment as Governor of Bengal because he was, in Jahangir's own words, 'so superior to any other in his talents ... indeed in all positive respects he was without peer'.[41] Nur-Jahan now contrived to have Mahabat-Khan sacked as Khan-Khanan and Commander-in-Chief, removed from Burhanpur, where he remained at the service of Pervez, and despatched in Asaf-Khan's place to the far eastern corner of the empire. Another official named Khan-Jahan Lodi, who had been adopted by Jahangir as his foster-son, was appointed in Mahabat-Khan's stead as counsellor to Prince Pervez.

The humiliation of this reverse – compounded by an apparent attempt to frame him for embezzlement – prompted Mahabat-Khan to stage his own mutiny, an extraordinary sequence of events in which the risks inherent in the Mughal structure of 'mobile government' were brutally exposed and which culminated in Jahangir's most experienced general joining the dissident Shah Jahan in exile. What emerges from the various accounts of the mutiny, however, is that it began in a spirit of absolute loyalty to the person of the emperor – despite, or perhaps because of, Mahabat-Khan's animosity towards both Nur-Jahan and Asaf-Khan. Certainly he never intended to take the drastic final step that would have transformed a mutiny into a true coup d'état: the killing of the emperor. Throughout the six-month crisis, in fact, Mahabat-Khan tried to persuade Jahangir to stand up for himself, arguing that the overweening influence of the queen was detrimental to the state. 'But the influence of Nur-Jahan Begam had wrought so much upon his mind,' reported one historian, 'that if two hundred men like Mahabat-Khan had advised him simultaneously to the same effect, their words would have made no permanent impression upon him.'[42]

This strange rebellion began on the Jhelum River in Kashmir on 24 March 1626, as the royal household and its entourage travelled between Lahore and Kabul.[43] Mahabat-Khan had travelled from Burhanpur to his Bengal posting before returning with a fortune in cash and jewels from the Jahangirnagar treasury, the best war-elephants from the provincial filkhana and several thousand Rajput fighters, recruited en route at Ranthambor Fort. His only aim was to locate the imperial entourage and plead his case with the emperor in person. But Jahangir, prompted by Nur-Jahan and her brother (and seemingly oblivious to the threat posed by Mahabat-Khan's substantial force) refused to grant a private audience unless the entire Bengal treasury were handed over first. Then the imperial Superintendent of Elephants, *Gajpat-Khan*, arrived to demand the handover of the Bengal herd. In what appeared to be a clear indication that Mahabat-Khan's prospects were finished, the cheeky elephant-keeper sneered, 'My lord khan, for what day are you keeping them; the boat of your life has sunk!'[44] Mahabat-Khan snapped at last.

Intercepting the royal retinue, the general observed immediately that an over-complacent Asaf-Khan had taken the majority of the army, the arsenal and treasury with him across the Jhelum, using a sturdy bridge of boats, leaving the emperor, still camped by the river, unprotected. Deploying a few hundred Rajputs on the river, he ordered them to burn the bridge, cutting off any possible rescue by Asaf-Khan. Then, with just a small mounted strike force, he made straight for the royal pavilions, abducted Jahangir and took him to the part of the camp where Shahriyar, prospective heir to the throne, had also been taken into custody. The first stage of the mutiny had been carried off perfectly, with one error: Mahabat-Khan had overlooked the queen. Over the next five days, Nur-Jahan mounted two brave but unsuccessful rescue attempts; at last, faced with the defeat of her remaining troops and the desertion of Asaf-Khan, who had fled to Attock Fort with a rump force of 200 men, Nur-Jahan surrendered and joined her husband in captivity.[45]

Mahabat-Khan moved briskly to consolidate his victory. First, he despatched an expeditionary force to besiege Attock and take Asaf-Khan into custody. Then he had several of Asaf-Khan's more experienced and valuable cronies beheaded.[46] After demonstrating such ruthlessness, however, what the victorious general did next confounded his enemies. He did nothing. Indeed, the most bizarre aspect of the entire mutiny was that its organiser did so little to influence the emperor's behaviour or administration in any way. His travel plans scarcely interrupted, Jahangir entered Kabul on 27 April 1626.[47] It was, to all intents and purposes, a normal imperial progress, even though the emperor was still technically in Mahabat-Khan's custody. To mark the occasion – it was, after all, his first visit to Kabul for nineteen years – Jahangir scattered coins to the crowds before making camp at the finest available garden. Over the following days, he paid his respects at the tomb of his great ancestor Babur and passed an agreeable time on the customary hunting trips.

It is hard to know what plan, if any, Mahabat-Khan had for consolidating this strange authority over the emperor. He had no allies of significance; nor did he appear to have designs to place an alternative candidate on the throne. Given such lack of clarity, it was perhaps inevitable that his hold on power was but brief. The final turning point was a violent squabble between the ahadi freelance troops in the imperial guard and Mahabat-Khan's Rajputs, who had 'turned unruly and conceited because of the dominance and power they happened to enjoy'.[48] What the arrogant Rajput mercenaries had forgotten, however, was that they were on unfamiliar and potentially very dangerous territory and that the hostile ahadi musketeers, despite their lesser number, were much better armed. So when tempers frayed and it came to a fight, the ahadis, with the advantage of firepower over swordsmanship, slaughtered the Rajputs in their hundreds. As the clash spiralled out of control and the surviving mercenaries fled into the side-streets and surrounding hillsides, they were gleefully rounded up by local Kabulis and Hazara tribesmen and sold in the slave markets. At a stroke, Mahabat-Khan was deprived of the cream of his personal army.

Jahangir and Nur-Jahan immediately assumed their proper positions and began again to dictate policy. The first step was an immediate departure from Kabul on 22 August. Shahriyar was ordered by the emperor to take a fast-moving force to the western fringes of the empire, because Shah Jahan had been reported to be advancing towards Thatta. The queen, however, countermanded this order, instructing her son-in-law instead to go to Lahore, where he must seize the treasury, and recruit another ten thousand soldiers by whatever means necessary. As the royal entourage made its slow way through the mountains, news arrived from the south that Prince Pervez was gravely ill. The doctors in the palace at Burhanpur had diagnosed severe epilepsy, brought on by too much drinking. The old family affliction, alcoholism, had reappeared. From Burhanpur, Khan-Jahan Lodi reported that, following protracted spells of unconsciousness, the doctors had ordered burning brands to be placed on the prince's forehead and temples. But there was also a more welcome arrival, also from the south. Shah Jahan's sons, Dara-Shikuh and Aurangzeb, reduced to the status of hostages by their father's ill-conceived rebellion, arrived at the camp with their gift of tribute: elephants, gems and jewelled utensils worth one million rupees. More money arrived to swell the royal treasury – more than two million rupees – when the Bengal treasury, with which Mahabat-

Khan hoped to transform his fortunes, was intercepted outside Delhi by a contingent led by the tireless veteran Anup Rai Singh-Dalan.

The mutiny ended as suddenly as it had begun and, ironically, at exactly the same Jhelum River campground, on 13 September 1626. This time it was Mahabat-Khan – his grip weakened by the death and imprisonment of so many of his followers – who injudiciously crossed the river first, allowing the emperor's loyal retainers to move in and protect the royal person. Mahabat-Khan, isolated on the wrong side of the water, was treated as if he were a lowly functionary, brushed off like a pestering fly. He was ordered to head south-west to the province of Thatta, to follow up on the latest reports of Shah Jahan's whereabouts. En route, he should locate Asaf-Khan and bring him to court to face Nur-Jahan's anger over his abrupt departure from the battlefield the previous March. And there was one last mission: to find two missing sons of the late Prince Daniyal – Tahmurath and Hoshang – and deliver them to Lahore.

So, by the end of October, the status quo ante had been restored. Securely lodged in Lahore Fort, the ailing Jahangir and his dominant wife presided over Akbar's ancient capital with renewed vigour. Shahriyar's position as heir apparent looked ever more secure, especially when Nur-Jahan secured the arrest and detention of Dawar-Bakhsh Bulaqi and news came from Burhanpur that Prince Pervez had died at the age of thirty-six.[49] Ordering no more than the most rudimentary obsequies for this loyal but undistinguished son, Jahangir commanded that the prince's body be transported to Agra and buried in his riverfront garden. Around the emperor were reassuringly familiar faces. The old retainer Abd-al-Rahim the Khan of Khans was there, his title reclaimed from Mahabat-Khan. Other senior officers, too, came forward to kiss the ground in loyalty to the true emperor. Asaf-Khan won some measure of rehabilitation with an appointment to the governorate of Punjab; based at Lahore, however, meant he was safely under the queen's watchful eye. It seemed that Jahangir could look forward to the 22nd year of his reign with a degree of optimism, even complacency.

While his father had been subjected to these traumas, Shah Jahan had himself been enduring a torrid time: prolonged illness, political uncertainty and arduous long-distance travel, all coming on top of the humiliation and despair brought on by seeing his life's ambitions reduced to ashes. News of Mahabat-Khan's mutiny now brought renewed hope and he resolved to head north. Apologists for the prince insist that he was 'outraged' by the coup attempt and was set on rescuing his father. It is far more likely, however, that he was, as one historian put it, 'trying to fish in troubled waters to his own advantage', although Shah Jahan had little reason to be optimistic that Mahabat-Khan, then in the ascendant, would merge his own mutiny with the prince's rebellion.[50] Equally, Shah Jahan had no love for Nur-Jahan. His own status as persona non grata within the empire had forced him to lie low in small, out-of-the-way settlements on the other side of the empire's southern border. At the time of the coup attempt, he was living with no more than one thousand armed retainers in the territory of his former enemy, the Nizam al-Mulk of Ahmadnagar, the westernmost of the Deccan kingdoms that he had once tried to hard to cow. Shah Jahan's base was Nasik, a small community south-east of Surat that remains hugely significance to the nation's Hindus.[51] From here, he set out on 18 June 1626 on his latest attempt to win the kingdom.

The journey got off to a bad start when Raja Kishan Singh, son of his trusted ally Raja Bhima and nephew of the Maharana of Mewar, died suddenly. Half of Shah Jahan's troops were Mewaris riding under Kishan Singh's banner and they promptly departed en masse to escort the raja's body home. His depleted army now effectively useless, the prince drifted northwards. He may have planned to head to Persia to seek help from Shah Abbas. Since his surrender to his father, Shah Jahan had maintained contact with the Persian ruler, hoping that, as Muhammad Hadi put it, 'by his affection and intercession the dust of strife and contention that had risen could be put down'.[52] More realistically, he may have hoped to secure the military support of the Maharaja of Jodhpur, his mother's kin. If so, he was to be disappointed; his plodding progress northward through the principalities of Rajasthan, retracing the route into exile taken by his great-grandfather Humayun in his darkest hour, produced no sensational recruitment. From Ajmer to Jodhpur he traipsed, then further west to Jaisalmer and the western fringes of the empire, finding all doors closed. No raja was willing to risk the anger of the Great Mughal by supporting this rag-tag band. And the rebel prince still had to face the grim expanse of the Thar Desert, 'a burning plain that caused horror as far as the eye could see … full of thorns and waterless.[53]

Surviving a horrendous six-day ordeal, Shah Jahan arrived at the provincial capital of Thatta in October to find the imperial fortress held against him by the governor, *Sharaf-al-Mulk*. Without the manpower to mount an effective siege of the citadel, the prince was forced to withdraw – but not before he had suffered a heart-stoppingly close call when Sharaf-al-Mulk ordered a deliberate salvo of artillery fire to be aimed at the royal camp, where Mumtaz-Mahal's own tent was shredded in the bombardment.[54] Nor, as now became grimly clear, could Shah Jahan expect any help from Persia. Successive messengers had brought back a succession of dusty answers. In response to his most recent appeal – 'I have, like my ancestors, turned for help to you and I hope you will give me proper advice at the proper time' – had come merely a bland assurance of goodwill and an earnest reiteration of the mildly scolding advice contained in the Shah's previous letters.[55] Shah Jahan had made a strenuous four-month, 850-mile journey for nothing.

All that remained was his ever-faithful family: Mumtaz-Mahal was of course still at his side; at Thatta she delivered another son, Prince Lutfallah.[56] Then, out of the blue, an imperial messenger found Shah Jahan's camp. Far from being a summons, it contained a rebuke and a warning from Nur-Jahan, whose spies had tracked his every move, mile by tortuous mile. The queen reminded him that his two beloved sons, Dara-Shikuh and Aurangzeb, were still in Mahabat-Khan's tender care. Any reckless advance by Shah Jahan, she suggested, might prompt a regrettably violent retaliation against the two lads. This blow extinguished any remaining hope. Heading south again four days after Lutfallah's birth and dragging both family and demoralised followers behind, Shah Jahan retreated. Stricken with illness, he travelled through Gujarat in a curtained palanquin, the kind of foppish luxury he usually despised. Like a beaten dog, tail between legs, he slinked back into the territory of the Nizam al-Mulk of Ahmadnagar, forced once again to accept his hospitality in the shape of a modest mansion at Junnar, some way south of his old haunts at Nasik.[57] On his way to this dismal exile, he passed just forty miles to the east of Surat, where every European trader had once been subject to his will. At the 'sudden rumour' of his approach, business ground to a halt while the portside business community held their breath. 'We could not proceed in any business in six or seven days following,' wrote the East India Company's senior factor, Thomas Kerridge, at the end of December, 'which time he spent in passing by, yet … proceeded in very peaceable manner unto his former rendezvous in Deccan; whereby it is generally conceived the King will pardon his former offence and receive him again into grace.'[58]

9

Killing the 'Tiger King'

In time of need, when no option remains,
The hand will grasp a sharp sword by the point.

Sheikh Muslih al-Din Sadi[1]

Sultan Khurram having now begun his way with blood, kept on the same course and never left until he had destroyed all others that might hinder his ambitions.

Peter Mundy[2]

'Tis obvious to every man of common sense that kingship knows no
    kinship
And no thinker can ever accept a partner for God or the monarch.

Haj Muhammad Jan 'Qudsi'[3]

Exiled at Junnar, deserted by past and potential allies and with his personal militia depleted to almost nothing, Shah Jahan's prospects were now seemingly non-existent. Military success, nationwide celebrity, wealth and acclaim – all seemed a world away, a lifetime ago. But the year 1627 was to prove a sudden and conclusive turning point. Far away in the northern mountains, the actions of one man, Abu-al-Hassan Asaf-Khan, wholly unprompted by Shah Jahan, would transform the prince's fate. On 11 March – nine days before the Nauruz festivities were due to mark the formal beginning of his twenty-second year on the throne – Jahangir ordered his courtiers to prepare once again to leave Lahore and make for 'the happy vale … the peerless perennial garden of Kashmir'.[4] The hot weather was proving even more trying than usual to the chronic asthmatic and the emperor's fragile constitution was suffering. It was to be his last holiday before making what the loyal officer Mutamid-Khan called the 'pilgrimage to the domain of non-existence'.[5]

During that long summer of 1627, Jahangir was in growing distress. Kashmir could ease the symptoms of his asthma but not even that tranquil paradise could provide the most powerful man in the land with a cure. The effects of a lifetime's dissipation were impossible to avoid. In the closing stages of his terminal decline, he fell into delirium, babbling incoherently and provoking acute anxiety among his courtiers. He was unable to keep food down, unable to swallow water and even developed an aversion to the opium that had been his constant companion for forty years. On the journey back to Lahore in late autumn, the imperial retinue passed into the low forested hills of western Kashmir and reached the palace fortress at Rajauri, one of many fine Mughal structures to grace the emperor's way into the mountains. It was here that the final crisis came – an attack of severe asthma – and it was here that Salim Jahangir, fourth of the Great Mughals of Hindustan, died on Sunday 7 November 1627. He was fifty-eight years old but sketches made in the months before his death show him gaunt and pale, a shadow of his former chubby, exuberant self. He had ruled over the multitudes of Hindustan and the mountains of the Hindu Kush for twenty-two years and five days. He had seen off rebellions by his two most capable sons and been shored up in the years of personal disintegration by the steely determination of one of the most ruthless queens in history. The year of his demise – 1037 by the Muslim calendar – was found in the simple epitaph: The World-Seizer left this world.[6]

Where Jahangir had failed, however, was in signalling an unambiguous succession. The intense and brutal power-struggle that followed was so swift in coming and so all-consuming that, amid the welter of conflicting ambitions, no one had time for the conventional etiquette of mourning. As when Akbar died, the political bonds of the old order were effectively destroyed; it was up to a new, emerging leadership to carve out new alliances and force, or buy, new allegiances. Only Jahangir's queen, the feared Nur-Jahan, was left to supervise as the body was washed, wrapped in a simple linen shroud and placed on the funeral bier. It was she and her fellow widows, as well as the other ladies of the household, who escorted the emperor's body down from the Himalayan foothills to one of the queen's favourite gardens, *Dilkusha*, about five miles from the citadel at Lahore. The funeral cortege arrived at the site (today known as Shahdara) on Friday 12 November and Jahangir was consigned to the earth.

Over the grave, Nur-Jahan ordered the construction of a large yet unostentatious tomb, a single-storey square edifice, of red sandstone with marble decorative motifs. At its four corners rose elegant towers, topped with white marble cupolas, while the vaulted compartments of the interior were a blaze of colour, embellished with bright floral frescoes and delicate pietra dura inlay work. On the white marble tomb itself was the inscription: Nur al-Din Muhammad Jahangir Padshah.[7] By the time of its completion – after ten years and the expenditure of more than a million rupees – it was truly a fitting tomb for an emperor. For the queen, the death of her husband was a crushing blow. She may not have been compelled to immolate herself, like some of her Rajput contemporaries; instead, she faced the threat of a long, slow extinction, years of oblivion, consigned to the stifling ennui and impotence that was the fate of lesser members of the harem.

'I am not the nightingale,' said Jahangir, 'to fill the air with my plaintive cries;
I am the moth that dies without uttering a single moan.'
'I am not the moth that dies an instantaneous death, replied Nur-Jahan;
'I suffer a lingering death like the candle that burns through the night without uttering a
single moan.' [8]

While Nur-Jahan grieved, her brother made his move. In seizing the initiative, Asaf-Khan's motives were clear. He had been humiliated by the entire episode of the Mahabat-Khan mutiny. He had been forced to give up any claim to their father Ghiyath al-Din Itimad-al-Daula's estate. Worse still, he had been entirely sidelined in the management of state affairs – despite his appointment by the late Jahangir shortly before the emperor's death as Governor of Punjab and as imperial Finance Minister, entrusted 'to control permanently all branches of administration, revenue and politics'.[9] So the inheritance crisis presented Asaf-Khan with a stark choice. Were Shahriyar to win the throne, as Nur-Jahan planned, the kingdom could expect many more years of her manipulations and machinations, more years of the expert and arrogant puppeteer behind the throne. The senior positions at court would go to a younger generation of sycophants and, at 55, Asaf-Khan would likely be surplus to requirements. But if Shah Jahan were to achieve an unexpected rehabilitation, Asaf-Khan's own daughter, Mumtaz-Mahal, would be queen and his own prospects immeasurably enhanced.

It was clear to Asaf-Khan that, in this moment of crisis, with Shah Jahan so far away, such a sudden reversal could only be achieved by his own prompt, ruthless and unilateral action. What would Shah Jahan not owe him in return for such a tremendous demonstration of loyalty? So Asaf-Khan struck, with courage and guile. It is no exaggeration to say that without him Shah Jahan would never have been emperor: he would have languished in impotent self-pity in his Deccan exile. The Mughal biographer Shahnawaz-Khan praised Asaf-Khan's tactics and sheer nerve, comparing him to the great viziers of the old days, who used boldness and deception in equal measures: 'Even Nizamul-Mulk, Yahya and Khalid Barmaki, each of whom has been a sign of perfection in ministership in the service of sultans of bygone ages, would be so to say a child in primary school as compared to him'.[10]

Asaf-Khan's plan required speed and great confidence, as well as political skill in reading and rearranging the political dispositions. At its heart was a gambit of breathtaking ruthlessness: a deception of unprecedented magnitude, for it would involve the deliberate murder of an emperor, a crime unprecedented in the Mughal era. His first move, on the very day of Jahangir's demise, was to send a messenger to Shah Jahan. For this extraordinary mission, to travel in secret the full length of the empire as fast as possible, he selected a Hindu accountant from Benares, usually responsible for running the Lahore Fort elephant stables: an insignificant figure that few would notice travelling the imperial highways, even in great haste. Banarsi's instructions were simple: to ride to Junnar, tell the prince that the Emperor is dead and advise him to proceed at once to Agra, the Seat of the Caliphate. It was too dangerous to carry a written letter; instead, Banarsi took with him a verbal message and Asaf-Khan's own signet ring as proof of its authenticity. Taking the first of a series of post-horses, Banarsi left at once by the southward road, out of the mountains and on through the imperial heartland to the Deccan 1,400 miles away.[11] Asaf-Khan was gambling that his plans would already be complete by the time Shah Jahan received the message and made his way to the capital.

Asaf-Khan's second move was to neutralise the threat posed by Nur-Jahan. Despatching a large force to intercept the funeral cortege – but not to stop it – he ordered that the queen's mobile quarters be immediately sealed off and kept under close guard. Access to Nur-Jahan herself was denied on pain of death. Letters appealing to her brother for a face-to-face meeting were ignored – although, significantly, Asaf-Khan did not stop her correspondence to others. This remorseless battle of wills between brother and sister was entertainingly described by Sir Thomas Herbert in a colourful account of his travels through the Indies. The treacherous Asaf-Khan is pitted against the wily queen, each offering assurances of fidelity while preparing the fatal blow. Nur-Jahan develops her own strata-gems against her brother, 'by which, while she bleared him with show of friendship, she might more easily kill him … on a sudden'. On discovering that she has been outmanoeuvred, 'she blamed her credulity and sorrowed that she had not strangled him'.[12]

The next and most crucial step for Asaf-Khan was to implement his stalling device. Declaring his desire simply to fulfil Jahangir's dying wish, that Dawar-Bakhsh Bulaqi be crowned his successor, Asaf-Khan now arranged a hasty but genuine coronation. With Nur-Jahan silenced, it was a straightforward matter to persuade the principal officers of the Mughal state to endorse the late emperor's nomination. The formal ceremony that placed Dawar-Bakhsh on the throne took place in an incongruous setting: a tiny farming settlement called Bhimar, high in the Himalayan foothills.[13] As the cream of the empire's nobility and military gathered in prayer, the khutba was read by the court's senior imam, stating unambiguously that the orphan prince had been elevated to the position of fifth Mughal Emperor

of Hindustan. The religious aspect properly concluded, the nobility filed forward to swear allegiance, 'accepting Bulaqi as the one who deserved the throne and paying their respects to him'.[14] The coronation was confirmed by a contemporary Persian historian, who noted that the court elite fell in with Asaf-Khan's scheme because it was 'in accordance with a testamentary disposition made by Jahangir at the time of his death'.[15] Still, the sixteen-year-old Dawar-Bakhsh must have found the speed of events difficult to comprehend. For all the oaths, for all the punctilious religious and secular formalities of the coronation, the young man may have felt that he was, in the words of Asaf-Khan's later biographer, 'nothing but a sheep for the feast'.[16]

Shahriyar, meanwhile, was in Lahore Fort, seeking urgent medical assistance. He had prematurely abandoned the Kashmir holiday because of some disfiguring and humiliating symptoms induced by venereal disease. The most visible side-effect of the ailment was acute alopecia, described by contemporaries as *da-al-salab*, 'fox-mange'. Prince Shahriyar had lost all his facial hair – beard, moustache, eye-brows and eye-lashes – and, some time before Jahangir's death, had dashed to Lahore for treatment, in the face of protests from Nur-Jahan, who was reluctant to see her candidate out of her sight. Now the one small flaw in Asaf-Khan's planning became clear. While physically containing Nur-Jahan and mollifying her personal influence at court, he allowed letters to escape. The queen was quick to exploit the error, writing to Shahriyar with strict orders to seize the provincial treasury in the heart of the citadel, with its hoard of more than seven million rupees. Then, scattering bribes like confetti and offering lavish salaries, Shahriyar set about recruiting an army. Bypassing any known or potential affiliates of Asaf-Khan, he was forced to conscript inexperienced

Silver rupee minted in the name of King Dawar-Bakhsh

officers for his senior command staff, placing at their head Prince Baisun-ghur, the third son of his late great-uncle Daniyal.[17]

Asaf-Khan, still en route to Lahore from the Kashmiri foothills, had failed to anticipate this rapid recruitment but he responded vigorously. The decisive battle between the two armies came on Saturday 19 November 1627, eight miles from the citadel walls. It was effectively the battle for Shah Jahan's succession. Given his lavish expenditure, Shahriyar must have been sorely disappointed at the dismal display put on by his fifteen thousand recruits. Asaf-Khan had fewer than ten thousand men marshalled in the field that day – but many of them had years of campaign experience and they were all physically much tougher, hardened by almost constant marching with the imperial entourage and led by veterans such as Mir Muhammad Baqr *Iradat-Khan* and Mutamid-Khan, who commanded the left and right flanks. Abu-al-Hassan Asaf-Khan himself rode a fine war-elephant in the vanguard. The young Emperor Dawar-Bakhsh was similarly mounted and behind him were Shah Jahan's sons, Dara-Shikuh and Aurangzeb, released from their confinement as court hostages. The encounter was less a battle than a severe thrashing. As his men scattered into the countryside, Shahriyar unwisely returned at the gallop to the fort, where he skulked in hiding in the women's quarters. Hot on his heels rode Iradat-Khan and Asaf-Khan's firstborn son, Mirza Abu-Talib *Shayista-Khan*. The luckless Shahriyar, bald and derided, was dragged out kicking and screaming, hands bound with his own cummerbund, by *Fairuz-Khan*, Jahangir's most trusted eunuch.[18] He was briskly blinded before being tossed back into a secure suite of rooms to await the fate of the loser.

Asaf-Khan's meticulous plans, laid 'with the wisdom of a fox and agility of an eagle', were nearly complete.[19] On Sunday 20 November, with the dead of the battle freshly interred, Dawar-Bakhsh Bulaqi was again formally enthroned, this time in the splendid surroundings of the ancient capital. Again, the khutba of kingship sounded across the battlements and mansions of the fortress plateau, confirming the fact of the coronation to the people of Lahore. In addition to the young man's full title – Abu-al-Muzaffar (Father of Victory) Dawar-Bakhsh Padshah – there was an additional, informal honorific accorded to the new ruler: *Shir-Shah*, the Tiger King.[20] But the reign of Dawar-Bakhsh would last just 72 days. The man who had placed him on the throne was already finalising details of his removal. Repairing to his private mansion south of the royal palace, Asaf-Khan summoned another messenger to carry a straightforward and unconcealed letter to Shah Jahan that reported the victory over Shahriyar and again summoned the prince to hasten to Agra.[21]

Asaf-Khan, Shah Jahan's father-in-law and king-maker

The news of Jahangir's death came to Junnar on 27 November with the arrival of Banarsi, the Hindu filkhana manager turned express rider. After leaving Kashmir twenty days earlier, the messenger had made incredible progress on a minimum of sleep, flogging a succession of post-horses through unfamiliar terrain, in search of a renegade prince whose location was not even known.[22] Those who received him at Shah Jahan's borrowed mansion were initially suspicious; perhaps this dusty traveller could be an assassin, sent by the queen to end the prince's hopes once and for all. But Asaf-Khan's signet ring settled all doubts. Banarsi was escorted straight from the road, without even washing, into the quarters of Mahabat-Khan, who, as an enemy of Shah Jahan's enemies Nur-Jahan and Asaf-Khan, had been welcomed into the prince's entourage with open arms. The news was swiftly relayed to Shah Jahan in his private apartments.

So soon as Sultan Khurram received those packets, he intends a speedy progress for the crown, which he gaped for, notwithstanding all his father's legacies. He first imparts his resolutions to his companion Mahabat-Khan ... to say truth, the best and most approved soldier through India, for many years a heavy and mortal enemy to Khurram and but lately reconciled unto him. By great persuasions and entreaties ... [Shah Jahan asks the general] to be his protector and with his army to safeguard him to the king's metropolis and royal seat Agra ... with this advantage, that in Mahabat-Khan's company (one much beloved and feared by the people) he might advance securely and without whom he could never have passed Ahmedabad, on the way to Agra, nor had hopes to enjoy the title of an Emperor, Khurram was so generally hated by the vulgar.[23]

Hated Shah Jahan may certainly have been – especially once Asaf-Khan's plans reached fruition and the fate of the rival claimants to the throne became widely known – but politics in the middle of a war of succession was a matter of pragmatism, not to say survival. The departure date from Junnar, Thursday 1 December, was chosen by the astrologers; there would be no time to indulge in more than the most basic ceremonies of mourning.[24] Before he left, he despatched two trusted servants with a coded message, acknowledging and returning Asaf-Khan's signet ring and conveying Shah Jahan's own message that he was on his way.[25] One contemporary Persian historian noted that allies were not slow in arriving.

The princes of the Deccan lent generous support and from all sides troops flocked to his side – Chagatays, Mongols, Afghans and Rajputs. Sultan Bulaqi's fortunes began correspondingly to decline and his principal officers of state and the wisest heads among his military leaders saw no future for a grandson now that an ambitious natural son of the late Emperor was in the contest for the throne. Their loyalty to Sultan Bulaqi wavered and they began to leave Lahore and go to Agra to join Shah Jahan, striving to outdo one another in the race to pledge their fealty and services. By the time Shah Jahan neared Agra, most of Sultan Bulaqi's nobles and troops had joined him.[26]

Making a steady but unhurried advance on the capital, Shah Jahan now began to act as emperor in all but name. Even before leaving Junnar, he had thought to secure loyalties among the Mughal southern command by writing a generous letter to Jahangir's Governor of the Deccan, Khan-Jahan Lodi, inviting him to stay in his post under the new emperor.[27] En route to the north, he began to issue imperial edicts and made further brisk rearrangements to the administration of provincial capitals as he passed through. One such *firman* ordered tax inspectors and collectors of the Islamic *zakat* tax not to harass Dutch traders based at Surat, who had recently requested preferential trading status.[28] At Ahmedabad, he ordered the minting of new coins, even though the only mould available at such short notice bore – irony of ironies – bore the name of his own father during his years of rebellion at Allahabad: Shah Salim.[29] At both Ahmedabad and Thatta, the incumbent governors were sacked and imprisoned, though the first of these dismissals involved some tricky family business. Mirza Safi *Seif-Khan*, 'Sword Master' and Governor of Gujarat, was married to Mumtaz-Mahal's sister Malika Banu but had remained loyal to Jahangir throughout Shah Jahan's failed rebellion. Indeed, it was his active involvement in the defeat of the rebel forces in 1623 that prompted Jahangir to award him his honorific and the governorship of Shah Jahan's old stamping-ground. In sacking this relative, however, Shah Jahan reckoned without forceful intervention from the harem. It did not take long for Mumtaz-Mahal, who was extremely fond of her sister, to argue for Seif Khan to be brought to court, pardoned and released.[30]

It was at Ahmedabad on 19 December that the new governor, Nahir Khan Tonwar *Shir-Khan*, relayed the news of Asaf-Khan's decisive victory at Lahore a month earlier.[31] Now confident of overcoming the remaining obstacles between himself and the throne, Shah Jahan ordered the court drummers to beat out a tattoo of victory and celebration. It was amid this mood of heady anticipation and barely restrained triumphalism that a party of English traders, venturing to approach the prince with a gift of two fine horses and two bales of scarlet silk and cloth of gold, saw the strength of his army: 'the choice horsemen whereof, being about 5,000, were divided into two squadrons, half a mile distant from each other, and himself with Mahabat-Khan, that time on horseback, with a troop of his principal servants in the middle twixt both'.[32]

There were two more crucial stops to be made during what was rapidly becoming a triumphal progress towards Agra. The first, on 11 January 1628, was in the Rajput kingdom of Mewar, for so long Shah Jahan's most dependable ally. Maharana Karna Singh rode from Udaipur to pay homage at Gokunda, north-west of the Mewari capital, just as his father, Amar Singh, had done after Prince Khurram's first victory a dozen years earlier. This time, however, the ceremony was one between partners and friends, not victor and vanquished. There were no humiliating rituals of submission beyond the customary obeisances of the vassal prince and any residual discomfort was assuaged by the generous presents lavished by Shah Jahan upon his friend, including a chest-ornament featuring a ruby worth forty-thousand rupees.[33]

After Mewar, Shah Jahan's entourage retraced the route taken during that 1615 campaign to the old expeditionary headquarters at Ajmer. The prince arrived at the Chishti shrine at Ajmer on 23 January, performing the final stage of the journey, as his father and grandfather had done before him, on foot. Remembering the pledge, made in the aftermath of the Mewar victory, to build a fine mosque to honour the authority of the ancient Sufi mystic, Shah Jahan allocated a generous budget, authorised initial architectural plans to be drawn up and construction initiated. The result, completed nine years later, would be one of the finest mosques in the entire empire, a small but exquisite white marble jewel, beside which Akbar's towering structure nearby loomed, chunky and devoid of taste.[34] Resting for a few days at his old lakeside headquarters – always preferred to the stifling solidity of Akbar's old fort – the prince allocated the revenue of the Ajmer fiefdom to Mahabat-Khan, de facto commander-in-chief, in gratitude for his muscular support.

With Shah Jahan now drawing nearer to Agra, the timing of the final moves in this complex game of political chess became ever more precise. Asaf-Khan had been following Shah Jahan's daily advance with care but it was not until he received the prince's final, deadly instructions that he sprang his trap. The letter ordering Asaf-Khan to kill the emperor was carried north by a third envoy, who departed on 2 January as his master was preparing to decamp from Ahmedabad for Mewar. But this was no ordinary messenger; it was a killer with a mission: Reza Ghulam Bahadur, the same executioner who had strangled Dawar-Bakhsh's father, Prince Khusraw, six year earlier, still on hand to finish off the son. 'Due to the exigencies of the affairs of state,' wrote Shah Jahan's court official biographer, Inayat-Khan, 'Reza Bahadur was sent off to eliminate the princes imprisoned in Lahore; and His Majesty despatched an edict to this effect in his own handwriting, along with a special jewelled sword and dagger for Yamin-al-Daula [Asaf-Khan].'[35] The death sentence was worded more poetically by Shahnawaz-Khan, though it bore the same finality: 'It would be well at this time, when the heavens were troubled and the earth was seditious, if Dawar-Bakhsh and the other princes were made wanderers in the plains of non-existence'.[36]

Reza Bahadur took twenty-seven days to reach Lahore – three and a half weeks in which Dawar-Bakhsh Bulaqi continued to be deluded as to his status. He was allowed to send out imperial edicts, headed as always with the royal seal bearing his full title. Raja Jai Singh – grandson of the old retainer Raja Man Singh – received such a letter in the name of Shir-Shah, the Tiger King.[37] Asaf-Khan's decoy even extended to the striking of new coins at the Lahore mint, bearing Dawar-Bakhsh's titles, the Islamic date 1037 and, on the reverse, the Muslim declaration of faith in the one God and his Prophet.[38] But the messenger's arrival signalled an end to this charade of kingship – and Asaf-Khan followed his new orders with alacrity. The first order of business was the declaration of a new emperor. On Saturday 29 January 1628, the khutba prayer sounded again over Lahore Fort, echoing out over the crowded city below exactly as it had ten weeks earlier. The difference was the deletion of the name of Dawar-Bakhsh and its substitution with the name of Khurram Shah Jahan.[39] The ousted young emperor was imprisoned; he had only two days to await his fate. For both Shah Jahan and Asaf-Khan, it was a time to settle scores definitively, to remove once and for all any obstacles in the path to the throne.

In the small hours of 2 February 1628, Dawar-Bakhsh was beheaded.[40] But he was not alone: the executioner Reza Bahadur also slaughtered Prince Shahriyar (making Shah Jahan the regicide a fratricide twice over), as well as Dawar-Bakhsh's brother Garshasp and two of Prince Daniyal's sons, Tahmurath and Hoshang.[41] Sir Thomas Herbert, feeling that the full sordid details of the murder were 'pertinent to rehearsal', reported how the five princes were butchered in a bathing suite to which Asaf-Khan, 'banishing all pity and loyalty from his heart, fleshed in former murders', had the only key. Reza Bahadur, Sir Thomas continued, 'straightaway cut all their throats and carried their heads as a trophy and sure testimony of his villainy unto Agra, where Khurram expected them'.[42] Another account attributes commendable calmness to the emperor as he is surprised by Reza Bahadur while playing chess with his brother. Punning on the meanings of similar-sounding Persian words, Dawar-Bakhsh observed dryly to Garshasp: 'Virtue (reza) has not come; it is your and our fate (qaza) that has arrived'.[43]

Word of the murders travelled fast. Gregory Clement, an English trader at Agra, reported this 'lamentable massacre' to his superiors, noting anxiously, 'what success may ensue this unnatural proceedings we leave to the divine disposures'.[44] But as they had done with the murder of Khusraw earlier, Shah Jahan's apologists glossed the brutal nature of the prince's regicide with the language of political necessity. The court poet Haj Muhammad Jan 'Qudsi' was, of course, quite aware that the reign of Shah Jahan began with the cloud of multiple murder hanging over it. In his long verse biography, the *Zafarnama*, therefore, he sought to distance the new emperor from the moral stain of the Lahore killings by deploying a variety of colourful images that strove to paint the event as a natural purging of undesirable elements.

He who knows virtue and vice, knows that intriguers ruin the country.
By distrust, the country is ruined; 'tis best to pluck the sapling of mischief by the roots.
The heads of political intriguers should be under the earth and the body-politic cleansed of all impurities. ...
Will the tree of desire yield good fruit if it is not pruned of its superfluous boughs?
With a double-edged sword 'tis best to strike off that head which is the source of dynastic strife.
Today the eaglet emerges from the egg and tomorrow it begins to prey. ...
If you admit that the King is the 'Shadow of God' on Earth, it follows that the One God cannot cast two shadows.
The King's mind was relieved of anxiety when the thicket was purged of its tiger-cubs.[45]

The very day of the Lahore murders, Shah Jahan's imperial cavalcade pitched camp at last on the outskirts of Agra at Jahangir's favourite garden at Dehrabagh, known to the late emperor as the *Nur-Manzil*, the 'House of Light'. The prince had travelled for exactly two months in stately fashion: fifty-five days had been spent on the road, with a one-week stop at Ahmedabad. And so, on 2 February 1628, Shah Jahan re-entered the city he had not seen for more than eight years.[46] On the 'auspicious Saturday', the fourteenth of Aquarius, he mounted his finest elephant, its howdah wrought of silver and gold, decorated with awnings of Chinese brocade and silk curtains in colourful flowery designs. His nobles picked their most magnificent Persian and Arab horses and had them accoutred with chased and ornamented saddles. On both sides of the procession marched Shah Jahan's senior generals and their loyal officers, bearing jewelled waist-daggers and maces plated with gold and silver.[47] As the emperor-to-be passed through the streets and bazaars of the capital, scattering gold and silver coins like monsoon rain, the people shouted out blessings – for the health of the emperor, for the prosperity of the nation and for the eternity of the empire. But the propitious moment for the prince to enter his citadel was not yet at hand. According to the precise calculations of the Greek and Indian astrologers, he had to wait another tantalising twelve days. And so, with the crowd still dinning in his ears, Shah Jahan repaired to the mansion that he had built during his princehood on the bank of the Yamuna, to finalise every detail of his coronation.

The day finally dawned on Monday 14 February 1628.[48] Prince Khurram, honoured for his exploits in war as first Shah Khurram then Shah Jahan, entered the royal fortress by the southern gate and passed in procession into the Exclusive Audience Hall.[49] Ascending to the royal balcony, he took the position that he felt so long had been denied him, settling with legs crossed on the comfortably padded low square stone throne. From the pulpit came the khutba sermon, confirming the announcement that had taken the people of Lahore by surprise two weeks earlier. The order went out that a new seal of state was to be placed on all imperial edicts, while new coins were to be struck in the name of the new emperor. On the reverse side of a particularly huge gold coin was a verse:

Since this coin was made in the name of the King
The value of the moon was reduced in the eyes of the star.[50]

The boy born Khurram the Joyous thirty-six years and one month earlier was now acclaimed sixth Mughal Emperor of Hindustan: Abu-al-Muzaffar *Shihab al-Din* (Star of the Faith) Muhammad *Sahib al-Qiran al-Thani* (Second Lord of the Happy Conjunction of Jupiter and Venus) Shah Jahan Padshah Ghazi. Still more epithets picked out the new emperor's secular and religious duties: Shah Jahan was not just *Khalifat Panahi*, Refuge of the Caliphate, but *Zill'Allahi*, the 'Shadow of God' on earth. Court poets and historians, including Mutamid-Khan, outdid themselves ins producing a torrent of praise.

He is the shooting star of the region and the empire-adorner of the nation.
He is emperor of high fortune, son of the sky of glory and magnitude
O king! You are the blessing of God, brightening the eye of the kingship.
O king! You are the eternal giver of bounty and the fruit of benevolence.
One hundred gardens blossom on your bright forehead;
Hundreds of victories and defeats are contained in your sleeve.
You give new glory to the crown and the empire![51]

Inayat-Khan was also effusive: Shah Jahan was 'that king of auspicious canopy who possesses the dignity of Jamshid, the magnificence of Solomon, the splendour of Faridun and the grandeur of Alexander, an unparalleled emperor of ocean-like bounty who is gifted with angelic nature and disposition'. He was 'that light of the eye of manliness and men who is to be praised with the words of the noble Koranic verse as one of "those who hold authority amongst you"'. He was 'that follower of the splendid laws of Islam and propagator of the illustrious creed of the Prophet … that distinguished eagle of auspiciousness … that proverb and manual of instruction for eliminating the infidels and patronising the poor'. In conclusion, wrote Inayat-Khan, 'may God perpetuate his kingdom for ever!' [52] There were also pithy chronograms to be composed to highlight the year of this auspicious event, among them Hakim Rukna Kashi's 'Remain in this world as long as the world endures'.[53]

The immediate aftermath of the coronation was an occasion for political consolidation and rewards for loyalty. Asaf-Khan, the man who had made all this possible, was still on his way south from Lahore; but promotion was granted, to the rank of Eight Thousand foot and Eight Thousand horse, and conveyed in a letter which Shah Jahan addressed to his 'Uncle Yamin-al-Daula'. Mahabat-Khan, whose army had protected Shah Jahan on the long march from the southern imperial frontier, was confirmed as Commander-in-Chief of the Mughal army and reinstated as the Khan of Khans. Official accounts list carefully the nobles and officers who lined up to pay tribute to their new monarch. The roll of honour lists veterans of the Jahangir administration, including the wily old diplomat Khan-Alam, Abu-al-Hassan Mashhadi *Lashkar-Khan* (the 'Army Master'), Raja Jai Singh and the indefatigable huntsman Anup Rai the Lion-Killer. Among the neophytes who rode Shah Jahan's coattails into the heart of the new order, many of whom had stuck with the renegade prince during the wilderness years, were Dilawar-Khan, Sayyid Muzaffar Khan Barha, Wazir-Khan and – most conspicuously – the executioner Reza Bahadur, now honoured with the title *Khidmatparast-Khan*, the 'Noble who Renders Service as if it were Worship'.

The coronation of Shah Jahan meant that his favourite wife, Mumtaz-Mahal, became First Queen of the Empire, a stature conveyed in her new title, *Nawab Mahd Aliya*. Substantial cash grants were handed out to her and the other ladies of the royal harem. Her Majesty Mumtaz-Mahal benefited to the tune of six hundred thousand silver rupees and two hundred thousand gold ashrafis. Her annual maintenance was set at one million rupees. Princess Jahan-Ara, now an eligible maiden of fourteen, was awarded a yearly maintenance grant of six hundred thousand rupees and a massive cash bonus, one hundred thousand ashrafis and four hundred thousand rupees, up front.[54]

The event that rounded off the coronation celebrations and confirmed

Shah Jahan's absolute status as head of the ruling dynasty was the reunification of his family the following month. On Tuesday 7 March, an excited procession drew near the outskirts of Agra and pitched camp near the tomb of Emperor Akbar at Bihishtabad. It was the last stop for the three eldest princes of the line – Dara-Shikuh, Shah-Shuja and Aurangzeb – on their long march from Lahore, which they had made under escort by Asaf-Khan and his full household. With the permission of the new emperor, an equally excitable group cantered out from the main gateway of Agra Fort and hastened north to greet the princes. At its centre was the queen herself, surrounded by her remaining children, unable to wait for the astrologers to determine the precise moment when the royal sons should be permitted to re-enter their capital. For Mumtaz-Mahal, of course, it was also a chance to see her beloved parents again, the first time in many a long year. As for her sons, she had bade them farewell at the lowest ebb of her husband's career, thousands of miles away, when it had been far from certain that she would see the three hostages again. 'In the workshop of rhetoric,' wrote Abd-al-Hamid Lahori, lump in throat, 'there is no expression that can convey such joy'.[55]

The following morning, Asaf-Khan and the princes moved in somewhat more restrained procession through the streets to the citadel. Around them rode the *crème de la crème* of the court nobility, who maintained their honour guard as the entire procession advanced into the ancient fortress before dismounting and entering the Ordinary Audience Hall, where the official greeting ceremony was to take place. The event was immortalised in paint by the great artist Bichitr, whose crowded and almost hectically colourful masterpiece states unequivocally both the continuity of the Mughal line and the loyal adoration of the nobility. The emperor is shown enveloping his eldest son, Dara-Shikuh, in a warm embrace, just as he had, in his hour of glory after the Mewar and Deccan campaigns, been embraced by his father Jahangir and Jahangir had before that by Akbar the Great. The royal balcony itself is resplendent with carved marble screens and rear wall painted in gorgeous floral motifs. There are just five figures accorded the ultimate privilege of sharing the imperial balcony: the three princes just in from Lahore, their younger brother, the four-year-old Murad-Bakhsh and – an avuncular hand on the shoulders of Shah-Shuja and Aurangzeb – the Master of Terror himself, Zamana Beg Mahabat-Khan, Shah Jahan's most senior general and another link to the old days. Below the balcony, its stone balustrade draped in a finely worked Persian carpet, stands a 'Who's Who' of the Mughal aristocracy. The artist worked painstakingly to realise the features of each in recognisable detail, allowing the discerning contemporary critic to pick out the real elite, clustered inside the inner rail of the courtyard – among them the Lord Chamberlain and learned Shiite mullah, Shukrullah Shirazi *Afzal-Khan*, the 'Superior Master', and the man in charge of military logistics, Mir Abd-al-Salam Islam-Khan.[56] Among the new arrivals from Lahore were depicted more veterans of Shah Jahan's cause, including Mutamid-Khan, Shahnawaz-Khan and Asaf-Khan's eldest son, Shayista-Khan. But, according to the contemporary account of Abd-al-Hamid Lahori, it was Asaf-Khan himself who received special treatment from the new monarch.

At the Emperor's signal, he went to the jharoka, which is a stairway as lofty as heaven, and placed his head in servitude at the imperial foot. The appreciative Emperor, who nurtured and cherished his servants, raised with his own hands the head of this leader of his sincere servants and embraced him in favour. Through this regal act of compassion Asaf-Khan's head was elevated to the skies. ... During that very assembly the Emperor gave him a robe of honour with a jewel-studded collar ... and a jewel-studded sword with a bejewelled scabbard ... which His Majesty Arshashyani [Akbar] had given to His Majesty Jannat-makani [Jahangir] and which Jahangir had given to the Solomonic emperor [Shah Jahan] for the conquest of the Deccan.[57]

So the king-maker received his due reward from the man he had, almost single-handedly, put on the throne. He was now Wakil, Chief Minister to the emperor, the second man in the land. With the rank went riches: a gift of one thousand gold mohurs – the same granted to the heir apparent, Dara-Shikuh, and considerably greater than those of the lesser princes – and another promotion to the rank of Nine Thousand foot and Nine Thousand horse: an unprecedented honour for one born outside the ruling family.

10

Emperor Shah Jahan and Queen Mumtaz

Greed, they say, is the root of all sin,
The source of disease and indigestion,
Even of life and death;
But it is love, alas, love
Which is the source of all our sorrows.

Banarasi Biholia[1]

When Mumtaz-Mahal left this world,
Fairies opened before her the Door of Paradise.
And angels composed the chronogram:
May Paradise be the abode of Mumtaz-Mahal!

Saida al-Gilani[2]

So began the thirty-year reign of Khurram Shah Jahan, during which the Mughal empire experienced a period of unprecedented prosperity and internal stability. Despite the enormous expense of protracted campaigns on the empire's northern and southern fringes, the new emperor presided over the most remarkable phase of architectural development seen since the Timurids fought their way over the mountains and into Hindustan. This profusion of sublime structures and extensions in white marble and elegant *pietra dura*, cut and carved with the finesse of the sub-continent's finest artisans, was approved – budget and design – at the very desk of the emperor himself. It was also a time for sweeping away the dead wood of the previous era. The succession of Shah Jahan provided the empire with its most profound administrative shake-up in decades. Unlike the transfer of power from Akbar to Jahangir, in which old retainers rubbed shoulders with the arrivistes of Salim's princely retinue, the political elite in Agra was now effectively recreated almost from nothing. After so many years in rebellion, Shah Jahan owed little to his father's loyalists and set about removing them from positions of responsibility, replacing them with his own tested companions.[3]

Following the new appointments in Gujarat and Thatta, made during Shah Jahan's march north to Agra, the remaining provinces of the empire were subjected to a root-and-branch administrative shake-up, in which the key posts of state were reallocated to a new generation, creating an establishment that was not just reinvigorated but indisputably loyal. It was a remarkably bloodless transition, too, in which even old enemies were forgiven. The new governor of Kabul, for example, was Abu-al-Hassan Lashkar-Khan, a veteran officer who had served in various parts of the empire since the turn of the century.[4] But Lashkar-Khan had been part of the Mahabat-Khan/Pervez expeditionary force that pursued the renegade prince Shah Jahan through the south. The relationship between emperor and governor was further complicated by the fact that Prince Shah Jahan had looted 900-thousand rupees from Lashkar-Khan's Agra home during his raid on the city in February 1623 (though the event was subsequently sanitised to infer that the money had been a donation).[5] One conspicuous exception to this generally conciliatory situation was Sharaf al-Mulk, the sacked governor of Thatta who had ordered his artillery to fire on the tent of Mumtaz-Mahal during the abortive siege of the city's fortress in October 1626: he was summarily executed.[6]

This reshaping of central and provincial government was matched by the character of the new Shah Jahan regime in general, a character that was strikingly and deliberately different from what had gone before. It was no less autocratic but it was more family-oriented and given to trusting few but the most proven confidants. Above all, Shah Jahan set new standards for religious conservatism in government. This ideological shift made for conspicuous alterations in the balance of religious authority at court, leading to a much more orthodox Islamic regime than Jahangir had presided over and certainly far from Akbar's universal tolerance. Confident of his ability to woo and retain the loyalty of India's Hindu sub-rulers and keen to establish a fresh new identity for the Mughal state, the new emperor abandoned the decades-old public image of inclusivity and instead grounded his authority and credentials firmly in his own faith. The new Shah Jahan coinage featured an unambiguous statement of the emperor's Islamic credentials. The name of Allah was stamped in the middle, arrayed around it the names of the four 'rightly-guided caliphs' who followed in the Prophet Muhammad's footsteps.[7] On the other side was the simple declaration of faith in the one God and his Prophet.

There were other symptoms of the prevailing orthodoxy. The new trend towards Islamism was visible in the re-branding of the Mughal military by royalty-sanctioned imperial historians like Inayat-Khan as 'the Army of God' and its campaign against Portuguese settlers on the Bengal coast, for example, as a 'crusade against the infidels'.[8] In September 1633, the Prophet Muhammad's birthday was marked with a pious celebration in the brand new forty-pillared *Chihil-Sutun* vestibule in front of the royal balcony. The guests of honour were not ambassadors, soldiers or aristo-crats but grey-bearded clerics, scholars and reciters of the Koran. Later still, in his tenth year on the throne, the old Zodiacal calendar, which had underpinned royal documentation since the birth of the Timurid dynasty, was abandoned once and for all; Shah Jahan's personal history was retro-spectively redrafted according to the Muslim calendar. And, in addition to the new coins of the realm, massive gold medallions would be minted to emphasise the emperor's credentials as Defender of the Faith.

There were complementary changes, too, in court protocol. Shah Jahan's very first edict as emperor was to ban the full-length prostration – a hangover from the Akbar era – decreeing that such an abject gesture should be reserved for God alone.[9] More appropriate, he ruled, was the taslim salute, in which the supplicant approached the emperor, touched the ground with the back of his right hand, then rose to bring his right palm up to the crown of his head. Religious figures, however, were exempted from even this courtesy and allowed to greet the emperor with the conven-tional al-salamu aleikum, 'Peace be with you', and depart with the recita-tion of the opening verse of the Koran: bismillah al-rahman al-rahim, 'In the name of God, the compassionate, the merciful'. In addition, Muslim holidays were accorded much greater pre-eminence, becoming occasions on which charitable donations in stipulated amounts were mandatory. On the Leilat al-Miraj, the night of the Prophet Muhammad's ascent to heaven, for example, two thousand rupees was judged appropriate. On the Ashura festival, sacred to the empire's Shiites, the date – 10 Muharram – was matched by the donation: ten thousand rupees.[10] The same principle made the anniversary the Prophet's birth the most expensive: 12,000 was the compulsory donation on 12 Rabi I. The leading figures of the orthodox Sunni faith, too, were given a much more central role under Shah Jahan. A typically detailed portrait shows the emperor holding a late-night audience for the ulama at the royal durbar hall. By bringing these elderly Islamic scholars inside the golden railing, a carpeted and canopied enclave that demarcated the heart of the Mughal state, Shah Jahan was demonstrating clearly to the aristocracy lined up dutifully below the balcony that this was the way forward.

This general prominence of Islamism, however, was breached in several ways, some more politically significant than others. The most important diversions from the trend to greater orthodoxy concerned the emperor's eldest son, Dara-Shikuh. Contrary to the new trend of laying down Islamic precepts for the edification of his Hindu subjects, Shah Jahan sought to borrow from the Rajputs one practice that might immeasurably improve the security of the state: the law of primogeniture. Making the eldest son the automatic heir apparent would reshape the Timurid dynasty

on less arbitrary and violent lines. The old Central Asian ways of leaving the succession as an open contest – allowing sons, nephews, brothers and uncles equal opportunity to recruit personal retinues sufficient to mount a physical challenge against all other contenders until only one was left alive – were dangerously unpredictable. His own rebellion, he vowed, would be the last. Dara-Shikuh, now just thirteen, would be groomed for greatness; he would also be allowed considerable latitude in his exploration of spiritual thinking.

The summer of 1628 was Shah Jahan's first opportunity in many years to be together with his family in an atmosphere of security and continuity. His children's education had, of necessity, been fractured. But Dara-Shikuh had maintained some continuity under the guidance of the Shiite cleric Mullah Abd-al-Latif Sultanpuri, in whose appointment Queen Mumtaz-Mahal had doubtless had the final say. Despite his tutor's sectarian affiliation, the young prince had shown a distinct leaning towards Sufism and had already studied its philosophy extensively. He would write in later years that the Sufi path was a matter less of choice than divine inspiration.

In the prime of my youth, an unknown voice addressing me four times said, 'God would give you such a gift which has not been bestowed upon any emperor of the world'. In course of time, the fore-shadowing of it began to manifest and day by day the veil was lifted little by little.[11]

That enthusiasm for mysticism echoed Shah Jahan's own lifelong (and hereditary) devotion to the great Sufi saint of Ajmer, Sheikh Muin al-Din Chishti. Like his father, he enjoyed arguing over the existential mysteries with intelligent and articulate debaters, be they Hindu sannyasis or living Sufi saints. Astrologers, too, were always consulted on all key decisions of state and family, with the emperor determined that Hindu and Greek experts should reach unanimity in their analysis of planetary guidance. The biennial lunar and solar Tuladan weighing ceremonies – borrowed long ago by Akbar from the Hindus – also remained a central part of court celebrations of royal birthdays. Shah Jahan, however, adapted the ritual to make it more acceptable to conservative Muslim sensibilities, making sure to include the ulama among the recipients of the proceeds and changing the materials against which he was weighed to substances more useful in the daily life of the poorer citizens who gained from the auspicious event.[12]

It was certainly not easy to ditch or proscribe the non-Islamic ceremonials that had become part of the fabric of the Mughal court. The Nauruz Festival, beginning the zodiacal month of Aries, had become an integral part of the 'court and social' calendar, effectively sanctified by habit. The

Shah Jahan honours Muslim dignitaries at court

first Nauruz of Shah Jahan's reign – just five weeks days after the coronation – was not an occasion for stinting. The emperor, knowing that he had
the vast wealth of an empire to play with, was even more flamboyantly
generous to his nearest and dearest than he had been at his crowning.
Contemporary accounts indicate an expenditure of nearly eighteen million
rupees between the coronation and the end of Nauruz, the bulk of it
lavished on Mumtaz-Mahal and her children.[13] At the centre of each event
– social, administrative and especially religious – was the new emperor,
presiding from his throne amid the silken drapery of a high holiday.

**The 'mass of clouds' canopy was erected in the courtyard of the Exclusive Audience Hall.
Underneath it stood majestic pavilions, the trellis work of which was of pure silver instead
of wood. These were draped in brocaded and gold-embroidered velvet. At intervals stood
small canopies set with gems and trimmed with strings of pearls; and in as many places
were deposited jewelled thrones and seats of gold. Carpets of many colours and figurative
patterns covered the floor, while the walls and doorways of the great quadrangle were
hung with brocaded velvets, European tapestries, Turkish and Chinese cloths of gold and
Gujarati and Persian brocades.[14]**

Shah Jahan knew that it was essential for the new royal family to play
a prominent role in the ceremonies, not least to emphasise the demise of
the old order of Nur-Jahan. The ousted queen, demoralised but still too
clever and dangerous to be left to her own devices at Lahore, had been
brought by her brother south to Agra – where she was not part of the
triumphal reception – and incarcerated. The foreign traders in Agra noted
that she lived 'privately in the castle', while all the coins issued in her
name were gathered up and removed from circulation, 'called in and not
to be uttered'.[15] Her days as a political force were numbered; dressing only
in the white of mourning, she retired on a modest allowance.[16]

Mumtaz-Mahal, meanwhile, was given powers equivalent to those that
her aunt had enjoyed and far greater personal resources. She may not have
had the personal ambition or degree of control over her husband that
Nur-Jahan had enjoyed for so long but Shah Jahan was perfectly content
for her to play an important part in decision-making. Indeed, her role grew
rapidly, until foreign ambassadors were heard to observe with disdain
that public business 'slept until it was referred to her', while the emperor
himself was 'governed and wound up at her pleasure'. She was appointed
as keeper of the royal seal, in exactly the way that Jahangir's chief queen
had been. In an unprecedented division of Muslim sovereignty, coins were
even struck in the name of the queen and, in an echo of the administrative influence of Nur-Jahan and Queen Guljar Maryam-Zamani before her,
Mumtaz-Mahal now began issuing royal edicts in her own name. These

orders were written under a circular seal, containing an elegant Persian couplet: 'By the grace of God, Mumtaz-Mahal became the companion in the world of Shah Jahan, the Shadow of God'. A typical edict from 17 October 1629, eighteen months after she became empress, contained strict instructions to provincial officials in Khandesh, far to the south, on how best to administer district lands recently reverted to Shah Jahan's administrative control. The document is a perfect illustration of how the imperial secretariat, part of which devolved to the office of the empress, micro-managed even the most parochial bureaucracy of empire.

It should be the endeavour of the above-mentioned Kanuji to adhere to the prescribed rules and regulations of His Majesty the Emperor: to treat the peasants and residents of that place in such a way that they feel satisfied and grateful to him and the population and cultivation of the district increase day by day and practise sincerity, honesty and devotion. He should try in such a way that not a single rupee of the Government in this regard is lost or wasted.[17]

Around Mumtaz-Mahal in the harem were placed a new generation of ladies, influential with or because of their husbands and independently wealthy. Huri Khanam Begum – wet-nurse to both Jahan-Ara and Aurangzeb – and the distinguished tutor, Sati al-Nisa Khanam, became central members of the royal household.[18] And at the heart of the harem was the royal family, subject, like the most ordinary family of the empire, to the triumphs and tragedies of life and death. On 9 May 1628, Queen Arjumand Mumtaz-Mahal gave birth to her twelfth child in sixteen years of marriage: a son, Daulat-Afza. But celebrations were muted: just days earlier, the seven-year-old Princess Thurayya had succumbed to smallpox – and five days after Daulat-Afza's arrival, his infant brother Lutfallah also 'departed to the asylum of the world beyond'.[19]

Determined as he was to enjoy family life and focus his attention on a vigorous programme of construction in all the key imperial cities, Shah Jahan was distracted by a succession of violent conflicts, against foreign and internal adversaries. The first outbreak came at the northern extreme of the empire, beyond the imperial provinces of Kabul and Kashmir. Regional tensions stemmed from a complicated triangular relationship between the Mughals, the Persian Empire – with which it had clashed over the ownership of Kandahar – and the rulers of *Turan*, an independent and very warlike Uzbek territory spread over the regions of Transoxiana, Balkh and Badakhshan.[20] Even Akbar the Great had been careful not to antagonise the

Uzbek clans on the other side of the Hindu Kush mountain range, the de facto border. Writing in June 1596 from Kabul, he had stressed that 'both parties should strive to strengthen the foundations of peace and concord', observing that, in the spirit of maintaining neighbourly relations, he had not only declined the request of a Mughal aristocrat for land in the border area but also turned down an appeal from the Shah of Persia himself for a joint expedition against the Uzbeks.[21]

Six years before Shah Jahan's coronation, the Persian occupation of Kandahar in June 1622 had triggered intensive diplomatic activity between the three rival powers. The Uzbek ruler, Imam Quli Khan, had wider territorial ambitions – specifically aspiring to regain the region of Khurasan, which Shah Abbas of Persia had occupied in 1598. In 1622, Imam Quli Khan had written to Jahangir to urge a joint assault on the Persian positions: 'If Prince Shah Jahan were to march north from the Deccan', he wrote, 'we also will hurry there … and shall fulfil the conditions of loyalty. After the victory, let us take Khurasan and whatever you wish of that country may be included in the imperial domains and the remainder granted to us.'[22] This amicable attitude towards Agra, however, did not last. Emboldened by Jahangir's inability to reclaim Kandahar and by Shah Jahan's rebellion, the Uzbeks abruptly changed tactics, mounting major incursions into Mughal territory in 1625 and 1626, both times being beaten back by Mughal forces.

Now in power himself, Shah Jahan resolved to negotiate an alliance with Turan.[23] He initiated an exchange of ambassadors to discuss details of a joint invasion of Kandahar, despatching envoys and lavish presents to Imam Quli Khan.[24] These overtures, however, were unsuccessful: ignoring the envoys and hoping instead to capitalise on any instability within the Mughal power structure at this crucial moment of handover, the Uzbeks launched an offensive against Kabul on 19 May 1628 from their bases in Balkh and Badakhshan. Ravaging the countryside as they advanced, they ran into determined resistance from Shah Jahan's garrisons and by early June were compelled to dig entrenchments around Kabul Fort in preparation for a long siege.

Facing his first military test with customary resolve, Shah Jahan sent Mahabat-Khan, the Khan of Khans, with a force of twenty thousand men buttressed by Rao Surat Singh, who was ordered to 'launch a campaign against the rebel in such a way that either he is arrested alive or his head is sent to the royal court'.[25] But even this well-planned and rapid reaction force, deployed in an efficient pincer movement, was outstripped by Lashkar-Khan, the new governor of Kabul. Advancing via Jalalabad, he smashed into the Uzbek siege lines, forcing the insurgents to withdraw hastily to Bagram. Demoralised by defeat and desertions, the Uzbek commander retreated homewards so precipitately that 'he traversed the heights and hollows, which he had formerly taken a month to travel through, in four days'.[26] Lashkar-Khan entered Kabul in triumph on 14 September 1628 to take up his appointment a little later than planned but in fine style. One hundred thousand rupees were distributed among the people of the despoiled province, while Lashkar-Khan was rewarded with royal favours. Other officers involved in the victory, like Raja Jai Singh, the grandson of Akbar's old Rajput retainer Raja Man Singh, were ordered to attend at court to receive their due honours.[27] And Abu-Talib Kalim, 'a poet of rare technique', rhapsodised on the theme of the perfect emperor.

O emperor … Your enemy gathered in a corner of your empire
But returned scattered.
He could not pick a bud out of the garden of Kabul
And returned with a heart full of thorns of despair.[28]

While dealing with the Turanis, the new Mughal emperor kept the Persians at arm's length, to the resentment but presumably not the surprise of the aging Shah Abbas. Indeed, Shah Jahan had been so angered by the complete lack of Persian support during his wilderness years that he did not even bother to inform Abbas that he had at last come into his inheritance. Abbas was reduced to complaining petulantly that he had only heard of Jahangir's death and Khurram's succession through his own spies.[29] It took the death of Shah Abbas in January 1929 and the succession of his nephew Shah Safi to prompt a renewal of diplomatic correspondence. Sayyid Hakim Haziq, a doctor of impeccable lineage (but notorious for his conceit and pomposity), was sent west from Agra in October 1629 with congratulatory messages and gifts, reminding Safi of the old friendship between the Safavid and Timurid houses. It was a shrewd but cautious manoeuvre on Shah Jahan's part, one that might just open a new era of mutual cooperation.

He had barely seen off the Uzbeks, however, when he was faced with two insurrections within the empire. The first was a rebellion led by one Jujhar Singh Bundela of the Hindu Orchha clan, son of the man who had murdered Akbar's wise counsellor Abu-Fadl Allami back in 1602. The uprising centred on the central Indian territory of Bundelkhand, where Jujhar Singh now set about 'raising forces, strengthening the forts, providing munitions of war and closing the roads.'[30] It was this last measure – denying imperial traffic access to transit routes to the Deccan – that made this more than just a minor affair. The emperor resolved to crush the rebellion with exemplary force, deploying three massive armies to surround the rebels and hit them from three directions. Mahabat-Khan, fresh from his fruitless march to relieve Kabul, moved from the north, while Pir Khan Khan-Jahan

Lodi – re-appointed as Governor of the Deccan holdings and still based at Burhanpur – attacked from the south. The third blow would be struck from the east by Firoz-Jang. This immense army under Mahabat-Khan's overall command now numbered twenty-seven thousand cavalry, six thousand infantry armed with the latest matchlock rifles and more than one thousand engineers, tasked with sapping the enemy fortifications: a sledgehammer to crack a nut.

Emulating his father's practice, Shah Jahan departed from the capital to follow the campaign from a closer vantage point. En route, he paused briefly at Fatehpur-Sikri – where the royal palace still survived, despite the decay of the city around it – to perform the traditional lunar birthday weighing ceremony on Sunday 26 November 1628.[31] Shah Jahan was exactly thirty-eight years old. The next stop for the royal camp was in the hills of Bari District, scene of the celebrated lion-hunt and his dramatic rescue of Jahangir eighteen years before. With three such able generals deployed to Bundelkhand on his behalf with such lethally large armies, it was hard to resist the temptation offered by a month of prime hunting in the temperate climate of a Rajasthani winter. Eventually, however, he felt the old compulsion to engage seriously in the important campaign underway. Departing from Bari at the end of December, the emperor made for Gwalior Fort, the notorious jail for the most serious political offenders. As a gesture of mercy to mark his first visit as emperor, Shah Jahan ordered a general amnesty. He could afford to be magnanimous.

The imperial forces closed in as planned from three sides, demolishing the resistance offered by rebel contingents in smaller fortresses with brutal efficiency. At Erach, Firoz-Jang's division breached the walls and slaughtered the defenders in their thousands. Finally appearing before the walls of Bundelkhand Fort, Mahabat-Khan's massed ranks presented Jujhar Singh's garrison with a terrifying sight. Completely intimidated, he capitulated, appealing to the Mughal commander that 'if a line of exoneration were drawn across the paper of his offences, he would come to court and not turn his head away from the halter of obedience and submission'.[32] The price for this subservience was a crippling burden of financial reparations: half a million silver rupees, one thousand solid gold coins and forty elephants. After submitting himself to a humiliating prostration before Shah Jahan at Gwalior, Jujhar Singh was graciously rewarded with provisional rehabilitation and appointed a junior officer in the Deccan campaign force, where he could be kept under a watchful eye.

By 17 February 1629, Shah Jahan was ready to leave for the capital, the eradication of the rebellion accomplished. But the Nauruz that spring, marking the first formal anniversary of his accession, was just a brief interlude and would be the last time in many years that the hardened campaigner would know peace, relaxation and undiluted contentment. The festival was celebrated in full glorious colour; as in Jahangir's day, the royal courtyards were draped with silk canopies, held aloft on gilded ebony poles, while the flagstones were scattered with a profusion of Persian carpets in the softest lambswool. Around the splendid figure of the emperor circulated a blizzard of gifts – at least two million rupees' worth from Mumtaz-Mahal alone, while Shah Jahan's sons and daughters sought to outdo each other in generosity and showiness.

Crucially, in keeping with Shah Jahan's determination to minimise threats to the imperial order and to the smooth succession of Dara-Shikuh, there is no word in the official annals of the emperor's other two wives, the Persian 'Kandahari Begum' or the daughter of Shahnawaz-Khan. They had long ago served their political purpose and were assiduously air-brushed from history. As Inayat-Khan dutifully put it, 'his whole delight was centred in this illustrious lady [Mumtaz] to such an extent that he did not feel towards the others one-thousandth part of the affection that he did for Her Majesty'.[33] Or, in the words of Abd-al-Rahim Lahori, the emperor's other wives were given the honour of doing service but were 'content with this illustrious connection in name only, being satisfied with merely this precious alliance'.[34] Kandahari Begum had borne just one daughter, Purhunar Banu, now seventeen years old; Shah Jahan's third wife had managed one son, Jahan-Afroz, who had died in his infancy. Any accidental children, by-blows of dalliances with harem concubines, were to be ignored, reduced to the status of anonymous minor aristocracy and kept in their place with deliberately parsimonious allowances. As for Queen Nur-Jahan, she was confined to quarters, her only remaining role in life the construction of Jahangir's tomb outside Lahore and her own most modest mausoleum not far away. The official message was clear: there was only one queen, Mumtaz-Mahal, and one ruling family, the offspring of Shah Jahan and Mumtaz-Mahal.

Given such sweeping changes at the core of the imperial administration, Shah Jahan should not have been surprised that the most serious rebellion came from a man who had risen high from humble beginnings under the old order: Khan-Jahan Lodi, the Governor of the Deccan who had recently supported Shah Jahan against the Bundelkhand rebellion. Born into an Afghan clan, Khan-Jahan had dabbled in both imperial politics and Sufism from a young age. Falling first into the circle of Prince Daniyal and then his brother Salim, he thrived in the back-stabbing hot-house of dynastic rivalry – so much so that, by the age of twenty, Jahangir had honoured him as a foster-son, accorded him a succession of titles and ordered a ring to be engraved with a special couplet describing him as the 'special son' and 'loyal follower' of the emperor.[35]

Jahangir showered upon Khan-Jahan an embarrassment of riches, offering him the additional title *Sultan-Jahan*, 'Prince of the World', as well as a special seat near the throne, free access to the imperial harem and the hand of the emperor's eldest daughter, Sultan al-Nisa, in marriage. In a contemporary biographical sketch, Shaikh Farid Bhakkari described how Khan-Jahan pragmatically appealed for moderation: 'The khan submitted that the title "Sultan" was exclusively for princes and it did not at all fit that slave and that "Khan-Jahan" was sufficient. Taking a seat in the august royal presence and going inside the seraglio too were appendages of princes and that slave should be exempted from the proposal of a matrimonial alliance with the chaste veiled lady *Padshah-Mahal* ['Great Queen of the Palace'].'
[36] Such discretion was certainly advisable, as the precipitate elevation of an outsider at the drunken whim of the emperor might have created powerful enemies for the upstart within the ruling family, but on the strength of such blatant royal favour, Khan-Jahan had flourished in the imperial administration and had begun to suffer delusions of grandeur.[37]

The division of the spoils after Shah Jahan's accession had left him resentful: instead of being brought to Agra to share in the glory of the new era as Commander-in-Chief – a title he had briefly enjoyed in Jahangir's final year – he was eclipsed by the equally arrogant Mahabat-Khan and fobbed off with the Deccan governorate, far from the hub of imperial politics. In fact, he was fortunate that Shah Jahan was so magnanimous, for even as Asaf-Khan, far to the north in Lahore, was engineering the brutal end-game that ensured Shah Jahan's succession, Khan-Jahan had already flirted with rebellion. Ignoring the letter sent by Shah Jahan in December 1627, which sought to confirm his support by reaffirming his position as Governor of the Deccan, he made an alliance with the old enemy, the Nizamshah of Ahmadnagar and – treason piled upon treason – handed over the Mughal territory of Balaghat in exchange for a massive bribe of three hundred thousand rupees.[38] 'Khan-Jahan is in open rebellion,' noted an East India Company merchant, 'seizing for himself the country about Burhanpur.' [39] So the brash noble's inclusion in the recent three-pronged attack on Jujhar Singh at Bundelkhand Fort had been a crucial test of loyalty.

Even when, in the aftermath of that victory, Khan-Jahan travelled to Agra to apologise for his misjudgement and accept the forgiveness of the new emperor in person, he remained insecure about his position in the new order, an anxiety that was not assuaged by Shah Jahan's repeated invitations to the royal apartments. What appears to have triggered the final split was a petulant remark from a junior official, who snapped at

Khan-Jahan's sons one night: 'Your bravery will be put to the test tomorrow when they put fetters on your father's legs and take ten million rupees from him'.[40] When the young men found their father – who was trusted enough to be even then on guard duty in the anteroom outside the royal apartments – Khan-Jahan panicked and fled. Two verdicts on his behaviour have survived. His admirers were appalled at the way that a distinguished imperial servant was hounded by lesser men, toadies to the new emperor, while the official version of events, as presented by Muhammad Hadi in his posthumous postscript to Jahangir's memoirs, was censorious and unforgiving.

In short, since his head had been turned by too much imperial favour ... he allowed himself to have outlandish fears and baseless imaginings. It went so far that he ran away and on the eve of Sunday 15 October 1629 he, his sons and a group of Afghans left Agra and took the road to wretchedness. ... Since it was nearly time for his downfall, he abandoned the right way, made himself a wanderer in the valley of error with his own vain notions and made a pact with [the] Nizam al-Mulk [of Ahmadnagar].[41]

Khan-Jahan's band of refugees, including his own household, fled for the Chambal River, making for the south. Hot on their heels came a compact rapid reaction force. The monsoon rains had swollen the Chambal to the extent that crossing would be slow and dangerous, so turning his back to the rushing water and selecting his ground near the outskirts of Dholpur, Khan-Jahan prepared to fight. It was a short, bloody and attritional encounter. Casualties were high on both sides but the Mughals could expect reinforcements in substantial numbers. Two of Khan-Jahan's four sons were shot dead: Hussein and Ismat Khan, the latter a lad of just twelve years of age. Among the fatalities on the imperial side was Reza Bahadur Khidmatparast-Khan. Shah Jahan's executioner had fought his last fight: he was shot in the temple and killed immediately. For Khan-Jahan, flight was the only option. Scrambling for anything they could find to bear them across the swollen river, he and his family and remaining followers dragged horses, carriages and what valuables remained through the mud and off to the south.

The renegade's options were now narrow indeed. He may have hoped for a sympathetic ear in Bundelkhand, lately seat of its own failed uprising. But Jujhar Singh was still deployed to the Deccan front, leaving his son, Vikramaditya, to salvage a modicum of family honour by accommodating the bedraggled fugitives for a brief period of recovery and fitting them out with an appropriately comfortable caravan of beasts and vehicles to take them further south to Khan-Jahan's old partner in conspiracy, the Nizamshah of Ahmadnagar. But the pursuit was not far behind. True to form, Shah Jahan authorised a massive force to crush this more serious rebellion. Khan-Jahan Lodi's betrayal was bad enough. The potential for upheaval in the southern districts, where the imperial border garrisons were inconsistent at best, would be greatly aggravated were he to permit a declared rebel with considerable local experience to escape.[42]

Commanding fifty thousand personnel in three divisions on this, the monarch's third Deccan campaign were three wily and hardened campaigners. The commanding general was Mir Muhammad Baqr Iradat-Khan, now granted the additional title Azam-Khan. His brigade generals were equally experienced: Raja Jai Singh – member of the Rajput warrior elite and representative of the empire's Hindu subjects – and Shayista-Khan. Their brief was simple: winkle the rebel Khan-Jahan out of his bolthole at Asir Fort, high on a mountain-top not far from the southern imperial capital at Burhanpur, and destroy the military threat from his Deccani allies once and for all. The emperor himself resolved to follow the action from as close a vantage point as possible. Tracing the old imperial highway via Ranthambor Fort, Mandu and over the Narmada crossings, by mid-March 1630 Shah Jahan had made his way to Burhanpur, where his 'victorious standard shaded the territory'. His movements were monitored by the beady eye of English traders at their base up the west coast at Surat. 'Yet is the King now in Burhanpur,' noted Thomas Wylde on 23 April, 'and it is said he will fall upon … Ahmadnagar, who, although they pay him yearly tribute, were never truly subdued, nor will surrender their fortresses or castles into the King's hands, as he has required. … Others say he will fall into Deccan, pretending a conquest of that country; which is likeliest.'[43]

The campaign dragged on through 1630, marred by a resurgence of the perennial problem within the Mughal military: rivalries within the senior officer corps. Shayista-Khan was recalled after falling out with Azam-Khan and replaced by Abdallah Khan. Back at Burhanpur Fort, household life continued along its routine path of daily court ritual, administrative chores, and seasonal festivals and weighings. On 23 April 1623, Queen Mumtaz-Mahal was delivered of another baby girl who was barely named – Husnara Begum – before she passed away.[44] The royal midwives must surely have observed that the queen's pregnancies had tended in recent years to result in sickly and failing infants at best, miscarriage or stillbirth at worst. But for Mumtaz-Mahal ending her annual production rate was never an option. Procreation was her duty – and would be her undoing.

Gloom inside the palace at Husnara's short life was eclipsed by the misery outside the castle walls. The countryside for miles around was suffering from the depredations of the vast Mughal army and the scorched earth policy pursued by the Ahmadnagaris. The southerners burned their homes and fled into the hills, leaving the imperial army desperately short of food. Shah Jahan's commanders made securing provisions their priority, stripping any community they found of grain and fodder for their livestock. This merciless but necessary tactic soon transformed the frontier territories into a starvation zone. For the merchants of the East India Company at Surat, constant conflict across the southern districts had 'stopped up all passages [and] the usual intercourse of trade'.[45] Another report to company head-quarters written on 22 November projected a gloomy forecast, warning that the management should expect 'no lively vend' of materials such as sandalwood. Such meagre hope for improvement, the author noted, rested on the appointment of Asaf-Khan as regional commander-in-chief, replacing Azam-Khan. The celebrated minister's 'subtle contrivance' might yet achieve some 'underhand composition of peace' – much along the lines of the earlier diplomatic solutions that had ended Deccan wars and salvaged a measure of dignity – and money – for the emperor.[46]

As so often, the observant English traders proved the value of main-taining a healthy network of informers at court, for Asaf-Khan was not formally appointed until three days after that report. The news of Asaf-Khan's imminent arrival galvanised Azam-Khan, who launched a series of blistering attacks on Khan-Jahan Lodi's positions. A decisive victory at Bir saw Khan-Jahan on the run again, fleeing into the hill country, a terrain that frustrated the imperial soldiers behind him. Falling back on Daulatabad, he was joined by the Nizamshah, who was perhaps regretting what must now have seemed a precipitate and ill-advised choice of ally. Recognising this lack of enthusiasm, Khan-Jahan decided to make a break from the fortress – apparently hoping to trek the full length of the empire to make alliance with Afghan clans then agitating in the northern regions around Peshawar and Kabul.

Again, however, Shah Jahan's pursuit force was swift and efficient. Under the command of Abdallah Khan and Sayyid Muzaffar Khan Barha, the Mughal soldiers caught the rebels near Sironj in early January 1631 and inflicted heavy slaughter.[47] At least four hundred of Khan-Jahan's Afghan loyalists were butchered. The man who had sheltered the fugitive on the run from Agra fifteen months earlier, Vikramaditya of Bundelkhand, had switched sides, swallowing a reprimand from his father but accepting the spurious title Jagraj, 'Lord of the World', as reward for his new alle-giance. Losing allies at every turn, Khan-Jahan gave himself up for lost and fled further north, where his escape route took him closer and closer to the imperial city at Allahabad. There, he was eventually brought to bay. The imperial forces sprang their last and most lethal ambush just seventy miles from the city on 1 February 1631.[48] The final encounter was short and merciless. Khan-Jahan, weary of flight and aggrieved at the loss of his sons, fought bravely but was speared by a soldier called Madhu Singh and beheaded. The fight went out of his remaining followers. Abdallah Khan despatched the severed head to Shah Jahan, who was now able to contemplate an empire largely at peace with itself, though still troubled by conflict on the southern frontier.

Away from the fighting, the royal family had been enjoying the comforts of Burhanpur Fort when, on 17 June 1631, Mumtaz-Mahal again went into labour.[49] It was her fourteenth full-term pregnancy in nineteen years of marriage. History does not record the number of intervening miscarriages. At the age of forty, she may have been well advised to avoid childbirth; after all, she had already well fulfilled her primary function of providing offspring for the Mughal dynasty. By the summer of 1631, the Persian lady had given her emperor seven sons, of whom four survived and six daughters, of whom just two still lived. In an indication of the precariousness of human survival, even in the most sumptuous of circumstances then possible, two children had died at birth, four more within the first three years of life and little Lady Thurayya had reached just six. But it would be this last emergency confinement, prompted by an incipient miscarriage at seven months, that would cost the life of the queen.

The first that Shah Jahan knew of the crisis was when his daily game of chess with his eldest daughter, Jahan-Ara, was interrupted by a messenger running from the queen's chambers with an urgent summons. The princess responded to the call to her mother's bedside, then ran back through the palace to convey grim news to her father: labour was progressing badly. The baby was refusing to emerge, despite her small size, there was a great deal of blood and the midwives were beginning to despair for the life of the queen. Even Shah Jahan's close friend, the skilled physician Hakim Alim al-Din *Wazir-Khan*, was powerless to alleviate her distress.[50]

The physicians who were the chosen ones of their time tried, they used all their medicines;
But it was not the will of God that this opportunity should be taken. ...
On one side, all the charm-writers were called and were chanting and calling upon the spirits;
On the other were the nurses and the scholarly doctors.[51]

This verse comes from an Urdu mini-biography of Mumtaz-Mahal, which gives us the fullest and most moving account of the emperor and queen's last separation. Replete with imagery of long-distance travel and death (in which 'friends come, empty the store of wine-jars and leave') it describes in vivid terms the 'bad delivery pains' and the 'delicious medicines' administered by the flustered servants and midwives, whose knowledge of pampering a queen evidently outstripped their familiarity with the science of a post partum haemorrhage.[52] Similarly, it narrates how the distraught Jahan-Ara, unable to help her stricken mother, fell back on superstition and began distributing gems to the poor in the hopes of accruing rapid divine credit. Still more plausibly, it describes both the fear of the courtiers that Shah Jahan, 'shedding tears like rain-water', might take his anger and grief at the queen's dismal condition out on them – and the powerlessness of the usually omnipotent emperor, doing his best to give encouragement to his beloved.

This account also endorses what might otherwise be dismissed as apocryphal tales, such as the queen's famous dying wishes and the story that, just before the birth was finally achieved, the sound of crying was heard in the womb itself. These stories were still circulating in vivid detail two hundred years later, when the poet Qasim Ali Afridi was alive.

Worshipper in Shah Jahan's mosque at Ajmer

Immediately on hearing the crying, the Begum despaired of her life, summoned the Emperor to her side and said in plaintive accents: 'It is well known that when the baby cries in the womb, the mother can never survive her birth. Now that it is my lot to leave this mortal sphere for the eternal home, o King, pardon every fault that I may have committed. ... I shared your lot at the time of your captivity [i.e. rebellion and exile] and other afflictions. Now that the Lord God has given it to you to rule the world, I have, alas, to depart in sorrow! Promise to keep my two last requests.' The emperor promised on his life and soul and asked her to state her wishes. She replied: 'God has given you four sons and four daughters [*sic*]. They are enough to preserve your name and fame. Raise not any issue on any other woman, lest her children and mine should come to blows for the succession. My second prayer is that you should build over me such a mausoleum that the like of it may not be seen anywhere else in the world.' Then, a moment after giving birth to Gauhar-Ara, she died.[53]

If we allow ourselves to suspend disbelief over these deathbed wishes, we may divine the astuteness of Mumtaz-Mahal. First, she showed herself to be a political pragmatist to the last. She knew all too well that family divisions and rival candidacies could be utterly destructive when it came to the next succession. Secondly, she gave him a mission that would enable him to channel his grief and loss into something that the whole empire might cherish – and that would stand as a lasting memorial to her relationship with the emperor. So, metaphorically handing 'all her treasure with her own hand to the king', she entrusted him to ensure that the Shah Jahan Mumtaz-Mahal dynasty alone would be charged with the future of the Mughal state.

As a Shiite, the grief of parting may have been somewhat eased by the knowledge that her marriage was eternal, lasting until Judgement Day; she was confident, then, of seeing her husband again in Paradise. As a Sunni, however, Shah Jahan had no such certain belief. He had known Mumtaz for more than twenty-five years and been married to her for a little over nineteen, during which she had maintained an unswerving loyalty through the most desperate of straits. So, even as the tiny baby Gauhar-Ara was taken off to a private chamber and fed with drips of water from a copper pot, he sat bewildered with sadness amid the rising panic of the medical staff and household servants. The anonymous Urdu biographer described the tearful denouement.

In this chaotic condition, the hands and feet of the begum became cold and there was lamentation and weeping on all sides.
The king lost his senses, crying without restraint.
Now the companions of life had become separated! How then could he restrain himself?
And then it was declared that Her Majesty had shifted from this world to the next and was now jesting with the houris in paradise.[54]

The court was as paralysed as the emperor by the death of the Primary Queen. More used to spinning their elegant chronograms on occasions of national celebration, the poets devoted themselves to the task of creating something special to mark this black day. While one observed bleakly that the Persian word for grief, *gham*, did the trick – its constituent letters adding up to the grim date, AH 1040 – Said Gilani produced the pithiest and most celebrated epigram: 'May the abode of Mumtaz-Mahal be Paradise'.[55]

The queen's body was consigned to the earth within the day, as Islamic law prescribes, after being ritually washed by the ladies of the court. Shah Jahan was too prostrated with grief to be involved. Besides, by the conventions of his Sunni faith, the marriage had ended with the death of Mumtaz, meaning that purdah was again effectively in force. Instead,

Jahan-Ara and her elder sisters led the senior wives at court in undertaking the sad task, in a special section of the palace mosque. The queen's body was then wrapped in a funeral shroud made of clean, white cloth, tied at the head and feet. So it was that the formal funeral prayers began where Mumtaz-Mahal had spent so much of her life, in the women's quarters of the citadel.

The burial ground was in the grounds of the old hunting-lodge at Zeinabad, on the opposite side of the river and in plain sight from the windows and parapets of Burhanpur citadel, enabling the emperor to maintain vigil even at a distance. Shah Jahan could pace the battlements and watch the sun rise over his beloved's tomb. At sunset, the mausoleum was lit by the dying glow of the setting sun. But how different was that last crossing of the Tapti for the family of Queen Mumtaz-Mahal. Instead of the merry picnic outings of former times, it was a doleful funerary barge that transported the bier to the Zeinabad side. The ahukhana – where Shah Jahan's uncle Daniyal had long ago whiled away his last years in an alcoholic stupor – was unoccupied these days and had made for a pretty spot for a private day out for the royal family, swimming in the large tank and strolling in the walled garden. Now, trees were cleared at the western end of the garden and a simple pillared cenotaph erected to house the body of the queen. Around the tomb were the placid waters of a deep formal pond and the customary flower, shrubs and trees of a tranquil Mughal garden.

It was hard for Shah Jahan to find any comfort in the death of his companion. The Prophet Muhammad is quoted as saying: 'After the death of a person, his [or her] actions stop, except for three things that he leaves behind. First, charity that continues to benefit the poor; second, knowledge from which some benefit may be obtained; third, a virtuous child who prays for him'.[56] As a religious man, the emperor would have found all three points to be applicable to his late queen. But her death left a vast hole at the centre of his life. The anonymous biographer of Mumtaz-Mahal gives the emperor a verse of compelling poignancy.

**How happy was the time when there was joy and mirth;
How wonderful a time it was. But it's gone; all that remains is regret.
We were friends and companions, sharing sorrows together.
But we were always doomed to face this parting.
These are the days of separation and the affliction of sundering.
Alas, I would have loved to look upon her grace just once more;
But today is the time to let her go.[57]**

The first week was a blur of grief, during which Shah Jahan remained in his private quarters. The affairs of state to which he had previously paid meticulous attention, the rituals of daily court life, large and small, all were forgotten. Then, on Thursday 26 June, nine days after her death, he paid his first visit to the grave at Zeinabad, stumbling through the obligatory funeral prayers and recitations. Thereafter, for as long as he stayed at Burhanpur, he visited the grave every Friday evening. But the trauma aged him. The official histories all agree that in the wake of the calamity, Shah Jahan gave up music and singing, even wearing fine linen, for at least two years. The big set-piece court holidays, such as the traditional Spring Festival and the two Eid festivals of Islam, triggered tears of nostalgia. He donned the white of mourning, a habit he returned to every year during the fateful month of Dhu al-Qada. Most extraordinarily – indeed, downright implausibly for a man of such single-minded ambition – contemporary accounts insist that he even contemplated abandoning the throne to Dara-Shikuh rather than suffer the 'weariness and pain' of ruling alone. Constant weeping forced him to use spectacles. And his beard and moustache began to turn white. Like many a vain middle-aged man, he had previously tweaked out the odd grey hair that sprouted on his face; now vanity was a thing of the past and within a week his beard had turned more than one-third white. And the poet Muhammad Jan Qudsi outdid himself in his flowery and senti-mental descriptions of a nation's grief.

When Bilqis made her departure from this abode of dust,
The Solomon of the Age sat in mourning.
When he was deprived of that rose-bouquet,
He donned white dress like that white rose stem. …
The King of Kings gave vent to unrestrained agitation and tumult.
When the ocean surges tempestuously, who will say nay?
No one prevented any other from lamentation,
For each was engaged in that task only. …
The musician's instrument went completely out of tune;
Its only sound was the sound of breaking hearts.
And the earth thought, from the profusion of indigo mourning robes,
That perhaps the blue sky had descended.[58]

11
The Illumined Tomb

Upon her grave – may it be illumined till the Resurrection! –
The King of Kings constructed such an edifice
That since the Divine Decree drew creation's plan
No-one has seen its equal in magnificence.

Abu-Talib Kalim[1]

All true art has its origin in sentiment … Moghal emperors were men,
they were not mere administrators. They lived and died in India, they
loved and fought. The memorials of their reign do not persist in the ruins
of factories and offices but in immortal works of art – not only in great
buildings but in pictures and music and workmanship in stone and metal,
in cotton and wool fabrics.

Rabindranath Tagore[2]

Presiding over the continuing Deccan campaign from his field headquarters at Burhanpur, Shah Jahan debated a return to Agra. There would be no festivities in the imperial capital, despite the eradication of the rebel threat and the relatively solid progress of Asaf-Khan's forces. Agra and the empire were draped in mourning and victory celebrations were banned. The emperor himself was weighed down with grief. He could not enjoy as he had before the luxuries of Burhanpur Fort's breezy apartments looking out over the Tapti, the sublimely decorated bathing suites or the cool garden laid out at the heart of the palace precincts; yet the idea of returning to Agra, so far from the walled garden the body of Mumtaz lay, must have seemed insupportable. The practical solution was to leave his southern armies to continue their efforts to subjugate the recalcitrant Deccanis and focus his attentions on the construction of a new, worthier mausoleum close to Agra Fort.

There were certainly many similarities between the two riverfront cities. The first priority, then, was to find an appropriate location in Agra that would mirror the situation at Burhanpur, where the citadel afforded a clear view over the tranquil Tapti to the tranquil funeral-garden beyond. In the capital, the entire river front – on both sides of the Yamuna – was a patchwork of mansions, multi-storey villas and, on the eastern bank, gardens, all belonging to the royal family or the aristocracy.[3] Directly opposite the royal citadel, following the inner curve of the river, was a succession of seven large imperial gardens. Here was the obvious first choice for the queen's final resting place, in direct line of sight across from the palace. Then, through the summer of 1631, Shah Jahan – still at Burhanpur – heard submissions from architectural experts, astrologers and masters of traditional Indian practices. As practical, aesthetic and philosophical ideas were pooled and synthesised, important cultural factors came to the fore, even on the question of location. According to one 12th century Sanskrit treatise on Hindu temple architecture, for example, the ideal building should have a north-south orientation. This tenet, from a completely different religious and cultural tradition, chimed perfectly with Islamic sensibilities, for such positioning placed the mosque that would eventually stand to one side of the mausoleum in the perfect place, its prayer-niche (*mihrab*) facing Mecca to the west.[4] Such important cultural assimilations served to emphasise the uniquely Indian character of Mumtaz-Mahal's tomb, taking Islamic Mughal architecture in a radical new direction. It also meant that the east bank just would not do.

Instead, the emperor's agents turned their attention to the short stretch where the river turned east, offering potential for a site with a north-south axis and a distant but clear view of the mausoleum from the palace windows. Here were the villas of distinguished imperial servants such as Mahabat-Khan and the veteran diplomat Khan-Alam. But one relative newcomer might be more biddable than his proud neighbours. On an area of high ground just around the elbow of the Yamuna stood a comfortable house on a patch of land belonging to the Mirza-Raja Jai Singh. According to Abd-al-Hamid Lahori's officially-sanctioned biography, the raja's home was a 'splendid domed building'.[5] This river-front estate had been handed down from generation to generation since the family – in the person of the staunch Rajput loyalist Raja Man Singh – was allocated the land in the days of Akbar the Great. Contemporary accounts insist that Jai Singh was willing to cede it back to the monarch as a gesture of loyal commiseration for his great loss. But documentary evidence indicating that the raja subsequently and deliberately sought to impede the construction process – perhaps even to sabotage it – suggests that he may have been reluctant to part with a river-front residence in a fashionable suburb of the capital.[6] The emperor, of course, had the power simply to commandeer the land and it was not until some time later that Shah Jahan retrospectively revised his strategy. After all, a land-grab was not the most laudable way to initiate a project that would, in cultural terms, define his reign. Somewhat belatedly, he arranged for no fewer than four villa properties to be handed to the disgruntled raja as compensation for the coveted riverside plot. It would not be until 28 December 1633 – by which time work on the site was well underway – that the king was able to issue the document finalising the land exchange, retrospectively dignifying the land acquisition and enabling his tame historians to state that the transaction had been concluded 'with that scrupulousness so requisite in worldly transactions'.[7]

In the meantime, Shah Jahan began to consider the tomb's detailed design, bearing in mind his queen's dying wish to be honoured with 'such a mausoleum that the like of it may not be seen anywhere else in the world'. The construction of what would be acclaimed as the 'Illumined Tomb' was the product of months of intensive planning, even before the first blocks of stone were laid. So extraordinary was the vision that arose beside the Yamuna that in no time stories began to circulate of its mysterious, even miraculous origins. One account even asserted that the tomb design had been presented wholesale to the royal couple by a Muslim holy man, while Mumtaz-Mahal was still alive.

One day, the king was out hunting with Her Majesty when they came upon a saint called Bilul Shah, living near a cemetery. With his hands, he was shaping a mausoleum out of clay. The king and queen were delighted to see his handiwork and begged, 'Give this mausoleum to us'. The holy man riposted: 'I will sell it for one thousand rupees'. They doubled the sum he demanded, giving him one thousand each and the holy man said, 'Send to me the imperial draughtsman, Adam'. Thereupon the architect Adam was summoned to stand before the saint, who said to him, 'Look under my armpit'. After one hour gazing at the armpit of the saint, the imperial draughtsman produced a finished design and brought it out to present before the king. The queen said, 'A mausoleum should be built according to this design given by the saint; it should be unique and have no parallel'. And the king accepted the queen's wishes.[8]

At every stage of the project development, detailed designs were drawn up on paper and submitted to the emperor for his comments. Shah Jahan devoted a vast amount of time that year to consultations with the leading draughtsmen of the *Diwan al-Buyutat*, the imperial department responsible for the design of new buildings and the maintenance of existing structures. The man picked to co-ordinate the process – shouldering the burden of not just the delivery of a peerless and unique monument but meeting the expectations of an irascible and grief-stricken emperor – was a Persian from Shiraz, Mullah Murshid *Makramat-Khan*, the 'Master of Noble Qualities'. The appointment was typical of Shah Jahan: despite his support for Sunni religious personalities at court, he did not hesitate to promote a qualified Shiite. Makramat-Khan was a senior ministry official with special responsibility for construction in and around Agra. He also happened to be Superintendent of the Imperial Astrologers.[9] The mullah's chief assistant was Mir Abd-al-Karim Mamur-Khan, the 'Doyen of Architects' who had done so much good work during the reign of Jahangir. Another senior colleague was Ustaz Ahmad of Lahore, an architect of distinction who appears to have supervised the actual design process.[10]

As the months passed, the design came into clearer focus, as plans were submitted by all the master architects of the land, considered and either incorporated or rejected. Around the project, supervisors collected a truly international team of specialists. One Persian manuscript reveals the geographical spread of expertise. From the Levant came Ismail Khan Rumi to design the dome and the scaffolding supporting it; his subordinates working on the superstructure were from Lahore and Samarkand. Among the other twenty-three named senior artisans were a squad of master-masons, including Ustaz Issa of Agra and Muhammad Hanif of Kandahar. The inlay workers were all Hindus from Kanauj, while the flower carvers came from Pokhara, far to the north in the Himalayas. The man in charge of inscriptions and calligraphy was the celebrated Abd-al-Haqq Qasim Shirazi, who had already been honoured with the title *Amanat-Khan*, 'Lord of Trust', for his work on the inscriptions at Akbar's Sikandra tomb. And to conclude the list – last but emphatically not least – there was Ram Lal of Kashmir as head gardener.[11]

Even as the consultation process continued, builders were already at work on the site. Their first job was to throw up a basic structure some way south of the Yamuna to protect the grave-site from prying eyes, much as the small edifice at Zeinabad had been quickly erected in the days after Mumtaz-Mahal's death. There, the queen's body could be temporarily re-buried with a modicum of dignity and without impeding the construction of the great mausoleum. In the words of the court historian Muhammad Salih Kamboh, the body would be 'entrusted to earth in the heaven-like tract of land ... and on top of the illumined grave, at first in haste, a small domed building was built so that the eye of a non-confidante does not fall on the holy precincts of the grave of that veiled one'.[12] This temporary tomb constructed, it only remained for the body itself to be exhumed and despatched to Agra.

The task was entrusted to Shah Jahan's second son, Shah-Shuja. The twenty-year-old prince was escorted by two trusted retainers, the late queen's doctor, Alim al-Din Wazir-Khan, and her chief lady-in-waiting, Sati al-Nisa Khanam. Leaving the Deer Park at Zeinabad behind them, de-commissioned as a grave-site but maintained as a pleasure garden for royalty, the cortège left Burhanpur on 11 December 1631 on its gloomy month-long journey to the capital.[13] All along the way, courtiers attending the convoy were ordered to distribute liberal quantities of gold and silver coins, as well as foodstuffs, to the people clustered along the roadside. Mumtaz-Mahal reached her penultimate resting-place on 15 January 1632

and was immediately consigned to the earth in the small structure that had *Mumtaz-* been prepared for her.[14] It must have been a dismal ceremony, conducted *Mahal's first* in haste, with few dignitaries present and surrounded by the chaos of an *burial-place at* enormous building site. Raja Jai Singh's villa had been demolished and *Burhanpur* the deep digging to prepare the necessary pilings and foundations of the vast funerary complex was already underway. The prince and his escort did not dally long in Agra, however. All the senior figures of court were with the emperor in the south and the fortress was staffed by a skeleton housekeeping team.

Back in Burhanpur, the design of Queen Mumtaz-Mahal's mausoleum was beginning to take shape. Given Shah Jahan's arrogant personality, it was inevitable that there was more than a hint of ego involved and that the monument contained elements of architectural autobiography. Nor was it just the emperor: the architects, draughtsmen, engineers, calligraphers and masons, all had undying reputations to gain. After all, as Muhammad Arif Qandhari had observed during the days of Akbar, 'the most skilful engineers and artists must be aware that the fame of emperors rises with their lofty edifices. Thus the well-known saying: "The names of kings remain alive for ages on account of their buildings".'[15] And there was much more than a tomb at stake. The final designs would envisage an elongated complex of buildings and gardens, a sequence of connected geometric modules, in squares and oblongs. First came the flat rectangle of the terrace looking over the water, with its white marble plinth and central tomb; then the vast square garden with its waterways and orchards; then a broad forecourt (the *jilaukhana*) the same size as the waterfront terrace; and finally, at the southern end, a huge square market complex, of the same dimensions as the garden and complete with four comfortable caravanserais positioned among the stalls and lanes of the biggest bazaar in the capital.

Even with the ancillary buildings on the periphery of the complex, style and scale were calculated to surpass anything that had gone before. The huge entrance-way between forecourt and garden, for example, sought to eclipse even the mighty gate at Akbar's tomb at Sikandra. The construction of coffered ceilings, arched doorways, columns, ventilation shafts and frescoes demanded sheaves of designs as the architects refined the building's detail, drawing sections and elevations for the ground floor, mezzanine and upper levels. As he signed off on each part of the design, the emperor ordered a meticulously accurate scale model to be carved in hardwood, so that any flaws could be spotted and rectified before the building work began.

While the great gateway, the mosque to the west of the central tomb and the pilgrim shelter to the west represented professional accomplishment at its highest level, it was the queen's mausoleum that would be the focal point of the complex, commanding the attention of every visitor – and demanding the most courageous leap of imagination that the Mughal era had yet seen. The queen's tomb was designed to be the zenith of the form, the ultimate refinement of everything that had gone before. Successful elements of earlier imperial structures were incorporated but always with a view to aesthetic improvement. It would be a masterpiece of architectural evolution and innovation, in which hitherto disparate styles would be merged as never before, presenting some surprising variations on established themes. So the mandate was of extraordinary breadth, complemented by an effectively limitless budget and timescale. Perfect proportion was to be observed, especially in the pure white exclamation of unprecedented simplicity and emotional power that would draw the eyes and capture the hearts of visitors for centuries to come – but the design was also to be daring and radical.

Thus the architects set about confounding the conventional wisdoms of tomb-garden design. Instead of being set at the centre of the foursquare *chaharbagh* garden, like those of Akbar at Sikandra and Jahangir at Lahore, the tomb would stand north of the conventional quadrangle, honouring the ancient Hindu principal of the 'drawn outline' – *rekha* in Sanskrit – and presenting the perfect profile of a building on the horizon. Only at the leading edge of the complex, set against the great open space behind, could the tomb serve as a screen on which the effects of light reflected off the water would play and the never-ending vicissitudes of the weather and sunlight be mirrored. 'That which appears to be renewed moment by moment is beautiful', elaborated Pandit Jagannath, one of the emperor's favourite Sanskrit-language wordsmiths, a Hindu honoured with the title *Mahakavirai*, 'Great Master of Verse'.[16] Only poised above the Yamuna could that principal of ceaseless renewal be achieved, permitting a display of the building's ever-changing moods. Shah Jahan's consultations with architectural experts from traditions far beyond those of his own clan and religion were paying unexpected dividends.

Other established ideas were boldly set aside. Mughal tombs were conventionally square structures; Shah Jahan's designers chamfered off the corners, creating an irregular octagon and allowing for another narrow face of ornamental arches.[17] The minarets habitually placed atop the corners of the tomb – like Jahangir's pillars at Shahdara with their yellow and white zigzag motif, or the stubby pillars gracing Itimad-al-Daula's beautiful mausoleum upriver – were instead pushed outwards to stand independently at the corners of the main plinth, which itself was constructed in careful proportion to the whole. Each monumental porch, or *pishtaq*, was inscribed with flawless inlaid calligraphy, black against white. As well as asserting the value of this most cherished Mughal art form, the use of the holy Koran reclaimed some of the Islamic credibility lost in the adoption of so many other innovations.[18] Indeed, restating its sacred usage as part of the fabric of the tomb may have been aimed at mitigating grumblings among the orthodox at court that tomb architecture of any kind – let alone so grandiose – was contrary to the Prophet Muhammad's expressed concern that building over a grave might make it a place of worship.[19] Further guaranteeing a (perhaps somewhat defensively) minimalist level of ornamentation, the designers decided on bas-reliefs, coloured stone inlay and pietra dura panels, on a much more modest scale than had been seen on, for example, either Itimad-al-Daula's tomb or that of Afzal-Khan, Shah Jahan's Persian finance minister, whose mausoleum featured a blaze of tiling in vivid blues, greens and reds. Still, the precious stones inlaid into the surfaces were commissioned from as far away as Yemen, Persia, Sri Lanka and the River Nile.[20]

The single greatest innovation – and the one that has ensured the mausoleum's lasting fascination – was the decision to encase the basic brickwork structure in blinding white marble. The inspiration for this came from the southern provinces of the empire: Mandu, where Shah Jahan had spent many months on campaign. The two-hundred-year-old tomb of Hoshang Shah Ghuri, lying in the centre of the royal complex on the plateau, is believed to be the first structure to be built entirely of white marble in all India. Predating the Mughal invasion, let alone the architectural fancies of Shah Jahan, the mausoleum was a model of restrained sophistication – even if some architectural critics disdain its slightly dumpy proportions.[21] The influence of this simple monument, much smaller and absolutely plain, on the core design of what would become the Illumined Tomb of Mumtaz-Mahal was later clearly stated by a small group of Shah Jahan's architects. Passing through Mandu on their way in 1659, not long after the completion of the mausoleum, they had a simple tribute carved into the right-hand lintel of the tomb's only entrance.[22] Shah Jahan had also seen examples of more refined secular structures in white marble at Udaipur, the Mewari capital, where he had been sheltered by his ally Rana Karna Singh during his ill-starred rebellion. Completed comfortably before the queen's tomb at Agra was begun, the *Chandra-Mahal* 'Moon Palace', the assembly-rooms and other associated courtyards atop the sprawling lakeside palace at Udaipur were larger-scale examples of what could be achieved in this extraordinary medium.[23] But in Shah Jahan's defining architectural achievement, these precedents would be comprehensively surpassed.

Such an immense project, however, took a great deal of time. The formal opening ceremony would not happen for twelve years and final work on the detail would go on beyond that. But once the designs and wooden models had been approved by the king, construction began simultaneously in all quarters of the forty-two-acre complex. Even as the foundations of the mighty terrace were being sunk into the sandy riverbank, trees were planted in profusion so that the garden, once finished, would already have its cherished shade. Engineers began building the channels and cisterns that would feed the waterways befitting such a garden, so that, like the Gardens of Eternity of the Koran, it would have 'rivers flowing beneath'.[24] Still, a full year after the queen's death, there was little yet to see. The first *urs* – a traditional Indian Muslim anniversary marking Mumtaz-Mahal's 'marriage' with God – was marked by a ceremony held in the courtyard south of the garden, the only space available for the traditional tents and canopies of a big court occasion. In fact, the king missed the precise anniversary due to a slower than expected return journey from Burhanpur to Agra. On 22 June 1632, however, everything was in place for an appropriately solemn ceremonial and the official historian Jalal al-Din Tabatabai described how the massed ranks of the nobility, military officers and religious scholars all turned out for the occasion, which also featured the visiting Persian ambassador, Muhammad Ali Beg.[25] Other accounts described how the envoy, alongside the king's chief minister, Asaf-Khan, was charged with supervising the ceremony after Shah Jahan, overcome with emotion, retired to pray in seclusion, leaving the dignitaries to enjoy a lavish feast.[26]

There was rather more progress to report by the time of the second urs, by which time the ceremonies, including the annual reading of the entire Koran, took place upon the finished terrace where the mausoleum would rise. This was an impressive rate of work, for the imperial workforce had created a red sandstone platform thirty feet high and one thousand feet long, prompting Abd-al-Hamid Lahori to marvel that 'when the diggers, with stout arms and hands as strong as steel, had with ceaseless labour excavated down to the water table, the inventive masons and architects of remarkable accomplishment constructed the foundation very firmly of stone and mortar up to the level of the ground'.[27] This had then been topped with a second plinth, faced in white marble. On that vast white pavement on 26 May 1633 – this time precisely matching the lunar anniversary of the queen's demise – the full court again turned out in their finery. Again, royalty and nobility feasted and prayed amid splendid carpets, plump cushions and silk canopies.

Inspiration for the Taj Mahal: the tomb of Hoshang Shah at Mandu

The crucial difference was that the body of Mumtaz-Mahal had at last been moved from the small domed structure, which was promptly demolished, to her final resting-place: a small chamber created within the body of the marble platform and reached by a narrow descending stone staircase. Above her grave was a cenotaph, its top inscribed with quotations from the Koran, the sides decorated with the ninety-nine holy names of God, each etched into its own cartouche. Walls and dome, however, had yet to be built over the stark accommodation in which the queen's body lay, so the focus of the urs was the inauguration of an octagonal golden fence, crafted under the supervision of Said Gilani, Superintendent of Goldsmiths. Forged of more than one thousand pounds of solid gold, it was placed around the grave where – as Muhammad Amin Qavini pointed out in his biography of Shah Jahan – its pendant lamps would provide illumination for Jahan-Ara and the ladies of the harem when they came for midnight prayers.

The gold railing, on which the inscription, knobs and most of the flowers are inlaid in enamel, and which required forty-thousand *tolas* of gold, equivalent in cost to an amount of six hundred thousand rupees, was brought ... along with enamelled golden constellation-orbs and hanging lamps ... and submitted for His Majesty's most enlightened inspection. And at the most exalted order, the railing was set up and the aforesaid hanging lamps and constellation-orbs were suspended above ... the resting-place of that recipient of divine light.[28]

The Cornish traveller, Peter Mundy, who spent much of that summer and autumn in and around Agra, was also struck by the ostentatious wealth in the construction of the complex:

It goes on with excessive labour and cost, prosecuted with extraordinary diligence, gold and silver esteemed common metal and marble but as ordinary stones. He [Shah Jahan] intends, as some think, to remove all the city hither ... commanding merchants, shopkeepers, artificers to inhabit [the district] called by her name, Tage Gunge.[29]

Driven by the force of this royal will, the work ground steadily on. Across the vast project, masons carved elegant balustrades, inlaid bright semi-precious stones into sheets of white marble and chiselled delicate lacy fretwork into solid stone screens. Clouds of dust arose as slabs of red sandstone were manoeuvred into place by teams of labourers, overseen by deputies from Makramat Khan's staff. The calligraphers drew their painstaking designs, pencilling the sacred Koranic verses onto white marble before stepping back to verify that perspective was correct for viewing from ground level, adjusting their sketch and finally setting chisel to stone. Stories of the king moving incognito among the workforce to monitor progress and staff motivation in person have passed into Indian folklore.

To find out, he disguised himself as an old man and went to the site by the Yamuna River. There he came across a stone-cutter, whom he asked, 'What are you doing?' The stone-cutter was annoyed by the disturbance and said, 'Go away, old man, don't you see that I am busy?' The stone-cutter's dedication impressed Shah Jahan. He went to the next stone-cutter and asked the same question. The second stone-cutter was equally impatient and he told the disguised emperor, 'Cutting stone is a great art, old man, and I can't be answering questions and practising my art'. Again Shah Jahan was impressed; from his body language he could tell that the man was proud of his professional skills. Finally, the emperor went to the third stone-cutter, to whom he put the same question. 'I am building the Taj Mahal, old man, and if I keep answering idle questions I shall never be able to complete the most beautiful monument on earth.' Shah Jahan returned to his palace much pleased. Clearly the third stone-cutter had given the best answer. The first worker represented dedication to work – and honest day's work for an honest day's pay. The second showed professional excellence. The third symbolised the power of a shared vision.[30]

The white marble came from the Makrana quarries in Rajasthan and had been arriving in small quantities at Agra since the previous winter, hauled on massive six-wheeled carts by teams of buffalo. But Makrana lay in Amber, Raja Jai Singh's hereditary kingdom, and with the issue of his stolen land still to be resolved he had been reluctant to allow passage to the stone-transporters across his territory. Shah Jahan first wrote to him on 19 September 1632, politely but firmly requesting his assistance for the imperial convoy-master, Malik Shah, who had a blank cheque from the imperial treasury for both stone and bullock-carts. On 11 October, the emperor was forced to write again, reminding the raja of his obligations to his Mughal overlord and to 'arrange as many carts as possible on hire at the earliest possible time and despatch them to Makrana in order to transport marble to the capital'. Even the transfer of the four villas in compensation for his Agra estate appears not to have mollified the testy Rajput and on 30 June 1637, a plainly seething Shah Jahan tersely warned Raja Jai Singh against allowing his men to go on detaining stone-cutters on their way to the quarry, causing the work rate there to suffer.[31] With such obstacles, it was not surprising that the project was experiencing serious delays.

As the years passed, Shah Jahan monitored progress at the building site. In the early summer of 1634, he ordered a postponement of his annual holiday in Kashmir. It would not be appropriate, he declared, to be seen promenading among the trees, flowers and tranquil waterways of his recently completed Shalimar garden during Dhu al-Qada, the month in which he donned the white of mourning. So the astrologers were commanded to return to their almanacs and come up with a later, equally auspicious, date for departure to the Himalayan foothills. The fourth anniversary of Mumtaz-Mahal's death, on 5 May 1635, was marked by a return to formal ceremony, as near to the grave site as the on-going building work would permit. The urs was becoming an increasingly religious occasion, with far more emphasis placed on private prayer and Koranic recitation than collective ceremonial and feasting. The charitable donations were continued, each anniversary featuring a donation of fifty thousand rupees to deserving men and women. And as the royal family returned each year, they were able to see the walls rise a little higher, the precise geometry of the entire complex resemble the design, sketches and wooden models a little more closely. The imperial craftsmen were filling in the detail, too. The gold railing around the cenotaph was replaced by a white stone screen, meticulously carved and more in keeping with the minimal ostentation. By December 1637, Shah Jahan was able to reward the master calligrapher, Abd-al-Haqq Amanat-Khan, with an elephant – still a powerful symbol of royal patronage – for designs that eclipsed the imagination of all other specialists. Now, as the work gradually progressed, Amanat-Khan left his autograph inside the tomb chamber, then on the western exterior archway and finally – by the end of spring 1639 – on the main body of the mausoleum.[32] Still, however, Ismail Khan Rumi and his team had yet to complete their work on the mighty dome.

By January 1641, when Fr Sebastião Manrique, a zealous fifty-three-year old Portuguese Jesuit, visited Agra, the central structure was still unfinished. While he despised the Mughal empire's indigenous faiths, calling Muslims 'followers of the wicked Koran' and 'disciples of the perverse and lascivious precursor of Antichrist', he noted the complex's 'handsome, lofty, quadrangular wall of hewn stone of a reddish hue … crowned with strong spikes made of the same stone, instead of the usual battlements'.[33] Discussing the difficulties involved in transporting the slabs of white marble, he also gave a plausible assessment of the work-force at the site.

Some of these blocks, which I met on the way … were of such unusual size and length that they drew the sweat of many powerful teams of oxen and of fierce-looking, big-boned buffaloes, which were dragging enormous, strongly-made wagons, in teams of twenty or thirty animals. This great wall embraced a huge square-shaped enclosure, in the centre of which rose a vast, lofty, circular structure … made of glittering white marble. On this building, as well as other works, a thousand men were usually engaged, overseers, officials and workmen: of these many were occupied in laying out ingenious gardens, others planting shady groves and ornamental avenues: while the rest were making roads and those receptacles for the crystal waters, without which their labour could not be carried out.[34]

Some contemporary European travellers experienced a mixed response to the great mausoleum yet, despite often virulent disapproval of native mores, could not help but be moved and impressed by the sprawling yet elegant complex. The French traveller François Bernier was explicitly troubled by aesthetic uncertainties, haunted by a sense of cultural guilt at fancying something so alien to his own traditions. He inspected the mausoleum in 1659, by which time it was already a famous curiosity, a compulsory stop for every foreign visitor to Agra. His account, part of a voluminous letter to Jean-Baptiste Colbert, founder of the French East India Company, contains almost everything that a modern tourist could hope to know about the funerary complex. Vivid, detailed and rich with illustrative comparisons to celebrated buildings on a similar scale in Paris, Bernier's narrative could be fairly described as the prototype tour guide (at a time when entrance fees were not required) to the complex. Taking the reader through the eastern outskirts of Agra along 'a long, wide, or paved street, on a gentle ascent', past elegant gardens and caravanserais into the main complex, he notes cautiously of the vast entrance gate that it is 'a different and peculiar kind but not without something pleasing in its whimsical structure'. At last (and hesitating to confide his admiration to his French companion, lest his 'taste might have become corrupted' by his long residence in the Indies), Bernier reaches the mighty structure on the river-front.

This building is a vast dome of white marble … encircled by a number of turrets, also of white marble, descending the one below the other in regular succession. The whole fabric is supported by four great arches, three of which are quite open and the other closed up by the wall of an apartment with a gallery attached to it. There the Koran is continually read with apparent devotion in respectful memory of *Tage Mehale* [Bernier's italics] by certain mullahs kept in the mausoleum for that purpose.[35] The centre of every arch is adorned with white marble slabs whereon are inscribed large Arabian characters in black marble, which produce a fine effect. The interior or concave part of the dome and generally the whole of the wall from top to bottom are faced with white marble: no part can be found that is not skilfully wrought or that has not its peculiar beauty. … Under the dome is a small chamber, wherein is enclosed the tomb of *Tage Mehale*. It is opened with much ceremony once a year and once only; and as no Christian is admitted within, lest its sanctity should be profaned, I have not seen the interior, but I understand that nothing can be conceived more rich and magnificent. I leave you to judge whether I had not sufficient ground for asserting that the mausoleum of *Tage Mehale* is an astonishing work. It is possible I may have imbibed an Indian taste; but I decidedly think that this monument deserves much more to be numbered among the wonders of the world than the pyramids of Egypt.[36]

By this time, the Illumined Tomb of Shah Jahan's dreams had been long realised. Its official completion date can be stated confidently: Saturday 7 February 1643, the twelfth anniversary of the queen's death. Court historians, aided in their meticulous measurements by having the actual plans to hand, acclaimed the masterpiece with painstakingly detailed descriptions of the complex, from the tiniest chip of carnelian inlay on the royal sepulchre to the towering minarets, soaring one-hundred-and-fifty feet into the sky 'like accepted prayers from the heart of a holy person'.[37] Faced with such a challenge to their own verbal dexterity, the poets rose to the occasion. While Abu-Talib Kalim concentrated his efforts on the sublime merits of the builder's art, eulogising the expertly joined marble slabs and the inlaid flowers whose realism is only undermined by the absence of odour, Haj Muhammad Jan reached for some exquisite metaphors to underline the redemptive virtues of this holy spot.

How wonderful is the resting-place
Of the chaste lady who was Bilqis of her time!
This has become the abode of the lady of the universe.
This is the illuminated place, like the garden of paradise!
The perfume of paradise mixed with vapours of ambergris
And swept by the eyelashes of the houris.
Its walls are etched with colourful designs
And its atmosphere is fresh like the lustre of gems.
The creator of this sacred mausoleum has brought water
From the source-spring of bounty.
And on this holy exalted dome drips the cloud of blessing.[38]

Opposite this flawless tomb, directly over the Yamuna from his beloved Mumtaz-Mahal, the emperor created the delightful *Mahtabbagh*, or 'Moonlight Garden', as a viewing platform, from which he could gaze at the tomb after dark. It was laid out as a perfectly symmetrical mirror to the funerary complex; taking the place of the tomb was a large octagonal tank, flanked by single-storey pavilions in the round-roofed style pioneered by Shah Jahan – a souvenir of his days in exile in Bengal. Northwards lay a replica 'chaharbagh' quartered garden, of identical dimensions to its southward counterpart and planted with the same density of trees, shrubs and flowers.[39]

All that remained was to assess the cost of this mammoth undertaking, a calculation made on the occasion of the twelfth urs, as Murshid Makramat-Khan and Mir Abd-al-Karim formally signed off on their greatest triumph. The Illumined Tomb had cost the imperial treasury five million rupees. In the context of the virtually bottomless Mughal treasury and the vast sums awarded annually to members of the royal family, this was not

a wildly excessive sum. It certainly gave the lie to Fr Manrique's snide *The Taj Mahal* claim that Shah Jahan, presented with an earlier, more modest estimate for the construction, had snarled 'in his barbaric pride and arrogance' that it should be much, much more expensive.[40] But a monument of this scale demanded a continuing budget, not just to ensure a satisfactory level of maintenance and adequate premises for the resident holy men and Koranic reciters but to accommodate and feed the thousands of pilgrims who began to arrive at the mausoleum.

The rationale of attaching a market and caravanserai complex now became clear. On the twelfth urs, marking the formal end of construction, rent money from the entire bazaar district was requisitioned in perpetuity, yielding a total of two hundred thousand rupees a year. Half as much again came from Shah Jahan's allocation of the revenues from thirty villages in the vicinity of Agra, again as a maintenance grant. The taint of its commercial origins was removed by its formal identification as a religious endowment (*waqf*), to be administered by the appropriate imperial ministry. The man in charge of the complex was a court eunuch named Agah Khan, civil administrator for Agra district, who held the job until he 'rolled up the carpet of existence' in 1657. Jean-Baptiste Tavernier, who identified this orderly business precinct as 'the Tasimacan, where all foreigners come', described it as 'a large bazaar, consisting of six large courts all surrounded with porticoes, under which are chambers for the use of merchants, and an enormous quantity of cotton is sold there.'[41] The food aisles were richly stocked too, noted the Cornish traveller Peter Mundy, affording 'plenty of beef, mutton, partridge, quails, pigeons, turtle doves and sometimes geese and ducks; mangos, plantains and pineapples; raisins, almonds, pistachios, walnuts, apples, oranges, prunes, prunellas or dried apricots'.[42] From the 1650s until the present day, despite a drastic deterioration in the fabric of the complex south of the tomb's main gate, the *Taj-Ganj* – the 'Treasury of Mumtaz' – has remained one of the city's most important bazaars.

Once built, however, the tomb of Mumtaz-Mahal struggled to retain its magnetic power over Shah Jahan. She drew him back for two more anniversary visits, by now formulaic in their prayers and almsgiving. But the emperor's determination to create a new imperial capital at Delhi outweighed his need to keep a reminder of the mother of his children in daily sight. Once Agra was usurped as Seat of the Caliphate, return visits to the tomb were as rare as return trips to the redundant fortress in the city. Indeed, it is clear that even basic maintenance at the tomb began rapidly to slip. By 4 December 1652, when Aurangzeb was en route to take over provincial command in the Deccan states, the thirty-four-year-old prince stopped at Agra to pay his respects at his late mother's cenotaph. He found the entire complex in a shocking state of disrepair – less than ten years after its completion. The Mahtab Garden across the river had been inundated by the Yamuna; no one had thought to build up its embankments. Even the revered tomb itself was cracked and leaking. Five days later, Aurangzeb sat to compose an earnest letter to his father, lamenting the damage and chiding him, cautiously, for his negligence.

The buildings of this shrine enclosure of holy foundation are still firm and strong ... except that the dome over the fragrant sepulchre leaks during the rainy season in two places on the north side. Likewise the four arched portals, several of the recessed alcoves on the second storey, the four small domes ... have become dampened. The marble-covered terrace of the large dome has leaked in two or three places during this past rainy season and has been repaired. Let us see what happens in the coming rainy season. ...

Long-living protector! An extraordinary evil eye has struck this model of lofty buildings. If the rays of your august attention fall on the remedy to ward it off, it will be proper. ...

May the world-illuminating Sun of the Caliphate [Shah Jahan] remain shining upon the heads of the people of the world![43]

The spacious complex, however, did provide room for other royal burials. Tombs for Shah Jahan's first wife, Kandahari Begum, and his third, Izz-al-Nisa, were constructed in the southern corners of the courtyard outside the main gate. Ladies of the aristocracy who had been particularly close to the royal family, too, were accorded the honour of proximity in death. Mumtaz-Mahal's cherished lady-in-waiting, Sati al-Nisa Khanam, merited a simple octagonal memorial just outside the perimeter walls on the west side.

Shah Jahan's last visit occurred on 27 December 1654, during which he gave his eldest son and heir apparent, Dara-Shikuh, a tour of the funerary complex. He had not been there for more than ten years. Thereafter the king was first too distracted by war, then physically constrained by imprisonment. And when he made his next journey through the towering entrance gate, down the long shaded central avenue of the garden and up to the octagonal white domed shrine, it would be for his own low-key, furtive, almost secretive funeral.

12
Master of the 'Ornamented Throne'

> During the present reign, building activity has reached such a level that has neither been attained in any earlier era nor will ever be possible in the future.
>
> Muhammad al-Amin Qazvini[1]

> The light of the throne's rubies, mingling with the lustre of diamonds,
> Is like the reflection of illuminations in crystal water.
> Its antique emeralds are greener than fresh grass.
> With the fire of its rubies, a lamp may be lighted,
> Inextinguishable by water or by any gust of wind.
> It truly hath no price. But whatever else you desire, that it has:
> Dignity, majesty, glory, grandeur, grace and beauty.
>
> Abu-Talib Kalim[2]

The fact that Shah Jahan could spend five million rupees on his widow's tomb with such nonchalance is an indicator of the vast wealth at his disposal. The imperial balance sheet at the beginning of his reign puts that price tag in perspective. It shows that the average annual revenue from the empire's fourteen provinces was assessed at a little over thirteen million rupees each. The total was dragged down by under-achieving regions like Bihar, Oudh and Kabul but the really wealthy provinces such as Punjab, Khandesh in the south and Agra itself easily outstripped the average. Together, they brought Shah Jahan's total income during 1628, his first year on the throne, to nearly 190 million rupees.[3] Most of that money flowed directly into the imperial coffers as crown-land revenue. The remainder was allocated at the emperor's discretion to 655 named individuals: members of the royal family and the members of the nobility whose fiefdoms financed their private militias and lavish lifestyles.[4] In 1628–9 alone, allowances in cash and goods to 'the begums, the princes, the nobles, officers, sayyids, learned men and sheikhs' accounted for eighteen million rupees in cash and land grants.[5]

The Mughals' extravagant wealth dwarfed the exchequers of contemporary rulers. The annual revenue of their old rivals in Trans-Oxus Central Asia was assessed objectively at around three million rupees, a truly pitiful sum by Agra standards. And compared to Shah Jahan's annual income – worth nearly £25 million sterling at contemporary rates – the monarchs of Europe were struggling on paltry sums.[6] In 1635 Britain, even as Queen Mumtaz-Mahal's tomb was well underway, King Charles I was mired in financial crisis. Struggling to maintain his lavish court and household on an annual budget of half a million pounds, he was forced to resort to increasingly desperate and legally questionably taxes to drum up the cash needed to fund his unpopular military adventures. Perhaps, like his father, he should have sent an ambassador to Agra; with such an embarrassment of riches at his disposal, Shah Jahan could have helped him many times over and had plenty to spare for his own military and architectural expenses – although his general mistrust of foreigners made it most unlikely that he would have obliged.

Needless to say, the empire was divided between a very few 'haves' and a great many 'have-nots'. Fr Sebastiaõ Manrique was astonished at the opulence of the royal treasuries and the great incomes enjoyed by royalty and nobility. He noted that even merchants were allowed to take ingots of gold, silver or copper to the imperial mint and have them cast into coins of the realm: 'In some of their houses,' he reported, open-mouthed, 'I saw such vast sums of money piled up that if they had been covered over they would have struck the ordinary gazer as being merely heaps of grain rather than piles of anything so unusual.'[7]

The poor, by contrast, thronged every village, highway and urban back-street across the entire empire. In 1636, a labourer in Surat or a domestic servant in Agra could expect to be paid twenty-five rupees per year on average and certainly never more than fifty.[8] Such small fry rarely merited notice. The Dutch trader, Francisco Pelsaert, was an exception. On the land, he reported, peasants faced a bleak existence, 'cruelly and pitilessly oppressed'. If their villages were unable to pay the full amount of rent, they could be seized and sold – man, woman or child – or charged with fomenting rebellion. For in Mughal India defaulting was tantamount to treason. 'Some peasants abscond to escape their tyranny,' Pelsaert recorded with dismay, 'and take refuge with rajas who are in rebellion and conse-quently the fields lie empty and unsown and grow into wilderness. Such oppression is exceedingly prevalent in this country.'[9] Famine routinely stalked the land, driving up grain prices beyond the reach of most families outside the palaces and mansion walls of the wealthy elite. In early 1631, British merchants in the southern provinces noted grimly how trade had been disrupted by 'this direful time of dearth … the calamity having filled the ways with desperate multitudes who, setting their lives at nought, care not what they enterprise so they may but purchase means for feeding'.[10] And the urban poor were just as badly off.

This is a short sketch of the life of these poor wretches, who, in their submissive bondage, may be compared to poor, contemptible earthworms ... Now we shall write a little of the manner of life of the great and rich, but, in order to do so, we must entirely change our tune; for the pen which has described bitter poverty ... must tell that in the palaces of these lords dwells all the wealth there is, wealth which glitters indeed but is borrowed, wrung from the sweat of the poor.[11]

When the emperor was in Agra – between the military campaigns to north and south that would increasingly occupy his time, money and energy – the city blossomed. As the focus of the empire's wealth, it boasted wide avenues and covered markets with vaulted ceilings; productive mercantile districts, carefully partitioned according to métier and goods; and at least eighty caravanserais for the accommodation of travelling merchants, bringing their cargoes from the far reaches of empire and storing them in the security of these fortified lodgings. During Shah Jahan's reign, for those who were fortunate, wealth and security went hand in hand. As Chandrabhan the Brahmin counsellor recorded in his 'Rules Observed during Shah Jahan's Day', the Mughal state was careful to look after its most valued citizens.

Throughout the night, watchmen, sentinels, patrols, rounds, guards, emissaries, spies and news-gatherers are stationed in all quarters of the palace, the streets and markets. The respect for government and dread of its laws is such that all persons in the city and markets may sleep with their door open, without any apprehension of danger. ... And through the blessing of His Majesty's justice, there is such protection and safety on the roads and ways that merchants and travellers with their goods and packs come and go at all seasons with confidence and gladness.[12]

With the court in full session, the luxurious lifestyle of the wealthy spilled out from the fortress gates and the riverfront mansions. A dull day might be livened up by visiting the most spacious market square, just outside the castle's western wall. 'There is also in that place,' wrote Johann de Mandelslo in 1638, 'a high pole ... where the court-lords, and sometimes the Mughal himself [Shah Jahan], divert themselves with shooting at the parrot fastened at the top of it.'[13] There were more serious blood sports to enjoy, too. Mandelslo witnessed lions fighting tigers – and men were offered the chance to win the favour of the emperor by entering the arena with such beasts, armed only with a sword and shield. One individual, in extremis with the lion at his throat, pulled a hidden dagger from his waistband and cut the beast's throat. Unfortunately, Shah Jahan was outraged by such 'cheating'; berating the suddenly deflated champion, he ordered his summary execution.[14]

Inside the walls of Agra Fort, life for the royal family – the peak of this pyramidal society – continued in its daily round of duty and pleasure. There was already a generational shift in the air. As the young princes moved into adulthood, they accepted the responsibilities and rewards of their new status: military rank, civil administration and provincial governorship. Jahan-Ara, the emperor's eldest daughter, stepped into her late mother's position as de facto Primary Queen of the empire. In this role, however, the emphasis was less on political counsel than charitable donations: the princess organised almsgiving on the key days of state and religion, as well as famine relief and pilgrim convoys to Mecca. Jahan-Ara's financial endowments were commensurate with her status and she was, like her leading brothers, a millionaire – even if, given her propensity to Sufism and abstinence, it seems likely that her personal extravagances would have been minimal (though one account claimed that the entire revenue of Surat Port had been allocated 'to meet her expenditure on betel'!).[15]

The day-to-day business of court went on in as prescribed and formulaic a way as it had under Jahangir. Shah Jahan rose each morning to pray before making his obligatory sunrise appearance before the royal family, massed nobility and general public at the jharoka darshana viewing balcony. The only person who declined to attend this time-honoured event was the emperor's devout third son, Aurangzeb, who dismissed the whole thing as unislamic and therefore 'unlawful'; he also disapproved of those who celebrated the Nauruz 'like Persians'.[16] The affairs of state were handled in a series of businesslike audiences, circumscribed by time-honoured ritual, in which land-grants and estates were awarded, along with heavy silk robes of honour. The culture of mutual dependence between royalty and aristocracy – and even within the royal family – was emphasised again and again with the exchange of lavish gifts and tributes. Each recipient came forward, performing four deep taslim bows to their emperor. A typical ceremony was described by a Venetian adventurer, Niccolao Manucci, who was taken into the service of Prince Dara-Shikuh, the heir apparent. Enjoying the razzamatazz immensely and 'dressed like a Turk, with a turban of red velvet bound with a blue ribbon, and dressed in satin of the same colour; also a waist-cloth of gold-flowered pattern with a red ground', Manucci left a vivid and detailed account.

I noted that the throne on which the king, Shah Jahan, was seated stood in front of, and near to, the palace of the women, so that as soon as he came out of its door he reached the throne. It is like a table, adorned with all sorts of precious stones and flowers, in enamel and gold. ... Around the throne, at the distance of one pace, are railings of gold, of the height of one cubit, within which no one enters except the king's sons. Before they enter, they come and, facing the king, go through their obeisance, then enter the palace and come out through the same door from which the king issued. Arriving there, they again make obeisance, and upon a sign from the king they take their seat in the same enclosure, but at the foot of, and on one side of, the throne. Thereupon the pages appear with the umbrella, parasol, betel, spittoon, sword and fly-brusher.

Below the throne, several feet lower than it, a space is left, sufficient for the secretary (*wazir*) and the greatest officials of the court. This space is surrounded by a silver railing. Near it stand *gurz-bardars*, that is to say, the bearers of golden maces, whose duty it is to carry orders from the court to princes of the blood royal. After a descent of a few more steps there is another space of greater size, where are the captains and other officials, also the gurz-bardars with silver maces, who convey the orders of the court to the governors, generals and other princes. These are placed with their backs to a railing of wood painted vermillion, which surrounds the space.

The hall in which stood the royal seat is adorned with twenty highly decorated pillars, which support the roof. This roof stretches far enough to cover the spaces enclosed within the silver railing, and is hidden half-way by an awning of brocade. Further, a canopy over the king's throne is upheld by four golden pillars.

Outside the wooden railing is a great square, where, close to the railing, stand nine horses on one side and nine on the other, all saddled and equipped. Near to the pillars are brought certain elephants on every day that the king gives audience … And in the square a considerable number of soldiers stand on guard. At the end was a great hall, where were stationed the players on instruments and these, upon the king's appearing to give audience, played very loudly, to give notice that the king was already in the audience hall.

The silence preserved was astonishing and the order devoid of confusion. For this purpose there are officials whose business it is to see that the people are placed in proper order. Some of these officials held gold sticks in their hands and these came within the silver railing. The others carried silver sticks and they took great heed that throughout the court nothing was done which could displease the king.[17]

After such ceremonies of quotidian opulence, Shah Jahan resumed the business of office in greater privacy, returning to his divan in the Exclusive Audience Hall to write out, in his stylised 'broken *nastaliq*' Persian script, the edicts that drove the business of empire. The final daily session of court business was devoted to charity. Holy men of all faiths – ash-encrusted Hindu sadhus, Sufi mystics in white cotton robes – clustered into the royal presence, seeking to give blessings and receive alms. The emperor also distributed his royal largess, allocating hefty sums for the construction of mosques, religious madrasas, caravanserais and hospitals.

Evenings were dedicated to culture: the continuation of another family tradition. Less boozy than Jahangir's, less spiritually questing than Akbar's, nonetheless Shah Jahan's soirées were free-wheeling and open-minded explorations of the empire's literary, philosophical and musical traditions. Debate and performance went on late into the night. Sanskrit scholars like

Pandit Jagannath, the Great Master of Verse, recited verses in honour of Asaf-Khan, Prince Dara-Shikuh and Shah Jahan himself. One Sunday night in October 1634, encamped at Bhimar in Kashmir, the emperor awarded the poet his weight in silver as prize money for a cycle of twelve literary masterpieces. Similar honours awaited favoured Hindi poets, such as Hari Nath, who won an elephant, a horse and twenty-five thousand rupees in January 1640.[18] The masters of Persian poetry, indigenous and imported, also entertained with their ghazals, qasidas and chronograms.[19] Musicians, too, won titles and monetary reward with their compositions in Hindi and Persian. 'He listens to the recital of choice tales, pleasant sayings and authentic histories,' recorded Chandrabhan the Brahmin, 'delivered from the tongues of the companions, fluent readers and eloquent historians; which, together with delightful captivating Mughal, Kashmiri and Hindi songs, enliven the banquet till midnight; and the exhilarating sounds of the flute, viol … and other instruments reach the heavenly regions'.[20]

The most visible sign of the emperor's determination to put his stamp on the kingdom – evident from the very first year of his reign – was Shah Jahan's comprehensive and very expensive programme of building work. By the time he was toppled in 1656, he had spent at least twenty-nine million rupees – a consistent ten per cent of annual revenues – on architecture, the passion of his life. This could be seen simply as evidence of boundless self-absorption. Few beyond the royal family and court elite, after all, profited from the substantial modifications implemented by the Ministry of Construction at Agra Fort, at Lahore or at Burhanpur. New wings, gates, turrets and audience-chambers sprang up, often requiring the demolition or substantial reworking of existing structures. As always, the emperor was personally involved in sketching out the plans, while his father-in-law, Asaf-Khan, assumed responsibility for the final designs. Six million rupees were spent on changes inside Agra Fort alone, while Wazir-Khan, governor at Lahore, was granted another two million to expand the citadel to the west, with new buttressed towers, airy white marble apartments overlooking the Ravi and a splendid elephant stairway that enabled the royal family to ride from street level up to the palace plateau.[21] Another million was lavished on Jahangir's tomb outside the city. Further north, Kabul Fort was strengthened and the garden containing Babur's old tomb enlarged and enhanced by a modest little marble mosque in exquisite Shah Jahani style.[22] Not all these amendments worked. Worst were the redundant and meretricious little touches that clashed with existing structures and demeaned their dignity and integrity. The white marble round-

Shah Jahan's mosque near Babur's tomb, Kabul

roofed 'Bengali' shelters added to Akbar's tomb at Sikandra or Shah Jahan's old stone refuge on Jagmandir Island at Udaipur were errors of judgement, plain and simple, amounting simply to redundant superstructure.

In other respects, however, it could be argued that the emperor liquidated the seemingly limitless assets hoarded by his family and lavished them on the people in lasting structures for their pleasure and edification. Thus, far more important than thrones, tombs, pleasure-gardens or sequinned chambers, Shah Jahan gave his subjects mosques for their spiritual welfare, madrasas for their education, caravanserais to boost profitable trade, hospitals for their healthcare and fortresses to safeguard their security from foreign invasion and internal rebellion. Chandrabhan, the emperor's Brahmin counsellor, was only reporting the truth when he listed these public services, delivered 'though His Majesty's bounty'.[23] In 1638, during Shah Jahan's tenth year on the throne, the clutter of public buildings, shops and private houses outside the north-western gate of Agra Fort would be cleared to make way for 'a spacious plaza, which the natives of Hind call *chauk* … with a large bazaar laid out in octagonal Baghdadi style'. On the west side of this plaza, with its seventy-six arched trading chambers, was built 'a stately metropolitan mosque'.[24] This *Jamia Masjid*, or Friday Mosque – an unprecedented point of congregation for the faithful of the capital, capable of accommodating thousands of worshippers in its main courtyard – was funded entirely from Princess Jahan-Ara's personal allowance. The eulogies contained in the beautiful inscription, Persian script in black stone inlaid into the central arch of the inner sanctuary, make it clear that the princess outranked even the emperor's surviving wives. 'Supreme among Women of the Age', Jahan-Ara was labelled, as well as 'Mistress of the Ladies of the Realm' and even *Malika-Jahan*, 'Queen of the World'.[25] Despite the unprecedented irregularity of this secular hagiography, written in Persian, replacing the traditional Arabic verses of the Koran, the mosque stood proudly as an explicit statement of balance within the kingdom: a bulwark of religion complementing the mighty fortress on the other side of the octagonal plaza.

For at this time, Shah Jahan's religious attitudes were further hardening and his Islamic conservatism was becoming still more pronounced. At court, the emperor was under pressure from hard-line Sunnis who advocated Islamic revivalism and a clearer statement that Sharia Law was the empire's defining judicial and social principle. Such agitators sometimes saw Hinduism as the greatest threat to the security of a properly Muslim nation and, while Shah Jahan himself was far from a firebrand Islamist or stern puritan, he was inclined towards spasmodic outbursts of intolerance towards his own citizens. In January 1633, the emperor briskly ordered the demolition of as many as seventy partly-built temples at Benares, a Hindu holy site on the Ganges. His reasons may have been partly aesthetic; he may also have feared the local power of wealthy Hindus in the city. But his sectarian mission, as described by his own officials, was clear: 'the infidel-consuming monarch, who is the guardian of religion [i.e. Islam], commanded that at Benares and throughout the entire imperial dominions, wheresoever idol-temples had been recently built, they should be razed to the ground'.[26]

Shah Jahani religious architecture proliferated. A typical example of it at its peak is the compact and perfectly proportioned white marble mosque at Ajmer, the dusty Rajput town dubbed the 'Seat of Holiness' after the Chishti shrine that had drawn the emperor's fore-fathers like a magnet. Shah Jahan had less time for the Sufis than had Jahangir or Akbar – neglecting to visit Ajmer until his tenth year on the throne – but the mosque is a gem, quite deserving of its sixty-six-panel Persian eulogy and a worthy memorial to the man celebrated within as 'the religion-cherishing king, the Sun of Faith [who] has completely wiped away the tyrant of infidelity'.[27]

But the single most eye-watering extravagance of Shah Jahan's entire reign – an opulent indulgence that would be visible to just a tiny minority of courtiers, aristocrats and visiting dignitaries – was produced with a triumphant fanfare on 22 March 1635, the seventh formal anniversary of

his accession. This was a doubly auspicious occasion, for, in a rare meeting of the Muslim and Persian calendars, the Nauruz Spring Festival coincided exactly with the Eid al-Fitr, which celebrated the end of Ramadan, the holy month of fasting. The emperor and his court were returning from Kashmir and the astrologers divined that the third day of the festival would be the most auspicious for Shah Jahan to re-enter his capital and take his seat for the first time on his sensational new throne.

His father Jahangir may have been a man devoted to the pleasures of life but he had been content with a slab of black basalt, minimally engraved. Shah Jahan had eyed up the glut of gems in the royal treasury, hoarded over three generations, and decided that they were of greater use where they could be seen and appreciated. So he had commissioned from Said Gilani and his colleagues at the imperial goldsmiths' department a throne that was altogether more regal. Seven years in the making, the vast platform was more a miniature gazebo than any conventional western throne: eight feet deep, seven wide and fourteen feet to the crest of its golden canopy. It was created of more than two thousand six hundred pounds of solid gold – worth more than two million rupees – beaten and moulded into shape. Into it were fitted nearly nine million rupees worth of gems. It was an extraordinary indulgence, even by Mughal standards, costing twice as much as Mumtaz-Mahal's Illumined Tomb and woefully understated by its conventional label, the *Takht-Murassa*, or 'Ornamented Throne'.[28] The following description, based on the eye-witness accounts of Shah Jahan's courtiers, identifies the bird motif that prompted many historians retrospectively to label the masterpiece the 'Peacock Throne':

The inner roof was enamelled and had only a few stones set here and there; but the outside was covered with rubies, garnets and other gems. Twelve pillars of emeralds supported this roof. Above it were perched two figures of peacocks, facing each other with spread-out wings and studded with precious stones of every description. Between them was placed a tree set with rubies, diamonds, emeralds and pearls. Each peacock held a brilliant ruby in its beak and looked like a fire-eating bird.

Three jewelled steps led up to the Emperor's seat, which was surrounded on eleven sides with jewelled planks serving as railings. On these eleven panels the most splendid was the middle one, on which the emperor rested his arm reclining. It cost one million rupees; its central ruby alone being worth one hundred thousand. This ruby was a present from Shah Abbas, the Persian king, to Jahangir.[29]

The emperor's favourite poet, Haj Muhammad Qudsi, had been chosen to compose twenty verses that were inscribed in emerald and green enamel on the glistening fabric of the throne. Showering praise on the matchless skill of the artisans, the 'heaven-depleting grandeur' of its gold and jewels

Shah Jahan on the peacock throne

and the imperial majesty that it set off so well, Qudsi's poem climaxed with a chronogram that picked out the date in the letters of the phrase: 'The throne of the just king'.[30] Qudsi may have been on fine form, but he was comprehensively eclipsed by his colleagues. Abu-Talib Kalim was given six pieces of gold for each verse in his beautiful and image-packed celebratory poem of sixty-three couplets. And even he was outmatched by the master goldsmith himself, who had been summoned by Shah Jahan and showered with honours, including his weight in gold coins and the title *Bibadal-Khan*, the 'Peerless Master'. Said Gilani produced a poem of 134 couplets, positively packed with clever chronograms. The first twelve revealed the date of the emperor's birth, the following thirty-two the date of his first coronation; then came ninety couplets giving the date of the throne's inauguration.

Towards India he turned his reins quickly and went in all glory,
Driving like the blowing wind, dapple-grey steed swift as lightning.
With bounty and liberality, he returned to the capital;
Round his stirrups were the heavens and the angels round his reins.
A thousand thanks! The beauty of the world has revived
With the early glory of the throne of multi-coloured gems.[31]

For all the wealth and beauty of Shah Jahan's new building works, secular and religious, it was his decision to create a new imperial capital from scratch at Delhi, due north up the River Yamuna, that was his most radical initiative – and the one that would perhaps leave the most lasting impact on the empire. Given that Agra had not deteriorated in any way as a viable capital (beyond its byways becoming unpleasantly cramped and its riverbank eroded), it appears to be an entirely gratuitous projection of ego, wealth and power – or, in the words of one loyal historian, because 'exalted emperors always had it in their mind to adorn their reigns by some permanent records and signalise their times by the establishment of some everlasting landmarks'.[32] Perhaps Shah Jahan simply sought to emulate his beloved grandfather, Akbar; perhaps he thought that a new citadel in his likeness would mean a renewed empire in his likeness. Certainly the emperor's tame scribes had little to offer by way of motive beyond the desire to select 'some pleasant site, distinguished by its genial climate, where he might found a splendid fort and delightful edifices ... through which the streams of water should be made to flow and the terraces of which should overlook the river'.[33]

Great swathes of the Delhi area had fallen on hard times: it was now a jumble of old ruins and layers of rubble from previous occupants, including Shah Jahan's Mughal predecessors and their bitter rivals in the sixteenth-century wars, the Afghan Lodi dynasty. Passing by river in 1611, en route from Agra to Lahore on East India Company business, William Finch described the remains as a 'carcass', consisting of 'nine castles and fifty-two gates … [where] there are said to be four Delhis within five centuries'.[34] The only remaining structures of real significance were the tombs of Shah Jahan's great-grandfather, Humayun, and the venerated Sufi ascetic, Sheikh Nizam al-Din Chishti. The emperor, of course, knew Delhi mainly as a routine stop on the long, leisurely journeys to and from the northern provinces. Any trip to Lahore, Kabul or Kashmir necessitated a transfer at Delhi, from the royal barges that brought the court from Agra to the elephants, Arabian horses and palanquins that ferried them on into Punjab and the mountains. Emperor Jahangir, too, had always enjoyed stopping at Delhi's old Salimgarh fort, where the romance of the ruins, coupled with lovely gardens and the pleasant riverine climate, made for an agreeable location for protracted drinking parties.[35] Despite this sense of being past its prime, however, Delhi held a prominent place in the religious imagination of the people, who valued their visits to the shrines and tombs of the various holy men who gave the place its nickname: 'Threshold of Twenty-two Saints'.[36] It was also was a city large enough to merit status as the capital of a considerably wealthy province, rich in agriculture, serving as the permanent base of the incumbent governor, Gheirat-Khan, who was put in charge of the construction job.

The most likely vacant site lay at an historic junction where the ancient trade-route from the east – from the territories along the northern Ganges – crossed the Yamuna and divided: west on the long road to Lahore, south to Delhi and Agra. This, the emperor decided, would be the focal point of the city that would bear his name: Shahjahanabad.[37] The formal marking out of foundations began on Friday 29 April 1639, a date prescribed by the astrologers, and the first foundation stone of the new fortress was laid just two weeks later.[38] By the time the fort complex was complete in April 1648, twice as large as the old citadel at Agra, it was the centre of a model miniature city. At the heart of Shahjahanabad was the mighty red sandstone citadel, the *Qila Mubarak*, or 'Blessed Fortress'. A rare example of Shah Jahan returning to the practical but less aesthetically driven building materials and traditions of his grandfather's day, its two mile-long wall drew an irregular octagon around a parcel of prime building land. There were just two chief gateways, functional and unostentatious, to the west and south; 'the principal gate,' noted one European visitor with disappointment, 'has nothing magnificent about it'.[39] A third, smaller door at the northern end of the complex allowed a direct exit to the riverbank and the short crossing to the Salimgarh fort, while steps led down to the water from the rear of the Exclusive Audience Hall on the terrace above.

Within this enclosure rose the main palace and the sprawling mansions housing the emperor's surviving queens, his favourite daughters and his eldest sons. There were barracks for the citadel's permanent corps of guards and palace workshops and ateliers for the goldsmiths, portrait artists, tailors, embroiderers and all the myriad drones and functionaries whose invisible labours enabled the royal family to negotiate their daily life with such serenity and minimum effort. Ancillary buildings organised on a strict grid system of streets and lanes housed the royal mint and treasury, the administrative officers who ran the business of empire, the dogs and leopards for the royal hunts, the stables crammed with proud Arab stallions and, of course, the elephant-house, whose occupants would be paraded before the emperor, painted jet black and smeared from forehead to trunk with vermilion. Moored in the stream of the Yamuna below the castle walls, beyond the broad sandy bank that served both as elephant fighting arena and imperial parade-ground, bobbed a small fleet of gilded and brightly painted two-masted brigantines.

As the work progressed, oversight of the work changed with the governorship of Delhi province. With the foundations barely laid and stocks of red Sikri sandstone piling up on the riverbank, Gheirat-Khan was moved to Sind and replaced by another largely undistinguished character, Ilawardi Khan, who monitored the construction of the fortress walls before himself being replaced by one of the leading members of the team working on the Illumined Tomb at Agra: Mullah Murshid Makramat-Khan, the 'Master of Noble Qualities' himself. Now the work rate began to speed up, monitored by the emperor himself on short tours of inspection by boat from Agra.[40] In a little under nine years, wrote the Mughal biographer Shahnawaz-Khan, Shahjahanabad Fort 'had on all corners heavenly palaces and at every angle gardens and parks; in its layout and beauty it resembled a Chinese picture gallery but surpassed the latter in its grandeur'.[41] Not for nothing was the old verse of the thirteenth-century Persian poet Amir Khusraw appropriated and cut into the stone archways of the Exclusive Audience Hall, where the Ornamented Throne sat:

**If there is Paradise on face of the earth,
It is this, it is this, it is this.[42]**

Sturdy and relatively affordable as it was, the fort nevertheless drained another six million rupees from the imperial treasury. The luxury and craftsmanship of the spacious pillared halls – especially the central *Shah-*

Mahal or 'Imperial Palace', with its roof plated in silver – was unprecedented and very expensive. Nearly a million rupees were spent on gold decorations for the emperor's bathing-chamber ceiling. Such extravagance prompted comparisons with Baghdad, Cairo and Damascus, even with the awe-inspiring architecture of ancient Mesopotamia. Mullah Tughra, a Persian from Mashhad who had travelled the length and breadth of Shah Jahan's empire, took as his point of comparison an extraordinary 110-foot-high throne room at Ctesiphon on the River Tigris. Referring to this already ancient wonder, from where kings had once presided over the largest city in the world, he opined sycophantically: 'Two hundred Arches of Ctesiphon do not make a single brick of the city-walls of Delhi'.[43]

Exaggeration apart, Shahjahanabad was truly a remarkable undertaking. With the advantage of starting from scratch, the emperor's draughtsmen were able to fix all the perceived problems of Agra, where decades of uncontrolled growth had compressed boulevards to alleys and piled ramshackle bazaar against shambolic housing estates, or Fatehpur-Sikri, where drought had been the town's undoing. The most crucial development was the establishment of a predictable water supply for the body of the city and the fields in the surrounding countryside. This canal, named the 'River of Paradise', was the culmination of an ancient seventy-five-mile long waterway, once fallen into disuse but now repaired and extended to take water right to the very halls of the emperor.[44] After entering the city, the channel forked. One branch took water through a succession of royal gardens and on into the palace fortress, where it was forced under pressure through courtyard and hall in marble conduits and artificial rills to delight and cool the inhabitants, before spilling out to replenish the stone-lined moat around the castle's western side. The other channel was diverted into the heart of the city.

Water, space and fine buildings were the key ingredients in making Shahjahanabad a fresh and vital experience, a city of order but of great character and atmosphere. A weary caravan-master, arriving at night-fall with his train of truculent camels and still grumpier footsore baggage-handlers, would pass through the inevitable military cordon and customs post into a town where all the latest refinements of urban comfort and security were on offer to those who could afford them. There was spacious and safe accommodation to be found in one of the many caravanserais, refuges within the greater refuge and often endowed by ladies of the royal household. Foreigner travellers like François Bernier were certainly appreciative of such facilities, noting that they served as 'the rendezvous of the rich Persian, Uzbek and other foreign merchants, who in general may be accommodated with empty chambers, in which they remain with perfect security'.[45]

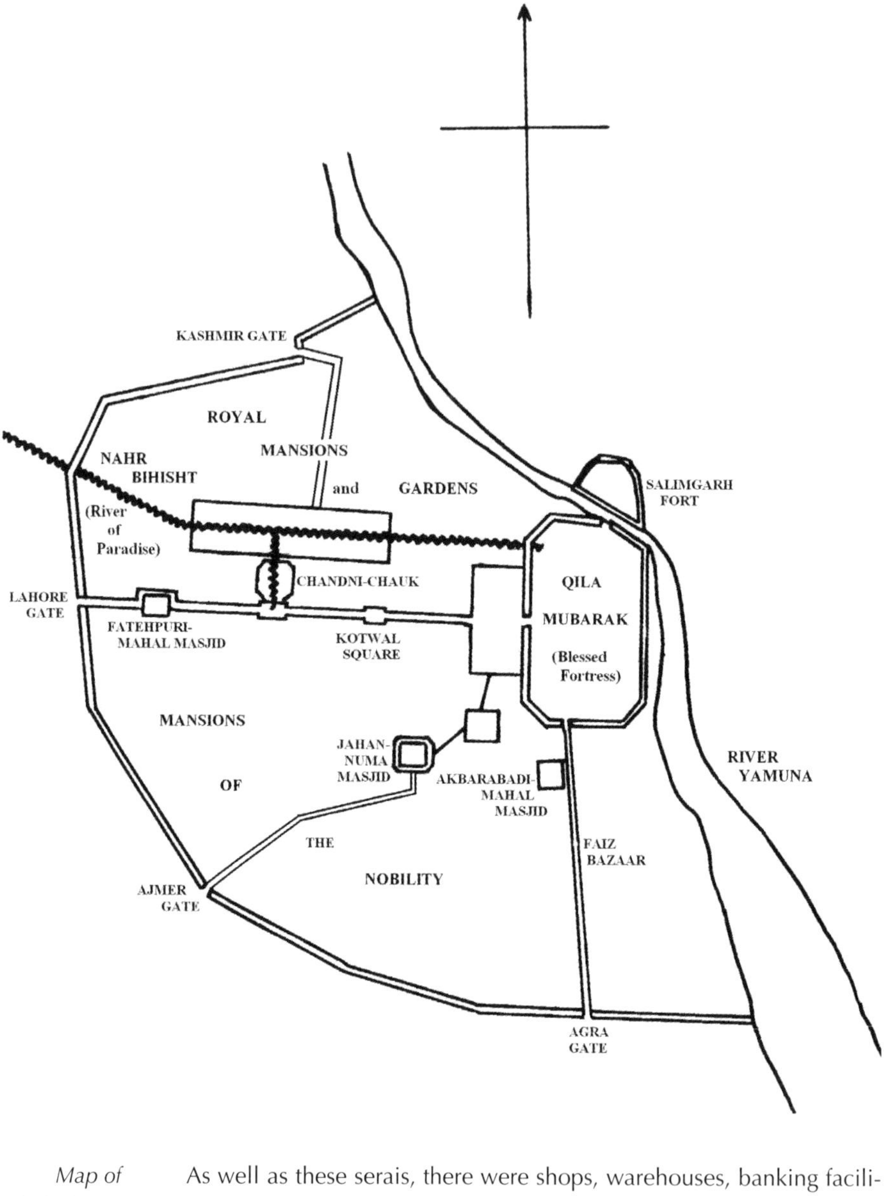
KASHMIR GATE
ROYAL
MANSIONS
and
GARDENS
NAHR
BIHISHT
(River
of
Paradise)
SALIMGARH
FORT
LAHORE
GATE
CHANDNI-CHAUK
QILA
MUBARAK
(Blessed
Fortress)
FATEHPURI-
MAHAL MASJID
KOTWAL
SQUARE
MANSIONS
OF
THE
NOBILITY
JAHAN-
NUMA
MASJID
AKBARABADI-
MAHAL
MASJID
RIVER
YAMUNA
FAIZ
BAZAAR
AJMER
GATE
AGRA
GATE

Map of Shahjahanabad, 1648

As well as these serais, there were shops, warehouses, banking facilities and restaurants aplenty, especially along the two great boulevards that ran due west and due south from the Great Square in front of the citadel: a fully modernised reincarnation of those ancient roads from the river-crossing. Forty yards wide, the western road was the largest and most important thoroughfare of the entire city. Traversing the entire breadth of the town, its centrepiece was the city branch of the 'River of Paradise' canal, bordered by an avenue of shady trees. On each side of the water was a roadway, again flanked by arcades housing more than one thousand shops, as well as the inns described so approvingly by Bernier – all of which were generously endowed by the emperor's eldest daughter, the spinster Jahan-Ara. Midway along its length was laid out a broad octagonal plaza with a square expanse of water in the middle, fed by a spur of the city canal. The tranquillity of this square after dark, when the night sky was reflected in the still waters of the pool, prompted the romantic name *Chandni-Chauk*, or 'Moon Plaza'.[46]

Jahan-Ara was not alone in splashing out some large sums on urban improvement. Among the stateliest buildings of the new city – completed a little later than the fortress – were a series of glittering mosques, each bearing the nickname of the lady who endowed it and each with domes and minarets sheathed in gilded copper. Between the Chandni-Chauk fountains and the western gate stood the Mosque of 'Fatehpuri-Begum', named for the imperial governess who had endowed the structure and whose moniker stated her origins in Akbar's old city. Standing foursquare facing up the boulevard to the fortress, the mosque complex forced travellers on the main road to divert around its northern side before resuming their westward journey to the city walls. Similarly, at the top end of the avenue leading south to Agra Gate was a substantial mosque built at the behest of Princess Purhunar's old nurse, 'Akbarabadi-Mahal'.[47] This north-south highway, the Faiz Bazaar, had as many as eight hundred shops in elegant vaulted arcades. Like every other large royal mosque, the Akbarabadi mosque sat on one side of a broad plaza graced with a pool, fountains, a well-appointed caravan-serai, a public bathhouse and a hospital.[48] Endowed by ladies of court, such mosque complexes were designed to be self-sustaining, the initial donors having formally yielded any financial return from the lucrative caravanserai market to the religious men of the mosque and to poorer citizens dependant on welfare.[49] But even these imposing complexes were overshadowed by the emperor's own gift to the city: the great congregational *Jahan-Numa-Masjid* – the 'World-Reflecting Mosque' – built on a conspicuous hillock south-west of the castle's main gate.[50]

The city's wide squares and plazas created a great sense of space but there was purpose, too. Halfway along the western avenue between the moonlit pond at Chandni-Chauk and the inner walls of the citadel was Kotwal Square, the venue for public court sessions and the brisk admin-istration of justice by the magistrates of Shahjahanabad and the Chief of Police, whose job description embraced social discipline, tax collection, census-taking and environmental cleanliness, as well as law and order. Outside the citadel, the Great Square served both as camp-ground for Rajput generals in the emperor's pay and charged with guarding the royal person and exercise arena for the imperial cavalry. Like other, less prominent squares in the city, it became at certain hours a crowded market, home to traders of all sorts. Another central market midway between the palace and the main city mosque was packed with storytellers, dancers, astrologers and quacks; the fact that the royal family had to make their way through this colourful scene earned the market the label of 'Exclusive Bazaar'.

Around and among the grand structures of empire and religion were dotted the mansions and gardens of the nobility, all of whom sought to emulate, in diminishing degrees of opulence, the luxury and space enjoyed by royalty. So the private premises of the most senior state functionaries included secluded household buildings for the immediate family, office space for administrative staff and accommodation for not just the plentiful servants but the dignitary's personal militia too. The French jeweller Jean-Baptiste Tavernier, in town to show his wares to the emperor, found Shahjahanabad a 'great straggling town', observing that 'all the houses of private persons are large enclosures, in the middle of which is the dwelling, so that no one can approach the place where the women are shut up'.[51] Each of these sprawling estates attracted its own dependent sub-district of servant accommodation and bazaars, evolving to become established *mohalla* neighbourhoods. But as size of property diminished, so too did quality of materials, resulting in the frequent fires among the cramped lanes of thatched mud-brick houses, as François Bernier observed:

More than sixty thousand roofs were consumed this last year by three fires, during the prevalence of certain impetuous winds which blow generally in summer. … Many of the inmates of the seraglio also fell victim to the devouring element; for these poor women are so bashful and helpless that they can do nothing but hide their faces at the sight of strangers and those who perished possessed not sufficient energy to fly from the danger. It is because of these wretched mud and thatch houses that I always represent to myself Delhi as a collection of many villages, or as a military encampment with a few more conveniences than are usually found in such places.[52]

The most surprising aspect of Shah Jahan's urban planning – and an indication that his own citadel was always the greatest priority – was not only that the surrounding city walls were so long in coming but that they were erected in such a slipshod manner. The first effort was simply washed away by a particularly heavy monsoon and it would not be until 1652 that the final barrier was completed, circumscribing the new city limits with a strong sandstone and mortar wall, running in a wide semi-circle around the western edge of town and meeting the riverbank at each end. Passage through this secure perimeter was restricted to four strong timber-and-iron gates, their huge hinges bedded into red sandstone. Through them travellers passed out onto the old highroads of empire: north to Kashmir, west to Lahore, south-west to Ajmer and south to Agra.[53] The freshwater Paradise Canal was channelled into the city through a secure culvert at the north-west corner. The encircling wall, the culmination of an ambitious project effectively realised, would not, however, be completed until after its designer's death.

Shah Jahan had dared to create a city from scratch and his architects had pulled it off with impressive speed. The formal inauguration of the Blessed Fortress at Shahjahanabad – nine years and two months in the making – came on Saturday 18 April 1648. It was an occasion for the full court to put on an impressive display and for poets like Yahiya Kashi to compose clever chronograms like the simple play on words 'Shah Jahan established Shahjahanabad', which produced the date of the celebrations.[54] The royal precincts at the heart of the splendid new palace were the focus of the celebrations, during which singers from the length and breadth of the empire – and beyond, from Persian and Central Asia – were invited to attend and entertain the massed dignitaries. The courtyard of the Exclusive Audience Hall was laid with luxurious carpets, while the walls were draped with swathes of silk and heavy brocade. Passing through the royal complex to the Ordinary Audience Hall, guests found themselves under another of the amazing fabric roofs thrown up for the most auspicious occasions of court: a vast canopy of velvet, hand-stitched in the imperial workshops at Ahmedabad. The thirty-thousand square feet of thick material was held seventy feet above the stone slabs of the courtyard by four columns like silver tree-trunks. It had taken three-thousand staff of the royal tent department a month to erect it and the historian Muhammad Waris boasted that 'until this joy-diffusing reign, which is the spring of good fortune and the daylight of life, no such tent of state, exalted to the heavens, has been pitched on the face of the earth'.[55] As at Agra, a silver railing around the courtyard perimeter defined the convention area for fully ten thousand men, the majority of Shah Jahan's imperial servants.

Above these lesser courtiers gathered under the immense tent were the core elite of the state, clustered around their emperor. Asaf-Khan, for so long Shah Jahan's right-hand-man, had died in late 1641, seven years earlier, and been buried not far from the late Emperor Jahangir outside Lahore.[56] In his place stood the emperor's new trusted counsellor, Saadallah-Khan, described by his biographer Shahnawaz-Khan as 'a man of great intelligence and judgement … unrivalled for his great learning and extensive knowledge of business'.[57] Shah Jahan himself sat on the balcony, cross-legged upon the sparkling new Ornamented Throne, while his heir apparent, Dara-Shikuh, stood to one side with his younger brother, Aurangzeb. The scene appeared to one of family unity and filial loyalty.

Since the mid-1640s, however, there had been signs that the fraternal rivalries of earlier generations – Akbar against Mirza Kamran, Salim against Murad and Daniyal, Khurram against Khusraw – were destined to be repeated. The mutually incompatible ambitions of Dara-Shikuh and Aurangzeb would lead to yet another cycle of Mughal internecine conflict, as each sought the highest seat in the land.

13

Like Father, Like Sons

It is not hidden from the hearts of the far-seeing that kings resemble
  gardeners.
As gardeners adorn gardens with trees, reject many, irrigate others,
extirpate bad trees and lop off evil branches … so do just and far-seeing
  kings
take care of their servants by instructing, educating and punishing them
and thereby light the lamp of wisdom and uprear the standard of
  guidance.

Sheikh Abu-al-Fadl Allami[1]

We have seen the ups and downs of the world;
We have observed the seasons of autumn and spring.
On the path of ambition one should move quickly;
We have seen the fast riding of skilful horsemen.

Chandrabhan Brahman[2]

For all the vast expense lavished on architecture public and private during Shah Jahan's thirty-year reign, nothing was quite as expensive as the business of making war. For the sixth Mughal Emperor was a man after his grandfather's heart: like Akbar, Shah Jahan was an emperor determined to preside over vigorous imperial expansion. The twenty-nine million silver rupees spent on construction would pale into insignificance beside the accounts of his northern and southern campaigns. The early years of internal rebellion were behind him and, from the time of his favourite wife's death in 1631, the thrust of military activity was outwards. Manpower and money were consumed in the struggle to push the empire into Central Asia via the important city of Kandahar and to assert definitive control over recalcitrant elements in the Deccan. But in this tireless campaigning were sown the seeds of Shah Jahan's own downfall. In his pressing need for a credible and loyal general he would enable Aurangzeb – third son of a rebellious third son – to develop a political power base and an independently loyal private army.

The chronic volatility of the south cried out for urgent action and a permanent solution. Shah Jahan had departed for Agra from the southern bridgehead at Burhanpur in 1632, a year after the death of Mumtaz-Mahal, with the Deccan war still unresolved. His initial strategy had been to isolate and destroy Ahmadnagar – the kingdom where Khan-Jahan had sought refuge in his treason – by forging an alliance with neighbouring Bijapur.³ But there were complex currents of political intrigue swirling in both these Deccan states. Muhammad Adilshah of Bijapur recklessly decided to gamble on both sides, teasing the Mughal general responsible for that front, Mir Muhammad Baqr Azam-Khan, with the possibility of a generous peace settlement while also secretly working on an alliance with Ahmadnagar.⁴ Led by the elderly and now chronically ill Zamana Beg Mahabat-Khan, the new governor of the Deccan frontier, the Mughal forces made some progress. Daulatabad Fort, the greatest stronghold in all Ahmadnagar, fell to the Mughals on 26 June 1633 after a fierce and prolonged campaign. But there were also disasters. During the blazing summer of 1633, a huge force was sent out to gather fodder for the imperial cavalry and baggage-animals. Shahnawaz-Khan described how the enemy exploited their vulnerability.

When they started loading the straw, the enemy took possession of a defile and started firing rockets. The straw caught fire from these rockets and many elephants, camels and bullocks were burnt and the whole plain was filled with flames and no way of escape was possible. They say that thirty-thousand quadrupeds and ten-thousand men were burnt, besides a numberless multitude who were half-burnt. … After the flames were extinguished the enemy made an attack and pressed the imperialist force hard.⁵

The catastrophe stopped Mahabat-Khan's Bijapur campaign in its tracks. Before he could regroup by gathering reinforcements from Agra, he was laid low with a terminal bout of illness and in late 1634 'rolled up the carpet of his life'.⁶ The loss of his most valued general forced Shah Jahan himself to take command, on what was to be his first and last expedition to the south as emperor. Departing from Agra, he travelled first to Daulatabad, bypassing Burhanpur 'on account of the fact that the inevitable demise of Her Majesty the Queen had taken place there'.⁷ Once based at Daulatabad fortress, the emperor executed an uncompromising policy that tackled all three Deccan states: Ahmadnagar, Bijapur and Golconda. Experience had proved that none could be trusted; indeed, his worst fear was a rebuilt tripartite alliance against him. So he divided his army into four divisions: three were deployed against the kings of Bijapur and Golconda to browbeat them into surrender and a resumption of the old tribute, while the fourth was charged·with the obliteration of Ahmadnagar. The plan was partially successful. Mughal forces fanned out from Daulatabad Fort, sweeping through Ahmadnagar with artillery, matchlock and sword. The Qutbshah of Golconda capitulated immediately, as he had a decade earlier, pledging to pay a fortune in tribute and recognise Shah Jahan as his overlord, both on the face of Golconda coinage and in the khutba prayers. Bijapur was not such a pushover but, after a succession of bloody encounters and further devastation of the countryside, Shah Jahan wrote an insulting letter to Muhammad Adilshah, threatening dire reprisals.

It is therefore requisite that … in the countries of Bijapur and Golconda and as far as the sea-shore, you make use of the khutba, the coin and the measure of Shah Jahan. … Otherwise having torn your skin and flesh with the talons of the swift royal falcon and his cruel beak, you will become a prey to the common kites. Listen therefore to these words with the ear of understanding and do not sleep like the hare while the eagle is in quest of her![8]

Muhammad Adilshah caved in, agreeing to reparations of two million rupees in exchange for a share in a partitioned Ahmadnagar. But by the time the peace treaty was signed, on 6 May 1636, its rigorous stipulations had been mitigated considerably, mainly because of a flood of emotional letters reminding Shah Jahan of how he had been helped by Bijapur during his years of rebellion. As a result, he now resisted the temptation to insist on full subjugation or annexation, settling instead for a treaty based on mutual trust and the territorial division of Ahmadnagar.[9] The emperor's personal presence appears to have made the crucial difference: two of the Deccan states had been neutralised, the third destroyed. So, just a fortnight after receiving Golconda's tribute of four million rupees in cash and kind, Shah Jahan decamped for the north, eagerly anticipating a rainy season on the high plateau at Mandu. And on 23 July 1636, three days after his father's departure, the eighteen-year-old Prince Aurangzeb took office as provincial governor of the Deccan.

The appointment was the latest stage in an unblemished career, during which Shah Jahan's third son had managed minor military campaigns and provincial appointments with aplomb. It was also evidence of just how different in character Aurangzeb was from his oldest brother, Dara-Shikuh. While Dara, now 21, had opted for a life at court, close to the person of the emperor, Aurangzeb had chosen the long, distant road of military glory. Each had made a calculated decision, a hard-headed assessment of the best route towards royal favour and then power. In the long, slow struggle that was to ensue, the relative merits of the soldier and the scholar, the Islamist outsider and the liberal court aesthete, would play a crucial part in the outcome of their contest for the throne – and would have traumatic implications for the fate of the emperor himself. In the summer of 1636, however, those years of insurrection and outright rebellion were still far off: Shah Jahan was forty-two year old and in only the eighth year of his reign. He would rule for a further twenty-two years but the seeds of rivalry between four of his sons – Dara, Aurangzeb, Shah-Shuja and Murad-Bakhsh – were already beginning to grow into mutual hostility.

While his younger brother moved to the Deccan, Dara-Shikuh stayed in Agra, secure in his formal recognition as Shah Jahan's heir apparent. Three year earlier, in October 1633, he had been awarded the Hissar Firoza estate, the time-honoured preserve of the Mughal Crown Prince. In addition to his administrative obligations at the capital, he pursued the life of a spiritual truth-seeker, motivated by his masters of the Qadirya Sufi sect. But in his spiritual quest he had wandered far from the path of Islam alone. He had delved into Christian thought, exploring the Gospels, the Psalms and the Pentateuch with the help of young Europeans like Niccolao Manucci. Aided by scholars from Benares, he had also produced Persian translations of the great Sanskrit texts of Hinduism, including the Upanishads and the *Bhagavad-Gita*. So far, indeed, had he gone in his investigation of possible common ground between the Muslim and Hindu faiths that he confided in one letter: 'The externals of Islam have fallen off from the heart of this fakir and the real infidelity has been revealed to me. I have become the wearer of the sacred thread [like a Hindu Brahmin], an idol worshipper.' [10]

By the time of the inauguration of Shahjahanabad in 1648, the thirty-three-year-old Dara-Shikuh had published at least three volumes of meditation on the Prophet Muhammad, saints and mysticism and his greatest works still lay ahead.[11] He was a Muslim but one in the mould of his great-grandfather, Akbar: an anomaly at a court where orthodoxy held sway. As he bowed to receive a heavy silk robe of honour and a formal military promotion, many looked askance at this pampered, probing prince. He in his turn was inclined to denounce the unquestioning conservatives as 'blockheads without insight'.[12] After all, he had the protection of his rank as the emperor's favoured son, the *Shah buland iqbal*: 'Prince of Good Fortune'. The problem was that while his rank – and thus the number of armed men under his direct authority – outmatched all three of his brothers combined, it was little more than theoretical. So, too, were his various postings as provincial viceroy of Allahabad and Punjab; after all, with the emperor determined never to let him leave court, Dara was the ultimate absentee landlord. It was no surprise, then that there was considerable animosity between the crown prince and the dynamic Aurangzeb.[13]

For his younger brother was, by contrast, a man of action. Not that Aurangzeb was stupid or uneducated; he had received the full attentions of the court's intelligentsia, indigenous and imported. Mir Muhammad Hashim al-Gilani and his tutorial team had steered the boy through all the conventional disciplines of an aristocratic schooling, from the Koran and the Sayings of the Prophet through mathematics and astronomy to archery, swordsmanship and elephant handling. Aurangzeb's innate linguistic abilities had enabled him to pick up a solid grasp of Hindi and Chagatay Turkish – the latter useful for northern campaigns – as well as the essential Persian and Arabic of high society and mainstream Sunni Islam.[14] So the conventional honorifics showered upon princes of the line – 'Precious Gem' and 'Prince of the World' – were matched by a sense of genuine respect, even if his haughty demeanour had won him few true friends among his loyal household.

An incident at the age of fourteen had singled him out for special attention by the emperor. The prince was officiating at an elephant fight on the sandbank below the jharoka window at Agra Fort in May 1633 when one of the tuskers ran amok. Coolly facing the beast down on horseback, Aurangzeb spiked the elephant's forehead with his spear. Enraged, it swiped the prince's horse from under him with a blow of its trunk. Undeterred, the youth scrambled to his feet and again faced the elephant with his spear. Reinforcements arrived in the nick of time, the prince's retinue hurling firecrackers to frighten the beast off into the deep water – but Aurangzeb's reputation was made. 'If the fight had ended fatally for me,' he told his father, 'it would not have been a matter of shame. Death drops the curtain even on emperors.'[15] In a mixture of admiration and relief, Shah Jahan had his son weighed against gold coins and presented with the treasure – along with the elephant that had nearly taken his life.

Since this incident, Aurangzeb had measured out his teenage years in steady progress through his lessons and military training. Shortly before his sixteenth birthday, he had been given the rank of Ten Thousand infantry and Four Thousand cavalry – and awarded the 'lal purdah', the scarlet silk curtain to draw across the entrance of his tent.[16] More significantly, he had been given real command responsibility, leading 20,000 men on an expedition to bring Jujhar Singh Bundela of the renegade Orchha clan back to heel. The Hindu prince had taken advantage of the mayhem in the Deccan, where he had been ordered into service as provisional reha-bilitation, to slip away and resume his harassment of Mughal officials and messengers. Aurangzeb handled the mission with commendable speed and efficiency, pursuing Jujhar Singh so relentlessly that the chieftain even-tually despaired, executed the women of his household and fled into the forest, where he was murdered by tribesmen.[17]

Such leadership credentials made the eighteen-year-old a strong candidate to take over the Deccan, newly subjugated and divided into four administrative territories.[18] All the evidence suggests that Aurangzeb, promoted again to the rank of Fifteen Thousand foot and Ten Thousand horse, was a good governor. Revenues were increased, highway robbers were mercilessly brought to justice and peripheral territories were brought under firm Mughal control. But there was envy in the wind: from Agra came a succession of sniping messages, penned by the emperor himself but apparently prompted by a jealous Dara-Shikuh. His viceregal autonomy effectively curtailed, Prince Aurangzeb was reduced to sending a stream of letters to the capital, alternately justifying his decisions and pleading for resources.[19]

Matters came to a head in March 1644, by which time Aurangzeb had administered the Deccan territories with increasing frustration for eight years. In a mysterious accident within the harem compound, Princess Jahan-Ara was badly burnt and, with the doctors despairing for her life, Aurangzeb hurried home to see the emperor's favourite daughter for what he thought would be the last time. Jahan-Ara survived – but the prince's precipitate return to Agra did not help his command prospects. Within two months, he had resigned his governorship, complaining against the animosity of Dara-Shikuh and the emperor's clear bias towards his eldest son. Shah Jahan's tame chroniclers did their best to cover up what was to them a wilful assertion of independence. Abd-al-Hamid Lahori claimed that Aurangzeb had been 'duped by his foolish companions', while Muhammad Salih Kamboh pointed to Aurangzeb's conservative religious beliefs: 'The prince, having been charmed by the holy company of the ascetics, wanted to renounce the world; but, since such conduct was not appreciated by the emperor, he degraded him from his rank'.[20] Resignation was dressed up as dismissal and Aurangzeb was temporarily in the wilderness. The power struggle was now in the open.

The consolidation of the south in 1636, meanwhile, had prompted Shah Jahan to re-examine his northern frontiers, which now looked decidedly vulnerable. The fortress towns of Kandahar and Kabul were effectively the twin pillars of the Gateway to India from the north, the route by which invaders from Alexander of Macedon to Babur of Central Asia had fought their way into the plains of Hindustan. Persia had besieged and captured Kandahar in June 1622 and Kabul had been menaced by the Uzbek incursions of 1625 and 1628. But beyond the practicalities of maintaining secure frontier outposts – especially when they accrued revenues from lucrative trade routes – Shah Jahan was not immune from the longing experienced by his father and grandfather for the 'ancestral homeland' of Central Asia.[21] Regular funds were sent to maintain the black jade tomb of the Amir Timur the Lame at Samarkand.[22] Despite his many achievements, there remained a deep-rooted sense of incompleteness, of destiny left unfulfilled. So, for Shah Jahan, war in the north had a double aim: to smack down the rival ambitions of the Persians and the Uzbeks, while reclaiming territory – Balkh, Badakhshan, perhaps even Samarkand and Pokhara – that in some atavistic sense still 'belonged' to his family.

Kandahar, completely unexpectedly, fell into the emperor's lap like a ripe plum. To give him due credit, Shah Jahan had begun the necessary detailed groundwork for either a diplomatic option – forging an alliance with Persia to secure his left flank for an assault on Central Asia – or for a military resolution. Sayyid Khawaja Qasim *Safdar-Khan* was sent to Persia in 1636 to 'gather valuable data on the relative military strength of the Safavids'.[23] Along with a delegation of appropriate grandiosity, the ambassador carried with him letters from his monarch, packed with the usual flowery sentiments and drafted by Shah Jahan's Chief Minister, Afzal-Khan. It turned out that there was no need for espionage when two years later, on 7 March 1638, the Persian governor of Kandahar, Ali Mardan Khan, abruptly surrendered the city to the Mughals.[24]

A man in his eighties, the governor had been a great favourite of the Persian ruler, Shah Abbas, but had fallen out with his successor, Shah Safi. His defection was rewarded with recognition by Shah Jahan as his 'faithful friend', half a million rupees in cash, lucrative estates around Herat and appointments as governor of first Kabul then Lahore.[25] Khawaja Abid *Qulij-Khan*, a Turani northerner who had been Shah Jahan's loyal follower, 'attached to the royal stirrups', since his princehood, was sent to accept Ali Mardan Khan's surrender and take over the administration of the border area, backed by his personal militia of one thousand heavily-armed Uzbek tribesmen.[26] A contemporary painting shows Ali Mardan Khan, on foot and bowing humbly from the waist, surrendering the keys of the city to Qulij-Khan, who towers haughtily over the Persian delegation on his white horse, heron feathers tucked into his turban.[27] After sixteen years, Kandahar Fort was once again a Mughal possession.

Shah Jahan hastily consolidated this surprise acquisition, though not before sending an urgent letter to the Persian ruler, justifying the re-occupation of Kandahar, apologising for any inconvenience caused and – the crowning insolence – advising Shah Safi in haughty tones to forget the whole thing.[28] In case of swift Persian retaliation, however, reinforcements were pressed from available contingents across the northern empire and rushed to Kandahar. By December 1641, Fr Sebastião Manrique, the zealous Portuguese Jesuit now travelling in the northern mountains, found a city 'enclosed on the west by a lofty, rugged and precipitous mountains, on the south and east by a strong wide wall furnished with many powerful cannon'.[29]

This easy acquisition of Kandahar gave Shah Jahan the confidence to plan a robust campaign into Central Asia. The Persians watched with dismay at the show of force on their north-eastern borders. Nor were they alone in their alarm at Shah Jahan's expansionist ambitions. The Ottoman emperor at faraway Constantinople, Sultan Mehmet IV, wrote with an urgent appeal to the Mughals to curtail their Central Asian adventure. The selection of a distinguished Sufi, Sayyid Muhi al-Din, as his ambassador indicates Mehmet's awareness of Dara-Shikuh's influence at court.[30] But the message fell on deaf ears.

Shah Jahan's initial target was the small mountain kingdom of Balkh, a territory under the leadership of Nazr Muhammad Khan. The first attack force was placed under the command of Prince Murad-Bakhsh, now twenty-four years old and hoping to position himself as a general of good standing in his father's eyes. Shah Jahan himself advanced to make Kabul his front line headquarters. Defying his reputation for being a drinker and party-goer, Murad mounted an effective offensive in 1646, driving back the Uzbek opposition. When he entered Balkh in triumph, Shah Jahan threw a party at Kabul that lasted eight days.[31] Nazr Muhammad Khan sought refuge in Persia.

Unfortunately, Murad then promptly withdrew to Kabul, declaring the campaign a success and ignoring the chiding letters from the emperor that ordered him to stay and secure the 'key to the conquest of Turan'. Aurangzeb, the only real general in the family, did his best to follow developments from his new base at Ahmedabad, far away on the west coast. He owed this partial rehabilitation to Jahan-Ara, who, on her recovery, had appealed to Shah Jahan to give Aurangzeb the governorship of Gujarat.[32] But Aurangzeb now strained at the leash, outraged at his brother's pathetic behaviour:

His Majesty wanted to keep Balkh, Badakhshan, Herat and Khorasan under his control. He sent armies for the same purpose at several times and those places were conquered. Murad-Bakhsh left the region without his permission and the Mughals lost those places. The financial resources were wasted for nothing. That is why someone has rightly said that a daughter is better than a wicked son. If the father is not able to complete the job, then it is the duty of the son to do it.[33]

The dutiful son was now given his chance. Qulij-Khan had been rushed in to fill the gap left by the disgraced Murad-Bakhsh – an Uzbek set against Uzbek clansmen – but a prince of the line outranked even a successful general. Early successes in 1647–8 were, however, spoiled by interference from the capital, where Dara-Shikuh sought relentlessly to undermine his brother's prospects. As a result, the Central Asian front degenerated into first muddle then defeat. Heavily armed Mughal battalions were unable to crush the more mobile enemy, who played to the advantage of their rugged and familiar terrain, harassing the invaders with hit-and-run raids. Morale deteriorated as desertions by Rajput troops were compounded by harsh winter conditions, inadequate supply lines over the mountains and financial difficulties. As Aurangzeb and Dara-Shikuh bickered and squabbled for command glory and, by extension, their father's benign attention, disaster loomed. Failure became inevitable when their adversaries, reverting to a strategy last tried twenty years earlier, forged an urgent alliance with Persia in late 1648. Shah Jahan's efforts to keep the two fronts separate – including a somewhat smug and patronising letter to the new Persian ruler, Shah Abbas II, urging him to expel Nazr Muhammad Khan to Mecca – had failed.[34]

The extent of that failure was revealed when the Persian army retook Kandahar on 23 February 1649 after a two-month siege. With breathtaking cheek, the new Shah wrote to Shah Jahan observing that as he had asked the Mughal emperor to hand over the city and was 'certain that the noble uncle would not grudge this': the refusal of the garrison to surrender had been an act of wilful disobedience to both rulers and its forceful recapture a decision 'taken on the basis of mutual accord'.[35] It was a stunning blow to Shah Jahan's aspirations on the north-west frontier.

Aurangzeb was given conditional command of the first campaign to relieve the city the following year, accompanied at all times by the emperor's own man, Saadallah Khan. Without heavy artillery, however, the campaign was doomed and Aurangzeb was forced to retreat before the winter snows. The second campaign fared little better, with the prince compelled to relay every decision back to Shah Jahan at Kabul, who usually authorised Saadallah Khan to veto it. Even when the commander's decisions were endorsed, the procedure ate up time, sapped morale and crushed any spontaneity in the field. Projects to drain the moat and undermine the massive walls were abandoned for want of proper digging equipment. And Dara-Shikuh continued to snipe from the rear, poisoning the emperor's mind against his brother and agitating for his own appointment as supreme commander in the mountains. Shah Jahan himself wrote a series of snide letters to Aurangzeb, saying that one who has failed does not deserve a second chance and rejecting the prince's pleas to be allowed more time or even to be permitted to serve as a junior officer under Dara. 'Had I considered you competent to take Kandahar,' he wrote, witheringly, 'I would not have summoned my forces back.'[36]

It can have come as no surprise that Dara-Shikuh's follow-up campaign was a complete debacle, destroying any pretensions to military competence that he may have nursed. This was a man who had the assets of five provinces at his personal command, his own army of sixty thousand infantry and forty thousand cavalry – in addition to the imperial levy conscripted especially for the campaign – and, above all, the absolute faith of the emperor. He also had the cream of the imperial officer-class at his disposal. Yet all was squandered. Dara's progress north only confirmed the gossip about his superstition and credulousness. During the march from Lahore Fort to Kandahar, his entourage included not only a number of Sunni scholars and Sufi holy men but also Hindu and Muslim magicians and miracle-workers. One such wizard, claiming to have forty genies at his beck and call, was 'entrusted to secure the reduction of Kandahar by prayers and magic'.[37] Perhaps desperate times required desperate measures. But it fell far short of the military discipline and leadership needed. Dara-Shikuh's ultimatums to the besieged garrison, the documents scrolled around arrow-shafts and fired over the walls, were contemptuously disregarded.

Three attempts to retake Kandahar had failed and Shah Jahan's Central Asian territorial ambitions lay in ruins. By the time it was finally abandoned in 1653, the northern campaign had brought Shah Jahan modest gains at best. The Uzbeks were damaged as a military force and shattered economically; Kabul itself would be safeguarded from attack for nearly a century. But Kandahar was lost, as was the myth of Mughal invincibility. The frontier had been pushed just thirty-five miles north. And it had all cost a fortune: almost forty million rupees, more than the construction of the Illumined Tomb, the Ornamented Throne and the new capital at Delhi combined. Revenue collection from the conquered territories never amounted to more than two million per year. It was a colossal misjudgement and more than just money and reputation was wasted. A contemporary chronicler from north of the border, Muhammad Yusuf bin Khawaja Baqa, travelled south into Hindustan the following summer and saw 'strewn all along the route animal and human bones; at places there were piles of them'.

Prince Aurangzeb sought to put as much distance as possible between himself and this military disaster. Accepting a new appointment as Governor of the Deccan – along with a promotion to the rank of Twenty Thousand infantry and Fifteen Thousand horse – he departed the north on 27 August 1652 without even giving his soldiers time to recover from their exhaustion.[38] Arriving in Daulatabad the following January, he discovered that the six men who had administered the territory since his own sudden resignation nearly eight years before had gradually allowed the Deccan to slide into a state of lawlessness and poverty.[39] Worse from the perspective of an eternally greedy imperial exchequer – not to mention the courtiers whose estates were no longer yielding enough to meet household and military expenses – the Deccan was drying up as a supply of revenue. Good taxes required good agriculture and the combination of economic stagnation and insecurity meant that 'much cultivated soil had lapsed into the jungle, the cultivators had declined in number and the revenues had fallen off greatly'.[40]

Unexpectedly, then, Aurangzeb became a Mughal governor whose priority was economic development rather than territorial expansion. His secret weapon was Murshid Quli Khan, a keen administrator from Khorasan who implemented a series of clever measures, including concessions for settlement of wild land, special government loans and taxes capped at 25% of agricultural production.[41] The reforms yielded quick results and before long, Aurangzeb was able to report a thirty-three per cent increase in revenues. But the sniping resumed from court, by now relocated to Shahjahanabad. First, Aurangzeb's closest followers were transferred one by one to the new capital; Shah Jahan knew better than anyone the dangers of allowing a rival power base to build up. Then came the financial pressure: the Deccan administration was ordered to implement pay-cuts: another tactic of Dara-Shikuh to undermine local support for his brother. Aurangzeb proposed offsetting some of the salary burden from his own estate holdings in Malwa and Gujarat, an offer roundly rejected by Shah Jahan at Shahjahanabad. In fact, Aurangzeb was already suffering financially. The combination of his recent promotions, which required the maintenance of tens of thousands of soldiers and their equipment, and the allocation of less wealthy estates meant that the prince was incurring an annual loss of 1.7 million rupees – nearly as bad as the province-wide deficit.[42]

Shah Jahan's rebellious sons: Shah-Shuja, Aurangzeb and Murad-Bakhsh

As a way of replenishing his coffers, Aurangzeb now eyed the territories of Bijapur and Golconda with an acquisitive eye. There were sound commercial reasons for desiring to expand south and east, not least because the Bijapuris held fifty per cent of the former kingdom of Ahmadnagar and because Golconda controlled access to the Coromandel Coast, where ports like Machilipatnam were enjoying the benefits of lucrative international trade in indigo and textiles. There were diamond mines and iron ore to be found there, too, and fertile territory on the Godavary and Krishna rivers. Politics and religion, as so often, were both also involved. Both Bijapur and Golconda were tied to the Mughal Empire by sworn treaty whose security obligations should have been mutual. But they were also Shiite kingdoms, frequently in direct maritime contact with Shah Jahan's enemy, the Shah of Persia. Their wealth could help prop up the struggling economy of the Mughal Deccan holdings; their occupation would remove a direct threat on the southern border; the subjection of the Shiite would be pleasing to the Sunni conservative Aurangzeb.

Despite such pragmatic reasoning, Aurangzeb knew he could not count on his father's unequivocal support for an invasion so he attacked without asking permission. It was a considerable gamble. The hostility of Dara-Shikuh to all his schemes was taken for granted. But success, he knew, would win over Shah Jahan – especially if it involved the kind of booty, cash and jewels that Prince Khurram had so enjoyed seizing in the old days. And he had a secret ace up his sleeve. Mir Muhammad Amin was a diamond merchant originally from Isfahan, who had emigrated to Golconda in 1630 and worked his way up to become Prime Minister to its ruler, Abdallah Qutbshah, honoured with the title *Mir-Jumla*. This deter-mined character had already acquired military experience overseeing the conquest of lands in the Karnataka for his king but – mainly because he had taken the opportunity to carve out a sizeable piece of fertile land for himself – he had fallen out with the Qutbshah. Persona non grata in Golconda, he now offered his services to Aurangzeb, pledging to work in secret to undermine resistance to the invasion.

The Mughal army was led by Aurangzeb's eldest son, Muhammad Sultan, who left Daulatabad with the command to take the Qutbshah by surprise and 'lighten his neck of the burden of his head'.[43] It was a brisk offensive: on 24 January 1656, the young general entered Bhagnagar and authorised the wholesale plunder of the city. Abdallah Qutbshah was besieged within Golconda Fort; his letters, 'craving pardon' and offering to marry his daughter to Muhammad Sultan in exchange for peace were rejected by Aurangzeb, who only wished 'to send him to the wilderness of destruction'.[44] But this impressive success proved to be the last straw in the long dispute with Dara-Shikuh. Even as Aurangzeb wrote to Shah Jahan to report on his victory and urge the complete annexation of Golconda, messengers were racing north from Abdallah Qutbshah to Dara's office, appealing for his support. Even the empire's enemies knew how best to capitalise on the divisions within the royal family. As before, there was no contest. Shah Jahan, ever anxious to shore up the Crown Prince's position at the expense of any possible rival, overruled Aurangzeb and ordered a humiliating withdrawal. The occupation had lasted barely two months.

Before the end of the year, however, the incorrigible Aurangzeb sniffed his next opportunity. Muhammad Adilshah of Bijapur died on 4 November 1656, leaving an eighteen-year-old son, crowned as Ali II. But rumours about the boy's true parentage began to swirl, provoking divisions inside the Bijapuri court and inviting the attentions of the prowling young Mughal at Daulatabad. Aurangzeb wrote immediately to Shahjahanabad, requesting permission for a full-scale invasion. His confidence that this time would be different was boosted by the presence of Mir-Jumla at court. Shah Jahan had maintained his practice of siphoning off the best talent to the capital; welcoming the Shiite on 7 July 1656, the emperor promoted him to the powerful rank of Six Thousand and handed him the job of Chief Minister, replacing the recently deceased Saadallah Khan.[45] But Mir-Jumla's valuable Deccan experience and evident abilities were not the only factors in prompting his dizzyingly swift rise to power: a gift of an enormous diamond that immediately took pride of place in Shah Jahan's jewellery collection may have helped seal the deal.[46] So, in early December 1656, Aurangzeb's invasion was approved. Residual doubts about tearing up the twenty-year-old treaty were squashed. Any moral debt to Bijapur, Shah Jahan argued, had been owed to the late emperor, not to his callow successor. It was time for the sovereignty of the Mughal Empire to be recognised.

Backed by reinforcements from Shahjahanabad under the personal leadership of Mir-Jumla, Aurangzeb launched his attack on Bijapur on 2 March 1657. Refusing to heed his father's calls for moderation, compromise or negotiated surrender, the prince pursued a brutally aggressive campaign against the Shiite southerners, pressing siege after siege and capturing great swathes of territory. But again, with victory in sight, orders came from the capital to Aurangzeb's generals to return to Shahjahanabad post haste, without even consulting their field marshal. This time the brake appears to have been applied on the emperor's initiative alone. Shah Jahan knew the risks of allowing a potential claimant to the throne to grow too strong: Aurangzeb must be reduced and removed from the Deccan. Before his plans could be developed, however, the emperor fell gravely ill.

The sixteenth of September 1657 was effectively Shah Jahan's last day as unchallenged ruler of the Mughal Empire, secure in his unrivalled authority. The illness struck with speed and intensity, confining him to bed for seven full days. He had no intention of surrendering power, or even loaning it to Dara; instead, he stubbornly continued to receive ministers and correspondence in his private chambers.[47] But this period of recuperation produced the most dangerous symptom of all: invisibility. When the emperor no longer made his daily appearances at the jharoka darshana, there was consternation at court and it spread like the plague. Soon all Shahjahanabad believed he was dead and by the time he staggered weakly to his window to show his face to the people on 24 September, the rumour of his passing had already swept into the countryside.

Fast-riding couriers brought the news to the princes of the royal line: Aurangzeb at Daulatabad, smarting at his latest reverse; Murad-Bakhsh in Gujarat, equally outraged by a recent intrigue on the part of Dara-Shikuh to demote him and send him south; and finally Shah-Shuja away east in Bengal, the emperor's second son but a man equally frustrated by Dara's endless machinations. For the past five years or more, the three brothers had maintained an informal triple entente in the face of Dara's increasing high-handedness. Aurangzeb had been the prime mover, arranging 'chance' meetings with Shah-Shuja and Murad and an exchange of coded letters. The alliance between two of the conspirators had been cemented by the arranged marriage in 1652 of Aurangzeb's first son, Muhammad Sultan, and Gulrukh Banu, eldest daughter of Shah-Shuja. But now the throne was at stake and alliances were cast aside. The secret messages continued for a while, but each man was now considering which strategy might further his own candidacy.[48] Their father's own bloody path to the throne had shown that the only motto sufficient unto the battle ahead was 'Kill or be killed'. Later, looking back on the events of that time and describing the fratricidal struggles that had broken the imperial family, generation after generation, the Jesuit priest António Botelho quoted Aurangzeb's sharp rejoinder when asked about his intentions vis-à-vis his brothers in the event of the death of the emperor. The prince was characteristically laconic and devoid of mercy: 'I will do as my father did'.[49]

14

Prisoner of the Royal Tower

Little thought this prince that one day he would be forced
to live at Agra … and far less still that he should be prisoner there
in his own palace and so end his days in affliction and trouble.

Jean de Thévenot [1]

Shah Jahan kard wafat: The King of the World has died.
Razi Allah: May God be pleased with him.

Ashraf Khan [2]

What are the qualities of an Emperor?
To do justice and to take care of the people.
He should be a hardworking and pious person.

Prince Aurangzeb [3]

Now began a brutal and prolonged end-game. The first of the princes
to lay open claim to the imperial crown – the first to violate the 'triple
entente' of Dara-Shikuh's younger brothers – was Shah-Shuja in Bengal.
At forty-one, the prince would have known that his last, probably his
only, chance at the throne was at hand. Shah-Shuja was the only one of
Shah Jahan's children to espouse explicitly his mother's faith: as Arjumand
Mumtaz-Mahal had been a Shiite, the legacy of her Persian forebears,
so Shah-Shuja publicised his own adherence to the alternative path of
mainstream Islam. In doing so, he may have hoped to win the support
of an influential minority within the Mughal court and military, playing
on hitherto suppressed sectarian divisions.[4] On 30 November 1657, he
declared himself emperor, with appropriately grandiose titles: *Abu-al-
Fauz* ('Father of Victory') *Nasr al-Din* ('Protector of the Faith') Muhammad
Timur II, Alexander III, Shah-Shuja Bahadur Ghazi. Coins were minted at
Rajmahal in his name, with the Muslim declaration of faith on one face.[5]
For the past twenty years, Shah-Shuja had been content to build his own
power-base in the east, adding Orissa to his Bengal fiefdom in 1642 but
failing, thanks to Dara's ever-increasing watchfulness, to acquire Bihar.

The French merchant François Bernier describes the opening gambits
of the long conflict, less war of succession – for the emperor still lived –
than fratricidal Battle of the Usurpers:

Sultan Shah-Shuja was the first who took the field. He had filled his coffers in the rich country of Bengal by utterly ruining some of the rajas or kinglets of that region and by plundering others. He was therefore able to raise a numerous army and confiding in the support of the Persian umara [Shiite generals], whose religious views he had embraced, advanced rapidly on Agra. He issued a proclamation which set forth the death of his father by poison from the hand of Dara and declared his determination both to avenge so foul a murder and to occupy the vacant throne.[6]

The advance of Shah-Shuja from the east triggered an acceleration of his brothers' plans. At Ahmednagar on 15 December, the youngest of the clan promptly declared himself emperor, minting his own coins in the name of Muhammad Murad-Bakhsh Padshah Ghazi.[7] He executed Shah Jahan's provincial finance minister, Ali Naqi, emptied the treasury and raided Surat to plunder the warehouses of the foreign traders. Far to the south, meanwhile, Aurangzeb set his own, more careful plans in motion. Exactly as his father had done in his years of rebellion, the prince now calculated how best to advance his own cause by disposing of his rival brothers on a priority basis. Shah-Shuja had treacherously broken ranks first; if Dara at Shahjahanabad failed to crush the advance from the east, he himself would have to tackle the renegade later. So first he attempted to appease Murad-Bakhsh with assurances that his claim to autonomous sovereignty over the western half of the empire – a vast territory including Gujarat, Punjab, Sind and reaching up into Kashmir – would be recognised if he would make a military partnership with Aurangzeb. Unwisely, Murad accepted the blandishments in his brother's correspondence at face value.[8]

As for Dara-Shikuh himself, no compromise was possible. Aurangzeb's strategy was two-pronged: to maintain Shah-Shuja's fiction that Emperor Shah Jahan was dead, despite all evidence to the contrary; and to proclaim that the crown prince at Shahjahanabad was a traitor to his own religion and possibly a murderer – in either case, a thoroughly unworthy successor. Meanwhile, Aurangzeb's army, the cream of the southern command, was intact, although the loyalty of several officers was in doubt. With rumours of the emperor's death sill unconfirmed, they, like the princes, had a choice to make. Some elected to follow Dara-Shikuh and return to the capital. Many, however, including veterans like Khawaja Abid Qulij-Khan, read the political situation astutely, chose to stay with Aurangzeb and took their battle-hardened divisions on the long march from Daulatabad to Shahjahanabad.[9]

By mid-February 1658, they were encamped on the banks of the Narmada, where they waited to make rendezvous with Murad-Bakhsh and the garrisons of Gujarat. Faced with a powerful imperial intervention force

– sent by Dara-Shikuh in his father's name but led by Muhammad Qasim-Khan – Murad-Bakhsh, who had been in correspondence with the Shah of Persia for some time, sent a coded letter to Isfahan urging a diversionary attack, a 'deployment of reinforcement and aid', across the north-west frontier. Shah Abbas was lavish in his promises of 'swift and comprehensive action'; troops were being mobilised from across the empire, he wrote. From the thirty-thousand-strong Kandahar garrison to the distant outposts of Azerbaijan, a massive force would be rallied for an assault on Kabul. A contingent of musketeers was already at sea, heading for Surat, he told Murad. But the promised help never arrived.[10]

In Shahjahanabad, the ailing emperor had done his best to reassert control. Well aware of his diminished strength, Shah Jahan had convened a special meeting of the court elite at the Exclusive Hall of Audience to declare that Dara-Shikuh – formally nominated as his successor – would bear responsibility for the defence of the realm against the would-be usurpers. The Venetian adventurer, Niccolao Manucci, was then serving in Dara's army as an artilleryman; his memoir provides some of the most vivid accounts of the conflict.

The king, finding himself in bodily weakness and desirous of pleasing Dara … transferred to him all his powers and dignities and ordered everyone to yield him obedience. He wanted to try if, by this means, he could rid himself of all the ills from which he suffered, including the danger in which he stood of being captured by Aurangzeb and dispossessed of his authority.[11]

It is far from clear, however, that Shah Jahan intended to abdicate – though such an impression may have been seized upon by Aurangzeb loyalists, the better to justify his insurrection. Certainly the accounts written during Aurangzeb's subsequent reign as emperor struck a harshly negative tone, denouncing Dara for 'beating the drums of his conceit and selfishness' and for leaving 'nothing of the administration except for the name of sovereignty to Shah Jahan'.[12] Nevertheless, amid a murmur of consternation from his courtiers, Shah Jahan gave orders that the imperial household would decamp for Agra. The emperor's health should improve in the relative tranquillity of the ancient fort and he had always sought the closest vantage-point from which to monitor an on-going campaign. On 28 October 1657, Shah Jahan departed from his capital for the last time, his lean and weakened body reclining in a silver palanquin, inlaid with gold and enamel. His fate was in Dara's hands.

Dara-Shikuh's first strike was a great success. A large force was sent east, under the nominal leadership of his eldest son, Suleiman-Shikuh, to confront Shah-Shuja. The actual commanders, including Raja Jai Singh of Amber and Jalal al-Din Daudzai *Diler-Khan*, a Pathan from the north, were tough and wily campaigners. They made rapid progress, using the power of the Ganges to take great barges of troops, cannon and elephants as far as Benares before setting their ambush. The brisk and bloody finale to Shah-Shuja's ambitions came on 24 February 1658 at Bahadurpur, five miles east of the Hindu holy city. The Mughal army trounced the insurgents, leaving loyal chroniclers to lampoon the defeated prince. 'Shah-Shuja,' one wrote, 'who was always subject to sensual pleasures and was exceedingly careless and knew nothing about planning and reflection, was terrified and fled. Without attempting to fight he behaved in a childish manner and got on board a boat and fled towards Patna.' [13] His hopes were destroyed. Suleiman-Shikuh was ordered to pursue Shuja eastwards in hopes of negotiating a truce that would allow the rebel to resume office in Bengal and Orissa, solely by way of shoring up the eastern front. It was a fatal mistake. Instead of leaving the disgraced prince to an ignominious retreat and returning to buttress the defence of the capital, Suleiman-Shikuh, his generals and his men were all wasted.

The continued absence of Suleiman-Shikuh and Raja Jai Singh compelled Dara to put together a second army to face the joint advance of Aurangzeb and Murad from the south. This was primarily comprised of Rajput militias, under the overall leadership of Maharaja Jaswant Singh of Jodhpur.[14] Dara had hoped to win unanimous support from influential Rajput rulers, building on his reputation as a sympathiser to Hindus, though not all were persuaded that his was the star to follow.[15] Still, Jaswant Singh brought seven thousand of his own followers and gathered more from Rajput clans as he advanced. Several thousand additional reinforcements under Qasim-Khan joined them before they made final camp at Dharmat, not far from Ujjain, where they dug deep trenches in boggy ground and waited for Aurangzeb and Murad-Bakhsh to approach.[16]

The rebel princes crossed the Narmada – the river again becoming the Rubicon of Mughal politics – in huge numbers on 13 April 1658 and swarmed forward towards Ujjain. In command of the vanguard was Zulfiqar-Khan and responsible for the artillery was Aurangzeb's veteran administrator, Murshid Quli-Khan. On the morning of 25 April, with the battle-lines drawn up, artillery exchanges began. Aurangzeb's gunners – led by a variety of European mercenaries – exploited their superior firepower to great effect, blasting holes in Jaswant Singh's ranks. To escape the carnage, the Rajput cavalry charged forward – but the muddy ground that was to be their defensive shield proved to be their undoing in the attack. The bravery of Jaswant Singh's warriors was beyond question, however, and only undermined by the lesser commitment of their clansmen who obstinately picked different points of attack, breaking the momentum of the whole.

The charge foundered and Jaswant's generals forced their king from the field, persuading him that it would be better to live and fight for their own homeland than to die in a squalid fratricidal war whose outcome would not alter Rajput servitude to the Mughal overlord.[17] Even as the survivors galloped from the field, Qasim-Khan and his reinforcements were already in full retreat along the road north to Agra.

Shah Jahan's throne at the Red Fort in Shahjahan-abad

This dramatic early victory handed Aurangzeb a powerful propaganda weapon. Was not the crown prince's abject dependence on Hindu soldiery proof of his treachery to Islam? There were many at court who had objected to Dara-Shikuh's dabbling in religious syncretism. Now, as proof of his brother's apostasy, Aurangzeb could brandish a copy of Dara's latest heretical volume, *The Mingling of the Two Oceans*. Published three years earlier, this philosophical work went far beyond an investigation into the similarities between Sufism and Hindu mysticism, expressing a deep appreciation of the fundamental truths discovered by the author outside Islam and espousing a new idea of universal brotherhood.[18] To Aurangzeb, a conservative Sunni raised by the strictest ulama, this was anathema. Besides, it was sound politics to denounce such extremism. It was clear, Aurangzeb now wrote to doubters at court, 'that if Dara-Shikuh obtained the throne and established his power, the foundations of the Faith would be in danger and the precepts of Islam would be changed for the rant of infidelity and Judaism'.[19] The apostasy argument buttressed Aurangzeb's repeated assertion that Dara had cynically usurped power from an emperor in the terminal stages of illness. When news came from Agra – Shah Jahan's new base – that a huge festival had been held on 15 December to celebrate the emperor's full recovery, it was disregarded as running counter to the manifesto behind Aurangzeb's rebellion. It suited his purpose to insist that the emperor was dead, the crown prince a usurper, the throne vacant.

Dara now faced a critical test of his character. The grim news of the disaster at Dharmat took eleven days to find him, alongside the recuperating Shah Jahan en route from Agra back to the capital. Dara's confidence in the security of his southern front was abruptly shattered – and Sulaiman-Shikuh's success in the east was now meaningless as the continued absence of experienced generals like Raja Jai Singh, still on a wild goose chase after Shah-Shuja, left the centre dangerously exposed. To continue to Shahjahanabad would be too risky; instead, the emperor and his chosen successor doubled back downstream, electing to make the final stand in defence of Shah Jahan's rule at Agra, where the capacious treasury was thrown open to fund Dara-Shikuh's campaign. In his desperation, he even wrote to the old enemy, Shah Abbas II of Persia, for 'moral and military assistance': all he received for his trouble was an invitation to visit – an offering of a bolthole that Dara may have done well to accept.[20] For now, though, there was a battle to fight, another army to raise: infantry, cavalry, field artillery, armoured elephants and camels bearing swivelling eight-pounder guns. As Niccolao Manucci reported, the departure of this new army on 24 May 1658 was an impressive spectacle. Dara-Shikuh, the commanding general, mounted his auspiciously-named elephant *Fateh-Jang* – 'Victor in War' – with the cry: 'Mercy to the humble, to the haughty death!'[21]

Prince Dara amidst his squadron appeared like a crystal tower, resplendent as a sun over all the land. Around him rode many squadrons of Rajput cavalry whose armour glittered from afar and their lance heads with a tremulous motion sent forth rays of light. There were other squadrons of cavalry armed with lances, in front of whom went many ferocious elephants clad in shining steel with chains on their trunks, their tusks encrusted with gold and silver and broad cutlasses affixed thereto by rings. ... A marvellous thing was it to behold the march, which moved over the heights and through the vales like the waves of a stormy sea.[22]

Even as Dara left, with Shah Jahan bidding an emotional farewell to a son he feared never to see again, there were profound anxieties. All involved knew that this was probably the last throw of the dice and that the men manning the artillery, straddling the war-horses and marching under the colourful banners of the imperial army were not battle-hardened soldiers at all. Dara had been forced to dragoon into service all and any civilians left in Agra, sending for additional conscripts from Shahjahanabad and the other northern cities. His officers, a composite of the empire's great variety – Hindustan-born Muslims, Hindu Rajputs, Central Asians and Persian migrants – were thrown together at a time when the glue of compelled loyalty was proving less than binding. And their leader was a man for bookish seminars, not sword-thrust, broadside and cavalry charge, tainted by the ridiculous superstitions of his disastrous Kandahar campaign.

It was the Battle of Samugarh that would sound the death-knell for the era of Shah Jahan. Dara's strategy appears to have been unambitious: merely to hold the crossings of the Chambal at Dholpur, thirty-five miles west of Agra, and inhibit the advance of Aurangzeb and Murad-Bakhsh until his son could rejoin the offensive. He therefore set his men to work on elaborate defence works on the sloping land above the riverbank, while his artillery commanded the water. What he had not anticipated was a classic out-flanking manoeuvre. Aurangzeb discovered a little-known crossing further east, where the Chambal passed through difficult terrain, rocky and forested. Untroubled by opposition from the local raja, who reneged on his promise to hold the fords for Dara, he resumed his march on Agra. Panic-stricken, Dara-Shikuh broke position and hurried his forces east until the two armies were face-to-face at Samugarh, just ten miles from the ancient citadel where Shah Jahan awaited news. But at this crucial moment, treasonous advisers cited astrological warnings and counselled delay: instead of pressing home a swift attack against an army already weary from its long forced march from the south, the crown prince dithered, merely parading his forces under the fierce sun and allowing the rebels to recover their wind and make their dispositions for the following day.[23]

The decisive battle on 8 June 1658 was fought by well-balanced forces – each side had between fifty and sixty thousand men – but the imperial army was badly demoralised by their leader's reluctance to attack. Aurangzeb deployed his armies in three sectors, quickly and decisively. Murad-Bakhsh commanded the left wing, facing an Uzbek general named Khalilallah Khan, a man of fragile loyalty. The right wing was led by Bahadur-Khan, pitched against Rustum-Khan, an Afghan. In the centre, the rebel vanguard was commanded by Aurangzeb's own son, Sultan Muhammad, whose forces were ranged against the cream of Dara's remaining Rajput allies, under the leadership of Rao Chhatrasal Hada of Bundi. The encounter lasted several hours and exceptional bravery was displayed on both sides; but Aurangzeb's experience in deploying his heavy artillery decimated Dara's forces. The valour of the Rajput cavalry prompted suicidal charges into the thickest ranks of the enemy, where one distinguished cavalier made it as far as Aurangzeb's own elephant before being cut down. Worse, Dara-Shikuh allowed his central vanguard to stray far to the right, blocking his own artillery's line of sight and allowing himself to be comprehensively outflanked. Then Dara was persuaded by the treacherous Khalilallah Khan to dismount from his elephant to go after Aurangzeb on horseback. Khalilallah had already held his division of fifteen thousand troops in position, ignoring the order to advance, 'as he had secretly made promises of service and loyalty' to Aurangzeb.[24] Now, the Mughal army, seeing Dara's howdah empty, assumed the worst and despaired. By late morning, retreat had turned to rout.

Dara fled the field, escaping to his private mansion outside Agra Fort to gather what money, supplies and followers he could before galloping north on the road to Shahjahanabad. The people of the city, alerted by the arrival of surviving stragglers from the imperial army, watched with dismay as the prince's small retinue passed the sandstone gate of the fortress without entering. Dara-Shikuh must have been simply too ashamed to face his father within the walls. Shah Jahan and Jahan-Ara instead sent out trusted eunuchs, bearing not just sacks of gold coins and jewels but messages of encouragement and forgiveness – but it was clearly safer for Dara-Shikuh to remain outside the citadel and make his last stand somewhere to the north, alongside the remaining imperial army still commanded by his eldest son. At this desperate stage, loyalty was at a premium, for Aurangzeb had written personally to many courtiers, claiming their allegiance: few now stood by their emperor. And the rebel prince was hard upon Dara's heels.

Having put paid to Dara and maintaining the fiction of their alliance, Aurangzeb now congratulated Murad-Bakhsh on the beginning of his reign.[25] Aurangzeb's plan had worked perfectly: he had successfully bamboozled one brother, watched with amusement from afar as the second was chased away and comprehensively destroyed the military pretensions of the third. He was emperor in all but name and the road to Agra and the Ornamented Throne at Shahjahanabad lay open before him.

Mughal chroniclers, working to the orders of their incumbent ruler, scarcely troubled to record the activities, let alone the thought processes of the defeated. Little is known, then, of the atmosphere within the fortress at Agra as Aurangzeb drew near. Shah Jahan must have been aware of the irony of his predicament: the rebellious son rebelled against, the biter bit. He may have hoped that Shahjahanabad Fort would still hold firm, open its treasury to Dara-Shikuh and form the base of resistance to Aurangzeb's advance – but in the meantime he had to face his son. Aurangzeb reached the outskirts of Agra on 12 June 1658 and settled into the comfortable pavilions of his grandfather's favourite Nur-Manzil garden, where he received oaths of allegiance from a succession of Shah Jahan's defeated officers. For ten days, letters between victor and vanquished were carried through the heavily-guarded western gate by Shah Jahan's chamberlain, an astrologer and skilled engineer from Khorasan called Mullah Ala-al-Mulk *Fazil-Khan*.

The opening rounds of correspondence were cordial enough. The emperor conveyed mild reproach and offered complete forgiveness in return for an immediate redeployment of Aurangzeb's forces to the Deccan front. Sensible of his overwhelming advantage, the prince repeated his claim that the campaign had been a just war for the throne. Shah Jahan replied with an invitation to face-to-face talks, noting that 'as he had recovered from a severe illness and in fact had had a second life conferred on him, the ardours of affection had risen high and he desired that he might soon be comforted by an interview'.[26] He enclosed with the letter a lavish gift of jewels and a celebrated family heirloom, a mighty sword known as *Alamgir*, the 'Seizer of the Universe'. Aurangzeb, however, spurned the offer, declaring that he would not visit his father until the fortress garrison had been replaced with his own personnel. At this, Shah Jahan ordered the gates to be sealed and the impregnable fort readied for siege. But Aurangzeb was far too wily to waste time on an impossible siege: he simply cut off the water supply.

On 19 June, Shah Jahan capitulated. Throwing open the gates, his garrison was marched out and replaced by Aurangzeb's men, under the personal command of the de facto crown prince, Sultan Muhammad. The emperor was denied access to the greater part of the fortress and confined to the harem quarters behind the General Audience Hall. The man who had ranged thousands of miles during his reign, from Kabul to the Deccan, was pent up in a space of just a few hundred square yards. His splendid apartments had become a cushioned, gilded, white marble prison. Nor yet had the father faced the rebellious son. Even the softly-spoken Jahan-Ara could not persuade her brother to enter the fort. For Aurangzeb, no reconciliation was possible until the apostate Dara-Shikuh was hunted down and the fight for the succession settled. Besides, there was always the fear that one of the eunuchs or female harem guards would make an attempt on his life. Shah Jahan tried to maintain an open line of communications with Dara – now believed to be organising a counter-attack from Shahjahanabad – but after a secret letter from the emperor to his eldest son was revealed to Aurangzeb, all contact with the outside world was cut. All that the emperor had to read was a series of self-justifying letters that consigned his own sovereign status emphatically to the past.

So long as you held the reigns of government, I never did anything without your permission, nor did I ever step beyond my jurisdiction. May the Searcher of Hearts be my witness![27] During your illness, Dara usurped all power, girt up his loins to promote Hinduism and destroy Islam and acted as king, totally setting you aside. I was compelled out of regard for the next world to undertake the heavy load of this task and engage in looking after the interests of the populace and peasantry. If you had not helped in various ways and raised to a position of trust your eldest son ... and if out of regard for him you had not failed to make any provision for the safety of your other sons, then all the brothers would have lived together peacefully and the fire of civil war would not have blazed forthwith.[28]

Shah Jahan was now held entirely captive. At sixty-six, he was already much older than his father or grandfather had been at their deaths. Troubled by nagging ailments and deprived of all but the most basic luxuries, the days of incarceration stretched ahead of him, empty days only given meaning by hours of prayer in the flawlessly elegant miniature Gem Mosque, by conversation with Jahan-Ara, by restless pacing around the enclosed gardens of the ladies' quarters – and by gazing out over the Yamuna at the magnificent mausoleum that he had seen finished fifteen years earlier. Now, perhaps, unable to tread the cool marble slabs of that consecrated precinct or pray beside the meticulously engraved cenotaph of that most loyal wife, he may have come to regret that he had found time for just one visit in all those long years.

Viewed in the hazy distance from the carved stone windows of the *Burj al-Muthamman*, the octagonal 'Royal Tower' that formed part of the harem precincts where Shah Jahan was to spend the rest of his days, the Illumined Tomb was a daily reminder of the power, luxury and content-ment that had been and was now lost. Shah Jahan's jailers were not above their own petty vindictiveness. Pen and ink were taken away; letters could only be dictated and were subsequently opened and censored. Some castle employees delighted in humiliating the former emperor by forcing him to wear the most demeaning clothing and the cheapest labourer's shoes. Worse, exploiting Aurangzeb's order that only constant vigilance would ensure no contact with the outside world, Agra Fort's new masters subjected the emperor and all his companions to relentless and intrusive surveillance. Niccolao Manucci, spared punishment for his loyal service to Prince Dara-Shikuh, returned to Agra to witness the smirking triumphalism of Shah Jahan's prison warders, working on the orders of the fort's new general manager, Itibar-Khan.

There passed not a day ... that there did not come under-eunuchs to whisper into his ear an account of all the words and acts of Shah Jahan and even what passed among the wives, ladies and slave-girls. Sometimes, smiling at what the eunuchs told him, he would make the company sharers in what was going on inside, adding some foul expressions of disparagement of Shah Jahan. Not content with this even, he sometimes allowed it to be seen that he treated him as a miserable slave. ... He smiled over it as if he had done some great deed; and it *was* a great deed, being after the nature of his friend Aurangzeb, who ... selected him to receive charge of his greatest enemy in the world, his father, for that by force of ill-treatment the wretched old man might die.[29]

The emperor did not yet die – but Aurangzeb, camped outside the red stone fortress, wasted no time in tying up loose ends. His first requirement was money, essential to reward loyal followers and win over new acolytes, as well as financing the next, inevitable fight with either Dara-Shikuh or his son. So he began systematically looting the castle treasury. Agra may have been replaced as the empire's capital – and the finest gems in the land had already been subsumed into the fabric of the Ornamented Throne at Shahjahanabad – but the castle vaults still contained a fortune in provincial revenues and army funds. There were nearly three million rupees worth of jewels belonging to Dara-Shikuh alone, a quantity far too large for him to bring away in his hasty retreat from the debacle at Samugarh. In his arrogance, Aurangzeb even demanded from Shah Jahan his diamond ring of kingship and a string of ninety-nine pearl prayer-beads, dulled with tolling the names of Allah but still worth nearly half a million silver rupees. Chastised by his powerless father, Aurangzeb responded with characteristic piety. 'You have written that it is contrary to the Muslim faith to seize another's property', he replied. 'Know that the royal property and treasures exist for the good of the people. A kingdom is not a hereditary private property! The king is merely God's elected custodian and trustee of his money for the good of the subjects.' [30]

The second inconvenience to be dealt with was Murad-Bakhsh, still apparently under the delusion that Aurangzeb had yielded him the throne. The younger brother had demonstrated impressive personal bravery in the last battle, incurring at least five serious wounds. But his suspicion that he had been duped was growing. His request for half the Agra treasure was laughed off, though Aurangzeb 'received him kindly and praised his courage, which deserved, he said, the first empire in the world'.[31] But the pretence was wearing thin. Instead of being allowed to make his way west to recover fully at Ahmedabad, which was to be his new imperial capital, Murad was invited to a banquet in Aurangzeb's Nur-Manzil camp. It was to be his last meal as a free man. Just as Dawar-Bakhsh Bulaqi had

Top surface of Shah Jahan's tomb (detail)

been ruthlessly used and cast aside in Shah Jahan's drive for the throne, so too was Murad's naivety rewarded with imprisonment and death. Handcuffed and closely guarded against any rescue attempt by his Gujarati garrison, Murad-Bakhsh was smuggled out of Aurangzeb's camp and taken to Gwalior Fort to await his fate.

There were now few obstacles between Aurangzeb and the throne. In early June – even before Shah Jahan's surrender of the citadel – he had begun convening formal audiences in the Nur-Manzil gardens in exactly the style of the emperor in the General Hall of Audience. There he welcomed the senior officers of Dara's clique who came to swear allegiance to their new master. He also started to make appointments to provincial governorships, the army high command and the key ministries of central government. All that remained was to take his place on the Ornamented Throne at Shahjahanabad. The physical transfer was easy enough to achieve: Aurangzeb was still travelling light, in full campaign mode and with none of the conventional impedimenta of the court. One minor inconvenience arose when the highest judge in the land, the Qadi al-Islam, declined to perform the coronation ceremony because he refused to accept that the true emperor was permanently incapacitated. Besides, he observed, any physical difficulties suffered by Shah Jahan were surely the result of his imprisonment, which was the result of Aurangzeb's own actions.[32] The Qadi was removed and replaced.

On 31 July 1658, a date selected by the astrologers, the usurpation of power was completed. With less than two weeks to make the arrangements, it was a cursory and unostentatious affair by his father's standards. The stupendous jewelled throne was brought out from the new fortress at Shahjahanabad and installed under cover of a silk pavilion in the royal gardens to the west of the mighty walls. Abrogating absolute power to himself, the third son of Shah Jahan adopted the royal name of Muhi al-Din Muhammad Aurangzeb Bahadur Alamgir Padshah Ghazi. To the people of the Mughal Empire, he would be simply Alamgir, Seizer of the Universe, the name appropriated from the great sword that his deposed father had sent out from his prison. So the blade, the name and the kingdom passed from father to son – and Shah Jahan's reign was abruptly cut off. He had ruled for thirty years, five months and seventeen days.

Once enthroned, Aurangzeb Alamgir moved swiftly to recreate the state in his own likeness, imposing the stamp of a still stricter Sunni orthodoxy upon the court and the administration of state. In addition to the complete proscription of the solar zodiac calendar, he abolished celebration of Nauruz. Special guardians of public morals were introduced to watch out for alcohol consumption and sexual impropriety; other officials were appointed to monitor Islamically correct practise in the market, on building sites and in the courtroom. The formal infrastructure of government and imperial finance, including taxation, was realigned on the lines of strict Hanafi law.[33] Over the next few years, other family traditions – including the annual weighing ceremonies and the daily appearances at the jharoka darshana balcony – were trimmed away, without protest from his sycophants at court.[34] Relations with Persia stabilised rapidly. Shah Abbas wrote with fulsome congratulations on Aurangzeb's accession and a brisk cross-border trade resumed; learning of a sizeable order for Persian tents and baggage materials, the Shah threw in fifty camels and a few golden utensils gratis to his new Mughal friends.[35]

There only remained Dara-Shikuh to be dealt with. After his hasty retreat from Samugarh, the crown prince had dashed for the north. With Shahjahanabad already held against him, denying him access to treasure, arms or men, his last-ditch hope was to consolidate all available forces at the ancient bastion of Lahore Fort. Arriving on 13 July and using the treasure from the old capital to buy the best men available, Dara had swiftly amassed a force of twenty-thousand cavalry. Urgent letters went out eastward: to Shah-Shuja in Bengal, offering to divide the empire after the defeat of Aurangzeb; and to Suleiman-Shikuh at Allahabad, commanding an immediate march to Lahore via the foothills of the Himalayas, avoiding the main cities along the Ganges and Yamuna that had already gone over to Aurangzeb.

The new emperor moved his forces with characteristic precision and speed. Following in the wake of two fast-riding advance strike forces under Shayista-Khan and Bahadur-Khan, he himself set out for the Punjab with the main army just six days after his accession. At the Sutlej River, he was joined by Raja Jai Singh, who had defected from Suleiman-Shikuh and pledged allegiance to the new power in the land. It was now shatteringly clear to Dara-Shikuh that he could not hope to defeat so many men under such talented leadership. He fled, abandoning Lahore at the end of August and making for Multan, on the mighty Indus. In a bizarre repeat of Shah Jahan's own wandering in the wilderness more than thirty years earlier, Dara now fled through the deserts and salt marshes of north-western Hindustan, haemorrhaging discontented troops and with Aurangzeb's armies snapping at his heels. By the time he reached Ahmedabad in January 1659, he was down to three thousand men. But he was to be given one last throw of the dice.

The end-game in the protracted war of succession was long drawn out and messy, involving repeated betrayals, switching loyalties and two last battles. On the strength of an earlier personal slight, Dara-Shikuh was able to persuade the new governor of Ahmedabad, Shahnawaz-Khan, to defect and open the coffers of the Gujarati capital to buy a new army. But with the force still too small to take on Aurangzeb's full army, Dara fled, first to a secure position in the dusty hills outside Ajmer, then to Gujarat and on into the grindingly hot northern districts of Sind. Dara's spirit was finally crushed by the death of his wife, Nadira Begum. Ordering his remaining men to safeguard her body on the long road to find a burial-place in Lahore, he was easy pickings for Aurangzeb's taskforce. It fell to Raja Jai Singh and Bahadur Khan to claim the credit for seizing the runaway. By the time Dara-Shikuh and his remaining allies were brought to Shahjahanabad in early September 1659, Aurangzeb Alamgir had prepared a suitable reception. The travel-stained and weary prisoners were paraded through the streets of the capital for the entertainment of the masses. The irony of his being chained atop a fine imperial elephant was designed to add to Dara's humiliation; in fact, it added to the gravitas of a man wholly crushed by fate, maintaining his dignity in the face of spite.

Dara surely knew the penalty for failure in a Mughal contest for the succession. The standard for ruthlessness had, after all, been set by his own father. There remained only the questions of method and degree of openness. True to form, Aurangzeb Alamgir declined to authorise the skulking secretive murders that had been his father's speciality. Instead, on the very night of Dara's capture, he turned to his advisers on Islamic law, putting to them a formal question: had Dara-Shikuh vilified the religion of God and allied himself with heresy? The new emperor produced a list of damning evidence, not least his brother's absorption in the 'unholy work' of translating sacred Hindu texts and the fact that he wore a ring with the simple word *Prabhu*, 'Lord', engraved on it in the ancient *devanagari* script.[36] The new emperor demanded a ruling that convicted Dara of being an 'unbeliever in the Faith, a manifest enemy who did not have even a hint of being a Muslim'.[37] As expected, the fatwa was concise and unequivocal, pronouncing the champion of inter-cultural exploration guilty of the crime of infidelity and apostasy. The sentence was death.

Awaiting his fate with measured calm in a darkened cell, Dara-Shikuh wrote one last appeal for mercy to his brother, arguing that his spiritual quest had been a genuine personal search and that he was now so diminished that he posed no threat.

My brother and my king,
I think not of sovereignty. I wish it may be auspicious to you and your descendants. The idea of my execution in your lofty mind is unnecessary. If I am allotted a residential place and one of my maids to attend to me, I would pray for Your Majesty from my peaceful corner.[38]

Emperor Alamgir was in no mood to be magnanimous. He scribbled a terse rejoinder on the back of the letter, berating his brother one last time for disobedience and sedition, before sending it back to the prison. Before dawn broke on 3 September, the jailers entered the cell, overpowering Dara-Shikuh and taking his severed head to the emperor. After one last act of spiteful vengeance – another parade, this time of a headless corpse – Dara-Shikuh, scholar, aesthete, would-be philosopher king, was consigned to an unmarked grave within the tomb complex of Emperor Humayun outside the city walls.[39]

Shah Jahan lived on, confined to his tiny quarters over the Yamuna and reduced to a monkish existence, free of status, comfort or wealth, for another seven years. In the women's quarters across the small complex remaining to him, Jahan-Ara and the other ladies eked out a similarly meagre life, effectively nuns whose only comfort was religion. These were women whose whole lives had been defined by their connection with the emperor, among them his eldest daughter, Lady Purhunar, now fifty-five years old and unmarried, and her faithful elderly governess Akbara-badi-Mahal. Perhaps the emperor, too, placed all his remaining hope in improving his prospects for the next life: certainly his constant companion was Mir Sayyid Muhammad of Kanauj, a scholar ready to discourse at all hours on the Koran and the Traditions of the Prophet.[40]

His captors revelled in bringing him the latest snippets of news that sounded the death-knell for any lingering hopes of liberation. First had come news of the disappearance and presumed death of Shah-Shuja. In January 1659, even as Dara continued to elude his vengeful pursuers, Shah-Shuja had made one last attack from Bengal. Driven back a second time, he was chased further and further east, beyond the mouth of the Ganges and the Bengali port at Chittagong into the jungles of Arakan, where he and his family disappeared into the swampy woodlands.[41] Then came the execution of Dara-Shikuh: the death of a favoured son who had remained at the emperor's side for so many years was truly a crushing blow. Then, on 13 December 1661, Murad-Bakhsh was executed at Gwalior. The son of the Ali Naqi – the imperial governor murdered at the beginning of Murad-Bakhsh's bid for the throne – had pressed for vengeance and Aurangzeb was only too happy to oblige. The prison qazi passed a death sentence, promptly carried out by two slaves with swords.[42] Suleiman-Shikuh, captured after hiding in Kashmir for more than a year and incarcerated with his uncle at Gwalior, followed six months later, succumbing to the slow poison of forcibly administered opiates.

Shah Jahan's only correspondence was now an intermittent series of bitter and petulant letters from Emperor Alamgir at Shahjahanabad. The two had still not met face-to-face once since Shah Jahan's overthrow and Aurangzeb's refusal to visit ensured that they never would again. Instead, his letters blamed the old man for everything from the civil war to his own childhood, deprived of paternal love. Attempting to justify his own conduct in the face of reproach from the prisoner of the Royal Tower, Aurangzeb Alamgir taunted him caustically with his own past crimes: 'How do you still regard the memory of Khusraw and Shahriyar, whom you did to death before your accession and who had threatened no injury to you?'[43]

For seven and a half long years, blanketed against winter chills and exposed to the dripping breathless sweaty unendurable heat of summer, Shah Jahan endured this life of enforced contemplation. He had much to think over. Considering his life with the objectivity conferred by time and humility, he may have had to come to terms with a brutal reappraisal of his own merits. He had moved through the jungle of conflicting rivalries and ambitions with ruthlessness but no great skill. The spoiled Prince Khurram had won fame, title and great wealth on the back of military victories secured for him by better men. His own rebellion against Jahangir had been a pathetic failure – not least when set against his son Aurangzeb's carefully measured application of brute force and pragmatic duplicity in his campaign for the throne. Shah Jahan's own seizure of the kingdom would have been impossible without the deft manoeuvring of his father-in-law, Asaf Khan. He had been adrift in the wilderness, beyond hope, when the sudden reversal of his fortunes gave him the opportunity to return to power. In doing so, he revealed the dark side of his character in the merciless order to slaughter all and any who threatened him – and in so doing set a new low in terms of regicide and fratricide for Mughal internecine conflict.

His legacy to the people of the empire was also mixed. He had bequeathed his son a state of astonishing wealth. One record of Alamgir's early years reveals that the nineteen provinces yielded a total of 231 million rupees.[44] Yet, as father to his great nation, Shah Jahan had shown no greater concern for the sufferings of the poor than other rulers of his time. The vast majority of that sum went straight into the coffers of the royal family and aristocracy. Famine relief and emergency grants to farmers had troubled the imperial treasury far less than the annual allowances of the pampered princes and princesses of the royal household. Few would mourn the death of an emperor who cared so little for his people.

Jahan-Ara's humble grave

Yet Shah Jahan could be confident of outliving all his critics: for the great structures scattered across his empire – the fortresses, mosques, schools, hospitals, merchants' hostels and tombs – were invested with the wealth of the imperial revenues and the talent of the nation's finest craftsmen, and revealed both his own generosity and his personal attention to the tiniest detail.

It remained, however, a rather bleak epitaph. Death can only have come as deliverance. On 17 January 1666, Shah Jahan was stricken with fever and dysentery, accompanied by distressing symptoms such as the urgent need to urinate constantly. Doctors, including Rizqallah Taqarrub and a Hindu surgeon from Vrindavan, were summoned to intervene to ease the discomfort with herbal medicines and opiate pain-killers.[45] Aware that his end was nearing, the white-bearded Shah Jahan formally gave away what meagre possessions he still had and did his best to offer reassurance to the women who had remained so steadfast through all these years of confinement that they would be cared for in the new empire of Aurangzeb Alamgir. With the words of the Koran on his lips – 'Lord, give us good in this world and good in the hereafter and defend us from the torment of the fire!' – he died on 31 January 1666.[46] Only his faithful Jahan-Ara was on hand to witness his passing, amid a storm of tears.

O Sun of mine now hidden from the eyes,
When will there be a dawn to end this night of separation?
O King of the universe and Axis of the world,
Open the eye of compassion and see my wretched state.
I cry from grief like a reed, with only wind to grasp;
I burn from sorrow like a candle, but only smoke rises from my head.[47]

Once emperor over countless millions, sovereign Mughal overlord to whom proud Rajputs bowed, the man responsible for the most sensational and most lasting architectural achievements on the sub-continent, Shah Jahan died almost alone and almost wholly unmourned. Jahan-Ara may have hoped to see a full-scale royal funeral procession, supervised by the nation's highest religious authorities and featuring lavish charitable donations by all the luminaries of central government. But her brother Alamgir dismissed the proposition out of hand and declined even to travel from Shahjahanabad. Not a single member of the aristocracy came to Agra to attend the funeral of Shah Jahan, which was carried out hurriedly and in total secrecy. The only dignitaries on hand were the loyal Sayyid Muhammad, tutor and companion for so many months, Hoshdar Khan, Superintendent of Agra Fort, and the city's Chief Justice, Qadi Muhammad Qurban, to take charge of the formalities.[48]

For the last time, one of Shah Jahan's flotilla of gaudy little river-boats pulled up at the water-gate of Agra Fort under cover of darkness, waiting patiently while the emperor's shrunken body was washed, swathed in clean white linen and encased in a sandalwood coffin. The bier was marched aboard by menial eunuchs from the fortress staff, accompanied by the obligatory security detail. For the last time, he travelled along the lazy brown stream of the Yamuna. And for the last time, as dawn broke on 1 February, he passed into the enormous mausoleum complex, burial place these last thirty-five years of the woman who had given him daughters of boundless fidelity and sons of equally limitless treachery. Beside the body of Arjumand Mumtaz-Mahal was finally laid to rest that of her husband, the sixth Mughal Emperor of Hindustan: Father of Victory, Star of the Faith, Muhammad the Second Lord of the Conjunction, Shah Jahan King of Kings, Warrior of Islam, Refuge of the Caliphate and Shadow of God on Earth. The cascade of mighty titles meant little now, as the corpse of the old man was borne into the white stone enclosure of the Illumined Tomb. But few kings had attained such a resting place.

Chronograms of the Mughal Empire

Mughal poets were irrepressible in their enthusiasm for chronograms, an erudite art-form in which poetic verve and emotional effect were matched by the author's cleverness in working only with letters that added up to the desired total. As we have seen, they were used throughout the reign of Shah Jahan. The letters of the Persian alphabet were matched with numerals according to a system based on the so-called *abjadi* sequence, which pre-dated the modern alphabet:

$$ا = 1, ب = 2, ج = 3, د = 4, ه = 5, و = 6, ز = 7, ح = 8, ط = 9,$$
$$ي = 10, ك = 20, ل = 30, م = 40, ن = 50, س = 60, ع = 70,$$
$$ف = 80, ص = 90, ق = 100, ر = 200, ش = 300, ت = 400,$$
$$ث = 500, خ = 600, ذ = 700, ض = 800, ظ = 900, غ = 1000$$

Thus, on one occasion, the Sultan of the Ottoman Empire in Constantinople wrote to the Mughal capital, chastising Emperor Shah Jahan for retaining the honorific 'King of the World' that he had been granted while still a prince. Surely, wrote the Sultan, he was really only *Shah-al-Hind*, 'King of India'. The court poet Abu-Talib Kalim defended his patron's title with a short verse, pleading justification by chronogram.

Since Hind and Jahan are numerically identical [5+50+4/3+5+1+50=59], His Majesty's right to be called 'King of the World' is established.

On another occasion, a poor man seeking alms won land, a horse and a robe of honour from a highly gratified Jahangir after pointing out that the king's name [3+5+1+50+20+10+200=289] was numerically equivalent to the Muslim exhortation *Allahu Akbar*, 'God is Great!' [1+30+30+5+1+20+2+200=289].

Chronograms also existed in contemporary European inscriptions, which used prominent letters (rather than every letter) to express the date. The motto on a medal struck by Gustavus Adolphus, for example, highlights Latin numerals in capitals: ChrIstVs DVX; ergo trIVMphVs. Addition of the numerals produces the date, 1632.

Appendix 2
Inscriptions on the Taj Mahal

Tomb exteriors

South arch: The Koran, Surat Ya-Sin (36/1–21)
West arch: Surat Ya-Sin, (36/22–44)
North arch: Surat Ya-Sin, (36/45–66)
East arch: Surat Ya-Sin, (36/67–83)
South door: Surat al-Takwir (81/1–29)
West door: Surat al-Infitar (82/1–19)
North door: Surat al-Inshiqaq (84/1–25)
East door: Surat al-Beina (98/1–8)

Tomb interiors

Upper register: (from SE to E to NE to N) Surat al-Mulk (67/1–12) (from NW to W to SW to S) Surat al-Mulk (67/12 cont'd-24)
Inscription: 'Written by the son of Qasim al-Shirazi, Abd-al-Haqq, called Amanat-Khan, in the year 1045'
Southeast arch: The Koran, Surat al-Mulk (67/24 cont'd-30); Surat al-Fateh (48/1–5)
East arch: Surat al-Fateh (48/5 cont'd-11)
Northeast arch: Surat al-Fateh (48/11 cont'd-17)
North arch: Surat al-Fateh (48/17 cont'd-25)
Northwest arch: Surat al-Fateh (48/25 cont'd-29)
West arch: Surat al-Fateh (48/29 cont'd); Surat al-Insan (76/1–8)
Southwest arch: Surat al-Insan (76/8 cont'd-22)

South arch: Surat al-Insan (76/22–31); Surat al-Zumar (39/53–4)

Inscription: 'Finished with His help; written by the humble *faqir* [poor man] Amanat-Khan al-Shirazi, AH 1048, in the 12th year of His Majesty's august accession'

Upper cenotaph of Mumtaz-Mahal (hall)

Top: The Koran, Surat Fusilat [or Ha-Mim] (41/30); Surat al-Mumin (40/7–8)

East side: Surat al-Tatfif (83/22–8)

South end: Surat al-Tatfif (83/8 cont'd); Surat Fusilat (41/30)

West side: Surat Fusilat (41/30 cont'd); Surat al-Baqara (2/286)

North end: Surat al-Baqara (2/286 cont'd); Surat al-Hashr (59/22)

Lower moulding: Inscription: 'The illumined tomb of Arjumand Banu Begum, entitled Mumtaz-Mahal, who died in the year 1040'

Lower cenotaph of Mumtaz-Mahal (crypt)

Top: The Koran, Surat al-Zumar (39/53); Surat Al Imran (3/185); Surat al-Muminun (28/118)

South end: Inscription: 'The illumined tomb of Arjumand Banu Begum, entitled Mumtaz-Mahal, who died in the year 1040'

North end: The Koran, Surat al-Hashr (59/22)

East/West sides: The 99 names of Allah (individual cartouches)

Upper cenotaph of Shah Jahan (hall)

Lower moulding: Inscription: 'This is the sacred grave of His most Exalted Majesty, *Firdos-Ashyani* ['Dweller in Paradise'], the second *Sahib-al-Qiran* ['Lord of the Happy Conjunction'], Shah Jahan Padshah Ghazi, may it ever flourish! AH 1076'

Lower cenotaph of Shah Jahan (crypt)

South end: Inscription: 'This is the illumined grave and sacred resting place of the Emperor, dignified as Ridhwan, residing in eternity, His Majesty, having his abode in Illiyun, Firdos-Ashyani, the second Sahib-al-Qiran, Shah Jahan Padshah Ghazi; may it be sanctified and may Paradise become his abode. He travelled from this world to the banquet-hall of eternity on the night of 26 Rajab 1076'

Gateway

South arch: The Koran, Surat al-Fajr (89/1–30)

North arch: Surat al-Dhuha (93/1–11); Surat al-Shirah (94/1–8); Surat al-Tin (95/1–8)

Inscription: 'Finished with the help of Him the Most High, AH 1057'

Mosque

Mihrab: The Koran, Surat al-Shams (91/1–15)

Discs: Surat al-Ikhlas (112/1–4)

Chronology of the Life of Khurram 'Shah Jahan'

1592

Birth of Prince Khurram (later 'Shah Jahan', at Lahore)	15th January
Formal start of Emperor Akbar's 37th year on the throne	20th March

1593

Birth of Lady Arjumand (later 'Mumtaz-Mahal')	16th April

1596

Khurram's 'maktab' ceremony	18th May

1599

Death of Khurram's uncle, Prince Murad (aged 28, in the Deccan)	11th May
Khurram and royal harem rejoin Akbar at Agra	19th June
Akbar departs from Agra on Deccan campaign (with Khurram)	27th September

1600

Crown Prince Salim begins rebellion against Akbar	10th August

1603

Salim ends first rebellion and returns to court	(after 31st March)
Salim sent to rejoin Mewar campaign but renews rebellion	12th October

1604

Suicide of Queen Man Bai 'Shah Begum' (mother of Khusraw)	24th May
Death of Akbar's mother 'Maryam-Makani'	9th September

1605

Death of Khurram's uncle, Prince Daniyal (aged 31, in the Deccan)	20th March
Death of Emperor Akbar	26th October
Salim 'Jahangir' formally crowned as 4th Mughal Emperor (at Agra, aged 36)	2nd November

1606

Khusraw flees from Agra to begin rebellion	15th/16th April
Capture of Khusraw	7th May

1607

Khurram granted rank of 8,000/5,000 and Hissar Firoza fiefdom (at Lahore)	30th March
Khurram betrothed to Lady Arjumand (at Lahore)	4th April
Khurram weighed on 16th lunar birthday (at Kabul)	30th July
Khusraw's assassination plot foiled; disgrace of 'Itimad-al-Daula' and family	11th–13th September

1609

Prince Pervez sent to the Deccan	12th October
Khurram betrothed to 'Kandahari Begum'	12th December

1610

Khurram's 1st marriage, to 'Kandahari Begum' (at Agra)	9th October

1611

Khurram promoted to rank of 10,000/5,000	7th April
Jahangir's 4th marriage, to Mihr al-Nisa (later 'Nur-Mahal' and 'Nur-Jahan')	3rd June
Ghiyath al-Din 'Itimad-al-Daula' appointed Wazir	4th August
Birth of Khurram's 1st child (to 'Kandahari Begum'): Princess Purhunar	21st August

1612

Khurram promoted to rank of 12,000/6,000	7th April
Khurram's 2nd marriage, to Lady Arjumand 'Mumtaz-Mahal'	10th May

1613

Birth of Khurram's 2nd child (to Mumtaz): Princess Hur al-Nisa	30th March
Imperial court leaves Agra for Ajmer	17th September
Khurram appointed to lead Mewar campaign	26th December

1614

Abu al-Hassan Ghiyath al-Din given title 'Asaf-Khan'	22nd March
Birth of Khurram's 3rd child (to Mumtaz): Princess Jahan-Ara	1st April

1615

Rana of Mewar surrenders to Khurram	5th February
Birth of Khurram's 4th child (to Mumtaz): Dara-Shikuh (at Ajmer)	29th March
Khurram promoted to rank of 15,000/7,000	3rd May

1616

Khurram promoted to 20,000/10,000	7th April

Death of Khurram's 2nd child, Princess Hur al-Nisa (aged 3)	14th June
Birth of 5th child (to Mumtaz): Prince Shah-Shuja (at Ajmer)	2nd July
Khurram given title 'Shah'	10th November

1617

Shah Khurram arrives at Burhanpur	13th March
Birth of Shah Khurram's 6th child (to Mumtaz): Princess Roshan-Ara (at Burhanpur)	2nd September
Shah Khurram's 3rd marriage, to daughter of 'Shahnawaz-Khan' (at Burhanpur)	2nd September
Shah Khurram given title 'Shah Jahan' and rank of 30,000 (at Mandu)	11th October
Jahangir and Shah Jahan leave Mandu for Gujarat tour	25th October

1618

Jahangir and Shah Jahan both ill (at Ahmedabad)	14th June
Birth of Shah Jahan's 7th child (to Mumtaz): Prince Aurangzeb (at Dohad)	3rd November

1619

Death of Shah Jahan's mother 'Jagat Ghosain' (at Agra)	18th April
Imperial court returns to Agra (after absence of 5 years, 7 months)	19th April
Birth of Shah Jahan's 8th child: Prince Jahan Afroz (at Agra)	25th June
Prince Khusraw released from prison and pardoned	5th November
Birth of Shah Jahan's 9th child (to Mumtaz): Prince Umid-Bakhsh (at Sirhind)	16th December

1620

Imperial court arrives at Srinagar (166 days from Agra)	30th March
Jahangir suffers first of a series of illnesses	5th October
Conquest of Kangra Fort	26th November

1621

Shah Jahan sent to the Deccan in response to uprising	13th January
Imperial court returns to Agra (after absence of 1 year, 5 months)	4th March
Prince Shahriyar (aged 16) promoted to rank of 8,000/4,000	20th March
Death of Shah Jahan's 8th child: Prince Jahan-Afroz (at Burhanpur)	(March)
Shah Jahan enters Burhanpur to relieve the besieged Khan-Khanan	4th April
Prince Shahriyar married to his step-sister, Ladli Begum	23rd April
Birth of Shah Jahan's 10th child (to Mumtaz): Princess Thurayya	11th June

1622

Death of Itimad-al-Daula (en route to Kashmir)	5th February
Death of Shah Jahan's 9th child, Umid-Bakhsh (aged 2, at Burhanpur)	February/March
Murder of Sultan Khusraw (aged 34, in the Deccan)	26th February
Jahangir orders Shah Jahan to march from Burhanpur to Kandahar	27th March
Shah Jahan arrives at Mandu, refuses to join Kandahar campaign	(April)
Persian forces under Shah Abbas capture Kandahar	21st June
Prince Shahriyar promoted to 12,000/8,000 for Kandahar campaign	23rd August
Birth and death of Shah Jahan's 11th child: unnamed boy (at Mandu)	(late 1622)

1623

Shah Jahan's rebel army reaches Fatehpur, finds Agra well defended	(before 19th February)
Jahangir's forces defeat Shah Jahan's army	28th March
Prince Dawar-Bakhsh (son of Khusraw) made Governor of Gujarat	21st May
Shah Jahan defeated and flees into the Deccan with close family	(before 30th October)

1624

Fifth defeat of Shah Jahan's forces (near Benares)	(before 27th June)
Mahabat-Khan appointed 'Khan-Khanan'	(after 27th June)
Imperial court leaves Kashmir for Lahore	15th September
Birth of Shah Jahan's 12th child (to Mumtaz): Prince Murad-Bakhsh (at Rohtas fort)	8th October

1625

Shah Jahan retreats from Bengal back to the Deccan	(before February)
Jahangir and imperial court arrive in Kashmir	7th May
Shah Jahan sends his sons as hostages and surrenders Rohtas fort	(before 21st October)

1626

Victory against Uzbek uprising north of Kabul	4th February
Shah Jahan writes to Jahangir offering surrender	2nd March
Mahabat-Khan mutinies and abducts Jahangir (on the Jhelum river)	24th/25th March
Shah Jahan leaves the Deccan, heads north to Thatta (via Ajmer)	18th June
Death of Prince Pervez (aged 36, at Burhanpur)	28th October
Birth of Shah Jahan's 13th child (to Mumtaz): Prince Lutfallah (in Thatta)	4th November

1627

Death of Emperor Jahangir (aged 58, en route from Kashmir to Lahore)	7th November
Asaf-Khan proclaims Dawar-Bakhsh 'Bulaqi' emperor (at Bhimar)	8th November
Asaf-Khan defeats Shahriyar	19th November
Dawar-Bakhsh formally crowned 5th Mughal Emperor (at Lahore, aged 17)	20th November

1628

Asaf-Khan proclaims Shah Jahan emperor (at Lahore)	29th January

Execution of Emperor Dawar-Bakhsh, Shahriyar and other princes	1st February
Shah Jahan formally crowned 6th Mughal Emperor (at Agra, aged 36)	14th February
Princes Dara-Shikuh, Shah-Shuja and Aurangzeb return to Agra	7th March
Death of Shah Jahan's 10th child, Princess Thurayya (aged 7, at Agra)	28th April
Birth of Shah Jahan's 14th child (to Mumtaz): Prince Daulat-Afza	9th May
Death of Shah Jahan's 13th child, Lutfallah (aged 1, at Agra)	14th May
Uzbeks besiege Kabul	9th June
Second coronation of Emperor Shah Jahan	15th August
Imperial troops under Lashkar-Khan lift siege and enter Kabul	14th September

1629

Death of Shah Jahan's 14th child, Daulat-Afza (aged 1, at Agra)	14th May
Khan-Jahan Lodi flees Agra and begins rebellion	15th October
Imperial court leaves Agra for Burhanpur	18th November

1630

Birth and death of Shah Jahan's 15th child (to Mumtaz): Princess Husn-Ara (at Agra)	23rd April
Appointment of Asaf-Khan as commander of Deccan campaign	25th October

1631

Death of Khan-Jahan Lodi	3rd February
Birth of Shah Jahan's 16th child (to Mumtaz): Princess Gauhar-Ara (at Burhanpur)	17th June
Death of Queen Mumtaz-Mahal in childbirth (aged 38, at Burhanpur)	17th June

1632

Mumtaz Mahal reburied at Taj Mahal	7th January

1633

Capture of Daulatabad in the Deccan	26th June
Dara-Shikuh granted Hisar Firoza as heir apparent	(October)

1634

Death of Mahabat-Khan	(October)

1635

Inauguration of 'Ornamented Throne'	22nd March
Shah Jahan leaves Agra on 2nd Deccan campaign	21st September

1636

Peace treaty with Bijapur and Golconda	6th May
Aurangzeb appointed Governor of the Deccan	23rd July
Formal start of Shah Jahan's 10th year on the throne (using Muslim calendar)	30th October

1638

Surrender of Kandahar by Persian governor	7th March

1639

Foundations of Shahjahanabad laid	29th April

1641

Death of Asaf-Khan (at Lahore)	14th November

1643

Completion of Taj Mahal; 12th anniversary ceremony of death of Mumtaz	7th February

1644

Princess Jahan-Ara nearly killed in harem fire	(March)

1645

Prince Aurangzeb appointed Governor of Gujarat	26th February
Death of Queen Nur-Jahan (at Lahore, aged 72)	18th December

1647

Aurangzeb promoted to rank of 15,000/10,000	30th January

1648

Formal inauguration of Shahjahanabad Fort	18th April

1649

Kandahar falls to Persian army	23rd February
Aurangzeb returns to the Deccan as Governor	27th August

1655

Prince Dara-Shikuh reconfirmed as heir apparent	15th February

1656

Mir-Jumla made Chief Minister	7th July

1657

Shah Jahan falls seriously ill (at Shahjahanabad)	16th September
Shah Jahan leaves Shahjahanabad for Agra for the last time	28th October
Prince Shah-Shuja declares himself emperor (in Bengal)	30th November
Prince Murad-Bakhsh declares himself emperor (in Gujarat)	15th December
Festival held in Agra to celebrate Shah Jahan's recovery	15th December

1658

Dara-Shikuh defeats Shah-Shuja (near Benares)	24th February
Formal start of Shah Jahan's 32nd year on the throne	5th March
Aurangzeb and Murad-Bakhsh cross the Narmada	13th April
Aurangzeb and Murad-Bakhsh defeat Jaswant Singh at Battle of Dharmat	25th April
Dara-Shikuh defeated by Aurangzeb and Murad-Bakhsh at Battle of Samugarh	8th June
Aurangzeb reaches Agra and beseiges Shah Jahan	12th June
Shah Jahan surrenders and is imprisoned	19th June
Aurangzeb 'Alamgir' crowned as 7th Mughal Emperor (at Shahjahanabad, aged 39)	31st July

1659

Execution of Dara-Shikuh (at Shahjahanabad)	3rd September

1661

Execution of Prince Murad-Bakhsh (at Gwalior)	13th December

1665

Formal start of Alamgir's 7th year on the throne	16th May

1666

Shah Jahan's final illness	17th January
Death of Shah Jahan (at Agra)	31st January

Glossary

Ahadi	Irregular trooper based at court, unaffiliated to individual *mansabdar* (q.v.)
Alishan	High Majesty
Amir	Noble of high rank; from Ar. 'prince'
Ataliq	Mentor, tutor, guardian
Bakhshi	Defence Minister (see also *Mir Bakhshi*)
Banu	Lady
Begum	Lady, madame
Crore	Ten million; one hundred lakhs (q.v.)
Farashkhana	Ministry of Carpets and Tents
Filkhanah	Elephant house
Firman	Imperial edict
Ghazi	Warrior of the Faith; term for senior Muslim figure
Jagir	Allocation of revenue-yielding land (usually to noble)
Jharoka darshana	Viewing window, where the emperor appeared before the people three times a day
Khilat	Robe of honour (Ar.)
Khutba	Declaration (e.g. of kingship) from mosque's pulpit
Khawaja	Honorific for (often Sufi) religious personality
Koka	Foster-brother
Korunush	Obeisance before the emperor (Turk.)
Kos	Unit of distance (about 2½ miles)

Kotwal	Chief of Police
Lakh	One hundred thousand
Mahal	Palace; harem complex
Mansab	Rank in Mughal administrative hierarchy, sub-divided into *zat* (q.v.) and *sawar* (q.v.)
Mansabdar	Holder of a *mansab*
Manzil	One day's journey for a caravan or body of troops
Mihrab	Niche at west end of mosque, indication direction of Mecca
Mirza	Noble of old Central Asian family
Mohur	Gold coin (of varying weight)
Nauruz	Spring Festival (Persian)
Peshkash	Offering to the king, often in cash, jewels or livestock
Qasida	Poetic panegyric
Sachiq	Wedding gift or pledge, usually in cash (Turk.)
Sannyasi	Ascetic (Sanskrit *sannyasin*)
Sawar	Indication of (usually cavalry) troops to be provided by a *mansabdar* (q.v.)
Sayyid	Honorific
Shab-i-Barat	Muslim festival (on 14 Shaban)
Shahi Qila	Royal Fort, used of Lahore
Sharia	Islamic law
Sheikhzada	Son of a distinguished religious personality
Silsilah	Sufi order (from Ar. 'chain of authority')
Sipahsalar	Commander-in-Chief
Suba	Province of the Mughal Empire
Subedar	Governor of a *suba*
Taslim	Obeisance before the emperor
Tilaka	Religious marking on the forehead (Sansk.)
Tughra	Stamped signature on imperial edict
Tuladan	Weighing ceremony
Wakil	Chief counsellor to the Emperor
Wazir	Chancellor, responsible for all imperial finances
Zat	Personal status and salary entitlement of a *mansabdar* (q.v.)

Notes

1. Prince of Good Fortune

1 Talib al-Amuli was Jahangir's poet laureate, 1619–27 (AH 1028–36). S.A.H. Abidi, 'Talib-i-Amuli: His Life and Poetry', *Islamic Culture*, 41/1 (1967), p. 120. The 'seven regions' or climes were adopted by Persian and Arab scholars from the geographical system outlined by the Alexandrian mathematician Ptolemy in the second century AD. The earth was divided into seven climatic zones, from south to north; the central zones, i.e. the greater part of the Indian sub-continent, were considered to be the most desirable climes.

2 Quoted in epilogue to Jahangir's memoirs; *The Jahangirnama: Memoirs of Jahangir, Emperor of India*, trans. and ed. Wheeler M. Thackston (Washington, Smithsonian, 1999), p. 455.

3 The Rajputs (Sanskrit, *raja-putra*, 'king's son') were hereditary Hindu warrior dynasties in Rajasthan (Sanskrit, *raja-sthana*, 'place of kings').

4 Muhammad Sharif Mutamid-Khan, *Ahwal al-Shahzadagi Shahjahan* ('Description of the Princehood of Shah Jahan'), British Library, MS Or. 3271, ff. 13–15. Charles Rieu, in his *Supplement to the Catalogue of the Persian Manuscripts in the British Museum* (Longmans, 1895), p. 53, argues that this must be a different Mutamid-Khan to the author of a biography of Jahangir known as the *Iqbalnama*, on the grounds that he refers to himself by name instead of as 'the present writer'; no contemporary Mughal sources, however, indicate that two individuals ever bore the same honorific at the same time.

5 'The sort of trees are Neem [*nim*; margosa], Peeplee (like great Pear trees) [*papal*; ficus religiosa], Dhaca [*dhak*; butea frondosa] and Bhurr [banyan; ficus Indica] …' Sir Richard Temple (ed.), *The Travels of Peter Mundy, in Europe and Asia, 1608–1667*, Vol. 2 (Hakluyt Society, 1914), p. 83.

6 12 Rabi II 1015. See Note on Transliteration and Calendars.

7 For much of his late teens and early twenties, Jahangir had been a raging alcoholic, consuming vast quantities of double-distilled liquor every day; doctor's advice helped reduce this fearsome intake down to a carefully regimented evening allowance; Thackston, *Jahangirnama*, p. 184; *Tuzuk-i-Jahangiri or Memoirs of Jahangir*, trans. Alexander Rogers, ed. Henry Beveridge (2 vols, Delhi, Atlantic Publishers, 1989), vol. 1, p. 307.

8 The title referred to the Koran's admiration of Mary as a paragon of purity and beauty: Surat Al-Imran (3/25–7).

9 Ellison Banks Findly, 'The Lives and Contributions of Mughal Women', in *The Magnificent Mughals,* ed. Zeenut Ziad (Karachi, OUP, 2002), p. 28.

10 The Hindi name Mass of Clouds (*dal-badal*) evokes an image of fertility; Muhammad Salih, quoted in Peter Alford Andrews, 'The Generous Heart or the Mass of Clouds: The Court Tents of Shah Jahan', *Muqarnas: An Annual on Islamic Art and Architecture*, 4 (1987), p. 152.

11 William Hawkins in Sir William Foster, *Early Travels in India 1583–1619* (Delhi, Oriental Books Reprint Corporation, 1985), pp. 117–8; also Abdul Aziz, 'A History of the Reign of Shah Jahan', *Journal of Indian History*, 7 (1929), part 3, p. 339 fn.

12 Mutamid-Khan, *Ahwal*, f. 48. Salim Jahangir's grandmother was Emperor Humayun's wife Hamida Banu 'Maryam-Makani', who naturally attended the 'showing of the face' (*unama*) ceremony marking the birth of a prince. The rupee (from Sanskrit *rupya*, 'silver') was the staple coin of Mughal administration and commerce; Irfan Habib, 'The Currency System of the Mughal Empire (1556–1707)', *Medieval India Quarterly*, 4 (1961), pp. 2–6.

13 Thackston, *Jahangirnama*, pp. 61–2 fn 83; *Tuzuk*, vol. 1, p. 76. Khurram banned the prostration (*sajida*) when he became Emperor Shah Jahan.

14 Thomas Coryat in Foster, *Early Travels*, p. 283.

15 The imperial provinces were: Agra, Ajmer, Allahabad, Bengal, Bihar, Deccan (Ahmadnagar), Delhi, Gujarat, Kabul (including Kashmir), Khandesh and Berar, Malwa, Orissa, Oudh, Punjab and Sind (including Thatta and Multan). Akbar introduced the *suba* (province) system in 1586; each province had a viceroy and a complete administrative staff.

16 Shamsam-ud-daula Shah Nawaz Khan, *The Maathir-ul-Umara: Being Biographies of the Muhammadan and Hindu Officers of the Timurid Soveeigns of India From 1500 to about 1780 A.D.*, tr. H. Beveridge, (2 vols, Calcutta, Baptist Mission Press, 1922), vol. 2, pp. 837–9. Zahiruddin A. Desai, *Nobility Under the Great Mughals: Based on Dhakhiratul Khawanin of Sheikh Farid Bhakkari: Parts 2 and 3* (Delhi, Sundeep Prakashan, 2003), pp. 3–5. Ghiyath al-Din means 'Succour of the Faith'. Honorifics could either be generic or specific; examples of the latter included a favoured horse-dealer dubbed *Tijarat-Khan*, 'Master Merchant', and Jahangir's favourite 'Master Architect', (*Mamur-Khan*). Edward Terry noted that, when the emperor 'gives advancement, he adds a new name [which is] pithily significant'; Foster, *Early Travels*, p. 327.

17 Ali Quli came from the Istalju tribe in north-eastern Persia and had served Shah Ismail II before travelling to the Mughal Empire and taking service with Abd-al-Rahim Khan-Khanan before joining Prince Salim's coterie then, finally, switching to the late Emperor Akbar's own entourage; Ellison B. Findly, *Nur Jahan: Empress of Mughal India* (Delhi, OUP, 1993), pp. 14–16; Mohammad and Razia Shujauddin, *The Life and Times of Noor Jahan* (Lahore, Caravan Book House, 1967), pp. 19–29; Nawaz Khan, *Maathir*, vol. 2, pp. 1073–5.

18 Arjumand's age is deduced from Qazvini's history, which says she was born fourteen years, four months and twenty-three days before her engagement ceremony (4 April 1607), which puts her day of birth (by the Gregorian calendar) as 11 November 1592.

19 Mina is literally 'enamel', hence bangles and other fine things. There may have also been a pun involved. The bazaar was traditionally laid out in two parallel aisles, an arrangement based on the account of a miracle performed by the Prophet Muhammad, in which he split the moon in two by pointing at it. This is said to have happened at Mina in the Arabian peninsula. It took place on *Khusroz*, the 'Day of Joy'; Soma Mukherjee, *Royal Mughal Ladies and Their Contributions* (Delhi, Gyan, 2001), pp. 102–3.

20 Foster, *Early Travels*, pp. 278–9. See also William Foster (ed.), *The Embassy of Sir Thomas Roe to the Court of the Great Mogul, 1615–1619* (2 vols, Hakluyt, 1899), vol. 1, pp. 104–5 fn for details of Coryat's adventures.

21 *Salatin shahzadagan … khawatin*; Iradat Khan 'Wazeh', *Mina Bazar* (Delhi, Muhammadi Press, 1851), p. 1, marginalia.

22 Ibid, pp. 5–11.

23 Thackston, *Jahangirnama*, pp. 29–30, 33, 48 and 58; Rogers and Beveridge, *Tuzuk*, vol. 1, pp. 16 and 70. Also Khawaja Kamgar Ghairat-Khan's *Maasir Jahangiri*, as translated in Francis Gladwin, *The History of Hindoostan, During the Reign of Jehangir, Shahjehan, and Aurungzebe* (Calcutta, Stuart and Cooper, 1788), vol. 1, pp. 2 and 10.

24 This number was known as the noble's *zat* ranking. A second, *sawar* ranking represented the number of cavalry troopers that he was expected to contribute. This system could involve further complexities when cavalrymen were permitted to have a string of two or three horses (*duhespa trihespa*). Only the royal family ever achieved a ranking above 7,000. One account notes that during Shah Jahan's reign, 'an officer of the rank of 3,000 foot with 3,000 horse [only] had to present 1,000 horse for branding'; Nawaz Khan, *Maathir*, vol. 2, p. 640. See also the chapter 'New Light on Mughal Cavalry' in Rafi Ahmad Alavi, *Studies in the History of Medieval Deccan* (Delhi, Idarah-i Adabiyat-i Delli, 1977), pp. 20–63. For a comprehensive analysis of the role of the princes' retinue, see Munis Daniyal Faruqui, 'Princes and Power in the Mughal Empire, 1569–1657' (unpublished Ph.D. thesis, Duke University, 2002).

25 *Sahib al-risalagi kul*; Wayne E. Begley and Zahiruddin A. Desai, *The Shah Jahan Nama of Inayat Khan* (Delhi, OUP, 1990), p. 5.

26 The vast majority of imperial taxes went to estate-holders in this way. Figures for the late seventeenth century show that, of 231 million rupees raised in revenue, 187 million (81%) went to jagir-holders among the royal family and nobility; the rest went to the central treasury; *Mirat Alam* of Bakhtawar-Khan in Sir Henry Elliot and John Dowson, (eds), *The History of India, As Told by Its Own Historians* (7 vols, Trübner, 1873–7), vol. 7, pp. 163–4.

27 Summary translation of Qazvini's *Padshahnamah*, British Library (BL), Add. 30,779, f. 24.

28 16 Aries in the Ilahi calendar, corresponding to 7 Dhu al-Hijja 1015 in the Muslim reckoning.

29 Adam Olearius, *The Voyages and Travels of the Ambassadors from the Duke of Holstein … whereto are Added the Voyages & Travels of J. Albert de Mandelslo … into the East-Indies*, tr. John Davies (Dring and Starkey, 1642), p. 44.

30 William Finch in Foster, *Early Travels*, pp. 165–6.

31 Wayne E. Begley and Zahiruddin A. Desai, *Taj Mahal: The Illumined Tomb: An Anthology of Seventeenth-Century Mughal and European Documentary Sources* (Seattle, University of Washington Press, 1989), p. 2.

32 Francis Gladwin, *The Persian Moonshee* (Calcutta, Chronicle Press, 1795), pp. 69–73. This is a translation of the first and most important section of Chandrabhan Brahmin's *Chahar chaman* ('Four Orchards'), entitled *Quwad al-sultanat Shah Jahan*, or 'Rules Observed During Shah Jahan's Day', which was formally presented to the emperor in 1645.

33 Joannes De Laet, *The Empire of the Great Mogol*, trans. J.S. Hoyland, ed. S.N. Banerjee (Delhi, Oriental Books Reprint Corporation, 1974), p. 55.

34 Edward Terry in Foster, *Early Travels*, p. 329.

35 Ibid, p. 106.

36 Ibid, p. 18; De Laet, *Great Mogol*, p. 55.

37 Richard Foltz (tr. and ed.), *Conversations with Emperor Jahangir by 'Mutribi' al-Asamm of Samarqand* (Costa Mesa, Mazda, 1998), p. 37.

38 Jahangir had in fact taken the throne on 2 November 1605 but his first year on the throne was considered to have formally begun on the following Nauruz (20 March 1606); see Chronology.

39 Thackston, *Jahangirnama*, p. 81; Rogers and Beveridge, *Tuzuk*, vol. 1, p. 115.

40 Afzal Husain, *The Nobility Under Akbar and Jahangir: A Study of Family Groups* (Delhi, Manohar, 1999), pp. 27–44.

41 Nawaz Khan, *Maathir-ul-Umara*, vol. 1, pp. 50–65; also Zahiruddin A. Desai, *The Dhakirat ul-Khawanin of Shaikh Farid Bhakkari (A Biographical Dictionary of Mughal Noblemen): Part 1* (Delhi, Idarah-i Adabiyat-i Delli, 1993), pp. 22–45.

2. The Millennial Child

1 Anon, 'A Selection from the History of Shahjahannamah Written by Moonshee Hamad Ameen [Qazvini]', BL, Add. 30,779, f. 23.

2 Mutamid-Khan, *Ahwal*, f. 58.

3 Thackston, *Jahangirnama*, p. 7 (Preface by Muhammad Hadi).

4 The various tributes are recorded in Banarsi Prasad Saksena, *History of Shahjahan of Dihli* (Allahabad, Indian Press, 1932), pp. 1–2. Official historians recorded two of the chronograms as particularly worth highlighting: *Shah rawi zamin wa Shah Jahan* ('King of the face of the earth and monarch of the universe'; 300+1+5, 200+6+10, 7+40+10+50, 6, 300+1+5, 3+5+1+50) and *lamia aftab Alamgir* ('A ray of the world-penetrating sun'; 30+40+70, 1+80+400+1+2, 70+30+40+20+10+200); Begley and Desai, *Shah Jahan Nama*, p. 5. However, the use of Shah Jahan and Alamgir, the future royal titles of Khurram and his son Aurangzeb respectively, prompts suspicion that these chronograms were honed considerably later and inserted retrospectively as a birthday invention.

5 BM, Add. 30,779, f. 24.

6 Hadi Hasan, *Mughal Poetry: Its Cultural and Historical Value* (Aligarh, 1952), pp. 10–11; Faydi (a Muslim) was Akbar's poet laureate 1580–96 (AH 988–1004) and translated into Persian several important Sanskrit works, including large sections of the greatest epic of all, the *Mahabharata*, and the *Kathasaritsagara* ('Ocean of Streams of Stories'), a vast anthology of folk tales and legends.

7 Letter from Fr. Anthony Monserrate (n.d.), in John Correira-Afonso, *Letters from the Mughal Court: The First Jesuit Mission to Akbar (1580–1583)* (Bombay, Gujarat Sahitya Prakash, 1980), p. 36.

8 Joseph Fletcher, 'Bloody Tanistry: Authority and Succession in the Ottoman, Indian Muslim and Later Chinese Empires', paper for the Conference on the Theory of Democracy and Popular participation, Bellagio, Italy, 1978, cited in Geoff Watson, 'Interpretations of Central Asian Influence on Mughal India: The Historical Debate', *South Asia: Journal of South Asian Studies*, 18:2 (1995), p. 5 fn; John Emerson, 'The Nomads in Eurasian History', draft article online at www.idiocentrism.com/turan.nomads.htm#_edn8.

9 *Hubb al-watan min al-iman*; Foltz, *Conversations*, p. 89.

10 Khurram's great-great-grandfather Zahir al-Din Muhammad Babur was dubbed *Firdos-Makani*, 'He Whose Place is in the Garden of Paradise'; Babur's eldest son Nasr al-Din Muhammad Humayun became *Jannat-Ashyani*, 'He Whose Nest is in Heaven'.

11 Foster, *Early Travels*, p. 271.

12 Some have observed similarities in the assumption of similar status and privileges by sixteenth-century Ottoman and Persian leaders; Colin Paul Mitchell, *Sir Thomas Roe and the Mughal Empire* (Karachi, ASCE, 2000), pp. 11–12.

13 Elliot and Dowson, *History of India*, vol. 5, pp. 524, 527 and 534.

14 Letter to Fr Everard Mercurian, dated 18 July 1580, in Correira-Afonso, *Letters*, p. 56.

15 Posthumously, Manmati was called *Bilqis-Makani*, the 'Bilqis of the Place', a reference to the name given in Arabic tradition to the Queen of Sheba (Saba, in what is now north-eastern Yemen). Her relationship with King Solomon

is described in the Bible (Kings 10:1–13) and in the Koran, Surat al-Naml (27/22–44).

16 Ashvini Agrawal, *Studies in Mughal History* (Delhi, Motilal Banarsidass, 1983), p. 91.

17 Husain, *Family Groups*, pp. 90–6.

18 One rupee was worth two shillings and threepence sterling, making the value of the dowry approximately 22,500 pounds, an incredible fortune by European standards. In contemporary England, a courtier's income would rarely exceed £3,000 a year, while a village parson might live on £20 per annum. Foster, *Sir Thomas Roe*, vol. 1, p. 95 fn.

19 Findly, *Nur Jahan*, pp. 124–7; also Ram Nath, *The History of Mughal Architecture* (4 vols, Delhi, Abhinav, 1982–2005), vol. 2, p. 72.

20 James Tod, *Annals and Antiquities of Rajasthan* (Delhi, M.N. Publishers, 1978), pp. 68–74.

21 Manmati crops up in later accounts only in respect of her fractious and mutually hostile relationship with Salim's last and most influential wife, Nur-Jahan.

22 Anon, 'History of Shahjahannamah', BL, Add. 30,779, f. 22.

23 Thackston, *Jahangirnama*, p. 30; Rogers and Beveridge, *Tuzuk*, vol. 1, p. 20.

24 16 October 1591 (28 Dhu al-Hijja 999); Elliot and Dowson, *History of India*, vol. 5, p. 460. Murad was widely known by the nickname 'Pahari' (indicating his birthplace at Sikri among the Aravalli hills) and occasionally 'Pahari Jiu', the second element of which comes from the Sanskrit *jiv*, 'long live!'.

25 Muhammad Arif Qandhari, *Tarikh-i-Akbari* ('The History of Akbar'), ed. and tr. T. Ahmad (Delhi, Pragati, 1993), p. 172.

26 Mutamid-Khan, *Ahwal*, f. 4.

27 Rogers and Beveridge, *Tuzuk*, vol. 1, p. 124; Nawaz Khan, *Maathir*, vol. 1, p. 180; Desai, *Bhakkari*, pp. 179–80; T.W. Beale, *An Oriental Biographical Dictionary*, H.G. Keene (ed.) (Delhi, Manohar Reprints, 1971), p. 151. Hakim Ali died of ulcerated lungs on 10 April 1609, when Khurram was seventeen.

28 Details of the sheikh's life and scholarship can be found in Desai, *Bhakkari*, pp. 22–45.

29 Muzaffar Alam and Sanjay Subrahmanyam (eds), 'The Making of a Munshi', *Comparative Studies of South Asia, Africa and the Middle East*, 24:2 (2004), pp. 62–72.

30 Beni Prasad, *History of Jahangir* (Oxford University Press, 1922), pp. 2–5. Loyal services performed by Raja Salivahan (corrupted in Persian to 'Salbahan') are mentioned in Salim Jahangir's memoirs: Thackston, *Jahangirnama*, pp. 12 and 45; Rogers and Beveridge, *Tuzuk*, vol. 1, p. 46.

31 Mubarak Ali, 'The Mughul Filkhanah', in *Historical Studies: Articles on the History of the Mughuls and Sind* (Lahore, Book Traders, 1987), pp. 87–95. The 'Overthrower of Elephants' label came from the poet Kahi, who hoped that 'elephant-loads of silver' would be bestowed on court bards; Hasan, *Mughal Poetry*, p. 38.

32 Ahmadnagar was ruled by the hereditary *Nizamshah* dynasty (which the Mughals often called *Nizam al-Mulk*); the ruling family of Bijapur, to the south, bore the label *Adelshah* and, to the east of Bijapur, Golconda was led by the hereditary *Qutb al-Mulk*.

33 A sum worth approximately 440,000 pounds sterling in contemporary England; see Note 18, above.

34 Qandhari, *Tarikh-i-Akbari*, p. 181.

35 *The Akbar Nama of Abu-l-Fazl*, tr. Henry Beveridge (3 vols, Calcutta, Bibliotheca Indica, 1917–21), vol. 2, p. 118; comprehensive details of the fort's construction can be found in Nath, *Mughal Architecture*, vol. 2, pp. 102–18; also Ebba Koch, *Mughal Architecture: An Outline of Its History and Development, 1526–1858* (Munich, Prestel, 1991), pp. 53–5.

36 Lt.-Col. C. Eckford Luard (ed. and tr.), *Travels of Fray Sebastien Manrique, 1629–1643*, 2 vols (Oxford, Hakluyt, 1927), pp. 159–60 and 165–6, includes a vigorous analysis of the provenance and fate of the Hathi Pol statues.

37 W.H. Moreland and P. Geyl, P. (tr.), *Jahangir's India: The Remonstrantie of Francisco Pelsaert* (Cambridge, W. Heffer and Sons, 1925), pp.1–4.

38 Sir William Foster, *The Journal of John Jourdain 1608–1617* (Cambridge, Hakluyt, 1905), pp. 162–4.

39 Nath, *Mughal Architecture* , vol. 2, pp. 156–73; Koch, *Mughal Architecture*, pp. 56–61.

40 The sheikh arrived at Ajmer from eastern Persia, aged 52, in 1190 A.D. and attracted a huge following. His tomb, embellished with silver and jewels, as well as Koranic quotations and Persian inscriptions, is known as the *Mazar al-Sharif* (Holy Sepulchre) and the wider tomb complex as the *Dargah*. *Sultan-ul-Hind Hazrat Khwaja Moinuddin Hasan Chishty* (Ajmer, Dargah Sharif, 2004), p. 13.

41 Hasan, *Mughal Poetry*, pp. 39–40. Today, Indian personalities often undertake a prolonged pilgrimage on foot (*padyatra* in Hindi), for political and religious reasons.

42 Qandhari, *Tarikh-i-Akbari*, p. 185.

43 Here I presume to disagree from Professor Ram Nath, who insists that the water supply and drainage were well thought out and efficient; Nath, *Mughal Architecture*, vol. 2, pp. 173–7.

44 Foster, *Early Travels*, pp. 149–50.

3. Salim's Rebellion

1 Mutamid-Khan, *Ahwal*, f. 13.

2 Khwaja Kamgar Husaini, *Maasir-i-Jahangiri: A Contemporary Account of Jahangir*, ed. Azra Alavi (New York, Asia Publishing House, 1978), p. 27.

3 Mutamid-Khan, *Ahwal*, f. 6.

4 The Deccan campaigns are covered at length in Beveridge, *Akbarnama*, vol. 3, pp. 995–1220.

5 M.A. Nayeem, *External Relations of the Bijapur Kingdom (1489–1686 A.D.)* (Hyderabad, Bright, 1974), pp. 52–61. Also Masoom Raza Kazimi, 'The Genesis of Iranian Diplomacy in the Deccan', *Proceedings of the Indian Historical Congress, 29th Session (Patiala, 1967)*, pp. 152–7.

6 Extract from Nizam al-Din Ahmad's *Tabakat-i Akbari*, in Elliot and Dowson, *History of India*, vol. 5, pp. 467–8.

7 Burhan Nizamshah died on 26 April 1595 (18 Shaban 1003) and Ibrahim before September the same year; B.G. Tamaskar, *The Life and Work of Malik Ambar* (Delhi, Idarah-i Adabitat-i Delli, 1978), pp. 32–4.

8 The Maharana had recently inherited the kingdom from his distinguished father, Pratap Singh; Husaini, *Maasir-i-Jahangiri*, p. 27. Also D.R. Mankekar, *Mewar Saga* (Delhi, Vikas, 1976), p. 81.

9 Payne, *Akbar and the Jesuits*, pp. 88–9.

10 Desai, *Bhakkari*, p. 54.

11 Sheikh Abu-al-Fadl had been sent to bring Murad back to the capital, a mission obviated by the prince's death; Beveridge, *Akbarnama*, vol. 3, p. 1144.

12 Mankekar, *Mewar Saga*, p. 81.

13 Thackston, *Jahangirnama*, pp. 55–6; Rogers and Beveridge, *Tuzuk*, vol. 1, pp. 24–5.

14 Surendrea Nath Sinha, *Subah of Allahabad under the Great Mughals (1580–1707)* (Delhi, Jamia Millia Islamia, 1974), pp. 34–7.

15 William Finch (account dated February 1611) in Foster, *Early Travels*, pp. 177–8. For details of Allahabad's 'Palace of the Queens', see also Koch, *Mughal Architecture*, pp. 61–2. Temple, *Peter Mundy*, p. 109, has a sketch of 'the principal outer gate of Fort Allahabad' (drawn in 1632).

16 *Muzaffar al-Dunya wa'l-Din*.

17 Order dated 19 February 1603 (1 Pisces 1011); Jalaluddin, 'Sultan Salim (Jahangir) as a Rebel King', *Islamic Culture*, 47/2 (1973), pp. 121–3.

18 Lal, *Mughal Glory*, p. 101.

19 Thackston, *Jahangirnama*, p. 13.

20 Elliot and Dowson, *History of India*, vol. 6, p. 442.

21 Thackston, *Jahangirnama*, p. 33; Rogers and Beveridge, *Tuzuk*, vol. 1, p. 25.

22 4 September 1602 (7 Rabi I 1010); Elliot and Dowson, *History of India*, vol. 6, p. 155; also Amir Ahmad, 'Murder of Abul-Fazl: A Reappraisal', *Journal of the Research Society of Pakistan*, 37 (2000), pp. 53–9.

23 Beveridge, *Akbarnama*, vol. 3, p. 1219.

24 Husaini, *Maasir-i-Jahangiri*, p. 31.

25 It was Muhibb Ali who completed his mentor's immense work; Beveridge, *Akbarnama*, vol. 3, p. 1242.

26 William Hoey, *Memoirs of Delhi (Being a Translation of the 'Tarikh Farahbakhsh' of Muhammad Faiz Bakhsh)* (Allahabad, 1888), p. 10.

27 Nawaz Khan, *Maathir*, vol. 1, p. 327.

28 In several accounts, the Sanskrit name 'Apurva' has evolved into 'Abrup'.

29 Nawaz Khan, *Maathir*, vol. 1, p. 183 (biography of Dr Ali Gilani). The identical quotation is used by Muhammad Hadi in Thackston, *Jahangirnama*, p. 15 and in Mutamid Khan, *Ahwal*, f. 10.

4. Jahangir's New Order

1 Thackston, *Jahangirnama*, p. 49; Rogers and Beveridge, *Tuzuk*, vol. 1, p. 52.
2 Foltz, *Conversations*, p. 89.
3 Nawaz Khan, *Maathir*, vol. 1, p. 180; also Desai, *Bhakkari*, p. 180.
4 There was even a story that Akbar had accidentally poisoned himself after preparing a lethal pill for a dissident courtier and consuming it by mistake; Brij Narain and Sri Ram Sharma, *A Contemporary Dutch Chronicle of Mughal India* (Calcutta, Susil Gupta, 1957), pp. 31–2. This account is a hybrid, compiled from the recollections of three employees of the Dutch East India Company: Francisco Pelsaert (based at Agra), Pieter van den Broecke and Johannes de Laet (both based at Surat).
5 Thackston, *Jahangirnama*, pp. 48–9; Rogers and Beveridge, *Tuzuk*, vol. 1, p. 51.
6 Elliot and Dowson, *History of India*, vol. 6, p. 169.
7 Thackston, *Jahangirnama*, p. 18.
8 Hoey, *Memoirs of Delhi*, p. 11.
9 Accounts of the struggle for succession are in Nawaz Khan, *Maathir*, vol. 1, pp. 327–8 (a profile of Mirza Aziz Azam-Khan), also Elliot and Dowson, *History of India*, vol. 6, pp. 169–72 (account of Asad Beg); and Thackston, *Jahangirnama*, pp. 17–18.
10 Shujauddins, *Noor Jahan*, p. 21.
11 Thackston, *Jahangirnama*, p. 17.
12 Anon, 'History of Shahjahannamah', BL, Add. 30,776, f. 69.
13 Banarasi Biholia, *Ardhakathanaka* ('Half A Tale'), tr. Mukund Lath (Jaipur, Rajasthan Prakrit Bharati Sansthan, 1981), p. 28.
14 This suggests that the French Jesuit, Fr Pierre du Jarric, was wrong to say that, 'some wished to pray for him in the Saracen [Muslim] manner; others did not dare to; and in the end neither Saracens, nor Gentiles [Hindus], nor Christians would claim him as theirs, so that he had the prayers of none'; Payne, *Akbar and the Jesuits*, p. 208.
15 Akbar was known posthumously as *Arsh-Ashyani*: 'He Whose Nest is on the Divine Throne'; Beveridge, *Akbarnama*, vol. 3, pp. 1261–2.
16 Nath, *Mughal Architecture*, vol. 3, pp. 359–95.
17 Narain and Sharma, *Chronicle*, pp. 33–4.
18 Foltz, *Conversations*, p. 30.
19 Faruqui, 'Princes and Power', pp. 50–65.
20 Riazul Islam, *A Calendar of Documents on Indo-Persian Relations, Vol. 1 (1500–1750)* (Isfahan, Islamic Culture Foundation, 1979), pp. 173–5. Husain, *Family Groups*, pp. 191–2, however, argues that the allegation of undue

favour is not borne out by scrutiny of the fiefdoms held by the different ethnic groups.

21 Nawaz Khan, *Maathir*, vol. 1, p. 328.

22 Thackston, *Jahangirnama*, p. 285; Rogers and Beveridge, *Tuzuk*, vol. 2, p. 52.

23 Gulam Husayn Zaydpuri, *The Riyazu-as-Salatin: A History of Bengal*, tr. Maulavi Abdus Salam (Calcutta, Asiatic Society, 1902–4), section 34, pp. 1–2; online translation courtesy of the Packard Humanities Institute (http://persian. packhum.org).

24 Milo Beach and Ebba Koch (eds), *King of the World: The Padshahnama*, tr. William Thackston (Washington, Azimuth, 1997), p. 161.

25 C.H. Payne (ed. and trans.), *Jahangir and the Jesuits: From the Relations of Father Fernão Guerreiro S.J.* (Routledge, 1930), pp. 36–7.

26 Entry for 19 August 1616 at Ajmer; Foster, *Sir Thomas Roe*, vol. 1, pp. 227–8.

27 The cauldron (*deg*) could hold more than 2,400 kilograms of rice but was still smaller than one presented earlier by Akbar, which held more than 5,000 kilos; both survive and are used in the Dargah today; *Sultan-ul-Hind*, p. 12; Thomas Coryat in Foster, *Early Travels*, p. 280; also described by Jahangir himself in Thackston, *Jahangirnama*, pp. 154–5; Rogers and Beveridge, *Tuzuk*, vol. 1, p. 256.

28 Sayyid Akbarali Ibrahimli Tirmizi, *Mughal Documents Vol. I: 1526–1627* (Delhi, Manohar, 1989), p. 83. The edict (dated 14 April 1610, corresponding to 26 Aries/Farwardin 1019) followed the visit of a Jain deputation led by Udayaharsha; it also contains a portrait of the 18-year-old Prince Khurram.

29 Thackston, *Jahangirnama*, p. 111; Rogers and Beveridge, *Tuzuk*, p. 171.

30 7 Dhu al-Hijja 1014; Ahmad Nabi Khan, 'Lahore During the First Regnal Year of Mughul Emperor Jahangir (1605–1606)', *Journal of the Research Society of Pakistan*, 22 (1985), p. 50. See also a full account in John d'Silva, 'The Rebellion of Prince Khusru According to Jesuit Sources', *Journal of Indian History*, 5/2 (1926), pp. 267–81.

31 Payne, *Jahangir and the Jesuits*, p. 4.

32 Thackston, *Jahangirnama*, p. 49; Rogers and Beveridge, *Tuzuk*, vol. 1, p. 52.

33 Narain and Sharma, *Chronicle*, p. 37.

34 Thomas Coryat in Foster, *Early Travels*, p. 279.

35 Anon ['Written and certified by Persons of good Import, who were Eye-witnesses of what is here reported'], 'A True Relation, Without all Exception, of Strange and Admirable Accidents, Which Lately Happened in the Kingdom of the Great Magor, or Mogul', in W. Oldys and T. Park (eds.) *The Harleian Miscellany: A Collection of Scarce, Curious and Entertaining Pamphlets and Tracts* (John Murray, 1808), p. 260.

36 Narain and Sharma, *Chronicle*, pp. 38–9.

37 Faruqui, 'Princes and Power', p. 137.

38 Payne, *Jahangir and the Jesuits*, pp. 8 and 11.

39 Gladwin, *History of Hindoostan* vol. 1, p. 9.

40 The Mughals did not have a permanent 'Foreign Office'; ambassadors were despatched on a case-by-case basis, usually when the emperor had

commercial or territorial ambitions to pursue. So, while envoys were sent to Persia, the Deccan states and even (with a view to forging an anti-Persian alliance) to the Ottoman capital at Constantinople, no ambassadors were ever sent to western Europe; N.R. Farooqi, 'Diplomacy and Diplomatic Procedure under the Mughals', *Medieval History Journal*, 7 (2004), pp. 59–86.

41 Islam, *Indo-Persian Relations*, p. 143.

42 Ibid., pp. 130 and 149.

43 Eskander Beg Monshi, *Tarik-e Alamara-ye Abbasi* ('History of Shah Abbas the Great'), tr. Roger M. Savory (2 vols., Boulder, Westview Press, 1978), vol. 2, p. 661. Muzaffar Hussein Mirza subsequently fell out with Akbar but was not allowed to return to Persia before his death in 1600.

44 Abdal-Rahim, 'Mughal Diplomacy from Akbar to Aurangzeb', PhD thesis, University of London, 1932, p. 52; also Mitchell, *Sir Thomas Roe*, p. 16.

45 Thackston, *Jahangirnama*, p. 58; Rogers and Beveridge, *Tuzuk*, vol. 1, p. 70.

46 Islam, *Indo-Persian Relations*, pp. 151–3.

47 Mankekar, *Mewar Saga*, p. 81.

48 Letter from Thomas Kerridge at Ahmedabad to Sir Thomas Roe, dated 1 December 1615; Foster, *Sir Thomas Roe*, vol. 1, p. 91 fn.

49 Shujauddins, *Noor Jahan*, pp. 22–3, has full details of the conspiracy. See also Narain and Sharma, *Chronicle*, p. 33.

50 Nawaz Khan, *Maathir*, vol.. 2, p. 1074. Also de Laet, *Great Mogol*, pp. 178–9.

51 By the time these histories were compiled, Arjumand Mumtaz-Mahal was the primary queen and co-residents of Khurram Shah Jahan's harem were largely ignored.

52 Both Jahangir's memoirs and Qazvini's later *Padshahnamah* give 17 Scorpio as the date of the feast, equating to 7 November. Qazvini, however, is wrong to equate it to 'the auspicious month of Rajab': it must have been 21 Shaban. Thackston, *Jahangirnama*, pp. 114–5; Rogers and Beveridge, *Tuzuk*, p. 180.

53 Begley and Desai, *Illumined Tomb*, p. 3.

5. The Shadow of Nur-Mahal

1 Zaydpuri, *History of Bengal*, section 34, p. 3; http://persian.packhum.org.

2 W. H. Siddiqi, (ed.) *Waqa-i-uz-Zaman (Fath Nama-i-Nur Jahan Begam): A Contemporary Account of Jahangir by Kami Shirazi* (Rampur, Rampur Raza Library, 2003), p. 256. The author, a Persian-born poet known by the nom de plume *Khallaq al-Mani* ('Creator of Ideas'), was an ardent apologist for Nur-Mahal/Nur-Jahan; he rejected criticism of the queen, especially the 'Nur-Jahan junta' theory.

3 Beach and Koch, *King of the World*, p. 76.

4 Payne, *Akbar and the Jesuits*, pp. 79–80.

5 Desai, *Nobility*, p. 134; Nawaz Khan, *Maathir*, vol. 1, pp. 262–3.

6 Jahangir himself describes the incident in detail in his memoir (though makes an error in the date, suggesting it happened earlier, around 20 December

1610 (early Shawwal)): Thackston, *Jahangirnama*, pp. 117–18; Rogers and Beveridge, *Tuzuk*, vol. 1, pp. 185–7.

7 William Finch in Foster, *Early Travels*, p. 154.

8 Beach and Koch, *King of the World*, pp. 76–8; translation by Thackston.

9 Raja Man Singh, another Khusraw supporter, was given the governorship of Bengal.

10 The encounter happened on 30 May 1607. Elliot and Dowson, *History of India*, vol. 6, p. 397; also Findly, *Nur Jahan*, pp. 27–30. No reliable indigenous source mentions the widely held but unsubstantiated belief that Jahangir deliberately had Ali Quli murdered because the emperor had loved Mihr al-Nisa for many years but had been denied her hand by Akbar, who disapproved of the match.

11 Thackston, *Jahangirnama*, p. 79; Rogers and Beveridge, *Tuzuk*, vol. 1, p. 114.

12 14 Gemini (Khurdad); hand-written note by Jahangir in BL, MS Or. 3276, f. 132, cited in Rogers and Beveridge, *Tuzuk*, vol. 1, pp. 192 fn.

13 Elliot and Dowson, *History of India*, vol. 6, p. 398.

14 Muhammad Salih Kamboh, *Amal-i Salih* (3 vols, Lahore, 1967–72), vol. 1, pp. 163–8, cited in Ebba Koch, *The Complete Taj Mahal* (Thames and Hudson, 2006), p. 263, fn 41.

15 Claude Markovits (ed.), *A History of Modern India, 1480–1950* (Anthem, 2004), pp. 96–7.

16 Sayyid Akbarali Ibrahimli Tirmizi, *Calendar of Acquired Documents (1402–1719)* (Delhi, National Archives of India, 1982), p. 19.

17 Order to Raja Jai Singh dated 9 August 1620; Sayyid Akbarali Ibrahimli Tirmizi, *Edicts from the Mughal Harem* (Delhi, Idarah-i Adabiyat-i Delhi, 1979), pp. 20–27. The date on the letter itself was obtained by using the zodiacal calendar for day and month (Amurdad/Leo) but the Turkish duodenary (twelve-year) solar cycle. 1620 was the eleventh year in the cycle, the Year of the Dog. See Note on Calendars.

18 Undated order bearing another honorific, *Wali-Nimat* ('Lady of Blessing'); Tirmizi, *Edicts*, p. 12.

19 The noble in question was Mirza Aziz Kokaltash; Husain, *Family Groups*, p. 65.

20 Lal, *Mughal Glory*, p. 59.

21 Elliot and Dowson, *History of India*, vol. 5, p. 467.

22 Foster, *Sir Thomas Roe*, vol. 1, p. 215.

23 Hasan, *Mughal Poetry*, p. 79.

24 Mutamid-Khan, *Ahwal*, f. 17. This lady, also known as Akbarabadi Begum (a reference to her home or origins at Agra), was a *paristar khas haram serai izzat*, 'special nurse of the female apartment of chaste ladies'. Though her status was clearly differentiated in Lahori's *Padshahnama* from the royal family itself (whose members are described as *mukhadarat saraparda daulat*, 'virtuous ladies of the royal court'), Akbarabadi-Mahal has frequently been mistaken for one of Khurram Shah Jahan's wives; see Beale, *Biographical Dictionary*, p. 45. I am indebted to Dr Yunus Jaffery for this clarification.

25 William Hawkins, writing in November 1611, inflates the value of imperial income to 500 million rupees, probably double the real revenues; Foster, *Early Travels*, pp. 99–100 fn, estimates the contemporary exchange rate at one rupee to a little over two English shillings.

26 Ibid., pp. 225–6.

27 Foster, *Sir Thomas Roe*, vol. 1, pp. 114.

28 Foster, *Early Travels*, pp. pp. 98–9 (account of William Hawkins) and pp. 162–3 (William Finch).

29 Ibid., p. 119.

30 Ebba Koch, 'Diwan-i Amm and Chihil Sutun: The Audience Halls of Shah Jahan', *Muqarnas: An Annual on Islamic Art and Architecture*, 11 (1994), pp. 143–4.

31 Foster, *Early Travels*, pp. 184–5. Other accounts of Jahangir's daily routine include Captain William Hawkins (pp. 114–6), Thomas Coryat (p. 247) and Edward Terry (p. 326).

32 Diary entry for 10 January 1616 (when the court was at Ajmer); Foster, *Sir Thomas Roe*, vol. 1, pp. 107–8.

33 9 Rabi I 1021; 22 Taurus (Urdibihisht) of Jahangir's seventh Regnal Year.

34 Begley and Desai, *Illumined Tomb*, p. 4.

35 Ibid., p. 5.

36 This second visit occurred on 7 June (18 Gemini/Khurdad); Thackston, *Jahangirnama, p. 137; Rogers and Beveridge, Tuzuk*, vol. 1, pp. 224–5.

6. Soldier of the Empire

1 Sajida Sultana Alvi, *Advice on the Art of Governance: Mauizah-i* Jahangiri *of Muhammad Baqir Najm-i Sani: An Indo-Islamic Mirror for Princes* (Albany, State University of New York Press, 1989), p. 49.

2 'The Story of Rana Amar Singh', in S.O. Heinemann, *Poems of Mewar* (Gurgaon, Vintage, 1990), p. 291.

3 Thackston, *Jahangirnama*, p. 164; Rogers and Beveridge, *Tuzuk*, vol. 1, p. 273.

4 Narain and Sharma, *Chronicle*, p. 44.

5 Mankekar, *Mewar Saga*, p. 82. See also G.N. Sharma, *Mewar and the Mughal Emperors: 1526–1707 A.D.* (Agra, Shiva Lal Agarwala, 1962), pp. 113–14.

6 Desai, *Nobility*, p. 56.

7 Narain and Sharma, *Chronicle*, p. 44.

8 Thackston, *Jahangirnama*, p. 152; Rogers and Beveridge, *Tuzuk*, vol. 1, pp. 251–2.

9 Mutamid-Khan, *Ahwal*, f. 25; also Thackston, *Jahangirnama*, p. 154; Rogers and Beveridge, *Tuzuk*, vol. 1, p. 256.

10 Mirza Aziz was seconded from his base at Burhanpur, where he served as Governor of Malwa province.

11 Khawaja Kamgar Ghairat-Khan's account in Gladwin, *History of Hindoostan*, vol. 1, p. 28.

12 Foster, *Early Travels*, p. 225.

13 Desai, *Nobility*, pp. 119–21.

14 Nawaz Khan, *Maathir*, vol. 2, p. 344.

15 Gladwin, *History of Hindoostan*, vol. 1, p. 30.

16 Mankekar, *Mewar Saga*, p. 83.

17 Nawaz Khan, *Maathir*, vol. 2, p. 1021.

18 Ibid., vol. 1, pp. 260–1. Also Abidi, 'Talib-i-Amuli', pp. 124–5. The lady's name was an honorific of a typically hybrid linguistic nature (Sanskrit/Arabic): 'Virtuous among Women'.

19 The title had been available since the death of the previous holder, Mirza Jafar Beg, in 1612; Beale, *Biographical Dictionary*, pp. 80–1. The East India Company factor Thomas Kerridge observed that Asaf-Khan had curried favour by giving Jahangir exotic foreign presents, 'knowing the king's extraordinary delight in toys'; Foster, *Sir Thomas Roe*, vol. 2, p. 268 fn.

20 Mutamid-Khan, *Ahwal*, f. 30. The words used by Jahangir – *farzand jigad band* – are striking for their fulsomeness, especially when compared to his language when their relationship subsequently soured (see Chapter 7, Note 61).

21 Thackston, *Jahangirnama*, p. 161; Rogers and Beveridge, *Tuzuk*, vol. 1, p. 266.

22 Mutamid-Khan, *Ahwal*, f. 30.

23 B.D. Agarwal, *Rajasthan District Gazeteers: Udaipur* (Jaipur, Government of Rajasthan, 1979), p. 49.

24 The Hindu prince was named after an important personality in the *Mahabharata*; in the Sanskrit epic, Karna was a kshatriya hero born of the Sun God (from whom the Mewari royal family also claimed descent).

25 Beach and Koch, *King of the World*, p. 31; translation by Thackston.

26 Ibid, p. 28.

27 *Ain kawah varah fil Jahangir Padshah*; Sayyid Akbarali Ibrahimli Tirmizi, *Ajmer Through Inscriptions (1532–1852 A.D.)* (Delhi, Indian Institute of Islamic Studies, 1968), p. 32; Nath, *Mughal Architecture*, vol. 3, p. 95. The carved elephant still exists in the Hathibhata (Elephant Stone) district of Ajmer but it lies within private property and is the subject of legal action by the state authorities; it has also been painted and plastered and is worshipped as a representation of the Hindu deity Ganesh.

28 Translation by Dr Yunus Jaffery; see also Nath, *Mughal Architecture*, vol. 3, pp. 256–8. The lake has since receded a considerable distance from the complex. The chronogram (2,5,20,1,200 + 100,900,200 + 3,5,1,50,20,10,200,10 + 40,4,1,40 + 1,2,1,4 + 2,1,4) does not add up correctly to 1024.

29 Biholia, *Ardhakathanaka*, p. 81.

30 Extract from *Iqbalnama* in Elliot and Dowson, *History of India*, vol. 6, pp. 405–6.

31 Edward Terry, chaplain to Sir Thomas Roe's embassy, left a vivid account of the horrible symptoms and lethally rapid effect of this 'fiery trial': Foster, *Sir Thomas Roe*, vol. 2, pp. 505–6 fn.

32 In Thackston, *Jahangirnama*, p. 175, the emperor notes that 'an extra quarter' was added to Khurram's rank 'as a bonus and a prize' but it is not clear

whether this is an additional 25% of the 15,000 infantry rank, the 8,000 cavalry rank or both.

33 29 Safar 1024; Bikrama Jit Hasrat, *Dara Shikuh: Life and Works* (Calcutta, Visvabharati, 1953), p. 1, quotes Dara-Shikuh himself as saying (in his *Safinat al-Awliya*) that Khurram had prayed at the Chishti shrine in Ajmer as all his children had thus far been daughters.

34 The chronogram (20+30, 1+1+30+10+50, 20+30+60+400+1+50, 300+1+5+10) gives the Hijri calendar birth-date: 29 Safar 1024. Begley and Desai, *Shah Jahan Nama*, p. 6; also Hasan, *Mughal Poetry*, p. 38.

35 Thackston, *Jahangirnama*, pp. 196–7; Rogers and Beveridge, *Tuzuk*, vol. 1, p. 330.

36 The location was also known as *Hafiz Jamal*; Nath, *Mughal Architecture*, vol. 3, pp. 254–6.

37 Foster, *Sir Thomas Roe*, vol. 1, p. 138.

38 Ibid., vol. 1, pp. 256–8.

39 Thackston, *Jahangirnama*, p. 184; Rogers and Beveridge, *Tuzuk*, vol. 1, pp. 306–7.

40 Translation by Dr Yunus Jaffery. The Persian word for opium, *tiriak*, in the second line of the stanza comes from the Greek *therika*. Mutamid-Khan, *Ahwal*, f. 39; Gladwin, *History of Hindoostan* vol. 1, pp. 33–4; Begley and Desai, *Shah Jahan Nama*, p. 6. Avicenna was the shorthand name given in Europe to the Persian physician Abu-Ali al-Husseni ibn Abdallah ibn Sina.

41 The Koran, Surat al-Baqqara (2/219) says: 'They ask you about wine and gambling. Say: "In them is great sin and some profit for men. But the sin outweighs the profit".' Surat al-Maida (5/90) says: 'Oh you who believe! Intoxicants and gambling, idolatry and divination, are an abomination of Satan's handiwork.'

42 Foltz, *Conversations*, p. 45.

43 The emperor further ordered that Wednesday (the 'fourth day', *chaharshamba*) would henceforth be known as the 'Day of Loss' (*gumshamba*); Thackston, *Jahangirnama*, p. 194; Rogers and Beveridge, *Tuzuk*, vol. 1, pp. 326–8.

44 Mahabat-Khan and Khan-Jahan were sent on 26 and 30 September 1615 respectively (5 and 9 Libra/Mihr).

45 Foster, *Early Travels*, p. 131.

46 Hussein Beg Tabrizi 'The Tailor' was sent to the Qutb Shah at Golconda, Darwish Beg Marashi to the Nizam Shah at Ahmadnagar and Shahquli Beg to the Adel Shah at Bijapur; Monshi, *Shah Abbas*, vol. 2, p. 1079. See also the section on the rôle of Shah Abbas in the Bijapur–Mughal conflict; Nayeem, *Bijapur*, pp. 62–6.

47 Tamaskar, *Malik Ambar*, pp. 28–32.

48 Foster, *Early Travels*, p. 139.

49 Narain and Sharma, *Chronicle*, p. 47.

50 Foster, *Sir Thomas Roe*, vol. 1, p. 201. Sir Thomas had been in Burhanpur from 14–27 November 1615, during which he had an audience at the Red Fort.

51 Ibid., vol. 2, pp. 280–1.

52 The adventurer Thomas Coryat, who witnessed the arrival of the Bijapuri embassy, wrote in a letter from Ajmer dated Michaelmas Day (29 September 1615) that two of the elephants were 'so gloriously adorned as I never saw the like … for they wore four chains about their bodies all of beaten gold; two chains about their legs of the same; furniture for their buttocks of pure gold; two lions upon their heads of the like gold … and the whole present was worth ten of their lakhs [one million rupees]'; Foster, *Early Travels*, p. 250.

53 Thackston, *Jahangirnama*, p. 187; Rogers and Beveridge, *Tuzuk*, vol. 1, pp. 313–4.

54 Tamaskar, *Malik Ambar*, pp. 96–7.

55 Foster, *Sir Thomas Roe*, vol. 2, p. 267.

56 Begley and Desai, *Shah Jahan Nama*, p. 9.

57 Foster, *Sir Thomas Roe*, vol. 2, p. 293. Roe's MS gives the date of the handover as 17 (i.e. 27) October; Thackston, *Jahangirnama*, p. 199, and Rogers and Beveridge, *Tuzuk*, vol. 1, p. 336, give 4 Scorpio (25 October).

58 Jivanji Jamshedji Modi, *Dastur Kaikobad Mahyar's Petition and Laudatory Poem Addressed to Jahangir and Shahjahan* (Bombay, Fort Printing Press, 1930), pp. 177–8.

59 Tamaskar, *Malik Ambar*, pp. 97–8.

60 Thackston, *Jahangirnama*, pp. 221–2; Rogers and Beveridge, *Tuzuk*, vol. 1, pp. 380–1.

61 Foster, *Sir Thomas Roe*, vol. 2, p. 419 fn.

62 Mandu was described with amazement by contemporary travellers such as Ralph Fitch and William Finch; Foster, *Early Travels*, pp. 17 and 140–1.

63 Nawaz Khan, *Maathir*, vol. 1, pp. 414–5.

64 Narain and Sharma, *Chronicle*, p. 52.

65 Desai, *Nobility*, pp. 143–4.

66 2 Ramadan 1026; Begley and Desai, *Illumined Tomb*, p. 7. Jahangir does not mention the wedding in his journal, although he subsequently refers to the death of the only child from the union.

67 Foster, *Sir Thomas Roe*, vol. 2, pp. 404 and 407. Roe also says that 'the prince at Burhanpur had made a marriage without the King's consent and [as a result] gotten displeasure', though Jahangir does not mention this in his memoir.

68 Edward Grey, *The Travels of Pietro Della Valle in India* (London, Hakluyt, 1892), pp. 56–7.

69 Beach and Koch, *King of the World*, p. 166.

70 His full titular name, as given in a royal firman dated 1 December 1617, was *Alishan* (High Majesty) Khurram Shah Shah-Jahan Ghazi; Tirmizi, *Acquired Documents*, p. 17.

71 Mutamid-Khan, *Ahwal*, f. 45. Other accounts say that the chair was gilded or made of solid gold.

72 Begley and Desai, *Shah Jahan Nama*, p. 7.

73 Thackston, *Jahangirnama*, p. 232; Rogers and Beveridge, *Tuzuk*, vol. 1, p. 401.

7. The Wolf Cub

1 Herat's leading poet (1414–92); Thackston, *Jahangirnama*, p. 265; Rogers and Beveridge, *Tuzuk*, vol. 2, p. 15.

2 Foster, *Sir Thomas Roe*, vol. 2, p. 283.

3 Thackston, *Jahangirnama*, p. 249; Rogers and Beveridge, *Tuzuk*, vol. 1, p. 436.

4 Specifically, the zodiacal months of Aries (Farwardin) and Taurus (Urdibihisht); Mutamid-Khan, *Ahwal*, f. 48.

5 15 Dhu al-Qada 1027, corresponding to 12 Scorpio (Aban).

6 The respective Persian chronograms are *guhar taj muluk aurangzib* (20+6+5+200, 400+1+3, 40+30+6+20, 1+6+200+50+20+7+10+2) and *aftab alam tab* (1+80+400+1+2, 70+30+40, 400+1+2), both equalling 1027; Begley and Desai, *Shah Jahan Nama*, p. 8; Hasan, *Mughal Poetry*, p. 38.

7 Thackston, *Jahangirnama*, p. 282; Rogers and Beveridge, *Tuzuk*, vol. 2, p. 50.

8 Jahangir had finally returned to Agra on 19 April 1619, after an absence of five years and seven months (spent at Ajmer, Mandu, Gujarat and in prolonged transit). He had left for Kashmir on 15 October.

9 Desai, *Nobility*, p. 25.

10 Gladwin, *Persian Moonshee*, p. 73.

11 Nawaz Khan, *Maathir*, vol. 2, pp. 345–6.

12 The comet, known to astronomers as 'C/1618 W1' or (in older texts) '1618 II', was visible to the naked eye for about two months. It was first observed in China on 25 November 1618; the last sighting was in Germany on 22 January 1619. Thanks to Gary Cronk at http://cometography.com.

13 On Bilqis, See Chapter 2, Note 15.

14 Mutamid-Khan's *Iqbalnama-i-Jahangiri*, in Elliot and Dowson, *History of India*, vol. 6, pp. 406–7.

15 Born on 10 Muharram 1029, Umid-Bakhsh died at Burhanpur in the month of Rabi II 1031 (i.e. February/March 1622).

16 The co-called *Chini-ka Rauza*, or 'Chinese Tomb', at Agra (the burial place of Shah Jahan's finance minister, Afzal-Khan) is one of few remaining sites in India where original glazed tiles from Lahore and Multan survive.

17 Anjum Rehmani, 'Abul-Hasan Asaf Khan: Life and Achievements', *Journal of the Research Society of Pakistan*, 35 (1998), pp. 53–4.

18 Foster, *Sir Thomas Roe*, vol. 2, p. 426.

19 Desai, *Nobility*, p. 144; Thackston, *Jahangirnama*, p. 352.

20 Nawaz Khan, *Maathir*, vol. 1, p. 413; Raja Vikramaditya's Sanskrit name has often been corrupted in Persian to 'Bikramajit'. The title was a reward for service under Shah Jahan in the Deccan; Mutamid-Khan, *Ahwal*, f. 51.

21 Thackston, *Jahangirnama*, p. 287; Rogers and Beveridge, *Tuzuk*, vol. 2, p.56.

22 The Naqshbandis were an influential Sufi order that had followed Babur into Hindustan from Central Asia; see Richard Foltz, 'The Central Asian Naqshbandi Connections of the Mughal Emperors', *Journal of Islamic Studies*, 7 (1996), pp. 228–39; also Arthur Buehler, 'The Naqshbandiyya in Timurid India: The Central Asian Legacy', ibid., pp. 208–28. The hero of the January

1611 lion-hunt, Anup Rai Singh-Dalan (see Chapter 5), was appointed
Warden of Kangra Fort in May 1625.

23 *Masjid Shah Jahangir bud nurani*; Hasan, *Mughal Poetry*, p. 37. The
chronogram (40+60+3+4, 300+1+5, 3+5+1+50+20+10+200, 2+6+4,
50+6+200+1+50+10) gives 1031, the year of the visit in the Muslim calendar.

24 Monshi, *Shah Abbas*, vol. 2, p. 1159. Mutamid-Khan, *Ahwal*, f. 58, adds that
Shah Jahan (perhaps with a view to a future alliance) contributed a personal
gift of gems worth a quarter of a million rupees.

25 Narain and Sharma, *Chronicle*, pp. 48–50. This long and authoritative account
of the embassy to Persia is only spoiled by the use of the name 'Khan-Azam'
instead of Khan-Alam.

26 Firman dated 4 January 1621 and addressed to Raja Suraj Singh; Tirmizi,
Mughal Documents, vol. 1, p. 118.

27 Thackston, *Jahangirnama*, p. 355; Rogers and Beveridge, *Tuzuk*, vol. 2, p.190.

28 Mutamid-Khan, *Ahwal*, f. 59.

29 Niccolao Manucci wrote: 'The town is much frequented by Persian
and Armenian traders, on account of the many excellent kinds of cloth
manufactured there, chiefly sorts of women's head-dresses and cloths for veils,
scarlet and white, of exceeding fineness; also for the quantity of iron procured
there'; William Irvine (tr.), *A Pepys of Mogul India, 1653–1708: Being an
Abridged Edition of the 'Storia do Mogor' of Niccolao Manucci* (John Murray,
1913), p. 32.

30 Description by Jean de Thévenot on 9 [i.e. 19] December 1666; Surendranath
Sen, *Indian Travels of Thévenot and Careri* (Delhi, National Archives of India,
1949), p. 100.

31 Raja Bhima was named after one of the heroes of the *Mahabharata*, the
second son of Pandu.

32 Narain and Sharma, *Chronicle*, p. 53.

33 Tamaskar, *Malik Ambar*, p. 115.

34 Nawaz Khan, *Maathir*, vol. 1, p. 417.

35 Mutamid-Khan, *Ahwal*, ff. 61–3, says that Golconda paid two million rupees,
Bijapur 1.8 million and the remaining 1.2 million was paid by Ahmadnagar,
whose aggressive stance had triggered the war; also Tamaskar, *Malik Ambar*,
p. 116.

36 Thackston, *Jahangirnama*, p. 364; Rogers and Beveridge, *Tuzuk*, vol. 2, p. 207.

37 'The Manners of Kings' (1/42), in Sadi's *Gulistan* (1258), quoted by Jahangir in
Thackston, *Jahangirnama*, p. 202; Rogers and Beveridge, *Tuzuk*, vol. 1, p. 340.
The 1899 translation by Sir Edwin Arnold is available online at http://www.
sacred-texts.com/isl/gulistan.txt.

38 The title had become vacant with the death of Shah Jahan's third father-in-law,
Iraj Abd-al-Rahim, at the age of 33 in April 1619.

39 Nawaz Khan, *Maathir*, vol. 1, p. 418.

40 Gladwin, *History of Hindoostan*, vol. 1, p. 57.

41 The Persian word *nahallaf* indicates an undutiful son or, in one dictionary, 'degenerate progeny', a slur based on his mother being of low caste or inferior position at court.

42 Mutamid-Khan, *Ahwal*, ff. 64–5.

43 Muhammad Amin Hussaini, *Anfa-ul-Akhbar* (Asafiya Library, Hyderabad, MS 974, 42/18/9), f. 218, cited in Alavi, *Medieval Deccan*, p. 15.

44 Shujauddins, *Noor Mahal*, pp. 46–9, has analysis of 'Khusraw's mysterious end'.

45 *Maasir Qutb Shahi*, cited in Beale, *Biographical Dictionary*, p. 220. In his *Anfa-ul-Akhbar*, Muhammad Amin says the murder was suggested by Raja Vikramaditya and 'some short-sighted people'; Alavi, *Medieval Deccan*, pp. 15–16. In compensation for his loss, Jahangir made Khan-Azam the guardian of Khusraw's young son, Sultan Dawar-Bakhsh *Bulaqi*; Narain and Sharma, *Chronicle*, p. 55.

46 Moreland and Geyl, *Francisco Pelsaert*, p. 71: 'Some mendicants presumed to make a representation of a grave at the spot where the bier or corpse had rested for a night on the journey and … in various towns, such as Burhanpur, Sironj, Agra and Allahabad, both Hindus and Muslims went in procession every Thursday with flags, pipes and drums to his worship; he was accepted as a true pir, or saint'.

47 Letters from Nicholas Bangham of the E.I.C. at Burhanpur, dated 5 and 23 February 1622; Foster, *English Factories* (1622), pp. 30 and 41.

48 Muhammad Salih Kamboh, *Amal Saleh*, vol. I, pp. 137 and 163–5, translated in Saksena, *Shah Jahan of Dihli*, p. 35.

49 Letter from William Methwold, Matthew Duke and Francis Futter at Masalipatam, dated 30 June 1622; Foster, *English Factories* (1622), p. 98.

50 Abdul Aziz, 'A History of the Reign of Shah Jahan', *Journal of Indian History*, 6 (1927), part 1, p. 241 (citing Qazvini); also Lahori's *Padshahnama* in Elliot and Dowson, *History of India*, vol. 7, p. 5. Though derided by Shah Jahan's apologists, Shahriyar had his admirers. The English merchant William Hawkins describes how the prince refused to cry, 'even when hit hard and stabbed in the cheek. … There is great hope of this child to exceed all the rest'; Foster, *Early Travels*, p. 117.

51 Ghiyath al-Din died on 5 February 1622 (17 Aquarius/Bahman A.H. 1030); Thackston, *Jahangirnama*, p. 373; Rogers and Beveridge, *Tuzuk*, vol. 2, p. 222. Desai, *Nobility*, pp. 3–4, mentions the names of a few servants who received minor bequests. Nur-Jahan's mother, Asmat Begum, had died the previous October.

52 Nath, *Mughal Architecture*, vol. 3, pp. 406–20.

53 Islam, *Indo-Persian Relations*, pp. 171–2 and 182; also Nayeem, *Bijapur*, pp. 62–3.

54 11 Shaban 1031; Monshi, *Shah Abbas*, vol. 2, pp. 1194–6. The fall of Kandahar was also reported by the English trader Robert Hughes in Surat; Foster, *English Factories* (1622), p. 108.

55 Mutamid-Khan, *Ahwal*, f. 65.

56 Thackston, *Jahangirnama*, p. 377; Rogers and Beveridge, *Tuzuk*, vol. 2, p. 231.
57 Suheil was the Canopus Star, commonly used for navigation.
58 Mutamid-Khan, *Ahwal*, ff. 66–7.
59 Anjum Rehmani, 'Historical Research on Mughal Monuments in Lahore', in Massarrat Abid and S. Qalb-i-Abid (eds.), *Cultural Heritage of the Mughals* (Lahore, University of the Punjab, 2005), p. 179.
60 Begley and Desai, *Shah Jahan Nama*, pp. 10–11.
61 The phrase is *farzand bad shiar*, contrasting powerfully with Jahangir's earlier affection language: See Chapter 6, Note 20.
62 S. Muinul Haq, 'An Unpublished Letter of Jahangir Addressed to Prince Khurram', *Journal of the Pakistan Historical Society*, 2 (1954), pp. 303–4; also Tirmizi, *Mughal Documents*, vol. 1, p. 122.
63 Zaydpuri, *History of Bengal*, section 36, p. 1; http://persian.packhum.org. The envoy was *Afzal-Khan* ['Superior Master'], son of Sheikh Abu-al-Fadl Allami; outspoken in support of Shah Jahan, Afzal-Khan had his estates confiscated and transferred to Shahriyar; Mutamid-Khan, *Ahwal*, f. 69.

8. Rebellion and Exile

1 'Ambition vs. Contentment', in Bowen, *Golden Pomegranate*, p. 77.
2 Letter from Thomas Kerridge et al. at Surat, dated 20 [i.e. 30] January 1628; Foster, *English Factories* (1624–9), p. 226.
3 Nawaz Khan, *Maathir*, vol. 1, p. 288.
4 Grey, *Della Valle*, p. 121.
5 Thackston, *Jahangirnama*, pp. 387–8; Rogers and Beveridge, *Tuzuk*, vol. 2, p. 248. Mutamid-Khan, in taking up this new appointment, must have left Shah Jahan's service and travelled to Agra.
6 Islam-Khan 'Mashhadi' (indicating his town of origin) was a veteran servant of Khurram's interests as the prince's personal envoy to the court and to Bijapur; he later served as Governor of the Deccan. Shahriyar was also accompanied by Mirza Rustum, a relative of Shah Abbas who knew Kandahar well. Nawaz Khan, *Maathir*, vol. 1, pp. 694–6.
7 Desai, *Nobility*, pp. 21 (concluding, bizarrely, the biographical entry for Nur-Jahan); Mutamid-Khan, *Ahwal*, ff. 76–9, has a detailed account of the battle.
8 Extract from Kaviraj Shyamaldas, *Vir Vinod* (1886), in Hindi and English at Jagmandir Island. The text refers to the rana's family as *suryavanshi* (Sun-dynasty), reflecting the common belief that they were descended from the solar deity; also Mankekar, *Mewar Saga*, p. 88.
9 Islam, *Indo-Persian Relations*, p. 230.
10 Zaydpuri, *History of Bengal*, section 36, p. 4; http://persian.packhum.org (quoting Mutamid-Khan).
11 Translation from Koch, *Taj Mahal*, p. 18; see also Begley and Desai, *Illumined Tomb*, p. 14.

12 Islam, *Indo-Persian Relations*, pp. 220–1 and 232; the editor notes that the letter to Queen Nur-Jahan is 'the only one on record from the ruler of one empire to the queen of the other'. See also Abdal-Rahim, 'Mughal Diplomacy', pp. 73–5.

13 Monshi, *Shah Abbas*, vol. 2, p. 1237.

14 Known to the British as 'Masulipatam'; reports of Shah Jahan's emergence from Golconda did not reach Jahangir (then at Sirhind, en route to Kashmir) until 26 February 1624, an extraordinary breakdown in communications; Thackston, *Jahangirnama*, p. 414; Rogers and Beveridge, *Tuzuk*, vol. 2, p. 289.

15 Mirza Nathan, *Baharistan-i-Ghaybi: A History of the Mughal Wars in Assam, Cooch Behar, Bengal, Bihar and Orissa During the Reigns of Jahangir and Shahjahan*, tr. M.I. Borah (Gauhati, Narayani Handiqui Historical Institute, 1936), vol. 2, p. 688.

16 Letter dated 12 November 1623; Sir William Foster, *The English Factories in India 1622–1623* (Oxford, Clarendon, 1908), pp. 312–5.

17 Khondkar Mahbubul Karim, *The Provinces of Bihar and Bengal under Shahjahan* (Dhaka, Asiatic Society of Bangladesh, 1974), pp. 11–19. Also B.C. Ray, *Orissa Under the Mughals* (Calcutta, Punthi Pustak, 1981), pp. 41–2.

18 Zaydpuri, *History of Bengal*, section 37, p. 2; http://persian.packhum.org; similarly sturdy sentiments are expressed in Nathan, *Baharistan-i-Ghaybi*, vol. 2, p. 691; also Mutamid-Khan, *Iqbalnama-i-Jahangiri*, in Elliot and Dowson, *History of India*, vol. 6, pp. 408–9.

19 Karim, *Bihar and Bengal*, p. 19. Ibrahim Khan was the uncle of Ahmad Beg, governor of Orissa.

20 Jahangirnagar is today's Dhaka.

21 Not to be confused with the Rohtas Fort in the Punjab, this ancient citadel was modernised and strengthened by Raja Man Singh when he was governor of Bengal in 1558.

22 Mutamid-Khan, *Ahwal*, ff. 90–2; also Sinha, *Allahabad*, pp. 43–6.

23 In his memoir, Jahangir noted as early as October 1623 that the Golconda-Orissa-Bengal route 'seemed reasonable in terms of military strategy' but Pervez only departed from Burhanpur on 6 Aries/Farwardin; Thackston, *Jahangirnama*, pp. 409 and 418; Rogers and Beveridge, *Tuzuk*, vol. 2, pp. 280–1 and 296.

24 Nathan, *Baharistan-i-Ghaybi*, vol. 2, pp. 755–62, contains a detailed account of the battle and the array of Shahjahan's forces but is incorrect in placing it on 26 October; also Sinha, *Allahabad*, pp. 46–8.

25 Mutamid-Khan, *Iqbalnama-i-Jahangiri*, in Elliot and Dowson, *History of India*, vol. 6, pp. 413–4; see also Zaydpuri, *History of Bengal*, section 38, pp. 1–2; http://persian.packhum.org .

26 Muhammad Amin Hussaini's *Anfa-ul-Akhbar*, ff. 220–3, cited in Alavi, *Medieval Deccan*, p. 18. Later, once Shah Jahan was on the throne, the author prudently amended his manuscript: 'trouble-mongers' became 'the army' and the word 'rebels' was deleted and replaced with 'faction'.

27 Begley and Desai, *Shah Jahan Nama*, p. 71.

28 25 Dhu al-Hijja 1033; since the birth of Umid-Bakhsh in 1619, Mumtaz-Mahal had given birth to another daughter, Sorayya Banu, in 1621, and an unnamed child who was stillborn, in 1622.

29 Nathan, *Baharistan-i-Ghaybi*, vol. 2, p. 735. The chronogram *Murad Shahjahan Padshah din wa dawal* (40+200+1+4, 300+1+5+3+5+1+50, 2+1+4+300+1+5, 4+10+50, 6, 4+6+30) adds up to 1033.

30 Nathan, *Baharistan-i-Ghaybi*, vol. 2, p. 764; also Faruqui, 'Princes and Power', p. 273.

31 The execution was marked by the chronogram 'The wretched Darab became a pure martyr': *Shahid pak shud Darab miskin* (300+5+10+4, 2+1+20, 300+4, 4+1+200+1+2, 40+60+20+10+50 = 1034); Nawaz Khan, *Maathir*, vol. 1, p. 452.

32 Jahangir became quite indiscriminate in his allocation of titles: Mahabat-Khan was variously labelled *Rukn-al-Sultanat* ('Pillar of the Sultanate'), *Rukn-al-Daula* ('Pillar of the State') and *Madar-al-Sultanat* ('Axis of the Sultanate'); Thackston, *Jahangirnama*, pp. 377, 397 and 410; Rogers and Beveridge, *Tuzuk*, vol. 2, p. 282, only refers to the last example.

33 Siddiqi, *Nur Jahan Begam*, p. 100.

34 The Abyssinian had fallen out, this time irrevocably, with the Adilshah of Bijapur, thus incurring the enmity of Mahabat-Khan; Elliot and Dowson, *History of India*, vol. 6, pp. 393–6 and 411–13. Malik Ambar died on 21 May 1626 at the age of 80, 'at the zenith of his fame, glory and power'; Tamaskar, *Malik Ambar*, p. 142.

35 12 Isfandarmudh of Jahangir's twentieth year on the throne (3 Jumada II 1035); Karim, *Bihar and Bengal*, p. 38fn.

36 Muhammad Hadi's appendix to Jahangir's memoirs in Thackston, *Jahangirnama*, pp. 433–4.

37 Siddiqi, *Nur Jahan Begam*, p. 202.

38 The appointment (under the guardianship of his late father's champion, Mirza Aziz Azam-Khan) was made on 21 May 1623; Thackston, *Jahangirnama*, pp. 397 and 418; Rogers and Beveridge, *Tuzuk*, vol. 2, pp. 260–1 and 297.

39 Monshi, *Shah Abbas*, p. 1290.

40 Sir Thomas Herbert, *A Relation of Some Yeares Travaile into Afrique, Asia, Indies* (Amsterdam, Da Capo Press, 1971), p. 30.

41 Thackston, *Jahangirnama*, p. 410; Rogers and Beveridge, *Tuzuk*, vol. 2, p. 282.

42 Anonymous (possibly Sheikh Abd-al-Wahhab), *Intikhab Jahangir Shah*, in Elliot and Dowson, *History of India*, vol. 6, pp. 451–2; see also Markovits, *Modern India*, p. 100, and Husain, *Family Groups*, pp. 176–9.

43 Accounts of the mutiny include Nawaz Khan, *Maathir*, vol. 2, pp. 15–20; also Shujauddins, *Noor Jahan*, pp. 70–89 (based on Mutamid-Khan's *Iqbalnama*).

44 Nawaz Khan, *Maathir*, vol. 2, p. 16.

45 H.G. Raverty, *Notes on Afghanistan … Extracted from … the Histories of … the Mughal Sovereigns of the House of Timur and their Muhammadan Chronicles* (Secretary of State for India, 1888), p. 32, has a vivid description of the fortress as it was in its prime.

46 These included Muhammad Taqi and, most notoriously, Asaf-Khan's elderly tutor, Mullah Muhammad Thattvi, whose Koranic invocations were alleged to be muttered curses against Mahabat-Khan; Shujauddins, *Noor Jahan*, p. 83.

47 8 Taurus/Urdibihisht, according to Muhammad Hadi; Mutamid-Khan has 18 May (21 Shaban 1035).

48 Thackston, *Jahangirnama*, p. 444.

49 Pervez died on 28 October 1626 (7 Safar 1036); the chronogram 'The death of Prince Pervez' (*wafat shahzad Parviz*, 6+80+400, 300+1+5+7+1+4, 2+200+6+10+7) adds up to 1035, when Jahangir's 20th regnal year had begun.

50 Shujauddins, *Noor Jahan*, p. 90.

51 Nasik, one of the Kumbh Mela sites, owes its significance to an important incident in the *Ramayana*; Rama's wife Sita was carried off from here by the demon Ravana to Lanka. Trimbak, to the west of Nasik, is also an important location for worshippers of Vishnu; legend has it that four drops of *amrita*, the nectar of immortality, fell to earth here during a fight between Garuda, Vishnu's vehicle, and demons.

52 Thackston, *Jahangirnama*, p. 449.

53 Mutamid-Khan, *Ahwal*, f. 107.

54 Ijaz ul-Haq Quddusi, *Tazkira-i Sufiyya-i Sind* (Karachi, 1959), p. 303, cited in Faruqui, 'Princes and Power', p. 273fn.

55 Saksena, *Shahjahan*, pp. 54–5.

56 The baby was born on 4 November 1626 (14 Safar 1036).

57 Junnar lies today in Maharashtra, due east of Mumbai.

58 Letter from Thomas Kerridge et al at Surat, postscript dated 14 (i.e. 24) December 1626; Foster, *English Factories* (1624–9), p. 161.

9. Killing the Tiger King

1 'The Manners of Kings' (1/1), in Sadi's *Gulistan* (1258), quoted by Muhammad Hadi in his epilogue to Jahangir's memoirs; Thackston, *Jahangirnama*, p. 438; Arnold translation online at http://www.sacred-texts.com/isl/gulistan.txt.

2 Temple, *Peter Mundy*, pp. 106–7.

3 Qudsi (his nom de plume) was originally from Mashhad in Persia and composed a verse biography of Shah Jahan called the *Zafarnamah*; Hasan, *Mughal Poetry*, pp. 41–2.

4 1 Pisces/Isfandarmudh; Thackston, *Jahangirnama*, p. 454.

5 BL Add. 30778/32.

6 *Jahangir az jahan raft* (3+5+1+50+20+10+200, 3+5+1+50, 1+7, 200+1+80+400 = 1037); Begley and Desai, *Shah Jahan Nama*, p. 12.

7 Nath, *Mughal Architecture*, vol. 3, pp. 423–8.

8 Hasan, *Mughal Poetry*, p. 79.

9 Anjum Rehmani, 'Abul-Hasan Asaf Khan: Life and Achievements', *Journal of the Research Society of Pakistan*, 35 (1998), pp. 55–6.

10 Desai, *Nobility*, p. 10. Abu-Ali Hassan ibn Ali ibn Ishaq, known as 'Nizam al-Mulk Tusi', was prime minister to the 11th Century Seljuk dynasty in Baghdad and author of one of the most important treatises of the medieval era, *Siyasatnama*, 'The Book of Politics'. Yahya (John the Baptist) is mentioned in the Koran, Surat Maryam (19/2–15), as being the precursor to the prophet Jesus. Khalid bin Barmak (A.D. 705–82) was wazir to the Abbasid Caliph, again at Baghdad.

11 Mutamid-Khan, *Ahwal*, f. 115. Some accounts insist that Banarsi travelled on foot, a physical impossibility, given the distance from Kashmir to the southern frontier of the empire; indeed, one legend has it that he carried a spear and slept as he ran!

12 Herbert, *Relation*, p. 33.

13 Bhimar today lies in Pakistani-administered Kashmir, near the Line of Control.

14 Mutamid-Khan, *Ahwal*, f. 116.

15 Monshi, *Shah Abbas*, vol. 2, p. 1290. The reliability of this Persian chronicle was endorsed by one reviewer, who called it 'the outstanding achievement of Safavid historiography'; J.D. Gurney, 'Review' in *International Journal of Middle East Studies* (17/2, 1985), pp. 276–7.

16 Nawaz Khan, *Maathir*, vol. 1, pp. 289–90.

17 After his subsequent defeat, Baisunghur is believed to have made his escape and survived for some time in Central Asia. A letter from Thomas Rastell et al. at Surat, dated 10 (i.e. 20) June 1631, describes how Baisunghur married a princess in the 'Tartarian territories' and briefly laid claim to 'Kabul, Multan and all those parts towards Lahore'; Foster, *English Factories* (1630–33), p. 160. An impostor subsequently represented himself as the prince in Persia and at the Ottoman capital, Constantinople. Jorge Flores and Sanjay Subrahmanyam, 'The Shadow Sultan: Succession and Imposture in the Mughal Empire, 1628–1640', *Journal of the Economic and Social History of the Orient*, 47/1 (2004), pp. 90–1 and 110–11.

18 Fairuz-Khan was subsequently retained in service by Shah Jahan; Nawaz Khan, *Maathir*, vol. 1, pp. 564–5.

19 Rehmani, 'Asaf Khan', p. 56. This approving (and otherwise comprehensive) biographical essay completely glosses over the murderous denouement of Asaf-Khan's plot.

20 Monshi, *Shah Abbas*, vol. 2, p. 1293.

21 Saksena, *History of Shahjahan*, pp. 60–1.

22 The date of arrival was 19 Rabi I 1037; Mutamid-Khan, *Ahwal*, f. 118. Banarsi's average of seventy miles per day was a remarkable feat given that he rode alone the entire distance; the American Pony Express, by contrast, changed riders every 75 or 100 miles.

23 Herbert, *Relation*, p. 31.

24 23 Rabi I 1037; Begley and Desai, *Shah Jahan Nama*, p. 13.

25 The message may have been in a special code, in Persian or in the old family Turkish: the two messengers, Amanallah and Baiyadid, are only described as

'servants who understand the language' (*khidmatgaran zaban fahm budand*); Mutamid-Khan, *Ahwal*, f. 116.

26 Monshi, *Shah Abbas*, vol. 2, p. 1292.

27 The letter was carried by Kamal al-Din Hussein *Jannisar-Khan*; Khan-Jahan, however, had rebellious instincts and sent the messenger back without any reply; Nawaz Khan, *Maathir*, vol. 1, p. 749.

28 Order dated 18 December 1627 (9 Rabi II 1037); Sayyid Akbarali Ibrahimli Tirmizi, *Mughal Documents Vol. II: 1628–1659* (Delhi, Manohar, 1995), p. 41.

29 Letter from Joseph Hopkinson et al. at Ahmedabad, 31 January (i.e. 10 February) 1628; Foster, *English Factories* (1624–9), p. 232.

30 Temple, *Peter Mundy*, p. 108fn.

31 Mutamid-Khan, *Ahwal*, f. 120. Shir-Khan was formally awarded the governorate of Gujarat at a parade at Karkariya Reservoir outside Ahmedabad on 25 December 1627 (17 Rabi II 1037 or 5 Capricorn/Dai) ; Nawaz Khan, *Maathir*, vol. 2, pp. 839–40. The new governor of Thatta was Mirza Issa Tarkhan, who had helped Shah Jahan during his earlier retreat from Thatta with 'money, stores, horses and camels and so [laid] the foundation of good fortune for himself'; ibid., vol. 1, pp. 689–90.

32 Letter from Thomas Kerridge et al. at Surat, 4 (i.e. 14) January 1628; Foster, *English Factories* (1624–9), pp. 205–7. Letter from Nathaniel Mountney at Ahmedabad, dated 28 December 1627 [i.e. 5 January 1628v], describes Shah Jahan's departure six days previously; ibid., p. 188.

33 Makekar, *Mewar Saga*, p. 88; Karna Singh died two months later and was succeeded by his son, Maharana Jagat Singh.

34 Nath, *Mughal Architecture*, vol. 3, pp. 433–40. Shah Jahan inspected the finished mosque on 5 December 1636; Begley and Desai, *Shah Jahan Nama*, p. 195.

35 Begley and Desai, *Shah Jahan Nama*, p. 14.

36 Nawaz Khan, *Maathir*, vol. 1, p. 291.

37 Bikaner State Archive, New Serial No. 21, cited in Husain, *Family Groups*, p. 148.

38 Coins of the 'Tiger King' survive in the Ashmolean Museum at Oxford.

39 22 Jumada I 1037; Thackston, *Jahangirnama*, p. 460; Begley and Desai, *Shah Jahan Nama*, p. 14.

40 Monshi, *Shah Abbas*, vol. 2, pp. 1292–3. Despite the clear evidence of this regicide, an intriguing range of legends arose to suggest the survival of Dawar-Bakhsh (or at least one impostor) and his subsequent reappearance in southern India and Persia; Flores and Subrahmanyam, 'Shadow Sultan', pp. 106–7 and 117. Islam, *Calendar*, pp. 275–7, includes correspondence between Shah Safi of Persia and the bogus 'Sultan Bulaghi'.

41 One contemporary southern source, the anonymously-written *Tarikh Sultan Muhammad Qutbshah*, states that eight relatives were murdered, though it does not name the other three, who may have been infants; Iftikhar Ahmad Ghauri, *War of Succession Between the Sons of Shah Jahan 1657–1658* (Lahore, Publishers United Ltd, 1964), p. 10 fn.

42 Herbert, *Relation*, p. 34–5; in his enjoyment of the juicy tale, Sir Thomas goes too far in his accusations of villainy, attributing the 'traitorous killing and poisoning of Sultan Bulaqi's father [Khusraw] and the Mughal Jahangir himself' to Asaf-Khan.

43 Nawaz Khan, *Maathir*, vol. 1, pp. 811–12, in a biographical note on Reza Bahadur (under the title given him subsequently by Shah Jahan, *Khidmatparast-Khan*). The account does not mention his role in the murder of Prince Khusraw. The same aphorism is quoted in Desai, *Nobility*, p. 209.

44 Letter dated 17 (i.e. 27) February 1628; Foster, *English Factories* (1624–9), p. 240.

45 Hasan, *Mughal Poetry*, pp. 41–2. In his *Majalis al-Salatin*, Muhammad Sharif Hanafi states baldly that as 'it is well known to politicians that the throne of royalty can not remain vacant for a moment, the temporary enthronement of Dawar-Bakhsh was judged expedient'; Elliot and Dowson, *History of India*, vol. 7, p. 137.

46 Date of Shah Jahan's entry ('with his train very sumptuously') confirmed in letter from Gregory Clement et al. at Agra, postscript dated 23 January [i.e. 2 February] 1628; Foster, *English Factories* (1624–9), p. 229.

47 Begley and Desai, *Shah Jahan Nama*, pp. 15–17.

48 8 Jumada II 1037, corresponding to 25 Aquarius/Bahman; Mutamid-Khan, *Ahwal*, f. 123; Begley and Desai, *Shah Jahan Nama*, p. 17. Thackston, *Jahangirnama*, p. 460, has 7 Jumada II. Abd-al-Hamid Lahori in Elliot and Dowson, *History of India*, vol. 6, p. 6, is ten days out, giving 18 Jumada II. The official Coronation Day, marking the formal beginning of Shah Jahan's long reign, came the following Nauruz, on 20 March 1628 (12 Rajab 1037). During the tenth year of the reign, as Shah Jahan became increasingly conservative, the zodiacal calendar was abolished and the Islamic date 1 Jumada II was instated (retrospectively) as the official beginning of the regnal year.

49 Aziz, 'Reign of Shah Jahan', part 3, pp. 328–42, has a detailed and colourful account.

50 *Chon sekkeh benam shah pirasteh shud / dar cheshm setareh qadr mah kasteh shud*; Kabir al-Din, Abd al-Rahim and Lees, *Padshah Namah*, vol. 1, p. 91.

51 Mutamid-Khan, *Ahwal*, f. 124.

52 Begley and Desai, *Shah Jahan Nama*, p. 2. Shah Jamshid and Faridun were both legendary rulers from the *Shahnama* ('Book of Kings') by the tenth-century Persian poet Hakim Abu-al-Qasim Firdawsi; the quotation is from the Koran, Surat al-Nisa (4/59), which commands obedience.

53 *Dar jahan bad ta jahan bashad* (4+200, 3+5+1+50, 2+1+4, 400+1, 3+5+1+50, 2+1+300+4 = 1037); Aziz, 'Reign of Shah Jahan', part 3, pp. 330–1 (Persian); Begley and Desai, *Shah Jahan Nama*, p. 17.

54 Kabir al-Din, Abd al-Rahim and Lees, *Padshah Namah*, vol. 1, p. 96.

55 Beach and Koch, *King of the World*, p. 38; translation by Thackston.

56 Afzal-Khan, a Persian, travelled to southern India and became a loyal servant of Prince Khurram before the Mewar campaign. During Shah Jahan's wilderness years, he became separated from his master but served as Jahangir's steward. Most recently, during the struggle for the succession, he had served Shah Jahan's interests while masquerading as a supporter of Prince Shahriyar in Lahore; Nawaz Khan, *Maathir*, vol. 1, pp. 151–2.

57 Lahori's Padshahnamah (translated by Wheeler Thackston) in Beach and Koch, *King of the World*, p. 38.

10. Emperor Shah Jahan and Queen Mumtaz

1 Biholia, *Ardhakathanaka*, p. 78.

2 Hasan, *Mughal Poetry*, p. 37.

3 These included Asaf Khan, Itiqad-Khan, Khan-Jahan Lodi, Sayyid Muzaffar Bara, Bahadur Khan, Khidmatparast-Khan the executioner and others; Faruqui, 'Princes and Power', p. 274 fn; Saksena, *Shahjahan*, p. 64.

4 Lashkar-Khan replaced Khawaja Abu-al-Hassan. Among the other changes, Mirza Rustum Safavi in Bihar was replaced by Khan-Alam, Mir Abd-al-Razzaq Muzaffar-Khan Mamuri in Malwa by Amanallah Bahadur Khanazad-Khan (eldest son of Mahabat-Khan), Fidai-Khan in Bengal by Qasim Khan Juvaini (ex-governor of Agra), Mukhtar-Khan in Delhi by Qilij-Khan and Jahangir Quli Khan (son of Mirza Aziz Koka) in Allahabad by Jansipar Khan Turkman. Apart from Khan-Jahan, Asaf-Khan was kept on in Punjab, though in his absence Amir-Khan was the de facto administrator; Asaf-Khan's brother Itiqad-Khan remained in Kashmir and Baqr Khan Najm al-Thani in Orissa; Aziz, 'Shah Jahan', part 3, p. 333; Faruqui, 'Princes and Power', p. 274 fn; Saksena, *ShahJahan*, p. 64.

5 Nawaz Khan, *Maathir*, vol. 1, pp. 831–4. For the missing money, see Thackston, *Jahangirnama*, p. 388; Rogers and Beveridge, *Tuzuk*, vol. 2, p. 250; and (the sanitised version) Kabir al-Din, Abd al-Rahim and Lees, *Padshah Namah*, vol. 1, p. 189. A more condensed biographical note in Desai, *Dhakirat ul-Khawanin*, pp. 152–3, omits the entire Kabul incident. Lashkar-Khan was subsequently withdrawn as governor because the local Sunnis disapproved of his being a Shiite.

6 Faruqui, 'Princes and Power', pp. 273–5.

7 The *khulafa rashidun* were Abu-Bakr (A.D. 632–4), Umar (634–44), Osman (644–56) and Ali (656–61).

8 Begley and Desai, *Shah Jahan Nama*, p. 29; Faruqui, 'Princes and Power', p. 276fn.

9 Rai Bhara Mal's *Lubbu-t Tawarikh-i Hind* in Elliot and Dowson, *History of India*, vol. 7, p. 170.

10 The Ashura festival marks the anniversary of the death of Imam Hussein, the Prophet's grandson, at Kerbala (in modern-day Iraq) in A.H. 61. The Leilat al-Miraj falls on 27 Rajab.

11 Hasrat, *Dara Shikuh*, pp. 2–5. At the age of 21, Dara-Shikuh would join the Qadiriya order, which was named after its founder, the 11th Century mystic Abd-al-Qadir al-Gilani, and reached India via Central Asia.

12 On the solar event, the king was weighed against gold, silver, silk, perfumes, copper, mercury, medicines, ghee, rice-milk, grain and salt; on the lunar event, the materials were gold, silver, tin, bales of cloth, lead, fruit and vegetables; K.R. Qanungo, 'Some Side-lights on the Character and Court-life of Shah Jahan', *Journal of Indian History*, 8 (1929), pp. 45–52.

13 A second coronation was held on 15 August 1628 (15 Dhu al-Hijja 1037), because 'according to the far-sighted astrologers, no more auspicious hour than this existed in the cycle of the calendar'; Begley and Desai, *Shah Jahan Nama*, p. 26.

14 Aziz, 'Shah Jahan', part 3, pp. 338–9 (quoting Lahori's *Padshahnamah*); see also Andrews, 'Court Tents', pp. 151–2 (quoting almost identical extracts from Muhammad Amin Qazvini and Muhammad Salih).

15 Letters from Gregory Clement at al. at Agra, dated 17 (i.e. 27) February and 2 (i.e. 12) March 1628; Foster, *English Factories* (1624–9), pp. 241 and 247.

16 Nur-Jahan died at Lahore on 18 December 1645, aged 72, and was buried in a plain square tomb not far from Jahangir's at Shahdara outside Lahore; Nawaz Khan, *Maathir*, vol. 2, pp. 1078–9. Her daughter, Ladhli Begum, is buried beside her. Nur-Jahan's epitaph befits her disappointing end: 'Mine is a poor person's tomb on which no lamp is lighted and no flowers are offered. … Forlorn and desolate, such is my fate'; Nath, *Mughal Architecture*, vol. 3, pp. 429–32.

17 Dated 16 Libra (Mihra) in Shah Jahan's 2nd Regnal Year (1629); Tirmizi, *Edicts*, pp. 56–7.

18 The household major-domo was Ishaq Bag Yazdi. On the death of Mumtaz-Mahal in 1631, he was transferred to run the household of the Princess Royal, Jahan-Ara and was subsequently given the title *Haqiqat-Khan*, 'Master of Truth'; Nawaz Khan, *Maathir*, vol. 1, pp. 614–5.

19 Begley and Desai, *Shah Jahan Nama*, pp. 22–3.

20 Turan is an ancient Persian word indicating the territories of Central Asia in general; it has come to delineate more specifically the ethnic Turkic, Mongol and Ugric and linguistic groups in the region. In Turkey especially it has acquired nationalist ideological overtones.

21 Letter to Abdallah Khan Uzbek, dated 15 June 1596, in Mansura Haidar (ed. and tr.), *Mukātabāt-i-Allāmī (Inshā'i Abu'l Fazl): Daftar I* (Delhi, Indian Council of Historical Research, 1998), pp. 102–14.

22 Nawaz Khan, *Maathir*, vol. 1, p. 605.

23 Muhammad Athar Ali, *Jahangir and the Uzbeks* (Aligarh, Aligarh Muslim University, 1964), pp. 1–6; Begley and Desai, *Shah Jahan Nama*, p. 27.

24 Kabir al-Din, Abd al-Rahim and Lees, *Padshah Namah*, vol. 1, pp. 233–6 and Nawaz Khan, *Maathir*, vol. 1, p. 605, on the Persian mission of Dr Haziq; Yar Muhammad Khan, 'Foreign Policy of the Mughals (1526–1707)', *Journal of the Research Society of Pakistan*, 29 (1992), p. 45, and an Uzbek chronicle,

the *Tazkira-i-Muqim Khani*, on the embassy of Mir Baraka (originally from Pokhara) to Central Asia. See also Farooqi, 'Diplomacy', p. 76, on the careful selection of Mughal ambassadors, and Richard Foltz, *Mughal India and Central Asia* (Karachi, OUP, 1998), pp. 132–3.

25 Edict dated Taurus/Urdibihisht A.H. 1037, i.e. between 20 April and 20 May 1628; Tirmizi, *Mughal Documents*, vol. 2, p. 41.

26 Nawaz Khan, *Maathir*, vol. 1, p. 833.

27 Order dated 26 September 1628 (5 Libra/Mihr, corresponding to 28 Muharram 1038); Tirmizi, *Mughal Documents*, vol. 2, p. 42. The expedition was the beginning of a long and successful career for Raja Jai Singh, which culminated in the award of a hybrid title, *Mirza-Raja* ('Prince-King'); Nawaz Khan, *Maathir*, vol. 1, pp. 731–4, and Desai, *Nobility*, p. 237.

28 Begley and Desai, *Shah Jahan Nama*, p. 25.

29 Islam, *Indo-Persian Relations*, p. 230.

30 Lahori's *Padshahnama* in Elliot and Dowson, *History of India*, vol. 7, p. 7. Richards, *Mughal Empire*, pp. 129–30, discusses the rebellion in detail.

31 30 Rabi I 1038.

32 Inayat Khan notes that 'it was clear that the bramble of Jujhar's wickedness could easily be pulled out by the roots'; Begley and Desai, *Shah Jahan Nama*, p. 29.

33 Ibid., p. 71.

34 Begley and Desai, *Illumined Tomb*, pp. 21–2.

35 The word used is *murid*, which can also mean disciple; Nimat Allah, *Tarikh-i-Khan Jahan*, vol. 1, p. 77.

36 Desai, *Nobility*, p. 23; also Husain, *Family Groups*, p. 133.

37 The subsequent account is largely based on the detailed (and very similar) narratives in Desai, *Nobility*, pp. 25–36 and Nawaz Khan, *Maathir*, vol. 1, pp. 795–803.

38 Husain, *Family Groups*, pp. 143–7, argues that Khan-Jahan, a supporter of the candidacy of Dawarbakhsh, was merely securing his rear in advance of joining the new king at Lahore; Saksena, *Shahjahan*, p. 68 fn, analyses the relationship between Khan-Jahan and Ahmadnagar. Alavi, *Medieval Deccan*, p. 19, argues that this allegation was an invention of Shah Jahan, not supported by contemporary Deccan chronicles.

39 Letter from Gregory Clement at al. at Agra, dated 17 (i.e. 27) February 1628; Foster, *English Factories* (1624–9), p. 240.

40 The official, Mirza Lashkari, was a man 'notorious for his loquacity' and the son of a veteran courtier named *Mukhlis-Khan*, who had served with Asaf-Khan in the decisive battle against Prince Shariyar outside Lahore; Nawaz Khan, *Maathir*, vol. 2, pp. 250–1. Another account says that Khan-Jahan's house was levelled 'as a punishment for his insolence'; Sayyid Mufazzal Khan's *Tarikh Mufazzali* in Elliot and Dowson, *History of India*, vol. 7, p. 141.

41 The rebellion began on 28 Safar 1039; Thackston, *Jahangirnama*, pp. 453–4 and 458.

42 Ashvini Agrawal, *Studies in Mughal History* (Delhi, Motilal Banarsidass, 1983), p. 147.

43 Letter from Thomas Wylde at al. at 'Swally Marine', dated 13 (i.e. 23) April 1630; Foster, *English Factories* (1630–33), p. 33.

44 Begley and Desai, *Shah Jahan Nama*, p. 38.

45 Letter from Thomas Rastell et al. at Surat, dated 31 December 1630 (i.e. 10 January 1631); Foster, *English Factories* (1630–33), p. 129.

46 Thomas Rastell; ibid., p. 92.

47 Sironj (today in Madhya Pradesh) was close to the imperial trade route between Delhi and Gujarat.

48 13 Aquarius/Bahman; Sinha, *Allahabad*, pp. 50–2.

49 17 Dhu al-Qada 1040. Inayat Khan noted that 'that noblest of the daughters of Adam had for nineteen years, eight months and some days [i.e. by the lunar calendar] enjoyed in the imperial palace the prosperity of both worlds. She was in the fortieth year of her age when she hastened to the heavenly garden'; Begley and Desai, *Shah Jahan Nama*, pp. 70–1; also Anon, 'Selection from the History of Shahjahannamah', BL, Add. 30,779, f. 6.

50 Dr Wazir-Khan had joined Prince Khurram's household and remained with him, 'attached to the stirrups', through the years of exile; on Shah Jahan's accession, he had been given the rank of Five Thousand and one hundred thousand rupees; Nawaz Khan, *Maathir*, vol. 2, pp. 981–3.

51 School of Oriental and African Studies (SOAS), MS 41156, Anon, *Ahval khilasat Banu Begum mukhatab bak Mumtaz Mahal*, f. 7.

52 Post partum haemorrhage (PPH), in which excessive blood loss is caused by tears to the fabric of the womb or uterus, is still the leading cause of maternal death worldwide; in developed countries PPH is classed as an obstetric emergency, stabilised by transfusion, oxygen supply, etc. Thanks to the midwifery experience of my sister, Fiona Nicoll-Seifert.

53 Quoted from autobiography of Qasim Ali Afridi (1771–1827), in Jadunath Sarkar, *Studies in Mughal India* (Calcutta, Kuntaline Press, 1919), pp. 28–9. See also Nawaz Khan, *Maathir*, vol. 1, p. 294.

54 Anon, *Ahval … Mumtaz Mahal*, f. 16.

55 *Jay mumtazmahal jannat bad* (3+1+10, 40+40+400+1+7, 40+8+30, 3+50+400, 2+1+4 = 1040); Begley and Desai, *Shah Jahan Nama*, pp. 70–1. *Gham* would be reckoned simply 1000+40.

56 Hadith Muslim.

57 Anon, *Ahval … Mumtaz Mahal*, f. 8. Thanks to Hossein Moghaddam at Oxford University.

58 Begley and Desai, *Illumined Tomb*, p. 37; see also tributes by Qazvini, Lahori and Kamboh in ibid., pp. 12–14, 17–18 and 25–7, and by Inayat Khan in Begley and Desai, *Shah Jahan Nama*, p. 70.

11. The Illumined Tomb

1 Begley and Desai, *Illumined Tomb*, pp. 43–4.

2 Rabindranath Tagore, 'What Is Art?' in *Personality: Lectures Delivered in America* (Macmillan, 1917), p. 18.

3 This kind of villa was known as a *haveli*; the oldest surviving map illustrating this orderly sharing of the riverbank was made for the Maharaja of Jaipur in the 1720s; Koch, *Taj Mahal*, pp. 22 and 30–1.

4 Bhuvanadeva's *Aparajitaprccha*; conversation with Professor Ram Nath, Agra, November 2006.

5 *Imarat alishan wa gumbaze*; Kabir al-Din, Abd al-Rahim and Lees, *Padshah Namah* vol. 1, p. 403. Muhammad Amin Qazvini describes the area as 'a tract of land, which formerly was the house (*khana*) of Raja Man Singh', while Muhammad Salih Kambo calls it simply a 'heaven-like tract of land' (*sarzamin bihisht ain*); Begley and Desai, *Illumined Tomb*, pp. 41 and 43.

6 Tirmizi, *Mughal Documents*, vol. 2, pp. 31, 48–9, 53–4 and 61; also Begley and Desai, *Illumined Tomb*, pp. xxx-xxxi.

7 Order dated 26 Jumada II 1043, corresponding to 8 Capricorn/Dai (Shah Jahan was still using the Ilahi calendar at this time); the four havelis were acquired from Raja Bhagwan Das, Madhav Singh, Rupsi Bairagi and Chand Singh; Tirmizi, *Mughal Documents*, vol. 2, pp. 53–4. The document was witnessed by the master architect, Makramat-Khan. See also Begley and Desai, *Shah Jahan Nama*, p. 74.

8 Anon, *Ahval khilasat … Banu Begum*, f. 12.

9 *Dararaghi ahl tanjum*; Tirmizi, *Mughal Documents*, vol. 2, p. 148; in a detailed biographical note, Nawaz Khan, *Maathir*, vol. 2, pp. 264–76, notes that Makramat-Khan was deployed on other military duties after four years so his involvement must have been brief; the account describes the later construction of Shahjahanabad in detail but makes no mention of the Taj Mahal!

10 Uztaz Ahmad Lahori's central role is asserted in the *Diwan al-Muhandis*, a body of poems by his son 'Engineer' Lutfallah (himself an architect); Begley and Desai, *Illumined Tomb*, pp. xli-xliii; also Giles Tillotson, *Taj Mahal* (London, Profile Books, 2008), pp. 80–4. This latter work is a useful overview of the mausoleum's construction and status, as well as the main 'players' in the story. Fr Sebastiaõ Manrique obscured the picture by insisting that a Venetian named Geronimo Veroneo was involved in the design. Veroneo was a respected Agra-based jeweller and goldsmith on the emperor's payroll but there is no mention of him in any Mughal record; see the long and discursive footnote in Luard, *Manrique*, vol. 2, pp. 174–6.

11 MS in Calcutta's National Library, cited in Ernest Havell, *Indian Architecture* (John Murray, 1913), p. 31–3, See also P.S. Bhat and A.L. Athawale, 'The Question of the Taj Mahal', *Itihas Patrika* 5 (1985), p. 102. Qasim Ali Afridi identifies many of the same individuals in his memoirs, though Ustaz Issa is classed simply as 'mason'; Sarkar, *Studies*, pp. 30–1.

12 Qazvini says only that 'overseers … hurriedly covered the top of that grave … so that it remained hidden from the public gaze'; Begley and Desai, *Illumined Tomb*, pp. 42–4.

13 The cortège's journey lasted from 17 Jumada I to 15 Jumada II 1041 and Prince Shah-Shuja returned on 4 Rajab (corresponding to 6 Aquarius/ Bahman); Inayat Khan in Begley and Desai, *Shah Jahan Nama*, pp. 73–4; Qazvini and Lahori in Begley and Desai, *Illumined Tomb*, pp. 42–3 and Sarkar, *Studies*, pp. 29–30.

14 The site of the temporary burial lies in the north-west corner of what is now the garden, close to the marble plinth.

15 Qandhari, *Tarikh-i-Akbari*, p. 180.

16 Abd-al-Hamid Lahori's *Padshahnama*, cited in Qanungo, 'Court-life of Shah Jahan', p. 50. Lahori ignorantly refers to Sanskrit as 'the Karnatak language'.

17 The figure is known as *musamman baghdadi*, or 'Baghdadi octagon'; Koch, *Taj Mahal*, pp. 152–3.

18 See Appendix 2 for details of the Koranic quotations. Non-religious calligraphy was used at, for example, the congregational Friday Mosque at Agra, where the ornamentation is a panegyric in Persian to Shah Jahan and his eldest daughter, Jahan-Ara.

19 Commentary in the Hadith al-Bukhari and the Hadith Muslim suggests that Muhammad feared that his own grave 'might have been raised above ground [and] taken as a place of worship'; Thomas Leisten, 'Between Orthodoxy and Exegesis: Some Aspects of Attitudes in the Sharia toward Funerary Architecture', *Muqarnas*, 7 (1990), pp. 12–22, explores the issue in detail.

20 Qasim Ali Afridi in Sarkar, *Studies*, p. 31.

21 Alp Khan 'Hoshang Shah' Ghuri was the son of Dilawar Khan, Governor of Malwa under the Delhi-based Tughluq sultanate. In 1401, Dilawar declared independence and established his capital at Dhar. Hoshang Shah inherited the throne in 1405 and ruled for 27 years, during which time he moved the capital permanently to the mountain-top at Mandu. Patil, *Mandu*, pp. 7–9 and 37–9.

22 The finely scratched and barely visible inscription is dated 23 December 1659 (9 Rabi II 1070) and signed by 'this humble indigent Engineer Lutfallah, son of Ustaz Ahmad [the senior architect described above], Khawaja Jadu Rai, Ustaz Sivaram and Ustaz Hamid', who had all 'come for pilgrimage'.

23 It is less clear that the pietra dura work inside the top chamber of the Gol-Mahal on Jagmandir Island (where Shah Jahan is reported to have resided in exile) do in fact predate his own use of such styles, as claimed in Udaipur.

24 The Koran, Surat Al Imran (3/15) and Surat al-Beiyina (98/8).

25 4 Dhu al-Hijja 1041 (seventeen days after the actual anniversary); Shah Jahan had reached Agra on 19 June; Begley and Desai, *Illumined Tomb*, p. 47.

26 Inayat Khan in Begley and Desai, *Shah Jahan Nama*, pp. 83–4; almost identical accounts by Qazvini and Lahori in Begley and Desai, *Illumined Tomb*, pp. 48–50.

27 Retrospective account on the occasion of the twelfth anniversary of the queen's death; Koch, *Taj Mahal*, p. 256.

28 A tola was equivalent to 0.425 oz. Abd-al-Hamid Lahori uses almost identical phrases in his account; Begley and Desai, *Illumined Tomb*, pp. 51–4; also Inayat Khan in Begley and Desai, *Shah Jahan Nama*, p. 95.

29 The name is a phonetic corruption of *[Mum]taz-Ganj*, 'Treasury of Mumtaz'; Temple, *Peter Mundy*, vol. 2, pp. 213–4; also (in an edited version) John Keast (ed.). *The Travels of Peter Mundy 1597–1667* (Redruth, Dyllansow Truran, 1984), p. 24.

30 Gurcharan Das, *India Unbound* (Profile, 2002), p. 68.

31 Edicts dated 4 Rabi I 1042 (corresponding to 28 Virgo/Sharivar), 26 Rabi I 1042 (19 Libra/Mihr) and 7 Safar 1047 (9 Cancer/Tir); Tirmizi, *Mughal Documents*, vol. 2, pp. 48–9 and 61.

32 Amanat-Khan's signatures are dated AH 1045/AD 1635–6, 1046/1636–7 and 1048/1638–9 respectively; Koch, *Taj Mahal*, pp. 99–100 and 224–5; also Begley and Desai, *Illumined Tomb*, p. 62.

33 Manrique was born at Oporto in 1587, took holy orders at Goa in 1604 and was appointed to the Bengal Mission by Fr Luiz Coutiˉo, Father-Provincial for India, in 1629; Luard, *Manrique*, vol. 1, pp. xxvii-xxviii and vol. 2, pp. 141 and 146.

34 Ibid., vol. 2, pp. 171–2.

35 This is the first recorded example of the name 'Taj Mahal', though it clearly identifies the late queen, rather than the monument; its spelling here is dictated by French phonetics.

36 Letter to Colbert (first published in London in 1671), in François Bernier, *Travels in the Mogul Empire, AD 1656–1668*, ed. Vincent Smith, tr. Archibald Constable (Delhi, Munshiram Manoharlal, 1992), pp. 293–9. Bernier had been in Egypt from 1656–8, living in Cairo for more than a year.

37 Begley and Desai, *Illumined Tomb*, pp. 65–82.

38 Qudsi's verses are treated as being spoken by Shah Jahan in Anon, *Ahval khilasat … Banu Begum*, f. 18; translation by Dr Yunus Jaffery; see also Begley and Desai, *Illumined Tomb*, pp. 85–6.

39 The myth of a 'Black Taj', to be built for Shah Jahan himself, sprang from bazaar gossip reported by a French traveller who visited Agra much later, in 1664; Jean-Baptiste Tavernier, *Travels in India*, tr. V. Ball (2 vols, Delhi, Low Price Publications, 2000), vol. 1, p. 91. This exaggerated account includes Tavernier's statement that he witnessed both 'the commencement and accomplishment of this great work, on which twenty-two years have been spent, during which twenty thousand men worked incessantly'. The 'Black Taj' myth was further propagated by another Frenchman, Jean de Thévenot, who never even visited Agra; Sen, *Travels of Thévenot*, p. 49. Much more recently, a 'Black Taj' was recreated digitally for Shaad Ali's 2001 music video of 'Meri Jaan' by Vasundhara Das; Rachel Dwyer, 'Views of the Taj Mahal', draft paper, S.O.A.S., n.d., p. 4.

40 Luard, *Manrique*, vol. 2, p. 173.

41 Tavernier, *Travels*, vol. 1, p. 90. 'Tasimacan' is presumed to be a phonetic corruption of *[Mum]tazmakan*, 'Home of Mumtaz'. Conspiracy theorists, most

notably Purushottam Nagesh Oak, have argued that the name is a corruption of a Sanskrit phrase *tejomahalaya*, indicating that the Taj Mahal usurped a temple of Shiva. See Oak, *The Taj Mahal is a Temple Palace* (Delhi, Oak, 1974). Other works investigating the claim that the Taj Mahal was built on a Hindu site include Bhat and Athawale, 'Taj Mahal', pp. 98–109, and Marvin Mills, 'An Architect Looks at the Taj Legend' (a technical review of Begley and Desai's *Illumined Tomb*); online at *http://www.stephen-knapp.com/an_architect_looks_at_the_taj_mahal_legend.htm*.

42 Temple, *Peter Mundy*, vol. 2, pp. 215–6; Keast, *Peter Mundy*, p. 26.
43 Letter dated 9 December 1652 (8 Muharram 1063), in *Ruqaat Alamgiri*; Begley and Desai, *Illumined Tomb*, pp. 175–6.

12. The Ornamented Throne

1 Shireen Moosvi, 'Expenditure on Buildings under Shahjahan – A Chapter of Imperial Financial History', *Proceedings of the Indian Historical Congress, 46th Session (Amritsar, 1985)*, p. 286.
2 *Kulliyat al-Kalim*, in Hasan, *Mughal Poetry*, pp. 56–7.
3 Muhammad Sharif Hanafi's *Majalis al-Salatin* ('Assemblies of the Sultans') in Elliot and Dowson, *History of India*, vol. 7, p. 138. The account does not give a specific year but ends just after Shah Jahan's coronation. Hanafi's totals were compiled using the *dam*, a small copper coin that was the currency of the general population: Agra = 20,562,500 (822,500,000 dams; 40 dams equalled one silver rupee); Ajmer = 10,512,500; Allahabad = 7,675,000; Bengal = 12,500,000; Bihar (Patna) = 7,817,500; Deccan (Ahmadnagar) = 28,350,000; Delhi = 16,402,500; Gujarat = 12,660,000; Kabul (incl. Kashmir) = 6,250,000; Khandesh & Berar = 21,830,000; Malwa (Mandu) = 7,000,000; Oudh = 5,805,000; Punjab (Lahore) = 20,625,000; Sind (Multan and Thatta) = 10,000,000; Total = 187,990,000 rupees. See also Habib, 'Currency System', pp. 10–12 and 17–18.
4 T.N. Ninan, 'An Indian Century?', paper by the editor of *Business Standard*, Seminar on India 1999, Delhi, January 2000; http://www.india-seminar.com/2000/485/485%20ninan.htm.
5 Nawaz Khan, *Maathir*, vol. 1, pp. 678–9. This account calculates the annual income at 225 million rupees.
6 Contemporary English merchants calculated the exchange rate as 2s 3d to the rupee (making one rupee worth £0.1125); the French equivalent was 1.5 livres to the rupee; Tavernier, *Travels*, vol. 1, p. 305fn.
7 Luard, *Manrique*, vol. 2, pp. 155–7; see also Habib, 'Currency System', p. 1.
8 Najaf Haider, 'Prices and Wages in India (1200–1800): Source Material, Historiography and New Directions', paper given at conference 'Towards a Global History of Prices and Wages', Utrecht, 2004, pp. 67–8; http://www.iisg.nl/hpw/papers/haider.pdf.
9 Moreland and Geyl, *Francisco Pelsaert*, p. 47.

10 Letter from Thomas Rastell et al. at Surat, dated 31 December 1630 [i.e. 10 January 1631]; Foster, *English Factories* (1630–33), p. 129.

11 Moreland and Geyl, *Francisco Pelsaert*, p. 64.

12 Gladwin, *Persian Moonshee*, pp. 58 and 52. The veteran Brahmin courtier was 53 when Shah Jahan came to the throne and joined the emperor's staff when his employer Afzal-Khan died in 1639; S.A.H. Abidi, 'Chandra Bhān Brahman – His Life and Works', *Islamic Culture*, 40/1 (1966) pp. 79–95.

13 Olearius, *Voyages and Travels*, p. 45.

14 Ibid., p. 53. Despite providing detailed observations on life in Agra, Mandelslo apparently did not visit the Taj Mahal (then in its sixth year of construction). The omission may be explained by his premature departure from the city, prompted by a chance meeting with the relative of a man he had killed in Persia; fearing reprisals (and notwithstanding the efforts of servants and colleagues to lie on his behalf), he retreated to Lahore before continuing his journey to the Far East.

15 This may have been shorthand for total household expenditure but was more likely travellers' gossip; Irvine, *Manucci*, p. 31.

16 Aurangzeb opined in one letter that only 'two things are necessary, that is to have the knowledge of the condition of the empire and to remember God'. On another occasion, he urged one of his household officers: 'Keep your faith perfect'; S.M. Azizuddin Husain (ed.), *Raqaim-i-Karaim (Epistles of Aurangzeb)* (Delhi, Idarah-i Adabiyat-i Delli, 1990), pp. 21 and 26.

17 Ibid., pp. 44–6. Manucci arrived at Surat on 22 January 1656 and made his way to Delhi via Burhanpur and Agra.

18 Qanungo, 'Court-life of Shah Jahan', pp. 50–1.

19 Rahman, *Persian Literature*, pp. 129–35, gives details of many poets and other men of letters.

20 Gladwin, *Persian Moonshee*, pp. 57–8.

21 Moosvi, 'Buildings under Shahjahan', pp. 287–8 and 293–5.

22 Shah Jahan's mosque was commissioned in 1639 and completed in 1646; Salome Zajadacz-Hastenrath, 'A Note on Babur's Lost Funerary Enclosure at Kabul', *Muqarnas: An Annual on Islamic Art and Architecture*, 14 (1997), pp. 135–6; Nath, *Mughal Architecture*, vol. 1, p. 115.

23 Gladwin, *Persian Moonshee*, p. 56.

24 Inayat Khan insists that those whose property was demolished were compensated 'by receiving ten or fifteen times the actual value': Begley and Desai, *Shah Jahan Nama*, p. 206.

25 Nath, *Mughal Architecture*, vol. 4, pp. 453–4.

26 Begley and Desai, *Shah Jahan Nama*, pp. 89–90; Sri Ram Sharma, *The Religious Policy of the Mughal Emperors* (Asia Publishing House, 1962), pp. 86–7. J. M. Shelat, *The Tragedy of Shah Jahan* (Surat, Chunilal Gandhi Vidyabhavan, 1960), p. 9, argues that the emperor's hostility to Hindus was mitigated by Dara-Shikuh, whose 'pronounced sympathies towards the Hindus [and] generous patronage … concealed from the non-Muslim population the darker side of Shahjahan's rule'.

27 Completion of the mosque in late 1636 fulfilled the vow made during the Mewar campaign twenty-one years earlier; Nath, *Mughal Architecture*, vol. 4, pp. 433–40.

28 All contemporary accounts (which never knowingly downplay expenditure) agree on a total cost for materials of around eleven millions rupees, then worth approximately £1.3 million. The report of François Bernier (Bernier, *Travels*, pp. 223 and 268–9) that the throne was worth thirty or forty million rupees was exaggerated in either case. Jean-Baptiste Tavernier also saw the throne at a time when Prince Aurangzeb had seized power and imprisoned his father (at Delhi in 1665; Tavernier, *Travels*, vol. 1, pp. 303–5). His valuation, based on information from 'those who keep the accounts of the king's jewels', was little short of hysterical, multiplying the cost a thousand times. Neither they nor any contemporary Mughal historian referred to it as the 'Peacock Throne'.

29 Muhammad Baqir, 'The Peacock Throne: Romance and Reality', *Journal of the Research Society of Pakistan*, 3 (1966), pp. 27–32. The inauguration of the throne took place on 3 Shawwal 1044. See Lahori's *Padshahnama* in Elliot and Dowson, *History of India*, vol. 6, pp. 45–6; also Inayat Khan in Begley and Desai, *Shah Jahan Nama*, p. 147.

30 *Aurang shahinshah adil* (1+6+200+50+20, 300+1+5+50+300+1+5, 70+1+4+30 = AH 1044].

31 Hasan, *Mughal Poetry*, pp. 56–61; biography of Said Gilani Bibadal-Khan in Nawaz Khan, *Maathir*, vol. 1, pp. 396–9. The throne was seized during an invasion by the Persian ruler, Nadir Shah, in May 1739; following the Shah's assassination by his own officers in 1747, it was destroyed and its jewels and gold dispersed. An elderly Kurdish eye-witness is quoted as saying that 'when that king was murdered and his camp plundered, the Peacock Throne and the tent of pearls fell into our hands and were torn in pieces and divided on the spot, although our chiefs themselves little knew their value; many of us threw away the pearls as useless and our soldiers, ignorant of the value of gold, offered their yellow money in exchange for a lesser quantity of silver or copper'; James Fraser, *Narrative of a Journey into Khorasan in the Years 1821 and 1822* (n.p., 1825), p. 43, cited in Baqir, 'Peacock Throne', 34–41.

32 Remarks in biography of Mullah Murshid Makramat-Khan in Nawaz Khan, *Maathir*, vol. 2, pp. 265–6.

33 Inayat Khan's *Shahjahannama* in Elliot and Dowson, *History of India*, vol. 7, p. 85.

34 Journal entry for 9 [i.e. 19] January 1611 in Foster, *Early Travels*, pp. 155–6.

35 Thackston, *Jahangirnama*, pp. 91, 314, 370–1 and 412–3; Rogers and Beveridge, *Tuzuk*, vol. 1, p. 137 and vol. 2, pp 108–9, 218 and 287.

36 *Bais khawaja ki chaukhat*; Shama Mitra Chenoy, *Shahjahanabad: A City of Delhi, 1638–1857* (Delhi, Munshiram Manoharlal, 1998), p. 32; Stephen Blake, *Shahjahanabad: The Sovereign City in Mughal India, 1639–1739* (Cambridge University Press, 1991), pp. 27–9.

37 Eckart Ehlers and Thomas Krafft, 'The Imperial Islamic City: A Map of 19th Century Shahjahanabad', *Environmental Design*, 1–2 (1993), p. 171. A map of Delhi in 1857 is available at http://www.columbia.edu/itc/mealac/pritchett/00r outesdata/1800_1899/ghalib/delhimap/delhimap.html.

38 25 Dhu al-Hijja 1048 and 9 Muharran 1049 respectively; Inayat Khan's *Shahjahannama* in Elliot and Dowson, *History of India*, vol. 7, p. 85.

39 Tavernier, *Travels*, p. 79.

40 Begley and Desai, *Shah Jahan Nama*, pp. 403–4, describes a typical inspection on 29 December 1647 (3 Dhu al-Hijja 1057), shortly before the fort's inauguration.

41 Nawaz Khan, *Maathir*, vol. 2, p. 267. Makramat-Khan died at Shahjahanabad in 1649, the year after the official inauguration of the Blessed Fortress.

42 *Agar firdos bar ru-ay zamin ast/Hamin ast-aw hamin ast-aw hamin ast*. Shah Jahan would certainly have had the idea from the same inscription on Babur's grave in Kabul; the verse has also been ascribed to other iconic achievements of Mughal aesthetics, including the Taj Mahal and the Shalimar Gardens in Kashmir.

43 Hasan, *Mughal Poetry*, p. 9. Ctesiphon is in modern-day Iraq.

44 *Nahr bihisht*; Elliot and Dowson, *History of India*, vol. 6, p. 88. The canal was the work of Ali Mardan Khan, a Persian officer who defected to Shah Jahan in 1638 (see Chapter 12) and was also responsible for building the irrigation channels for Lahore's Shalimar Gardens; Desai, *Nobility*, pp. 198–9.

45 Letter to François de la Mothe de Vayer, dated 1 July 1663; Bernier, *Travels*, p. 281.

46 The architect responsible for the design of the boulevard and the octagonal plaza was Zafar Khan *Raushan-al-Daula*, 'Brightener of the State'; Nawaz Khan, *Maathir*, vol. 2, p. 273.

47 Like Fatehpuri-Begum, Akbarabadi-Mahal's moniker came from the old name for Agra.

48 Like many large structures in the city and inside the citadel itself, this mosque and its ancillary buildings were destroyed in the wake of the 'Indian Mutiny' in 1857; Ehlers and Krafft, 'Imperial Islamic City', p. 176.

49 Such *waqf* endowments were approved in the Hadith of the Prophet Muhammed, e.g. Sahih Muslim (13/4006): 'Thereupon Allah's Apostle said: "If you like, you may keep the property intact and give its produce as *sadaqa* [a voluntary gift]". So Umar gave it as sadaqa, declaring that the property must not be sold or inherited or given away as a gift. And Umar devoted it to the poor … and to the emancipation of slaves.' Most Muslim-majority nations today have a Ministry of Awqaf.

50 The foundations of the mosque (know known as the Jumaa Masjid, or 'Friday Mosque') were laid on 6 October 1650 (10 Shawwal 1060); it cost a million rupees to build over six years, under the supervision of the architects Saadallah-Khan and Khalilallah-Khan; Nawaz Khan, *Maathir*, vol. 2, p. 272. The chronogram 'The mosque of Shah Jahan has appeared to fulfil our needs' (*qiblah hajat amad masjid Shahjahan*; 100+2+30+5, 8+1,3+1+400, 1+40+4,

40+60+3+4, 400+1+5+3+5+1+50) gives AH 1067, the date of its completion
(A.D. 1656–7); Nath, *Mughal Architecture*, vol. 4, p. 478.

51 Tavernier, *Travels*, pp. 78–9.

52 Bernier, *Travels*, pp. 246–7; see also Blake, *Shahjahanabad*, pp. 44–5, on the accommodation of rich and poor.

53 Another three gateways were subsequently cut into the wall or its bastions: the Murree Gate at the northern end, the Kabul Gate (north-west) and the Turkman Gate, due south of the Friday Mosque. The Akbarabad (Agra) Gate was later renamed the Delhi Gate; Blake, *Shahjahanabad*, p. 32; Moosvi, 'Buildings under Shahjahan', p. 290.

54 The date was 24 Rabi I 1058; *shud Shahjahanabad az Shahjahan abad* (300+4, 400+1+5+3+5+1+50+1+2+1+4, 1+7, 400+1+5+3+5+1+50, 1+2+1+4 = 1058); Nawaz Khan, Maathir, vol. 2, p. 270. Also Begley and Desai, *Shah Jahan Nama*, pp. 407–9.

55 Quoted in Andrews, 'Court Tents', p. 160; see also Blake, *Shahjahanabad*, p. 31.

56 Abu-al-Hassan Ghiyath al-Din Itiqad-Khan Yamin-al-Daula Asaf-Khan died on 21 November 1641 (17 Shaban 1051); Abd-al-Hamid Lahori in Elliot and Dowson, *History of India*, vol. 7, p. 68.

57 Nawaz Khan, *Maathir*, vol. 2, pp. 637–44.

13. Like Father, Like Sons

1 Translation from the *Akbarnama*, quoted in Husain, *Family Groups*, p. 183.

2 S.A.H. Abidi, 'Chandra Bhān Brahman – His Life and Works', *Islamic Culture*, XL/1 (1966) (Hyderabad, Islamic Culture Board, 1966), p. 87.

3 Nayeem, *Bijapur*, pp. 157–67.

4 In Ahmadnagar, internecine fighting had seen Nizamshah Murtaza II murdered at the behest of Fateh Khan, son of the legendary Malik Ambar, even as the powerful Maratha clans were beginning to emerge as a force capable of taking over the territory; Agrawal, *Mughal History*, pp. 147–50.

5 Nawaz Khan, *Maathir*, vol. 2, pp. 23–5; a verbatim account is in Desai, *Nobility*, p. 196.

6 The fatal illness has been given variously as leprosy (Persian *bahakandar*, from Arabic *bahaq*, 'vitiligo'), fistula or tuberculosis; Desai, *Nobility*, pp. 51–3. The chronogram 'The Commander-in-Chief is gone' (*Sipahsalar raftah*, 6+2+5+60+1+30+1+200, 200+80+400+5) gives the year of his demise: AH 1044; Nawaz Khan, *Maathir*, vol. 2, pp. 26–8.

7 Shah Jahan reached passed Burhanpur on 28 January 1636 (19 Shaban 1045/9 Aquarius); account of Muhammad Salih Kamboh in Begley and Desai, *Illumined Tomb*, p. 59. He reached Daulatabad on 28 February (21 Ramadan); see Beach and Koch, *King of the World*, p. 19, for a comprehensive breakdown of all the movements of Shah Jahan and, by extension, his capital, from his accession in February 1628 to his imprisonment at Agra in June 1658.

8 Francis Balfour, *The Forms of Herkern (The Inshā'ī Harakaran of Harakaran Mutradas Kanboh of Multan)* (Calcutta, 1781), p. 23.

9 Nayeem, *Bijapur*, pp. 161–5, has details of the complex and bitter treaty negotiations.

10 Shelat, *Tragedy of Shah Jahan*, p. 8.

11 *Safinat al-Awliya* (AH 1049), *Sakinat al-Awliya* (AH 1052) and *Risala al-Haq Numa* (AH 1056); Hasrat, *Dārā Shikūh*, pp. 7–11.

12 Ibid., p. 10.

13 Ghauri, *War of Succession*, pp. 34–6.

14 Jadunath Sarkar, *History of Aurangzib* (Calcutta, M.C. Sarkar and Sons, 1912), vol. 1, pp.4–5; Ghauri, *War of Succession*, p. 39.

15 Hamad al-Din Khan's *Ahkam Alamgiri* ('Anecdotes of Alamgir'), quoted in Sarkar, *History of Aurangzib*, vol. 1, pp. 9–12.

16 Sarkar, *History of Aurangzib*, vol. 1, pp. 12–13.

17 R.C. Majumdar, J.N. Chaudhuri and S. Chauduri (eds), *The History and Culture of the Indian People, Vol. 7: The Mughul Empire* (Bombay, Bharatiya Vidya Bhavan, 1994), pp. 198–9; Sarkar, *History of Aurangzib*, vol. 1, pp. 14–19.

18 Berar, Daulatabad (seat of the provincial capital), Khandesh and Telingana; Ghauri, *War of Succession*, p. 40.

18 Alavi, *Medieval Deccan*, p. 73.

20 Ghauri, *War of Succession*, pp. 46–7.

21 *Mulk al-mawruthi*; Farooqi, 'Diplomacy', pp. 62–5; Foltz, *Central Asia*, pp. 133–4.

22 Begley and Desai, *Shah Jahan Nama*, p. 323; Foltz, *Conversations*, p. 45. See also RC Varma, 'Mughal Imperialism in Transoxiana', *Islamic Culture*, 22 (1948), p. 254; Watson, 'Central Asian Influence', p. 17.

23 Nawaz Khan, *Maathir*, vol. 2, pp. 665–7; also Aziz Ahmad, *Studies in Islamic Culture in the Indian Environment* (Delhi, OUP, 1999), p. 37.

24 21 Shawwal 1047; a letter from Shah Jahan to Sayyid Muzaffar Barha Khan-Jahan has full details of the handover and Mughal military reinforcement; Islam, *Indo-Persian Relations*, p. 257. Also Begley and Desai, *Shah Jahan Nama*, pp. 221–3.

25 Desai, *Nobility*, pp. 198–9; also account of Johann de Mandelslo in Olearius, *Voyages and Travels*, p. 22.

26 Qulij-Khan served as Governor of Kandahar for three years; Nawaz Khan, *Maathir*, vol. 2, pp. 541–4. The author notes censoriously that 'though there was much praying and fasting in his camp, gambling, sodomy, drinking and fornication were also prevalent'. The biographical entry in Desai, *Nobility*, pp. 214–5, is almost identical in judgemental tone.

27 The miniature, probably part of a copy of Lahori's *Padshahnama*, is in the Musée Guimet in Paris; online at http://www.museeguimet.fr/The-Surrender-of-Kandahar?id_document=259.

28 Majumdar, Chaudhuri and Chauduri, *Mughul Empire*, p. 204.

29 Luard, *Manrique*, vol. 2, pp. 261–2.

30 The Sayyid was a descendant of Sheikh Abd-al-Qadir Jilani, after whom
the Qadiriya sect to which Dara-Shikuh belonged was named; Farooqi,
'Diplomacy', p. 77.

31 Foltz, *Central Asia*, pp. 138–41, has interesting details on the internal rivalries
among the Uzbeks.

32 Nawaz Khan, *Maathir*, vol. 2, p. 638.

33 Husain, *Epistles of Aurangzeb*, pp. xvii-xviii and 26.

34 In his reply, Shah Abbas notes pointedly that 'power and pride, greatness and
grandeur befit only God and not his humble servants', before noting that Nazr
Khan 'has no intention of proceeding to Mecca and his sole purpose is to seek
help to avenge himself and liberate his country'; Islam, *Indo-Persian Relations*,
pp. 293–4 and 297–8.

35 The siege had begun on 25 December 1648, according to Persian sources;
ibid., pp. 305–6 and 312–13.

36 Ghauri, *War of Succession*, p. 51; see also Islam, *Indo-Persian Relations*,
pp. 396–7 for Aurangzeb's humble reply to one particularly virulent letter.

37 Hasrat, *Dārā Shikūh*, p. 40.

38 22 Ramadan 1062; Ghauri, *War of Succession*, p. 51.

39 The intervening governors were: Khawaja Sabir Ali *Khan-Dauran* (6 June
1644–2 July 1645), Raja Jai Singh (for one month), Abd-al-Salam Mashhadi
Islam-Khan (27 July 1645–12 November 1647), Shahnawaz-Khan Safavi
(December 1647-July 1648), Prince Murad-Bakhsh (25 July 1648-August
1649) and finally Shayista-Khan (14 September 1649-September 1652); Desai,
Nobility, pp. 71–2, 195–7, 197–8, 237; Ghauri, *War of Succession*, p. 52fn.

40 Agrawal, *Mughal History*, p. 150.

41 Special concessions to farmers, known as *taqavi* loans, have been a feature
of Indian agriculture ever since; Nawaz Khan, *Maathir*, vol. 2, pp. 304–9, see
also the chapter 'Murshid Quli Khan's Revenue Reforms in the Deccan' in
Alavi, *Medieval Deccan*, p. 19.

42 Ghauri, *War of Succession*, p. 52.

43 Agrawal, *Mughal History*, p. 153.

44 Shelat, *Tragedy of Shah Jahan*, p. 14. Bhagnagar is today known as
Hyderabad. The marriage between Sultan Muhammad and the Golconda
princess was subsequently brokered by Mir Jumla, on condition that any son
from the union should inherit the kingdom; Tavernier, *Travels*, pp. 136–7, has
comprehensive detail of the Golconda campaign.

45 Saadallah-Khan's estates were allocated in their entirety to Dara-Shikuh.

46 The diamond, produced from Mir-Jumla's mine at Kollur, was seen by Jean-
Baptiste Tavernier (himself an expert jeweller) at Shahjahanabad and labelled
the 'Great Mogul' after its new owner; Tavernier, *Travels*, p. xx. There has been
much debate over two questions: whether the diamond had in fact previously
been owned by the Emperor Babur and had made its way, by a circuitous
route, to Golconda; and whether the 'Great Mogul' was the same diamond
seized in 1739 by Nadir Shah (see Chapter 12, Note 31 on the Ornamented
Throne) and labelled *Koh-i-noor*, 'Mountain of Light'; Stephen Howarth,

The *Koh-i-Noor Diamond: The History and the Legend* (Quartet, 1980), pp. 61–5 and 86–7; Iradj Amini, *The Koh-i-Noor Diamond* (Delhi, Roli, 1994), pp. 94–7.

47 Sri Ram Sharma, 'Aurangzib's Rebellion against Shah Jahan', *Journal of Indian History*, 44 (1966), p. 111.

48 *Ruqaat Alamgiri* (Aurangzeb's letters during the rebellion), including mutual promises of assistance and the exchange of agents, cited in ibid., p. 115 fn.

49 Botelho's *Relação das cousas mais notaveis, que observei no Reino do Gram Mogor* (1670), in BL, *Add. Ms.,* cod. 9855, f. 34v, cited in Jorge Flores, '"I Will Do As My Father Did": On Portuguese and Other European Views of Mughal Succession Crises', *e-Journal of Portuguese History*, 3/2 (2005).

14. Prisoner of the Royal Tower

1 Sen, *Travels of Thévenot*, p. 49.
2 Both chronograms give the date AH 1076 (300+1+5+3+5+1+50, 20+1+200+4, 6+80+400 and 200+800+10, 1+30+30+5); Begley and Desai, *Illumined Tomb*, pp. 159–60.
3 Husain, *Epistles of Aurangzeb*, p. 33.
4 Bernier, *Travels*, pp. 8–10; Ghauri, *War of Succession*, p. 74, notes that 'the successive defeats of Shah Shuja … doomed for good the ambitions of the Shia for a supremacy in India'; this perceived failure was compounded by the subjection of the Deccan states and their ultimate overthrow by the Marathas. See also biographical note online at http://banglapedia.net/HT/S_0251.HTM. It is, however, surprising that, of all the rival brothers, only Shah-Shuja did not correspond with the Shiite Shah of Persia.
5 Jadunath Sarkar, *The History of Bengal, Vol. II: Muslim Period, 1200–1757* (University of Dacca, 1948), p. 336; coins online at http://www215.pair.com/sacoins/public_html/mughal/mughal_22_shahshuja.html.
6 Bernier, *Travels*, p. 26.
7 http://www215.pair.com/sacoins/public_html/mughal/mughal_21_murbak.html.
8 Sharma, 'Aurangzib's Rebellion', pp. 115–16.
9 Muhammad Sadiq's *Tarikh Shahjahani* lists 'twenty eminent chiefs' who stayed with Aurangzeb; in Ghauri, *War of Succession*, p. 76fn.
10 Islam, *Indo-Persian Relations*, pp. 426–32.
11 Irvine, *Manucci*, p. 51.
12 Comments in biography of Aurangzeb loyalist Murshi Quli Khan Khorasani; Nawaz Khan, *Maathir*, vol. 2, p. 305. Sharma, 'Aurangzib's Rebellion', pp. 111–12, reports that Muhammad Salih Kamboh's history was blatantly re-edited during Alamgir's subsequent reign to reinforce the fiction that Shah Jahan abdicated in favour of Dara-Shikuh.
13 Ibid., vol. 1, pp. 495–505. The battle was on 21 Jumada 1 1068; Begley and Desai, *Shah Jahan Nama*, p. 547.

14 The Maharaja had been made Governor of Malwa province in place of Shayista-Khan, who had defected to Aurangzeb's camp.

15 For example, an effort to woo Maharana Raj Singh of Mewar in late 1654 failed. The rana had begun rebuilding the ancient fortress at Chittor, in breach of his family's treaty with the Mughals; despite forestalling a retributive campaign by Sadallah Khan, Dara could not prevent the Mewaris from corresponding with Aurangzeb in secret; Ghauri, *War of Succession*, pp. 11–12; Agarwal, *Udaipur*, pp. 50–1.

16 Qasim-Khan had been given the governorship of Gujarat in place of Murad-Bakhsh and charged with dislodging him by force; Nawaz Khan, *Maathir*, vol. 2, pp. 500–3.

17 A concise but comprehensive account of the Battle of Dharmat can be found online at http://horsesandswords.blogspot.com/2006/01/battle-of-dharmat-ii. html; also Sarkar, *Aurangzib*, vol. 1, pp. 348–69.

18 Muhammad Dara-Shikuh, *Majma'-ul-Bahrain or The Mingling of the Two Oceans*, ed. M. Mahfuz-ul-Haq (Calcutta, Asiatic Society, 1929), pp. 37–75; see also Ahmad, *Islamic Culture*, pp. 191–6; Hasrat, *Dārā Shikūh*, p. 10–13.

19 Muhammad Qazim in Elliot and Dowson, *History of India*, vol. 7, p. 179.

20 Farooqi, *Diplomacy*, p. 75; Islam, *Indo-Persian Relations*, pp. 426 and 430–4.

21 *Gharib muaf, maghrur marg*; Irvine, *Manucci*, p. 54.

22 Ibid., p. 55.

23 The battle is described in detail at http://horsesandswords.blogspot. com/2006_01_01_archive.html and (in more partisan terms) Irvine, *Manucci*, pp. 59–69.

24 Nawaz Khan, *Maathir*, vol. 1, p. 769.

25 Ishar Das's *Fatuhat Alamgiri*, cited in Sharma, 'Aurangzib's Rebellion', p. 116.

26 Quoted in biographical entry for 'Fazil Khan'; Nawaz Khan, *Maathir*, vol. 1, pp. 550–3. Tavernier, *Travels*, p. 273, insists on Aurangzeb's steadfast refusal (purely as a stalling tactic) to accept that Shah Jahan was still alive.

27 Ironically, given Aurangzeb's loathing of other faiths, the label 'Searcher of Hearts' for God is common to Christianity, Sikhism and Bahaism, as well as Islam.

28 Shelat, *Tragedy of Shah Jahan*, p. 28.

29 Irvine, *Manucci*, pp. 111–12.

30 Shelat, *Tragedy of Shah Jahan*, p. 29.

31 Tavernier, *Travels*, p. 266.

32 Ali Muhammad Khan's *Mirat-i-Ahmadi* (a Persian history of Gujarat), cited in Sharma, 'Aurangzib's Rebellion', pp. 113–14.

33 Hanafi law, founded by Imam Abu-Hanifa during the eighth century, is one of four major legal schools (*madhadib*) in Sunni Islam (the others are Hanbali, Shafii and Maliki); the Ottoman Empire was also run according to the Hanafi code of law. Foltz, *Central Asia*, p. 147, notes that the compilation of the Hanafi *Fatawa al-Alamgiriyya* depended on Central Asian religious scholarship and sources: a legacy of the period of Timur.

34 Ahmad, *Islamic Culture*, pp. 197–9, has details of religious reforms during Alamgir's reign.

35 Islam, *Indo-Persian Relations*, pp. 441 and 447.

36 Prabhu is an epithet ascribed variously to Brahman, Indra and Shiva; Muhammad Kazim's *Alamgirnama*, in Elliot and Dowson, *History of India*, vol. 7, p. 179.

37 The phrase used by Alamgir in a letter to Shah Jahan was '*mulhid bi-din … dashman mobin … rang az muslimani nadashtah*' (translation by Dr Yunus Jaffery); Ghauri, *War of Succession*, p. 75fn.

38 Hasrat, *Dara Shikuh*, p. 104.

39 Begley and Desai, *Shah Jahan Nama*, pp. 558–60.

40 Muhammad Salih Kamboh's *Shahjahannama,* in Begley and Desai, *Illumined Tomb*, p. 142.

41 Arakan (Rakhine) is today part of Burma; the fate of Shah-Shuja is examined in Muhammed Nurul Karim, 'Fate of Shah Shuja – His Flight to Arakan and Death', *Journal of the Pakistan Historical Society*, 1/4 (1953), pp. 8–18.

42 Kamboh in Elliot and Dowson, *History of India*, vol. 7, pp. 131–2.

43 Shelat, *Tragedy of Shah Jahan*, p. 30.

44 *Mirat Alam* of Bakhtawar Khan in Elliot and Dowson, *History of India*, vol. 7, pp. 163–4. The provinces of the expanded empire are now listed as: Agra, Ahmedabad, Ajmer, Allahabad, Aurangabad, Bengal, Berar, Bihar, Kabul, Kashmir, Khandesh, Lahore, Malwa, Multan, Orissa, Oudh, Shahjahanabad, Thatta and Zafarabad.

45 11 Rajab 1076; Kamboh's *Shahjahannama,* in Begley and Desai, *Illumined Tomb*, p. 143.

46 26 Rajab; quotation from Surat al-Baqara (2/201).

47 Begley and Desai, *Illumined Tomb*, p. 147; Jahan-Ara returned to Shahjahanabad to live out her days in the imperial household once more; she was buried in the compound of Sheikh Hazrat Nizam al-Din Auliya. Her simple dusty grave, crowded into one corner of the complex, bears the simple epitaph 'When Death at last arrives to set / my prisoned body free / No vault shall claim my dust – but let / The green grass cover me'; translation in Bowen, *Golden Pomegranate*, p. 36.

48 The authorised account of Alamgir's rule, Muhammad Kazim's *Alamgirnama*, has plenty of useful details but is hypocritical in its fraudulent account of the king's grief at his father's demise; Begley and Desai, *Illumined Tomb*, pp. 149–58.

Bibliography

In all sections, primary sources are given first.
Abbreviations:
IC = Islamic Culture
JIH = Journal of Indian History
JIS = Journal of Islamic Studies
JPHS = Journal of the Pakistan Historical Society
JRSP = Journal of the Research Society of Pakistan
SI = Studia Islamica

Reign of Akbar

The Akbar Nāma of Abu-l-Fazl, tr. H. Beveridge, 3 vols, Calcutta, Bibliotheca Indica, 1917–21

De, B.N. (ed. and tr.). *The Tabaqat-i-Akbari of Khwajah Nizamuddin Ahmad, Vol. II*, Delhi, Low Price Publications, 1992

Haidar, M. (ed. and tr.) *Mukātabāt-i-Allāmī (Inshā'i Abu'l Fazl): Daftar I*, Delhi, Indian Council of Historical Research, 1998

Qandhari, M.A. *Tarikh-i-Akbari*, ed. and tr. T. Ahmad, Delhi, Pragati, 1993

Ahmad, A. 'Murder of Abul-Fazl: A Reappraisal', *JRSP*, 37 (2000), 53–9

Holland, C. 'Akbar and the Mughal State: the Quest for Legitimization in Hindustan' (unpublished B.A. thesis), University of Georgia, 2005

Khan, A.N. 'Lahore: The Darus Saltanat of the Mughal Empire Under Akbar (1556–1605)', in M. Abid, and S. Qalb-i-Abid (eds.), *Cultural Heritage of the Mughals*, Lahore, University of the Punjab, 2005

Shyam, R. 'Honour, Ranks and Titles Under the Great Mughals (Akbar)', *IC*, 47/4 (1973), 335–53

Reign of Jahangir

Alvi, S.S. *Advice on the Art of Governance: Mau'izah-i Jahāngīri of Muhammad Bāqir Najm-i Sānī: An Indo-Islamic Mirror for Princes*, Albany, State University of New York Press, 1989

Anon, 'Genealogy of Jahangīr', Bodleian Library, Oxford, MS Arch. Seld. a.54

Foltz, R. (tr.) *Conversations with Emperor Jahangir by 'Mutribi' al-Asamm of Samarqand*, Costa Mesa, Mazda, 1998

Husaini, K.K. *Ma'asir-i-Jahangiri: A Contemporary Account of Jahangir*, ed. A. Alvi, New York, Asia Publishing House, 1978

The Jahangirnama: Memoirs of Jahangir, Emperor of India, trans. and ed. W.M. Thackston, Washington, Smithsonian, 1999

Modi, JJ. *Dastur Kaikobad Mahyar's Petition and Laudatory Poem Addressed to Jahangir and Shahjahan*, Bombay, Fort Printing Press, 1930

Rogers, A. and Beveridge, H. (eds). *Tūzuk-i-Jahāngīrī or Memoirs of Jahāngīr*, Delhi, Atlantic Publishers, 1989

Siddiqi, W.H. (ed.) *Waqa-i-uz-Zaman (Fath Nama-i-Nur Jahan Begam): A Contemporary Account of Jahangir by Kami Shirazi*, Rampur, Rampur Raza Library, 2003

Ali, M.A. *Jahangir and the Uzbeks*, Aligarh, Aligarh Muslim University, 1964

—— 'Religion and State During the Reign of Mughal Emperor Jahangir (1605–27): Nonjuristical Perspectives', *SI*, LXIX (1989), 95–119

Jalaluddin. 'Sultān Salīm (Jahāngīr) as a Rebel King', *IC*, 47/2 (1973), 121–5

Khan, A.N. 'Lahore During the First Regnal Year of Mughal Emperor Jahangir (1605–1606)', *JRSP*, 22 (1985), 49–61

Prasad, B. *History of Jahangir*, Oxford University Press, 1922

d'Silva, J. 'The Rebellion of Prince Khusru According to Jesuit Sources', *JIH*, 5/2 (1926), 267–81

Reign of Shah Jahan

Abd-al-Hamid Lahori, *Pādshāhnāmah* (containing an anomalous fragment on Khurram's life from the age of 16 to his accession), Bodleian Library, Oxford MS Elliot 368

Beach, M.C. and Koch, E. (eds), *King of the World: The Padshahnama*, tr. W. Thackston, Washington, Azimuth, 1997

Begley, W.E. and Desai, Z.A. *The Shah Jahan Nama of Inayat Khan*, Delhi, OUP, 1990

Kabīr al-Dīn, M., Abd al-Rahīm and Lees, Major W.N. (eds). *The Pādshāh Nāmah of Abd al-Hamīd Lahawrī*, 2 vols, Calcutta, Biblioteca Indica, 1867

Muhammad Saleh Kamboh. *Amal-i Salih*, 3 vols, Lahore, 1967–72

Muhammad Sharīf 'Mutamid-Khan', *Ahwal al-Shāhzadagi Shāhjahān* ('Description of the Princehood of Shah Jahan'), British Library, London, MS Or. 3271

Ahmed, M.Z. (ed.), *Mughal Archives: A Descriptive Catalogue of the Documents Pertaining to the Reign of Shah Jahan (1628–1658)*, Hyderabad, State Archives, 1977

Ali, A.A. 'Objectives Behind the Mughal Expedition to Balkh and Badakhshan, 1646–7', *Proceedings of the Indian Historical Congress, 29th Session (Patiala, 1967)*, 162–7

Andrews, P.A. 'The Generous Heart or the Mass of Clouds: The Court Tents of Shah Jahan', *Muqarnas: An Annual on Islamic Art and Architecture*, 4 (1987), 149–65

Aziz, A. 'A History of the Reign of Shah Jahan', *JIH*, 6 (1927), 235–57; 7 (1928), 127–47 and 327–44; 9 (1930), 132–72 and 279–305

Bāqir, M. 'The Peacock Throne: Romance and Reality', *JRSP*, 3 (1966), 27–42

Blake, S. *Shahjahanabad: The Sovereign City in Mughal India, 1639–1739*, Cambridge University Press, 1991

Chenoy, S.M. *Shahjahanabad: A City of Delhi, 1638–1857*, Delhi, Munshiram Manoharlal, 1998

Ehlers, E. and Krafft, T. 'The Imperial Islamic City: A Map of 19th Century Shahjahanabad', *Environmental Design*, 1–2 (1993), 170–9

Ghauri, I.A. *War of Succession Between the Sons of Shah Jahan 1657–1658*, Lahore, Publishers United Ltd, 1964

Hasrat, B.J. *Dārā Shikūh: Life and Works*, Calcutta, Visvabharati, 1953

Karim, K.M. *The Provinces of Bihar and Bengal under Shahjahan*, Dhaka, Asiatic Society of Bangladesh, 1974

Karim, M.N. 'Fate of Shah Shuja: His Flight to Arakan and Death', *JPHS*, 1/4 (1953), 8–18

Khan, Y.H. (ed). *Selected Documents of Shah Jahan's Reign*, Hyderabad, Daftar-i-Diwani, 1950

Lal, M. *Shah Jahan*, Delhi, Vikas, 1986

Moosvi, S. 'Expenditure on Buildings under Shahjahan – A Chapter of Imperial Financial History', *Proceedings of the Indian Historical Congress, 46th Session (Amritsar, 1985)*, 285–99

Muinul Haq, S. 'An Unpublished Letter of Jahangir Addressed to Prince Khurram', *JPHS*, 2 (1954), 302–11

Quamruddin, M. *Life and Times of Prince Murād Bakhsh, 1624–1661*, Calcutta, Quamruddin, 1974

Qanungo, K.R. 'Some Side-lights on the Character and Court-life of Shah Jahan', *JIH*, 8 (1929), 45–52

Saksena, B.P. *History of Shahjahan of Dihli*, Allahabad, Indian Press, 1932

Sharma, S.R. 'Aurangzeb's Rebellion Against Shah Jahan', *JIH*, 44 (1966), 109–24

Shelat, J.M. *The Tragedy of Shah Jahan*, Surat, Chunilal Gandhi Vidyabhavan, 1960

Reign of Alamgir

Husain, S.M.A. (ed.). *Raqaim-i-Karaim (Epistles of Aurangzeb)*, Delhi, Idarah-i Adabiyat-i Delli, 1990

Joshi, R. *Aurangzeb: Attitudes and Inclinations*, Delhi, Manohar, 1989

Khan, K. *History of Alamgir (Muntakhab al-Lubāb)*, tr. S.M. Haq, Karachi, Pakistan Historical Society, 1875

Sarkar, J. *Akham-i-Alamgiri (Anecdotes of Aurangzib)*, Calcutta, M.C. Sarkar and Sons, 1912

—— *History of Aurangzib*, 5 vols, Calcutta, M.C. Sarkar and Sons, 1912

Queens and the harem

Anon, *Ahvāl khilāsat Bānu Begum mukhātab bak Mumtāz Mahal*, School of Oriental and African Studies, London, MSS 41156 (two versions)

Butenschön, A. *The Life of a Mogul Princess: Jahānarā Begam, Daughter of Shāhjahān*, Routledge, 1931

Chattopadhyaya, A. 'Identity of Jahangir's Mother', *JIH*, 68–71 (1989–92), 121–6

Chowdhuri, J.N. 'Mumtâz Mahall', *IC*, 51 (1937), 373–81

Farooqi, H.A. 'Nur Jahan', in M. Abid, and S. Qalb-i-Abid (eds.), *Cultural Heritage of the Mughals*, Lahore, University of the Punjab, 2005

Findly, E.B. 'The Lives and Contributions of Mughal Women', in Ziad, *Magnificent Mughals* (q.v.)

—— *Nur Jahan: Empress of Mughal India*, Delhi, OUP, 1993

Habib, I. 'The Family of Nur Jahan during Jahangir's Reign: A Political Study', in K.A. Nizami (ed.) *Medieval India: A Miscellany*, Asia Publishing House, 1969

Lal, R. *Domesticity and Power in the Early Mughal World*, Cambridge University Press, 2005

Mukherjee, S. *Royal Mughal Ladies and Their Contributions*, Delhi, Gyan, 2001

Shujauddin, M. and R. *The Life and Times of Noor Jahan*, Lahore, Caravan Book House, 1967

Tirmizi, S.A.I. *Edicts from the Mughal Harem*, Delhi, Idarah-i Adabiyat-i Delhi, 1979

Foreign diplomats, merchants, travellers, etc.

Bernier, F. *Travels in the Mogul Empire, AD 1656–1668*, tr. A. Constable, ed. V.A. Smith. Delhi, Munshiram Manoharlal, 1992

Correira-Afonso, J. *Letters from the Mughal Court: The First Jesuit Mission to Akbar (1580–1583)*, Bombay, Gujarat Sahitya Prakash, 1980

De Laet, J. *The Empire of the Great Mogol*, trans. J.S. Hoyland, ed. S.N. Banerjee, Delhi, Oriental Books Reprint Corporation, 1974

Foster, Sir W. (ed.) *Early Travels in India 1583–1619*, Delhi, Oriental Books Reprint Corporation, 1985

—— *The English Factories in India 1618–1669*, 13 vols, Oxford, Clarendon, 1906–27

—— *The Journal of John Jourdain 1608–1617*, Cambridge, Hakluyt, 1905

Grey, E. *The Travels of Pietro Della Valle in India*, Hakluyt, 1892

Herbert, Sir T. *A Relation of Some Yeares Travaile into Afrique, Asia, Indies*, Amsterdam, Da Capo Press, 1971

Irvine, W. (tr.). *A Pepys of Mogul India, 1653–1708: Being an Abridged Edition of the 'Storia do Mogor' of Niccolao Manucci*, John Murray, 1913

Keast J. (ed.). *The Travels of Peter Mundy 1597–1667*, Redruth, Dyllansow Truran, 1984

Letters Received by the East India Company from its Servants in the East, 6 vols, Sampson, Low and Co., 1896–1902

Luard, Lt.-Col. C.E. (ed and tr). *Travels of Fray Sebastien Manrique, 1629–1643*, 2 vols, Oxford, Hakluyt, 1927

Moreland, W.H. (ed.). *Peter Floris: His Voyage to the East Indies in the 'Globe', 1611–1615*, Hakluyt, 1934

Narain, B. and Sharma, S.R. *A Contemporary Dutch Chronicle of Mughal India*, Calcutta, Susil Gupta (India) Ltd., 1957

Olearius, A. *The Voyages and Travels of the Ambassadors from the Duke of Holstein … whereto are Added the Voyages & Travels of J. Albert de Mandelslo … into the East-Indies*, tr. J. Davies, Dring and Starkey, 1642

Payne, C.H. (ed. and trans.) *Akbar and the Jesuits: An Account of the Jesuit Missions to the Court of Akbar by Father Pierre du Jarric, S.J.*, Routledge, 1926

—— *Jahangir and the Jesuits: From the Relations of Father Fernão Guerreiro S.J.*, Routledge, 1930

Moreland W.H. and Geyl, P. (tr.). *Jahangir's India: The Remonstrantie of Francisco Pelsaert*, Cambridge, W. Heffer and Sons, 1925

Sen, S. *Indian Travels of Thevenot and Careri*, Delhi, National Archives of India, 1949

Tavernier, J.-B. *Travels in India*, tr. V. Ball, 2 vols, Delhi, Low Price Publications, 2000

Temple, Lt.-Col. Sir R.C. *The Travels of Peter Mundy, in Europe and Asia, 1608–1667*, 4 vols, Hakluyt Society, 1907–36

Daniell, T. *Oriental Scenery: Twenty Four Views in Hindoostan*, Historic Gallery, 1795

Mitchell, C.P. *Sir Thomas Roe and the Mughal Empire*, Karachi, ASCE, 2000

Nanda, M. *European Travel Accounts During the Reigns of Shahjahan and Aurangzeb*, Kurukshetra, Nirmal Book Agency, n.d.

Subrahmanyam, S. *Explorations in Connected History: From the Tagus to the Ganges*, Delhi, OUP, 2005

—— *Explorations in Connected History: Mughals and Franks*, Delhi, OUP, 2005

Imperial politics

Abd-al-Qādir bin Malūk Shāh 'Badauni'. *Muntakhab al-Tawārīkh*, tr. W.H. Lowe, 2 vols, Calcutta, Asiatic Society of Bengal, 1884–98

Balfour, F. *The Forms of Herkern (The Inshā'ī Harakaran of Harakaran Mutrādās Kanboh of Multan)*, Calcutta, 1781

Desai, Z.A. *The Dhakirat ul-Khawanin of Shaikh Farid Bhakkari (A Biographical Dictionary of Mughal Noblemen): Part 1*, Delhi, Idarah-i Adabiyat-i Delli, 1993

—— *Nobility Under the Great Mughals: Based on Dhakhīratul Khawanīn of Sheikh Farīd Bhakkari: Parts 2 and 3*, Delhi, Sundeep Prakashan, 2003

Elliot Sir H.M. and Dowson, J. (eds), *The History of India, As Told by Its Own Historians, Vols. V, VI and VII: The Muhammadan Period*, Trübner, 1873, 1875 and 1877

—— Papers including Anon, 'A Selection from the History of Shahjahannamah Written by Moonshee Hamad Ameen', British Library, London, MSS Add. 30,771–86

Hoey, W. *Memoirs of Delhi (Being a Translation of the 'Tārīkh Farahbakhsh' of Muhammad Faiz Bakhsh)*, Allahabad, 1888

Nawāz Khān, S.S. *The Maāthir-ul-Umarā: Being Biographies of the Muhammadan and Hindu Officers of the Timurid Sovereigns of India From 1500 to about 1780 A.D.*, tr. H. Beveridge, 2 vols, Calcutta, 1922 and 1952

Abdal-Rahim. 'Mughal Diplomacy from Akbar to Aurangzeb' (unpublished PhD thesis), University of London, 1932

Agrawal, A. *Studies in Mughal History*, Delhi, Motilal Banarsidass, 1983

Alam, M. and Subrahmanyam S. (eds). *Indo-Persian Travels in the Age of Discoveries, 1400–1800*, Cambridge University Press, 2007

—— *The Mughal State 1526–1750*, Delhi, OUP, 2005

Anon. 'A True Relation … of Strange and Admirable Accidents, Which Lately Happened in the Kingdom of the Great Magor, or Mogul', in W. Oldys and T. Park (eds.) *The Harleian Miscellany: A Collection of Scarce, Curious and Entertaining Pamphlets and Tracts*, John Murray, 1808

Athar Ali, M. *The Apparatus of Empire: Awards of Ranks, Offices and Titles to the Mughal Nobility, 1574–1658*, Delhi, Aligarh Muslim University, 1985

Bakshi S.R. and Sharma S.K. (eds), *The Great Mughuls*, 8 vols, Delhi, Deep and Deep Publications, 1999

Beale, T.W. *An Oriental Biographical Dictionary*, ed. H.G. Keene, Delhi, Manohar Reprints, 1971

Chandra, S. *Medieval India From Sultanat to the Mughals: Part Two: Mughal Empire (1526–1748)*, Delhi, Har-Anand, 2006

Eraly, A. *The Mughal Throne*, Phoenix, 2000

Farooqi, N.R. 'Diplomacy and Diplomatic Procedure under the Mughals', *Medieval History Journal*, 7 (2004), 59–86

Faruqui, M.D. 'Princes and Power in the Mughal Empire, 1569–1657' (unpublished Ph.D. thesis), Duke University, 2002

Flores, J. '"I Will Do As My Father Did": On Portuguese and Other European Views of Mughal Succession Crises', *e-Journal of Portuguese History*, 3/2 (2005)

—— and Subrahmanyam, S. 'The Shadow Sultan. Succession and Imposture in the Mughal Empire, 1628–1640', *Journal of the Economic and Social History of the Orient*, 47/1 (2004), 80–121

Foltz, R. *Mughal India and Central Asia*, Karachi, OUP, 1998

Gascoigne, B. *The Great Moghuls*, Robinson, 2002

Gladwin, F. *The History of Hindoostan, During the Reign of Jehāngīr, Shāhjehān, and Aurungzebe*, vol. 1, Calcutta, Stuart and Cooper, 1788

—— *The Persian Moonshee*, Calcutta, Chronicle Press, 1795

Habib, I. *An Atlas of the Mughal Empire*, Delhi, Aligarh Muslim University, 1982

—— 'The Currency System of the Mughal Empire (1556–1707)', *Medieval India Quarterly*, 4 (1961), 1–21

—— (ed.) *Medieval India: A Miscellany*, vol. 4, New York, Asia Publishing House, 1977

—— (ed.) *Medieval India 1: Researches in the History of India 1200–1750*, Delhi, OUP, 1992

Haider, N. 'Prices and Wages in India (1200–1800): Source Material, Historiography and New Directions', paper given at conference 'Towards a Global History of Prices and Wages', Utrecht, 2004, 1–80

Husain, A. *The Nobility Under Akbar and Jahāngīr: A Study of Family Groups*, Delhi, Manohar, 1999

Islam, R. *A Calendar of Documents on Indo-Persian Relations, Vol. 1 (1500–1750)*, Tehran, Islamic Culture Foundation, 1979

Keay, J. *India: A History*, 2 vols, Folio Society, 2003

Khan, Y.M. 'Foreign Policy of the Mughals (1526–1707)', *JRSP*, 29 (1992), 39–54

Lal, M. *Mughal Glory*, Delhi, Kornark, 1988

Majumdar R.C., Chaudhuri J.N. and Chauduri S. (eds). *The History and Culture of the Indian People, Vol. 7: The Mughul Empire*, Bombay, Bharatiya Vidya Bhavan, 1994

Markovits, C. (ed.). *A History of Modern India, 1480–1950* (tr. N. George and M. Hendry from *L'Histoire de l'Inde Moderne*), Anthem, 2004

Marshall, D.N. *Mughals in India: A Bibliographical Survey of Manuscripts*, Mansell, 1985

Medieval India: A Miscellany, 4 vols, Bombay, Asia Publishing House

Monshi, E.B. *Tārīk-e Ālamārā-ye Abbāsī* ('History of Shah Abbas the Great'), tr. R.M. Savory, 2 vols, Boulder, Westview Press, 1978

Mukhia, H. *The Mughals of India*, Oxford, Blackwell, 2004

Naqvi, H. 'Capital Cities of the Mughul Empire', *JPHS*, 13 (1965), 211–43

Perti R.K. (ed.). *Calendar of Acquired Documents (1352–1754) Vol. 2*, Delhi, National Archives of India, 1986

Raverty, H.G. *Notes on Afghanistan ... Extracted from ... the Histories of ... the Mughal Sovereigns of the House of Timur and their Muhammadan Chronicles*, Secretary of State for India, 1888

Richards, J.F. *Document Forms for Official Orders of Appointment in the Mughal Empire*, Cambridge, E.J.W. Gibb Memorial Trust, 1986

—— *The Mughal Empire*, Delhi, Cambridge University Press, 2002

Sarkar, J. *Studies in Mughal India*, Calcutta, Kuntaline Press, 1919

Schimmel, A. *The Empire of the Great Mughals*, Reaktion, 2004

Schwartzberg J.E. (ed.). *A Historical Atlas of South Asia*, New York, OUP, 1992

Tirmizi, S.A.I. *Calendar of Acquired Documents (1402–1719)*, Delhi, National Archives of India, 1982

—— *Mughal Documents*, 2 vols, Delhi, Manohar, 1989 and 95

Ziad, Z. (ed.) *The Magnificent Mughals*, Karachi, OUP, 2002

Regional politics

Nathan, M. *Bahāristān-i-Ghaybī : A History of the Mughal Wars in Assam, Cooch Behar, Bengal, Bihar and Orissa During the Reigns of Jahāngīr and Shāhjahān*, tr.

Zaydpuri, G.H.S. *The Riyazu-s-Salātīn: A History of Bengal*, tr. M. Abdus Salam, Calcutta, Asiatic Society, 1902–4

Agarwal, B.D. *Rajasthan District Gazeteers: Udaipur*, Jaipur, Government of Rajasthan, 1979

Alavi, R.A. *Studies in the History of Medieval Deccan*, Delhi, Idarah-i Adabiyat-i Delli, 1977

Ali, M. *Historical Studies: Articles on the History of the Mughuls and Sind*, Lahore, Book Traders, 1987

Alvi, S.S. 'Mazhar-i Shâjahâni and the Mughal Province of Sind: A Discourse on Political Ethics', in A.L. Dallapiccola and S.Z. Lallement (eds), *Islam and Indian Regions*, Stuttgart, Franz Steiner Verlag, 1993

Davenport, H. (ed.). *The Trials and Triumphs of the Mewar Kingdom*, Udaipur, Maharana of Mewar Charitable Foundation, 1975

Kazimi, M,R. 'The Genesis of Iranian Diplomacy in the Deccan', *Proceedings of the Indian Historical Congress, 29th Session (Patiala, 1967)*, 152–7

Khan, A. M. *History of Gujarat*, tr. J. Bird, Richard Bentley, 1835

Mankekar, D.R. *Mewar Saga*, Delhi, Vikas, 1976

M.I. Borah, 2 vols, Gauhati, Narayani Handiqui Historical Institute, 1936

Nayeem, M.A. *External Relations of the Bijapur Kingdom (1489–1686 A.D.)*, Hyderabad, Bright, 1974

Newell, Lt.-Col. H.A. *Lahore: Capital of the Punjab*, Bombay, H.A. Newell, 1921

—— *Three Days at Agra*, Bombay, H.A. Newell, 1922

Patil, D.R. *Mandu*, Delhi, Archaeological Survey of India, 2004

Pinhey, A.F. *History of Mewar*, Jodhpur, Books Treasure, 1996

Ray, B.C. *Orissa Under the Mughals*, Calcutta, Punthi Pustak, 1981

Raychaudhuri, T. *Bengal Under Akbar and Jahangir*, Delhi, Munshiram Manoharlal, 1966

Sarkar, J. *The History of Bengal*, 2 vols, University of Dacca, 1948

Sharma, G.N. *Mewar and the Mughal Emperors: 1526–1707 A.D.*, Agra, Shiva Lal Agarwala, 1962

Sinha, S.N. *Subah of Allahabad under the Great Mughals (1580–1707)*, Delhi, Jamia Millia Islamia, 1974

Tamaskar, B.G. *The Life and Work of Malik Ambar*, Delhi, Idarah-i Adabyat-i Delli, 1978

Tirmizi, S.A.I. *Ajmer Through Inscriptions (1532–1852 A.D.)*, Delhi, Indian Institute of Islamic Studies, 1968

Tod, J. *Annals and Antiquities of Rajasthan*, Delhi, M.N. Publishers, 1978

Ziad, Z. (ed.), *The Magnificent Mughals*, Karachi, OUP, 2002

Arts and culture

Abid, M. and Qalb-i-Abid, S. (eds.) *Cultural Heritage of the Mughals*, Lahore, University of the Punjab, 2005

Abidi, S.A.H. 'Chandra Bhān Brahman – His Life and Works', *IC*, 40/1 (1966), Hyderabad, Islamic Culture Board, 1966

—— 'Life and Poetry of Qudsī Mashhadī', *IC*, 38/2 (1964), 93–106

—— 'Tālib-i-Āmuli: His Life and Poetry', *IC*, 41/1 (1967), 119–31

Alam, M. and Subrahmanyam S. (eds). 'The Making of a Munshi', *Comparative Studies of South Asia, Africa and the Middle East*, 24:2 (2004), 61–72

Amini, I. *The Koh-i-Noor Diamond*, Delhi, Roli, 1994

Bhutta, M.I. 'Muslim Calligraphy in the Subcontinent', *JRSP*, 36 (1999), 43–59

Bowen, J.C.E. *The Golden Pomegranate: A Selection from the Poetry of the Mogul Empire in India 1526–1858*, Bombay, Thacker and Co. Ltd., 1957

Ghani, M.A. *A History of Persian Language and Literature at the Mughal Court: Part III: Akbar*, Allahabad, Indian Press, 1930

Hasan, H. *Mughal Poetry: Its Cultural and Historical Value*, Aligarh, 1952

Havell, E. *Indian Architecture*, John Murray, 1913

Heinemann, S.O. *Poems of Mewar*, Gurgaon, Vintage, 1990

Howarth, S. *The Koh-i-Noor Diamond: The History and the Legend*, Quartet, 1980

Irādat Khan 'Wazeh'. *Mīna Bazār* ('Jewel Market'), Delhi, Muhammadi Press, 1851

Koch, E. 'Diwan-i Amm and Chihil Sutun: The Audience Halls of Shah Jahan', *Muqarnas: An Annual on Islamic Art and Architecture*, 11 (1994), 143–65

—— *Mughal Architecture: An Outline of Its History and Development, 1526–1858*, Munich, Prestel, 1991

—— *Mughal Art and Imperial Ideology: Collected Essays*, Delhi, OUP, 2001

Nath, R. *The History of Mughal Architecture*, 4 vols, Delhi, Abhinav, 1982–2005

—— *Indigenous Characteristics of Mughal Architecture*, Delhi, Indian History and Culture Society, 2004

Rahman, M.L. *Persian Literature in India during the Time of Jahangir and Shah Jahan*, Baroda, University of Baroda, 1970

Stronge, S. *Painting for the Mughal Emperor,* VandA Publications, 2002

Zajadacz-Hastenrath, S. 'A Note on Babur's Lost Funerary Enclosure at Kabul', *Muqarnas: An Annual on Islamic Art and Architecture*, 14 (1997), 135–42

Mughal gardens

Crowe S. and Haywood S. *The Gardens of Mughul India*, Thames and Hudson, 1972

Dar, S.R. 'Two Unrecorded Mughal Gardens of Lahore,' *JRSP*, 33 (1996), 31–41

Dickie, J. 'The Mughal Garden: Gateway to Paradise', in O. Grabar (ed.) *Muqarnas III: An Annual on Islamic Art and Architecture*, Leiden, E.J. Brill, 1985

Petruccioli. A. (ed.). *Gardens in the Time of the Great Muslim Empires: Theory and Design*, Leiden, E.J. Brill, 1997

Villiers Stuart, C.M. *Gardens of the Great Mughals*, A. and C. Black, 1913

Wescoat, J.L. and Wolschke-Bulmahn, J. (eds). *Mughal Gardens: Sources, Places, Representations and Prospects,*. Washington, Dumbarton Oaks, 1996

Religion

The Holy Qur'an, trans. and commentary A.Y. Ali, Brentwood, Amana Corporation, 1983

Ahmad, A. 'The Role of Ulema in Indo-Muslim History', *SI*, 31 (1970), 1–13

—— *Studies in Islamic Culture in the Indian Environment*, Delhi, OUP, 1999

Buehler, A.F. 'The Naqshbandiyya in Tīmūrid India: The Central Asian Legacy', *JIS*, 7 (1996), 208–28

Dārā Shikūh, Prince M. *Majma'-ul-Bahrain or The Mingling of the Two Oceans*, M. Mahfuz-ul-Haq (ed.), Calcutta, Asiatic Society, 1929

Foltz, R. 'The Central Asian Naqshbandī Connections of the Mughal Emperors', *JIS*, 7 (1996), 228–39

Leisten, T. 'Between Orthodoxy and Exegesis: Some Aspects of Attitudes in the Sharia toward Funerary Architecture', *Muqarnas*, 7 (1990), 12–22

Sharma, S.R. *The Religious Policy of the Mughal Emperors*, Asia Publishing House, 1962

Sinha, H.N. 'The Genesis of the Din-i-Ilahi', *JIH*, 19 (1930), 303–29.

Sultan-ul-Hind Hazrat Khwaja Moinuddin Hasan Chishty, Ajmer, Dargah Sharif, 2004

General history

Muhammad Salih Kamboh, *Bahār al-Sukhan* ('Spring of Prose'), Punjab Public Library, Lahore, MS 876–9

Khwajah Ni'mat Allah. *Tārīkh-i-Khān Jahān wa Makhzan-i-Afghani*, S.M. Imam al-Din (ed.), 2 vols, Dacca, Asiatic Society of Pakistan, 1960 and 62

Bihola, B. *Ardhakathanaka* ('Half A Tale'), tr. M. Lath, Jaipur, Rajasthan Prakrit Bharati Sansthan, 1981

Das, G. *India Unbound*, Profile, 2002

Khan, M.A. 'The Mughul Encampment', *JPHS*, 23 (1975), 225–32

Khan, M.W. *Lahore and Its Important Monuments*, Lahore, Government of Pakistan, 1961

Nizami, K.A. (ed.) *Medieval India: A Miscellany*, vols. 1, 2 and 3, Asia Publishing House, 1969, 1972 and 1975

Rehmani, A. 'Abul-Hasan Asaf Khan: Life and Achievements', *JRSP*, 35 (1998), 45–70

—— 'The Tomb of Asaf Khan', *JRSP*, 31 (1994), 51–7

Reza, H.R. 'The Role of Iranian Migrant Scholars in the Advancement of Sciences During the Qutb Shai Period in Dakan', Islamic Research Foundation, Mashhad, 2005

Watson, G. 'Interpretations of Central Asian Influences on Mughal India: The Historical Debate', *South Asia: Journal of South Asian Studies*, 18:2 (1995), 1–22

Picture credits

Akbar's Eastern Gate at Lahore Fort. (*Author*)

Prince Khurram is weighed at Kabul, July 1607. (© *Copyright the Trustees of The British Museum*)"

Emperor Akbar and Crown Prince Salim (later Jahangir). (*Bodleian Library, University of Oxford. Douce Or.a.1, fol. 18v*)

Gold coins showing the signs of the Zodiac. (© *Copyright the Trustees of The British Museum*)

Prince Khurram firing a matchlock rifle. (© *The Trustees of the Chester Beatty Library, Dublin*)"

Forty-pillared hall at Allahabad Fort (18th century aquatint). (*Bodleian Library, University of Oxford. Douce Prints A.3*, fol. 8*)"

Prince Khurram as a young man. (*Credit to be confirmed*)

Jahangir's black stone throne (detail). (*Author*)

Queen Nur Jahan hosts Jahangir and Khurram in the harem. (*Freer Gallery of Art, Smithsonian Institution, Washington, D.C., Gift of Charles Lang Freer, F1907.258*)

Ghiyath-al-Din Itimad-al-Daula. (*Freer Gallery of Art, Smithsonian Institution, Washington, D.C., Purchase, F1948.20*)

Arjumand 'Mumtaz-Mahal'. (*Topfoto*)

Pushkar inscription marking Khurram's victory over the Rana of Mewar. (*Author*)

Surrender of the Maharana of Mewar. (V&A *Credit to be confirmed*)

The 'Picture Wall' at Lahore Fort (*Author*)

Burhanpur Fort, towering over the Tapti River (*Author*)

Sir Thomas Roe, Ambassador of King James. (*Courtesy of the National Portrait Gallery London*)

Jagmandir Island: Shah Jahan's refuge during his rebellion. (*Author*)

Abd-al-Rahim the Khan of Khans. (*Freer Gallery of Art, Smithsonian Institution, Washington, D.C., Purchase, F1939.50a*)

Silver rupee minted in the name of King Dawar-Bakhsh. (*Ashmolean Museum, Oxford*)

Asaf-Khan, Shah Jahan's father-in-law and king-maker. (*Staatsbibliothek zu Berlin – Preussicher Kulturbesitz, Orientabteilung, A.117*)

Shah Jahan honours Muslim dignitaries at court. (*Freer Gallery of Art, Smithsonian Institution, Washington, D.C., Purchase, F1942.18a*)

Worshipper at Shah Jahan's mosque at Ajmer. (*Author*)

Mumtaz-Mahal's first burial-place at Burhanpur. (*Author*)

Inspiration for the Taj Mahal: the tomb of Hoshang Shah at Mandu. (*Author*)

The Taj Mahal. (*Author*)

Shah Jahan's mosque near Babur's tomb, Kabul. (*Courtesy of Tarquin Hall*)

The 'Ornamented Throne' (*akg-images*)

Shah Jahan's rebellious sons: Shah-Shuja, Aurangzeb and Murad-Bakhsh. (*Credit to be confirmed*)

Shah Jahan's throne at the Red Fort in Shahjahanabad. (*Author*)

Top surface of Shah Jahan's tomb. (*Copyright © The British Library*)

Tomb of Jahan-Ara, Delhi. (*Author*)

Index

Chashma al-Nur, 94
Chatar Diwar Pass, 132
China, 15
Chittor, 84, 89
Chittagong, 23, 246
Christians, 3, 25, 52, 76, 193, 220
Clement, Gregory, 155–6
Colbert, Jean-Baptiste, 193
Constantinople, 52, 102, 224, 249
Coromandel Coast, 227
Coryat, Thomas, 8, 23
Ctesiphon, 211
Cuttack Fort, 133

D
Dal Lake, 110
Damascus, 23, 211
Daniyal, xvi, 27, 34 (birth), 36–43, 46,
    60, 142, 155, 171
Dar al-Khilafat, *see* Agra
Dar al-Sultanat, *see* Lahore
Dara-Shikuh, xvi, xvii, 93, 138, 141,
    144, 150, 159–60, 163, 165, 171,
    180, 197, 201, 203, 215, 216,
    219–20, 222, 224–46 (death)
Dargah, 33, 85
Darius, 93
Darwish Beg, 61
Dastur Kaikobad Mahyra, 100
Daulatabad, 116, 175, 218, 226,
    228–30, 232
Daulat-Afza, 167
Daulat-Bagh, 94
Daulat-Khan, 76
Dawar-Bakhsh Bulaqi Shir-Shah, x,
    xvi, 138, 142, 148, **149**, 150
    (coronation), 154–5, 241
Deccan, 18, 23, 31, 36, 41–3, 52, 60,
    62–4, 84, 86–7, 93, 96–9, 101–5,
    107, 112–14, 117–19, 121–3, 126,
    130–2, 135, 137, 143–4, 147–8,
    153, 159–60, 168–75, 181, 196,
    217–22, 226–9, 239
Dehrabagh, 156
de Laet, Joannes, 14
de Mandelslo, Johann Albrecht, 12, 200
Della Valle, Pietro, xv, 104, 127
Delhi (*see also* Shahjahanabad), 2, 11,
    22–3, 31, 33, 37, 45, 51, 103, 128,
    196, 208–10, 214, 226
de Thévenot, Jean, 231
Dhar, 2, 5

Dharmat, 234, 236
Dholpur, 124, 173, 237
Dilawar-Khan, 58, 87, 158
Dilkusha, 146
Din Illahi, 25–7, 51
Diwali, 23
Dod, John, 132
Dohad, 108
Dudhana River, 99
du Jarric, Fr Pierre, xv, 38
Dussehra, 23
Dutch, 153

E
East India Company, 12, 33, 76, 77,
    94, 96, 126, 132, 144, 172, 175,
    193, 209
Eid al-Adha, 23, 180
Eid al-Fitr, 23, 73, 180, 207
Erach, 170
Etawah, 42

F
Fairuz-Khan, 150
Faiz Bazaar, 213
Farah, 61
Farid al-Din Attar, Sheikh, 48
Fateh-Gaj, 86
Fateh-Jang, 236
Fatehpur-Sikri, 33–5, 170, 211
Farid Bakkhari, Sheikh, 108, 128
Farid Bukhari, Sheikh, *see* Murtaza-
    Khan
Faydi Mubarak, 21, 33
Fidai-Khan, 128
Finch, William, xv, 12, 35, 77, 96–7,
    209
Firdos-Makani, *see* Zahir al-Din Babur
Firoz-Jang, xvii, 85, 87, 105, 115, 128,
    133–5, 170, 175–6
French East India Company, 193

G
Gajpat-Khan, 140
Ganges River, 31, 33, 37, 40, 134, 205,
    209, 234, 243, 246
Garshasp, 155
Gauhar-Ara, 177–8
Genghis Khan, 4, 22, 60, 105
Gheirat-Khan, 209–10
Ghiyath al-Din Beg, *see* Itimad-al-
    Daula

Jalal al-Din Akbar
(1541-1605)   =   1. Ruqayya Begum (1544-1626)
3rd Mughal Emperor   2. Salima Begum (1552-1613)
(r. 1556-1605)   3. Guljar 'Maryam-Zamani' (15

Khanim = Mirza   Murad   Daniyal = Jana Beg
Sultan   Muzaffar   'Pahari'   (1572-1605)
                  Hussein   (1570-99)

[3 children]

Salim Jahangir
(1569-1627)   =   1. Rajakumari Man Bai (d. 1605)
4th Mughal Emperor   2. Sahib-Jamal
(r. 1605-27)   3. 'Malika-Jahan'
                                          4. Manmati Jagat Ghosaini (d.
                                          5. Mihr al-Nisa 'Nur-Jah

Sultan al-Nisa   Khusraw = d. Raja of Baglana   Pervez   = J.
(1586-1646)   (1587-1622) | Sultan Bahar   (1589-1626) |

Dawar-Bakhsh 'Shir-Shah' Garhasp   [2 children]   [3 childr
(1612-28)   (d. 1628)
5th Mughal Emperor
(r. 1627)

Purhunar   Jahan-Ara   Shah-Shuja   **Auranzeb 'Alamgir'**
(b. 1611)   (b. 1614)   (1616-58)   (1618-1707)
                                                          7th Mughal Emperor
          Hur al-Nisa   Dara-Shikuh   Raushan-Ara   (r. 1658-1707)
          (1613-16)   (1615-59)   (b. 1617)

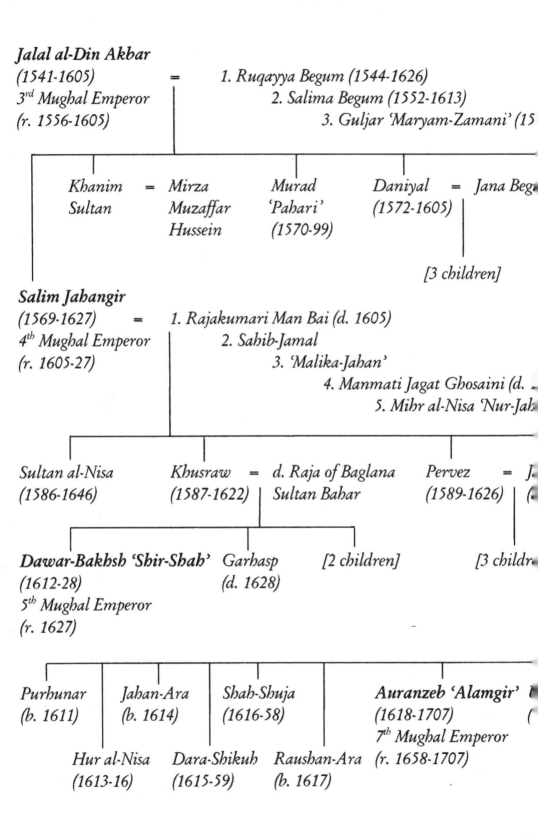